3551 0519

W9-AAL-716

HONOR BETRAYED

HONOR BETRAYED

SEXUAL ABUSE IN
AMERICA'S MILITARY

DR. MIC HUNTER

BARRICADE
BOOKS
Fort Lee, New Jersey

185 Bridge Plaza North
Suite 308-A
Fort Lee, NJ 07024

www.barricadebooks.com

Library of Congress Cataloging-in-Publication Data

Hunter, Mic
Honor betrayed : sexual abuse in America's military / Mic Hunter. — 1st ed.
p. cm.
Includes bibliographic references
ISBN-10: 1-56980-325-0 (hc : alk. paper)
ISBN-13: 978-1-56980-325-7 (hc : alk. paper)
  1.United States—Armed Forces—Women. 2. Gays in the military—United States.
    3. Sexual abuse victims—United States. I Title. II Title: Sexual abuse in America's military.

UB418.W65H86 2007

355.1'344—dc22
        2007003863

ISBN 13: 978-1-56980-325-7
ISBN 1-56980-325-0

First Printing
Manufactured in the United States of America

Dedicated to Dr. William F. Hunter,

Sergeant U.S.M.C., SP3 U.S. Army Reserve, U.S. Navy Reserve

TABLE OF CONTENTS

ACKNOWLEDGMENTS IX

PREFACE XI

PART I: WHY IT HAPPENS 1

1. INCENTIVES FOR ENLISTING 3

2. THE MILITARY CULTURE 13

3. "A BAND OF BROTHERS": THE CODE OF HYPERMASCULINITY 33

4. HAZING: "WHAT GOES AROUND COMES AROUND" 45

5. PROSTITUTION: THE NECESSARY EVIL? 63

6. A MAN'S HOME IS HIS CASTLE: ACCEPTANCE OF DOMESTIC VIOLENCE 73

7. WHEN JANIE COMES MARCHING HOME AGAIN: WOMEN IN THE MILITARY 85

8. THE FAG OF WAR: HOMOPHOBIA IN THE MILITARY 117

9. DÉJÀ VU: CHARACTERISTICS FOUND BOTH IN ABUSIVE FAMILIES AND IN THE MILITARY 143

10. "CAN'T YA TAKE A JOKE?": SEXUAL HARASSMENT 149

11. SEXUAL ASSAULT WITHIN THE RANKS 165

12. THE IMPACT OF SEXUAL ABUSE 177

13. FACTORS THAT AFFECT THE IMPACT OF SEXUAL ABUSE 185

14. THE OFFENDER MENTALITY 197

15. THE IMPACT OF SEXUAL ABUSE ON THE MILITARY AS A WHOLE 209

16. THE TIMES, THEY ARE A-CHANGIN' 217

17. WHAT THE MILITARY CAN DO TO REDUCE SEXUAL ABUSE 235
AND SECONDARY VICTIMIZATION

18. FINAL THOUGHTS 251

PART II: HOW IT HAPPENS—   **253**
PERSONAL STORIES OF SEXUAL ABUSE

    INTRODUCTION 255

    ANNIE D. 259

    DEAN 265

    THE REVEREND DOROTHY MACKEY 271

    GLORIA J. WILLIAMS 277

    GREGORY A. HELLE 281

    JON 289

    LYNDA K. ARNESON DOKKEN 293

    PAULA C. 301

    RACHEL JOHNSON 309

    RAYMOND D. 313

    ABOUT THE CONTRIBUTORS 317

END NOTES **319**

BIBLIOGRAPHY **335**

ACKNOWLEDGMENTS

MY THANKS to the reference staff of the St. Paul Library system, who never balked at my frequent requests for sometimes obscure information from difficult-to-locate sources; Dr. Chris Baldwin, who led me to my agent, Scott Edelstein, who was unrelenting in his efforts to find a publisher; Dr. Melissa Embser-Herbert for her comments on the chapter on women; Dr. Stephen Parker and Aaron Belkin for their comments on the chapter on homophobia; Ivy McFadden for making me look like a better writer; and Carole Stuart, who agreed to publish a book so many others feared to put into print.

Preface

UNACKNOWLEDGED CASUALTIES

BOOKS ON THE MILITARY rarely mention sexual abuse. Major General Jeanne Holm, who was the highest-ranking woman ever to serve in the U.S. armed forces, wrote a 544-page book on women in the military. Its index does not contain the words *abuse, harassment, rape,* or *sexual assault*. Likewise, General Tommy Franks, the Commander in Chief of U.S. Central Command, published a 536-page book in which none of these issues were mentioned.[1] When I revealed to colleagues that I was working on a book on sexual abuse in the military, many thought it was an obscure topic, believing that sexual abuse in the military is rare. I am familiar with such reactions. I faced similar responses when I was writing about the sexual abuse of males in the 1980s, when most people thought that was a rare phenomenon. Those who thought that the sexual abuse of boys was nearly nonexistent turned out to be wrong. Likewise, those who believe in the rarity of sexual abuse in the military are mistaken. It has existed since the beginning of military history and continues today. In fact, as you are reading this, somewhere a member of the U.S. military is being sexually harassed or assaulted. Only now are people, including high-ranking officers within the military, beginning to wake up to the reality of sexual abuse and to the conditions that engender it. It is my hope that this book will help to hasten this slow awakening.

History has shown us that soldiers can be noble, dignified, and self-sacrificing, even when engaged in wars that are petty and disgraceful. But some soldiers are capable of behaviors toward their comrades that violate the oaths they have taken, and that bring dishonor on themselves, the military, and the countries they serve.

My intention in *Honor Betrayed* is to draw attention to this previously taboo subject; to point out how the military has successfully responded to other psychological problems; and to encourage military leaders to make the American military a safer place for those who defend our country.

This book includes several firsthand accounts of sexual abuse suffered by U.S. military personnel. When I let it be known that I was seeking these personal stories, the first question asked was, "Are you a veteran?" When I disclosed that I have never been in uniform, I worried that people would decline to take part in the project and dismiss me with a comment such as, "Well, if you've never been a part of the military, then you wouldn't understand." Instead, I was shocked to hear this common response: "Oh, good. I was afraid you would be military and you wouldn't believe me."

The personal stories included in Part II of this book are in the words of those persons who lived through abusive experiences and, in many cases, continue to suffer from their effects. These people are brave and strong. They deserve our respect. They agreed to serve their country and were betrayed by their comrades. I hope this book helps to heal their wounds and prevents others from suffering the same pain.

I expect to be criticized by some as being disloyal, or as undermining the morale of our military by publishing this material. As Judith Herman noted some years ago, "Those who stand with the victim will inevitably face the perpetrator's unmasked fury." I stand behind what I have written and pose this question: What could be more supportive of our fighting women and men than exposing the forces that permit their mistreatment?

Dr. Mic Hunter

PART I
WHY IT HAPPENS

1

INCENTIVES FOR ENLISTING

IN AMERICA, JOINING THE MILITARY is entirely voluntary. In order to understand the military mentality we must first answer the question, what motivates someone to join the military? This question is particularly interesting when considering how many women and homosexual men enlist despite the military's history of intolerance of them.

Some people join the military to escape the civilian world, while others are attracted to some positive aspect of the military. David Browne Wood describes a unit of Marines:

> Many of them have fled dead-end jobs or stifling families or abortive attempts at college. All of them have fled the commonplace of shopping malls and interstate highways and fast-food drive-ins, seeking instead challenge and excitement, uncommon deeds, valor, glory. There is something else they seek; the sense of identity, of community, the sense of common principled purpose and the moral certainties that America, they believe, is losing.[1]

JOINING THE FAMILY BUSINESS

IN SOME FAMILIES, service in the military is expected, particularly if one or both parents have had military careers. It is common for children to join, in effect, the family business—the military. Nearly half of new recruits were raised in military families.

PATRIOTISM AND HONOR

"We civilians talk, we talk almost solely, of our rights, but in the army, [sic] it seems that men talk chiefly of their duties…"—William Dean Howells

THE DESIRE TO DEFEND one's country is a major reason people enlist in military service. Greg Helle, whose personal story appears in Part II, described his motivation for going to Vietnam, "Small town ideals were very important in my life. The center of our social world was the church; God and country were paramount. Raised in a good Christian family, defending the country was something that was not an option; I had a duty to my country."

"We teach them what there is in this country that is worth living for, worth fighting for, that is worth giving your life for."—General David M. Shoup, Commandant of the Marine Corps[2]

FULL CITIZENSHIP

WHETHER A NATIVE-BORN or naturalized citizen, being willing to "make the ultimate sacrifice" for one's country by contributing to the national defense is the definitive act of citizenship. This explains the efforts in the twentieth century of African-American men who, despite ongoing, stubborn resistance and prejudice from the military, strove to enlist for service and volunteer for combat duty. It continues to be common for recent immigrants and their offspring to enlist in the military to become "real Americans." Having a family member in the military is an indication that their new country has accepted them. Lieutenant Colonel Donna Alesch Newell explains why she sought to attend West Point: "My mother immigrated in 1949 to the United States from Ireland and she instilled several important concepts in me. One was that I should give something back to our wonderful country for the opportunities it had given me. Another was that in the United States, if you worked hard and trained hard, you could achieve anything."[3]

"All questions, all ambiguities, all contradictions in what it means to be a man or a citizen are banished in the creation of a warrior."—Leo Braudy[4]

TO GAIN A SENSE OF DIRECTION

"Join the Army, you can't make it anywhere else."—Advice given to Gregory Helle by his high school counselor

SOME JOIN THE MILITARY because they lack a sense of direction in their lives. In the military, they will be told when to get up, what to wear, what to do, and what to believe in. For a person without direction, this rigid structure can be seen as comforting rather than stifling. Lt. General C. J. Kennedy observed, "The Army took a lot of guesswork out of life."[5]

"Give me a chance—give the Marine Corps a chance—with these misguided kids, and we'll change them. We'll give them a purpose in life, and that's what they lack." —General Lewis Walt, Assistant Commandant[6]

ADVENTURE

"Join the Navy. See the world."—Navy recruiting slogan

PRIOR TO INTERNATIONAL commercial flights and ocean-going cruise ships calling at exotic ports, the best and perhaps only opportunity a lower- or middle-class person would ever have to travel extensively was to be a part of the military. When most Americans lived in small rural settings and were unlikely to travel even within their home state, those in the military were seeing distant lands.

"I joined the Navy, not because I was patriotic, just because I wanted to get off my block."—Bill Cosby

DEVELOPMENT COMPONENTS

Physical Fitness

THE MILITARY PROVIDES encouragement, training, equipment, and camaraderie geared toward physical fitness. In the first thirty-seven days of basic training at Parris Island, Walter Norton lost one-third of the 300 pounds he weighed when he arrived. "The military offered me a chance to change my relationship with my body. I thought, acted, and even walked differently than I had a few months before. I was afraid of nothing. The marines [sic] had reduced me to just what they wanted and nothing more: an efficient fighting machine."[7]

Education

Education in the form of career training, or funding for schooling before or after discharge, often motivates people to enlist in the military. This is particularly true of those from families who could not otherwise afford to pay for post–high school education. Opportunity for education is also an important reason service members reenlist. Education was the second most common reason given for female sailors to reenlist and fourth most common for males.[8]

Economic Opportunity

There continues to be a disproportionate number of enlistees from homes of lower socioeconomic status. For the underprivileged and undereducated, joining the military offers a guarantee of income, housing, food, and medical care. In 2005, when enlistment quotas were not being met, the Army National Guard signed an agreement with Labor Ready, a national temporary worker company, so that recruiters could more easily find unemployed Americans.[9]

Once the military became racially integrated, African Americans and other minority groups found that they could obtain positions of authority within the military that would have been unavailable to them in civilian organizations. In 1945, Frederick Branch became the first African-American commissioned officer in the Marines. To put this event in perspective, this was two years before Jackie Robinson "broke the color barrier" in major league baseball, and decades before the civil rights movement.[10] The military academies were racially integrated before public schools. The military is one of the most successful American institutions when it comes to race relations. In fact, sociologist Charles Moskos noted that in America, the only place it is routine for blacks to boss around whites is in the military, and that blacks in the military form the largest group of African American executives in the country.[11] The military has gone to great lengths to have its personnel view one another as members of the military first and members of different races second. One Marine described his comrades in a letter from boot camp to his mother, "One's black, here called a dark-green Marine, and the other's white, a light-green Marine."[12]

The American military has provided opportunities for women that would have been impossible in the civilian world. In 1918, O. M. Johnson became the first Caucasian woman to enlist in the Marines.[13] Such an opportunity was extremely impressive: American women would not have the right to vote for another two years. The military is one place where women can be paid at the same level as men. In the civilian world, women are paid 75¢ for every $1 a man makes. This pay gap is true even for educated women; even women with their bachelor's degree, master's, or doctorate (including physicians) make 38 percent less than similarly trained men.[14]

Maturity and Leadership

Recruitment slogans have long indicated that military service is a way to develop maturity and self-respect. Army recruitment slogans have included "The Army can really make you feel good about yourself" and "Be all that you can be." Many potential civilian employers view military experience as an indication of leadership skills. Lt. Cornell wrote of his combat experience in Vietnam:

> Commanding in combat is the greatest thing that's ever happened to me. . . . My sense of satisfaction comes from having been able to take care of my troops, to take care of my soldiers' lives. It was the ultimate challenge. There is no other job that even comes close. I learned so much about myself, my strengths and weaknesses. I learned how precious life is and how frail it is.[15]

Many people view a period of time in the military as a way to develop maturity. In some cases civilian judges have offered those convicted of minor offenses the choice of enlistment in the military instead of serving a jail sentence, with the idea that the experience of military service would teach the offender prosocial values and improve his self-respect, and thereby reduce the likelihood that further crimes would be committed.

"In a society that seems to have trouble transmitting values, the Marines stand out as [a] successful and healthy institution that unabashedly teaches values to the Beavises and Buttheads of America."—Thomas E. Ricks[16]

BEING A PART OF SOMETHING IMPORTANT AND BIGGER THAN ONESELF

"The tradition, and the respect—it makes you feel like you belong, and that you have worth as a person."—A Marine Corps Major[17]

THE MILITARY APPEALS to those who want to be part of something greater than themselves. Hedges wrote of the attraction to war, "Even with its destruction and carnage it can give us what we long for in life. It can give us purpose, meaning, a reason for living. . . . It gives us resolve, a cause. It allows us to be noble." [18]

For many people, like Lt. General Kennedy, membership in the military leads to cherished relationships: "The Army is more than a job; it's a life, a community of soldiers who become permanent friends."[19] General Colin Powell, former Chairman of the Joint Chiefs of Staff, described the relationships formed in the military as family "not bound together by blood relations, but an even closer family bound together by sacrifice, shared commitment, by being professionals in that proud group of Americans willing to serve their country."[20] The concept of the military as a family is encouraged from the beginning of training. When a recruit approaches his superior to report he had "problems with my family back home," his superior responded, "No, you don't have family back home. This [the military] is your family now."[21]

Military men, not usually thought of as emotionally expressive, go so far as to use the word "love" to describe the bond forged with comrades. In the book *All Quiet on the Western Front*, World War I infantryman Erich Maria Remarque wrote, "We don't talk much but I believe we have a more complete communication with one another than even lovers. . . . I belong to them and they to me, we all share the same life, we are nearer than lovers, in a simple, a harder way." Keith W. Nolan, a Vietnam veteran, stated, "There are few human experiences comparable to the camaraderie and brother-love of a Marine infantry unit in combat." Another Marine agreed, "The communication between [Marines in infantry battalions] is as profound as any between lovers. Actually more so." When William Manchester heard his unit was heading out on a dangerous mission he, although wounded and against orders, left his hospital bed and rejoined his comrades in battle.

> It was an act of love. Those men on the line were my family, my home. They were closer to me than any friends ever had been or ever would be. They had never let me down and I couldn't do it to them. I had to be with them, rather than let them die and me live with the knowledge that I might have saved them. Men, I now know, do not fight for flag or country, for the Marine Corps or glory or any other abstraction. They fight for one another.[22]

SACRED CALLING

TO SOME THE MILITARY is more than an organization, a paycheck, the ticket to an education, a way to see the world: it is sacred. Indeed, the motto of the Marine Corps is *Semper Fi*, Latin for "Always Faithful." A sign at the Parris Island training camp reads, "Surrender mind and spirit to harsh instruction and receive a soul."[23] The Marines sing *The Marines' Hymn*, not the Marines' song or anthem—the *hymn*. When new recruits arrive at boot camp one of the first things they hear is the Drill Instructor's Covenant with the senior drill instructor. It includes the statement

> I will treat you just as I do my fellow Marines, with firmness, fairness, dignity and compassion. As such, I am not going to threaten you with physical harm, abuse you, or harass you, nor will I tolerate such behavior from anyone else, Marine or recruit.[24]

This statement is referred to as a covenant, something that implies sacredness well beyond a mere agreement, contract, or even promise.

MANHOOD

UP TO THIS POINT all the listed motivations for enlisting in the military have been sex-neutral, appealing to both men and women. Now we will address a motivation that is sex-specific and plays a central role in understanding the military and sexual abuse. In order to fully grasp the military mentality, it is vital to understand gender role expectations. Unfortunately, when most authors address issues related to the military, they neglect to mention gender roles. A comprehensive survey of scholarship on thinking about war and peace found that only one-tenth of one percent even mentioned gender, and all those references were to women.

Many people, both men and women, have seen combat as the definitive proving ground for masculinity. In fact, the Greek word for cowardice, *anadreia*, is literally "unmanliness." Throughout history, men have worried that extended periods without war would damage their nation's character, particularly its masculinity. President Theodore Roosevelt advised Americans, "There is no place in the world for nations who have . . . lost their fiber of vigorous hardiness and masculinity" and concluded, "no triumph of peace is quite so great as the supreme triumphs of war." He welcomed the advent of the Spanish-American War, and when President Woodrow Wilson didn't enter World War I soon enough to please Roosevelt, he exclaimed, "Wilson has done more to emasculate American manhood and weaken its fiber than anyone else I can think of."[25] More recently, American presidents have also based their foreign policy on how it might affect their masculine image. President Lyndon Johnson and his advisors formulated their policies in Vietnam with the intent of gaining the respect of "men who were tough, real men."[26] Likewise, President Ronald Reagan intervened in Nicaragua because "America has to show a firmness of manhood."[27]

No other organization is as identified with providing a place to prove one's manhood as the military. General Robert Barrow, former commandant of the Marines, described the attraction of the Marines, "There is an inherent need in all males of the animal world to prove their masculinity or maleness. . . . The Marine Corps' reputation, richly deserved, for physical toughness, courage, and its demands on mind and body, attracts those who want to prove their manliness. Here the search ends."[28]

But for some men the search doesn't end with completion of boot camp. These are the men J. Calendo described as the "outcast, the jailbird, the hillbilly poor. Also the boy who's afraid he's queer, who thinks he'll be cured by baptism of fire into manhood."[29] Even after successfully completing boot camp, these men continue to question their masculinity, and with that questioning comes the need to prove, to himself and to others, that he is a "real man." One method of doing so is to prey on those of "lower" status: women and "faggots."

2

THE MILITARY CULTURE

COLONEL COX OF THE AIR FORCE described the military as a subculture: "The institutional military is further differentiated from other bureaucracies and exerts normative pressure on its members to conform to its unique institutional culture, a culture characterized by unconditional commitment to the mission, service before self, uncertainty and unpredictability in lifestyle, sometimes dangerous missions, frequent separations from family, and acceptance of a way of life without some of the constitutional protections commonly expected by American citizens."[1] The military has its own courts, police force, medical system, educational structure, and research facilities. It is powerful enough to be exempt from the laws that govern other institutions, even those that forbid discrimination.

Any culture has a set of norms and rules; some are overt, such as those written in manuals, while others are covert—unspoken but understood. Captain Mackey found there were actually three sets of rules: the ones civilians were told; those official rules that were actually enforced; and the unofficial rules that superseded all the other rules.*

CULTURAL INDOCTRINATION

"Culture is not a biologically transmitted complex."—Ruth Benedict, anthropologist[2]

---

* Captain Mackey's personal story appears in Part II.

"They're in culture shock now."—Drill Instructor Sergeant Carey, referring to his new recruits[3]

THE MILITARY'S MOST EFFECTIVE tool for indoctrinating recruits into the military culture is basic training ("boot camp"). Basic training is primarily about learning the culture rather than specific skills, which are taught later in specialized programs. Ben Shalit explained, "The basic training camp was designed to undermine all the past concepts and beliefs of the new recruit, to undermine his civilian values, to change his self-concept—subjugating him entirely to the military system."[4] Recruits are informed that whoever they were or what they did before enlistment is "absolutely, entirely, irrevocably irrelevant."[5] Basic training begins the process of building an effective unit from a random collection of strangers. In a few weeks, recruits are taught to do everything according to rules. To enforce the doctrine that everything *will* be done the military's way, recruits are told what clothes to wear and how to put them on. The recruits are told to put on their T-shirts as a group and then their right boots; if even one member puts on the left boot, the group is told to remove their boots and start over.[6]

Even though it has been over one hundred years since battlefield strategy consisted of soldiers standing in line firing at another mass of men, all armed forces still training using close order drill. Close order drill requires that each person pay attention to what others are doing in order to remain in step and moving in the same direction. All this marching has a practical application; the action of moving as one and immediately reacting together is teaching them to stop thinking of themselves as individuals and become a unit. In a civilian job review, the notation "displays an individual-type attitude" might be a compliment, but in the military getting such a comment on an evaluation can be reason for concern.[7]

Drill creates the instinct to respond immediately to an order. For it to work, every member of the formation must respond to the order to change direction at the exact same time. There can be no hesitating on anyone's part. Once the psychology of immediately, unquestioningly following an order and acting as a unit is instilled, this response generalizes to other actions. A Marine sergeant described his experience.

> When I went to boot camp and did individual combat training they said if you walk into an ambush what you want to do is just do a right face—you just turn right or left, whichever way the fire is coming from, and assault. I said, "Man, that's crazy. I'd never do anything like that. It's stupid." The first time we came under fire…we did it automatically. We done [sic] a right face, assaulted the hill—a fortified position with concrete bunkers emplaced, machine guns, automatic weapons—and we took it.[8]

The primary tool of boot camp is the drill instructor (DI):

> Martial virtues cannot be instilled in the absence of discipline, and discipline cannot be inculcated, let alone measured, in the absence of exacting standards. The responsibility for this crucial task lies with the drill instructor, the natural role model for every recruit. No other individual wields nearly as much power to inculcate martial values. For many recruits, especially those coming from broken homes or permissive school systems, boot camp may represent their first sustained encounter with an authority figure.[9]

Teams of DIs work together, each specializing in a specific type of instruction. The senior DI uses righteous anger to instill guilt, so the recruits will want to please him by improving their performance. As the father figure, he is permitted to smile and offer praise. The "Second Hat" or "Heavy A" relies on repetition as the primary teaching technique. The recruit who is performing the worst is taken out of the group, shown how to properly execute an act, and then ordered to repeatedly perform it. The "Third Hat" utilizes dread and physical pain to inspire compliance. Recruits who fail to properly perform are required to engage in Incentive Physical Training (IPT). The classic example is, "Drop and give me twenty [push-ups]." It can also consist of rapid bending, leg lifts, side lunges, and running in place.[10]

Until recently, the primary attitude was "break them down, so we can build them up our way."[11] Marine Colonel Fred Fagan described the process: "Military training exists to break [the recruit] down to his fundamental self, take away all that he possesses, and get him started out in a way that you want him to be. Issue him all new clothes, cut his hair, send his possessions home, and tell him he doesn't know a damn thing, that he's the sorriest thing you've ever seen, but with my help you're going to be worthwhile again."[12] The DIs' task is complicated, because, "In order to make Marines into disciplined fighting men who put the welfare of their unit above personal concerns, they must reform the recruits' cultural values. In today's society, these reforms often include eliminating the me-first ethic, the recruit's belief in the right to do whatever he pleases, systematical shirking of responsibility, immunity from punishment for antisocial or even criminal behavior, and the recruit's conviction that his every whim should be immediately gratified and every material acquisition within his grasp—now."[13] Captain D. Kaplan explained indoctrination this way: "Military socialization involves forms of discipline and domination that border on humiliation. The bodies of new recruits in basic training are putty in the hands of their commanders."

"You get the esprit de corps inside them and then whatever you tell them, they'll believe."—Staff Sgt. Marvin Frasier, Senior DI[14]

CULTURE AND LANGUAGE

"I'm becoming bilingual, English and Marine…"—A recruit in a letter from boot camp to his parents[15]

TO BE ACCEPTED INTO a subculture, one must learn its language: A bed becomes a rack or a bunk, the bathroom is now the latrine or the head, even left and right become starboard and port.* In boot camp a recruit learns new words for objects and a new interpersonal language in which they do not refer to themselves in the first person; there is no "I." They are allowed to refer to themselves only as "the recruit" or "this recruit," as in, "Sir, this recruit requests permission to go to the latrine."

New recruits are taught the history of their branch of the service to

---

* Although each branch of the American Military refers to its personnel with different terms (Air Force–airmen, Army–soldier, Marine Corp–marine, and Navy–sailor) throughout this book I will use the term soldier in the dictionary form of the word, "somebody who serves in an army or other military service" (Encarta Dictionary, 1999). I mean no disrespect to any branch of the service by this choice of words, and do so only to simplify the writing style. In quotes I used the language of the original author.

instill pride and the desire to be a part of a successful organization. The values of the culture are passed on from the old-timers to the newcomers through slang, stories, rituals, and songs. Military slang is highly sexualized (Sidebar 2-1). When a new pilot joined the 45th Medical Company in Vietnam, he was given a baseball-style cap with the unit insignia, and the "button" on the top was painted red to indicate he was only a "peter pilot," meaning he had not flown in combat.[16] Once his helicopter had been damaged by enemy fire, he removed the red button, demonstrating he had "lost his cherry." At West Point, the beginning of the academic year is formally termed the "reorganization week," but it is more commonly referred to as "re-orgy." In the dining hall each table is assigned a dessert corporal who must cut and serve desserts in pristine condition, or stand and shout, "Sir, the dessert has been raped, and I did it."[17]

Sidebar 2-1:
MILITARY SLANG[18]

• Sandwich meat	• Horse cock or fillet of mule tool
• Chopped beef on toast	• Creamed foreskins on toast
• Breakfast sausages	• Doggie dicks, poodle peckers, puppy peters or monkey dicks
• Untested gear or personnel	• Virgin
• Non-functional equipment	• Broke dick
• Being unproductive	• Dicking the dog
• Disorganized action	• Group grope or cluster fuck
• Beginning an undesirable task	• Tits Time
• Getting a distasteful assignment	• Bend over here it comes

Cadence calls, or Jody calls, are chants that recruits recite as they march or run to help them to keep time. The rhythm and repetition of Jody calls make them very memorable. Military personnel can repeat Jody calls decades after leaving basic training. Traditionally, most Jody calls—like those below—have involved sex, violence, or both:

I Wish

I wish all the ladies were bells in a tower.
I'll be the bellman and bang them every hour.
I wish all the ladies were pies on a shelf.
I'll be the baker and eat the pie myself.
I wish all the ladies were a cat in a tree.
I'll be a firefighter and get that nice pussy.[19]

Napalm

(To the tune of Jesus Loves the Little Children)
Napalm sticks to little children,
All the children of the world,
Be they yellow, black, or white.
Hear them screaming in the night,
'Cause napalm sticks to little kids.[20]

Lift Your Head*

Lift your head and hold it high,
Platoon ten thirty-six is running by,
Lift your head and hold it proud,
They're running hard and yelling loud.[21]

THE ACCEPTANCE OF VIOLENCE

"Your job is to learn how to kill people. . . . An M-16 can blow someone's head off at 500 meters. That's beautiful, isn't it?"—Sergeant Norman, Infantry Instructor[22]

THE MILITARY'S PRIMARY POWER comes from the ability to unleash massive violence. The stained-glass windows in the chapel at the Marine Corps' Parris Island facility depict airplanes firing their weapons and a flamethrower billowing multicolored flames. One veteran described his duties as, "Blow up things, and kill people."[23]

Although fewer than 25 percent of active duty personnel serve in combat roles, military culture aims to instill the combat value "Kill or be

---

* I include this one because I want to illustrate values other than sex and violence can be passed on using the same method.

killed" in all personnel. The drill instructor asks, "What is the motto of the bayonet?" The recruits answer, "To kill! To kill! To kill without mercy!"

Until very recently, violence between comrades began on the first day of basic training.

> For some reason, I pissed off a drill instructor to the point that he slapped me upside the head. I don't remember exactly what I did, but I did something wrong. "When I tell you to do something, I expect you to fucking do it!" I'll never forget that experience in my life. First time I'd ever been hit like that. Open handed, WHAP! Across the head, when I wasn't expecting it at all, standing straight at attention. "Oh, you're gonna flinch now, huh?" So he hits me again. He hit me three times. "What are you gonna do? Are you gonna cry? Are you a little pussy?"[24]

The acceptance of violence as a legitimate method for obtaining one's goals, whether with an enemy or with a comrade, creates a psychological environment where sexual abuse is likely to occur.* Sexual assault is best thought of as an act of violence rather than an act of sex. The point of the act is to invoke humiliation, pain, and terror in the victim.

THE ABILITY TO OBJECTIFY OTHER HUMANS

> *"The propagandist's purpose is to make one set of people forget that the other set is human."*—Aldous Huxley[25]

THE ABILITY TO OBJECTIFY other humans begins from the first day of basic training. Even before learning to objectify the enemy, recruits are learning to depersonalize their comrades because they are addressed not by name but merely as "recruit."

Empathy for the enemy makes killing harder. No leader is going to remind those under his command prior to a battle, "Now, let's remember, those we are going to face on the field of battle in a few moments are just like us. They have emotions. They have mothers and fathers. They love their kids. They feel pain and value life as much as you and I. All right, with that in mind, let's lock and load."

---

* When government uses violence as a means to an end, violence becomes more legitimized as a problem-solving technique for individuals as well. This helps explain the fact that following a war, whether the nation was defeated or victorious, the rate of homocide increases (Ember & Ember, 1994).

There are numerous forms of psychological "distance" that make killing and sexual assault psychologically easier.[26] One method is the use of neutral phrases, such as "target acquisition" or "target of opportunity." Sergeant Robert Hendrickson described his experience as a sniper, "[W]ithin one second prior to actual termination, a target would somehow seem to make eye contact with me."[27] Notice the person is described as "a target," which is about to be "terminated" rather than killed.

Another dehumanizing method is to cultivate the belief that the enemy is subhuman and does not value life; therefore, the soldier should have no qualms about killing him. One Vietnam veteran described the process, "You go through a progression, a stepwise regression, and sort of like, well, that's an enemy of my country. Those people—they're trying to kill me. They're subhuman. They're animals. They're going to rape our women and kill our children. They're in the way. Kill them."[28]

Psychological distance can be created through the use of derogatory names such as "gook," "zit," "zipper head," "dink," "slant-eye," "towel-head," "faggot," and "cunt." The victim is not some*one* but merely some*thing*. Male West Point cadets who sexually abused their female comrades viewed them as unlike "regular women." Regular women, such as their girlfriends, sisters, and mothers, were perceived as good and worthy of respect and protection. However, female cadets were not worthy of honorable treatment.[29] The use of derogatory names for the enemy is useful during war, but after a country is conquered, if the victors maintain this negative view, sexual assaults of citizens are more likely to be committed. During and after World War II and the Korean War, U.S. military courts executed American personnel convicted of rape. Squad leader John Smail said of rape in Vietnam, "That's an everyday affair. You can nail just about everybody on that—at least once. The guys are human, man."[30] It would be comforting to believe that sexual assaults occur during the heat of battle when emotions run high, but Americans commit 66 percent more sexual assaults when serving as an occupational army than as a combat force.[31]

"I then told him that in spite of my most diligent efforts, there would unquestion-ably be some raping, and that I should like to have the details as early as possible

so that the offenders could be properly hanged."—U.S. General George S. Patton, Jr.[32]

We ought not be surprised that rape takes place during war, because conditions are ripe for rape. Rhonda Copelon explained, "War tends to intensify the brutality, repetitiveness, public spectacle, and likelihood of rape. War diminishes sensitivity to human suffering and intensifies men's sense of entitlement, superiority, avidity, and social license to rape."[33] Many of the reasons for sexually assaulting the enemy in wartime are also factors that promote the abuse of comrades. Throughout history soldiers, particularly mercenaries, have viewed sexual assault as a form of reward for their services in battle. Some military commanders have viewed their troops sexually assaulting the enemy as a useful method for venting pent-up emotions. The ability to rape and kill is clearly an indication of power. During the Vietnam War, after members of the 11th Brigade had gang-raped and killed a woman, they would leave her body with her legs spread and an 11th Brigade patch between her legs.[34] When gang rape is committed, each man has knowledge of all the others' actions, and keeping their mutual crime a secret increases group loyalty.

Social distancing involves seeing the target of one's aggression as a member of a different social class. Someone with a working-class background can justify aggression against "an uppity college boy." Someone with an upper- or middle-class background can justify mistreatment of someone because "she's nothing but trailer trash." The military is very conscious of a form of social class—rank. The most obvious class difference is between officers and enlisted personnel. These groups are housed differently and drink their beers in separate clubs on military bases. All this segregation makes sexual abuse psychologically easier.

Moral distancing typically invokes religious superiority. Terrorist attacks of infidels and Jews are justified this way. Moral distancing is also used to justify the sexual abuse of women for "violating the role God intended for them," and homosexuals for being "ungodly."

A combination of cultural, social, and moral distancing was used during the "Rape of Nanking," when Japanese soldiers went on "an orgy of wholesale assault.[35]" Unarmed civilians were used for bayonet practice. Sixty-five percent of females between the ages of fifteen and twenty-nine were raped at least once.[36] Untold numbers of men were anally raped and then castrated.[37] Many of the rapes were gang rapes, after which the victims were left to die from their injuries. How did highly disciplined professional soldiers justify these acts? The Chinese were viewed by the Japanese as inferior people (cultural distance); civilians who had the financial means to flee had already left the city, leaving only the poor (social distance); and, most powerfully, the Japanese soldiers had God on their side (moral distance). One Japanese soldier explained, "I felt no shame raping and killing because I was a fighter for the emperor, who is a god, so I could do no wrong."[38]

Since the experience of war often overrides the usual social barriers of class, race, and religion, some combat veterans have difficulty believing it is possible to objectify comrades in arms. But most military personnel never experience combat and therefore are able to maintain their ability to objectify those comrades they view as being inferior to themselves. Even those service members who do experience combat may view the members of their unit as different from outsiders and therefore worthy of respect. ("She's not like other women, she's more like a guy"; "Sure he's gay, but he's not like regular faggots, he's all right.") Through this psychological compartmentalization, they are still able to objectify those outside their immediate unit as targets for sexual abuse.

OBEDIENCE TO THE CHAIN OF COMMAND

"Obedience to authority has always been a primary characteristic of military society."—Military Law[39]

"If the commander-in-chief tells this lieutenant colonel to go stand in the corner and sit on his head, I will do so."—Colonel Oliver North, 1987

IN ORGANIZATIONS WITH strict hierarchies the members tend to be highly attuned to how they look to others. This can induce members to perform to high standards, or lead to a situation where maintaining appearances and avoiding embarrassment become more important than doing what is in the best interest of the organization.

While in uniform, each person's rank is easily visible. Those with higher rank are entitled by that rank to order those of lower rank to engage in acts that may put them in harm's way and may even lead to their deaths. This is necessary for the functioning of combat units. Daniel Da Cruz noted the very first words heard by a group of recruits as they disembarked from a bus were on the topic of obedience.

> My name is Sergeant Bently. Now listen up, and listen good. Article 86 of the Uniform Code of Military Justice prohibits absence without leave. Article 91 prohibits disobedience to a lawful order. Article 93 prohibits disrespect to a senior officer. Burn those articles into your brains. You're going to live by them.[40]

Rituals such as saluting and responding "Sir, yes sir" are begun the first day of service and continue through one's enlistment. Military personnel take an oath to "protect and defend the Constitution of the United States against all enemies, foreign and domestic, and to obey the orders of the president of the United States and of the officers appointed over me." Recruits recite the names of the ten persons in their chain of command, beginning with their drill sergeant and ending with the President of the United States.[41] For eleven weeks, before every meal, recruits stand at attention and shout "D-I-S-C-I-P-L-I-N-E. Discipline, sir. Discipline is the instant willing obedience to all orders, [and] respect for authority."[42] Following orders without questioning them is a hallmark of effective training.

Stanley Milgram studied the effects of authority and willingness to inflict pain on another person. These studies were quite simple and straightforward: The subject was told to teach a list of words to a learner who was strapped into a chair in another room and to punish errors by giving an ever-increasing level of electric shock to the learner. The teacher sat at the controls of a "shock generator," with switches labeled from "slight shock" (15 volts) to "very strong shock" to "danger: severe shock" and finally "XXX" (450 volts). The researcher told the teacher to increase the shock by one level for each wrong answer given by the learner. Whenever the teacher flicked a switch to deliver a shock, lights flashed and there was an electric buzzing.

The "learner's" responses were actually tape-recorded so that incorrect answers occurred at predetermined points in the experiment. In response to the phony shocks the teacher heard the learner grunt, then at 120 volts announce, "Hey, this really hurts!" At 150 volts, "Experimenter! That's all. Get me out of here. I told you I had heart trouble. My heart's starting to bother me now. Get me out of here, please." At 165 volts he shouts, "I can't stand the pain. Let me out of here!" At 195 volts, "Let me out of here. My heart's bothering me. Let me out of here! You have no right to keep me here!" At 270 volts there were screams of agony after each shock. At 300 volts, "I absolutely refuse to answer any more. Get me out of here." At 315 volts, "I told you I refuse to answer. I'm no longer part of this experiment." At 330 volts and above there was no response, only silence.

If at any point the teacher asked the researcher if the shocks should continue, the researcher responded, "Please continue." If the teacher asked a second time, the researcher said, "The experiment requires that you continue." If the teacher again balked, the researcher said, "It is absolutely essential that you continue." At the fourth sign of hesitation the researcher said, "You have no other choice; you *must* go on." Sixty-five percent of the teachers, both males and females, continued to shock the learner until the maximum voltage was reached. They did so not only believing they were torturing an innocent person, but in spite of their own emotional discomfort, including nervous laughter, sweating, trembling, biting their lips, groaning, or stuttering. The teachers were volunteers who had answered an ad in a newspaper and had nothing to gain from continued participation in the experiment, yet they were more responsive to an authority figure they had just met than to the apparent suffering of another person who had done nothing to harm them in anyway. Lieutenant Colonel Grossman put the results of these experiments in perspective when he wrote, "if this kind of obedience could be obtained with a lab coat and a clipboard by an authority figure who had been known for only a few minutes, how much more would the trappings of military authority and months of bonding accomplish?"[43]

The results of Dr. Milgram's obedience studies foreshadowed the events that took place in the Vietnamese village of My Lai. In both places a person of authority directed that harm be done to people begging for mercy. One soldier who took part in the events of that day stated simply,

"[Lieutenant Calley] told me to start shooting. So I started shooting. I poured about four clips into the group. . . . They were begging and saying, 'No, no.' And the mothers were hugging their children and. . . . Well, we kept right on firing. They was [sic] waving their arms and begging…"[44]

Military personnel experience a double bind when it comes to following an order that they believe is morally or legally questionable. If they follow an order that upon later examination superiors determine to have been illegal, they are still held legally accountable. But if they refuse the order, and upon review it is determined to be a legitimate order, then they can face court marshal for not following orders. This was the situation Sergeant Javal S. Davis found himself in when he was stationed at Baghdad's notorious Abu Ghraib prison. He claimed intelligence officers who were preparing to interrogate prisoners gave him instructions to "rough them up" in order to "loosen them up" before questioning. Despite doing what he thought he was told to do, he was charged with conspiracy to maltreat detainees, dereliction of duty for failing to protect detainees from abuse, maltreatment of detainees, rendering false official statements, and assault. Davis told Army investigators he was "made to do various things" that he questioned on moral grounds but did anyway. He explained his actions by saying, "Yes, I could have said no to anything. But that would have been disobeying an order. So either you can get in trouble for not doing what you're told or get in trouble for doing what you're told."[45]

THE ISSUE OF VALID CONSENT IN A MILITARY SETTING

GIVEN THE IMPORTANCE placed on obedience in a military setting, the issue of consent is more complex than in a civilian setting. Philosopher David Archard determined an act is appropriate if everyone involved is competent to give valid consent and the reasonable interests of others are not significantly harmed.[46] That seems simple enough, but what constitutes valid consent? Capacity to give valid consent involves the ability to understand what is being proposed, the possible consequences, and the ability to make a conscious decision. Capacity is reduced by anything that interferes with a person's mental functioning, such as intoxication. Although, in most cases, a person consents to becoming intoxicated, that fact is not an indication of consent to be sexual.

Some individuals are particularly vulnerable to sexual harassment and assault due to a previous history of sexual abuse. Those who experienced incest in their immediate family are at greater risk of further sexual abuse as adults than are persons without these early experiences. A person who as a child assumed passive or frozen response while being sexually abused may involuntarily react the same way when faced with an unwanted or inappropriate sexual experience as an adult.

Consent that has been obtained through the use of threats or coercion is not valid consent. Nonvoluntary consent is an oxymoron, because "Fear invalidates the consent."[47] For the purposes of this book, this type of consent is most relevant due to the power of rank in military inter-actions. Threats can be explicit: "You do this or I will bring you up on charges of insubordination!" Threats can also be implicit, not spoken aloud but communicated through looks or body language.

An example of a situation that involved psychological vulnerability, intimidation, and physical isolation occurred in 1997 at the Aberdeen Proving Ground, where several male drill sergeants were eventually convicted of raping female trainees. The trainees were isolated with the drill sergeants at a small training area ten miles outside the main base so all people the trainees normally could have confided in (healthcare providers, chaplains, and company commander) were not on site, and in order to go off site, the trainees had to obtain permission from the very people who were abusing them.[48]

Is a Lack of Protest Consent?

Historically, men have been taught to assume that a woman who does not overtly protest is giving consent. However, if mere silence was the only criterion for determining consent, then a dead person could be said to be giving consent.[49] Women with conservative gender-role train-ing, and those who have histories of sexual abuse, have a tendency to acquiesce even to unwanted sexual attention.[50] If there is any doubt as to whether consent has been given, it is safest to assume that it has not been given.

> *"The harm to a woman of unconsented sex is much graver than that of the loss to a man who refrains from proceeding to have sex with consent."*—David Archard [51]

WARTIME MENTALITY

"If you believe the doctors, nothing is wholesome; if you believe the theologians, nothing is innocent; if you believe the soldiers, nothing is safe."—Lord Salisbury[52]

IN ORDER TO UNDERSTAND the mindset of the military it is helpful to contrast peacetime and wartime thinking. In contrast to civilians, military personnel are more prone to have a wartime perception of the world continuously, because they are always training for war. Wartime mentality involves dualistic, all-or-nothing thinking.

"The dualistic tendencies are evident: good vs. evil, capitalism vs. communism, a government of law and defense vs. the welfare state, the chosen nation vs. those in darkness."—James Nelson[53]

"In the army [sic] we weren't trained to give much attention to our feelings, or even to critical thinking. It was assumed that situations would be more or less black and white."—Sergeant Erik R. Saar[54]

"Soldiers are not, on the whole, warmongers, but the 'military mind'—the professional military perspective on human affairs—nevertheless exercises an enormous influence on how the business of mankind is conducted. The perspective is by no means arbitrary or narrowly self-serving; it is grounded in the military officers' recognition of the unpleasant realities of their profession."—Dr. Gwynne Dyer[55]

Army psychologist Lawrence LeShan has identified the steps that move a nation toward war:[56] enemy is identified; enemy is determined to be evil; presence of the enemy can no longer be tolerated; taking action against the enemy will lead to glory and improve the world; anyone who doesn't accept these facts is a traitor and supports the enemy.

These steps occur in the foreign policies of nations, but, more importantly for the purposes of this book, they are also apparent in the ways many in the military view women and homosexuals: gays and women have infiltrated our ranks; gays are evil, and women in the military, particularly in combat roles, are part of an evil plot to undermine the strength of the military; the presence of gays and women (except in limited roles) can no longer be tolerated; action, whether legal or illegal (harassment and assault), must be taken and will lead to personal glory, restore the military to its former glory, and thereby improve the world; and anyone who disagrees with this plan must be gay, a feminist, a traitor, or some combination thereof.

The Concept of Acceptable Loss

"Acceptability, Operation plan review criterion to determination whether a course of action is worth the cost in manpower, material, and time involved; is consistent with the law of war, and is militarily and politically supportable."—Department of Defense Dictionary of Military and Associated Terms[57]

"So what? What's the big deal, six fuckin' recruits drown?"—Marine recruiter when asked his reaction to the deaths of six recruits on an unscheduled march into a swamp

Even more than in other high-risk jobs, such as firefighters and law enforcement officers, military personnel accept the fact that, no matter how well missions are planned and carried out, some personnel are likely to be wounded, maimed, or killed. Even the much admired Admiral Chester Nimitz never lost less than 25 percent of the ships and 50 percent of the airplanes under his command in the four major engagements in which he led.[58]

The Organization Must Be Protected Even at the Cost of the Individual

"In the Marine Corps, if there's one single theme, or counsel, that goes throughout your career, it's 'Don't disgrace the Corps.'"—A Marine Corps Major[59]

The U.S. Supreme Court has repeatedly ruled that the purpose and organization of the military makes it necessary to subordinate the individual for the common good. In one case the justices wrote that the "very essence" of military service involves the "subordination of the desires and interests of the individual to the needs of the service."[60]

Historically, this attitude has contributed to the armed forces and Veterans Administration ignoring and suppressing reports of sexual abuse. Disclosure of sexual abuse within the ranks threatens to tarnish the reputation of particular units and the military in general. Therefore, evidence of abuse is overlooked, and those who attempt to call attention to it are discouraged, threatened, or punished. Those who dare discuss these "private matters" outside the military "family" are viewed with disdain, since the military is supposed to "take care of our own dirty laundry" without the interference of outsiders (civilians) who "don't understand." This dynamic is similar to what victims of incest experience. "If you tell anyone about what happened, Daddy will go to jail and then everyone in the family will suffer, and it will be your fault."

Thomas Powers, one of the officials with the Naval Criminal Investigation Service who was involved in examining the events that took place at the 1991 Tailhook Convention, was shocked that men who had sworn to protect and defend the Constitution of the United States would lie under oath to protect those involved in criminal acts. He noted, "It's as if they take an oath to the navy and not the nation."[61] The urge to defend the military's integrity is also apparent in documents that were produced in response to the scandal at Abu Ghraib prison.

> We should emphasize that tens of thousands of men and women in uniform strive every day under austere and dangerous conditions to secure our freedom and the freedom of others.[62]
>
> Although a clear breakdown in discipline and leadership, the events at Abu Ghraib should not blind us from the noble conduct of the vast majority of our Soldiers. We are a values-based profession in which the clear majority of our Soldiers and leaders take great pride. A clear vote of confidence should be extended by the senior leadership to the leaders and Soldiers who continue to perform extraordinarily in supporting our Nation's wartime mission. Many of our Soldiers have paid the ultimate sacrifice to preserve the freedom and liberties that America and our Army represent throughout the world.[63]

When one combines the concept of acceptable loss with the philosophy that the organization must be protected even at the cost of the individual, it is easy to see how the pain of an individual who has been sexually abused can be written off as "the price of doing business."

It's a Military Thing; You Wouldn't Understand

"Civilians cannot and will not understand us because they are not one of us. The Corps—we love it, live it, and shall die for it. If you have never been in it, you shall never understand it."—A U.S. Marines Lance Corporal[64]

Perhaps the ultimate expression of the military as a culture is the belief that anyone who is not a member of the military is incapable of understanding it. Therefore, whenever a civilian questions the military mentality, service members dismiss the critic as naïve, uninformed, and not creditable. Of course, when the critics are themselves members of the military, this dismissal is less effective.

The primary justification for the military being granted exception to the laws that govern the rest of society is that the military deals in death. At first glance this is a convincing argument, but it ignores the fact that those in other organizations such as law enforcement also risk their lives and use deadly force, and yet society and the courts have insisted that they conform to contemporary society.[65]

Warning: Social Experiments Ahead

"The Clinton Administration's penchant for social experimentation has unleashed a war against military standards and values."—J. H. Anderson[66]

A version of "It's a military thing; you wouldn't understand" is the discounting of attempts at modifying traditional military culture as a dangerous "social experiment." Military leaders described the racial integration of the armed forces as a dangerous social experiment. Army General George Marshall explained his opposition to the integration: "The War Department cannot ignore the social relationships between Negro and white, which have been established by the American people through custom and habit...such a social experiment would only bring a danger of efficiency, discipline, and morale."[67] Similar worries were voiced by military leaders when women entered the military and when it was proposed that homosexuals not be driven from the ranks.

Living in Separate Worlds

With the creation of the all-volunteer military, it is becoming increasingly true that much of American society truly doesn't understand military culture. Fewer Americans have first-hand experience of military service. During World War II, eight out of ten eligible males served in the military. By the Vietnam era, only four in ten males had served, even though there was still a draft. By the 1990s, fewer than one in ten men had military experience.[68]

Increasingly, members of Congress lack military experience. During the Vietnam War, two-thirds of the members of Congress were veterans. By the 1990s, only one-third had any military experience.[69] According to the Military Officers Association of America in 2006, only 31 percent of the Senate and 25 percent of the House had any military experience.[70]

ASSEMBLING THE PUZZLE OF SEXUAL ABUSE

IN ORDER FOR SEXUAL ABUSE to take place a number of factors have to come together: the abuser must be motivated to engage in abusive behavior, overcome any internal inhibitions to actually following through on the urge to abuse, overcome external inhibitions to abuse that are present in the unit, and overcome any resistance from the victim.[71] The extent to which sexual abuse takes place is greatly influenced by how abuse is viewed by leaders.

In units with leaders that deal proactively with sexual abuse, education is provided to all members of the unit. There are clear policies that are consistently and fairly enforced. Abuse is perceived as a problem for the entire unit. Those who report abuse are not punished, overtly or covertly, for doing so.

Less effective leaders perceive abuse as an individual problem ("Get over it. Learn to deal with it.") or as a problem between individuals ("You two learn to get along."). Those who make reports are usually seen as being troublemakers. Not surprisingly, a Department of Defense study found that, in units in which the men perceived their commanding officer was neutral or indifferent to abuse, there was more abuse than in units where the leaders were not tolerant of abuse.[72] The most salient predictors of sexual abuse in a unit were the absence of a grievance procedure, an unprofessional work atmosphere, and the existence and acceptance of a sexist attitude in the workplace.[73]

Unfortunately, there are units in which the leaders do not come to the aid of victims, but encourage abusers or even take part in abuse. In such units, anyone who dares to report abuse is punished.

3

"A BAND OF BROTHERS": THE CODE OF HYPERMASCULINITY

"We few, we happy few, we band of brothers, for he today that sheds his blood with me shall be my brother. . . ."—Henry V at the battle of Agincourt

ORGANIZATIONS THAT ENDORSE stereotypical masculinity exhibit much higher rates of sexual harassment and assault than do other organizations.[1] Therefore, to understand the context in which sexual abuse takes place in the military, one must understand the type of masculinity historically endorsed by many of its members.

A person is born male or female, but learns to be masculine or feminine.* Masculinity and femininity are taught to a child by its parents, siblings, and playmates, as well as through books, TV, movies, and school. The form of masculinity historically promoted in the military culture is an extreme one; therefore, I will use the term hypermasculinity to describe it. We will now examine this version of masculinity and its impact on the incidence and prevalence of sexual abuse.

"Masculinity is not something given to you, something you're born with, but something you gain. . . . And you gain it by winning small battles with honor." —Norman Mailer, *Cannibals and Christians*

---

* An ever-increasing number of persons are androgynous, meaning they are a balance of conventionally feminine and masculine tastes, values, and behaviors.

POLARIZED GENDER ROLES

A POLARIZED VIEWPOINT is apparent in the phrase "opposite sex" rather than "other sex."* According to this belief system, men are logical; therefore, women are emotional (as if a person couldn't be both logical and emotionally expressive). Polarized thinking holds that since men are strong, women must be weak. It follows that a man who is weak is less masculine and less deserving of respect or status. Drill instructors have long attempted to degrade, and thus motivate, male recruits by calling them girls or ladies.

> Interviewer: "What does masculine mean to you?"
> Marine Corporal: "Masculine means being able to act like a man."
> Interviewer: "How should a man act?"
> Marine Corporal: "Not like a woman."[2]

ENDORSEMENT OF PATRIARCHY

PERSONS WHO ENDORSE PATRIARCHY believe that males naturally are entitled to authority over females and that it is inappropriate for women to be in positions of authority over men.[3] In their view, when women outrank and give orders to men, it seems a violation of natural law. When the Women Army Corps was founded during World War II, it was made clear in the governing statutes that women were not to be in positions that permitted them to command male soldiers. Even in the 1970s, when female military officers had men under their command, they were not allowed to write their male subordinates' Efficiency Reports; it was considered demeaning for men to be evaluated by women. Of course, the military is not the only place where endorsement of patriarchy is found. Women make up more than half of the adult population of the United States but only 15 percent of the seats in Congress are held by women.

> *"Male power, especially over females, appears to be central to many men's definitions of themselves. With power they are men; without it they are no better than women."*—A. Kahn [4]

---

* The phrase "opposite sex" did not become widely used until the eighteenth century.

Marines in the lowest four ranks (E1-E4) who pride themselves on their hypermasculine image are half as likely to be married as males in the Air Force with the same rank.[5] When it comes to male-female relationships, hypermasculine men "wear the pants in the family" and avoid appearing "pussy whipped." When deployed at sea, some men compete to see how long they can hold out before "breaking down" and making a telephone call to their wives or girlfriends. Those who only last two weeks are viewed with disdain; those who last five weeks brag about their "stamina."

Natural Instinct to Protect and Defend Females

According to the membership of the Southern Baptist Convention, gender roles are "established by God" and men have a "gender-based responsibility to protect women and children."[6] Having women in the military, particularly in combat roles, violates this cherished role of men as protectors of the weak.

> Senator William Cohen: "Suppose you had a women pilot. . . of superior intelligence, great physical conditioning, in every way she was superior to a male counterpart vying for a combat position. Would. . . [you personally] because you would not want to see the risk to her life increased. . . pick the male over the female under those circumstances?"
>
> Air Force General Merrill McPeak: "That is correct."
>
> Senator Cohen: "So in other words, you would have a military less effective situation because of a personal view."
>
> General Merrill: "Well, I admit it doesn't make much sense, but that's the way I feel about it."[7]

Not everyone believes that males have an instinctual drive to protect females. Donna Dean wrote, "Natural protective instinct in males for the females? Oh, come now. Mass murder, rape, torture and other nasty things perpetrated against women (and children) by males, sometimes, but not always due to war, certainly proves the fallacy of that warm and fuzzy myth."[8] Certainly if all males were instinctually driven to protect women there would be no need for this book.

When American military personnel at the Abu Ghraib prison in Iraq wanted to humiliate their Iraqi prisoners, they made use of the prisoners' cultural view that women are inferior to men. What better way to humiliate a Middle-Eastern male than to have an American female lead him, naked, around on a leash and order him to masturbate while she watched?9 When these acts became public, many American civilians were shocked. The reports contradicted the belief that women's "mothering instinct" would make it impossible for them to frighten and debase a helpless person—let alone enjoy it. Those who are shocked by the idea that women could enjoy having—and potentially misusing—power over others have not been paying attention to history. After World War II, Irma Grese, a twenty-one-year-old woman who was the head of the Nazi SS guards at the Belsen concentration camp, was sentenced to death for atrocities she had committed at the camp. These horrible acts included beating prisoners to death, allowing dogs to attack and even feed on living prisoners, and binding together the legs of pregnant prisoners who were in labor and watching as the mothers and babies slowly and agonizingly died. Nor was she the only woman to take part in these acts: twenty-eight other female guards from this camp were found guilty of similar crimes.[10]

Restrictive Emotionality

Combat is a life-threatening situation, filled with extreme stress and uncertainty in which soldiers must perform assigned tasks while simultaneously controlling their emotions. As Mark Gerzon explained, "To embody courage under the most gruesome circumstances, the Soldier [sic] had to repress his fear. To embody strength, he had to repress his feelings of vulnerability. To embody toughness, he had to repress his sensitivity. To kill, he had to repress compassion."[11] Dr. Danny Kaplan noted, "The military role requires a restriction of personal identity and emotional experience. It is a cultural setting in which group performance and cooperation takes priority over individual expression of emotions. The mere thought of individual emotions may lead to uncontrolled action, and is therefore perceived as endangering the accomplishment of the military mission."[12] The most extreme example of this is when command structure falls apart, discipline disappears, and orderly retreat turns into a rout as individuals scrabble to save themselves.

Despite all the training males receive to ignore, suppress, and deny their emotions, men are still powerfully affected by combat. The psychological impact of combat has been called many things: shell shock, combat fatigue, and most recently, Post Traumatic Stress Disorder (PTSD). The number of psychological casualties is significant and can change the course of campaigns. During World War II, the U.S. Army alone sent home approximately 400,000 soldiers for "psychological reasons."[13]

Officers tend to suffer from trauma responses at four times the rate of enlisted personnel. One theory for this dramatic increase is that, in addition to the usual stresses of combat, officers are expected to uphold the hypermasculine ideal in order to keep morale high and motivate enlisted personnel.[14] The more involved service members are with killing or witnessing death, the higher their risk for psychological disturbances. Those personnel who personally take part in committing atrocities, such as raping civilians or comrades, are particularly at risk for trauma responses, particularly when their participation cannot be "rationalized in terms of some higher value or meaning."[15]

HIGH VALUE PLACED ON CONTROL, POWER, AND COMPETITION

WAR IS THE MOST EXTREME form of competition—to the winner go the spoils, and death to the loser. Hypermasculine males tend to view most interaction in terms of competition, with winners and losers. On board one ship, a group of the officers organized a competition to see who could go the longest without masturbating, while another group competed to see who could masturbate to ejaculation the greatest number of times in a twenty-four-hour period.[16] A hypermasculine male dare not engage in competition with a female, because nothing good can come of it. If he bests her, it is a hollow victory—after all, she is "only a woman." If he loses, he is less of a man because, as a male, he is supposed to be inherently better than any female. At the end of each academic year in the Naval Academy, members of the outgoing freshman class attempt to climb to the top of a twenty-one-foot greased obelisk to retrieve a sailor cap. There is a superstition that the person who actually removes the cap from the top will reach the rank of admiral. Since the goal is not only to retrieve that cap, but also to do so in less time than any previous class, the class works as a group, forming a human pyramid, with comrades clambering one on top of another in a frantic scramble to get someone to the top as quickly as possible. That is, unless the person getting near the top is a female, in which case her classmates toss her off, because none of them wants to be a member of the first class to be disgraced by having a woman reach the top first.[17]

Valuing control and power are useful attitudes when waging conventional war, but increasingly American foreign policy involves peacekeeping, which requires a different set of skills. Psychologist Diederik Stapel pointed out, "Competition activates a focus on differences between you and other people, and cooperation activates another mindset, where you focus on similarities."[18] Warriors need to focus primarily on competition, but peacekeepers are more effective when they concentrate on cooperation. Soldiers who value control and power, particularly if viewed as a sign of manhood, are frustrated by the restraints of peacekeeping. This frustration can be acted out in the form of sexual harassment, sexual assault, or other forms of violence toward local civilians or comrades.

THE VIEW OF PAIN

"Pain is good. Extreme pain is extremely good."—Sign on the ceiling of a barracks so as to be visible to those doing sit-ups

IN THE CIVILIAN WORLD, pain is bad. In the world of the military, pain is good. Drill instructors tell recruits, "Pain is weakness leaving the body." Military personnel are expected to continue to perform regardless of exhaustion, pain, or injury. Not to do so is a betrayal of masculinity and the military mentality.

MANDATORY HETEROSEXUALITY

"The men in Special Forces could be crude but in their opinion, faggots were the absolute scum of the earth, especially among the officer corps."—J. Hatheway, Green Beret and homosexual[19]

"The military isn't good about dealing with the realities of sexuality, either heterosexual or homosexual."—Colonel M. Cammermeyer, U.S. Army[20]

The hypermasculine male's heterosexuality must be constantly proven by making sexual comments about women. Real men are expected to always be ready to have sex.

Entitlement—"A Stiff Cock Has No Conscience"

Most people would agree that the longer sexual arousal is sustained, the more intense it becomes. The hypermasculine believe this sense of increasing urgency brings with it decreasing responsibility.[21] They believe there is a point of no return where sexual contact must take place, even if the other person has not agreed to that outcome. Historically, military personnel, particularly those of high rank, believed being warriors entitled them to sex on demand. Mary Reynolds Powell, a nurse stationed in Vietnam, wrote of getting a telephone call from a male captain "suggesting" that at least ten female nurses, not "too heavy," between five-foot-four feet tall and five-foot-seven, including blondes, brunettes, and redheads, ought to make an appearance at an upcoming party, and be "interested in having fun."[22]

The Pairing of Sex and Violence

"You've got to see it to believe it, fourteen outrageously sexy girls in string bikinis and high heels blasting away with the sexiest full auto machine guns ever produced."—Sexy Girls and Sexy Guns, videotape

One troubling aspect of hypermasculinity is the pairing of sex and violence, which makes sexual harassment and assault more likely to occur. In the videogame *Shellshock: Nam '67* the designers strove to make the battle scenes realistic and included an option where players could sexually abuse Vietnamese prostitutes.[23] The military has traditionally, actively paired sex and violence. Rifle practice is referred to as "fucking the targets."[24] A woman who is raped and then killed is referred to as a "double veteran." After the Tet Offensive in Vietnam, President Lyndon B. Johnson bragged, "I didn't screw Ho Chi Minh. I cut his pecker off!"[25] More recently, former President Richard Nixon described Saddam Hussein's defeat as being "militarily castrated."[26] During the second Gulf War, American aviators wrote "Bend over Saddam" on their bombs prior to dropping them.[27] Lt. Col. Dave Grossman recalled a Jody call that paired violence and sex: "I-Wanna-Rape-Kill-Pillage-and-Burn-and-Eat-Dead-Baaaabies!"[28] A Naval Academy cadence call that goes beyond pairing sex with violence, crossing over into misogyny, is "The S&M Man,"* sung to the tune of *The Candy Man.*

> Who can take a chainsaw, cut the bitch in two, fuck the bottom half, and give the upper half to you...[Chorus] The S&M man, the S&M Man, The S&M Man 'cause he mixes it with love and makes the hurt feel good! Who can take a bicycle, then take off the seat, set his girlfriend on it ride her down a bumpy street...[Chorus] Who can take some jumper cables, clamp them on her tits, jump-start your car, and electrocute the bitch...[Chorus] Who can take an ice pick, ram it through her ear, ride her like a Harley, as you fuck her from the rear...[Chorus][29]

Misogyny

"Chivalry is the most delicate form of contempt."—Albert Guerard

Misogyny occurs when the achievement of masculinity moves from being defined as that which is not feminine to demeaning that which is feminine. Misogyny is to sex as racism is to race: members of a particular group viewed as inferior, not because of who they are as individuals, but because they are members of the group. A misogynistic man may not think of himself as hating women. In fact, he may proclaim and even believe he respects women. But he actually respects the ideal of woman. Those who do not fit his narrow definition are not worthy of respect—quite the opposite. They are to be distained and punished. In 1991, when Specialist Melissa Rathbun-Nealy was captured by Iraqi troops, a reporter asked former World War II POW Sally Millett if she thought Mathun-Nealy would be "mistreated" (read: raped). Millet responded, "They don't hate women any more or as much as American men hate women."[30]

Historically, the military has focused on defining masculinity in contrast to women (and homosexual men). When a drill sergeant wished to insult his male recruits he would call them "a bunch of girls" or refer to them as "ladies." As one serviceman described it,

---

* S&M stands for sado-masochism, obtaining sexual pleasure from inflicting psychological or physical pain.

The lessons on manhood…focus less on creating what the Army wanted than on defining what the Army did not want. This is why calling recruits faggots, sissies, pussies, and girls had been a time-honored stratagem for drill instructors throughout the armed forces. The context was clear: There was not much worse you could call a man.[31]

Mary Reynolds Powell, an Army nurse who served in Vietnam, observed the effect that insulting men by referring to them as women had on their view of women: "When boot camp instructors call soldiers 'girls' or 'ladies' to insult them, it is impossible for the same soldiers and their officers to regard women as anything but inferior."[32] In 2005, American military personnel in Afghanistan broadcast taunts over a loudspeaker as they burned the corpses of Taliban fighters. The Americans had laid the bodies facing west to mock the Islamic requirement of facing Mecca during prayers, and burned them because Islam does not allow cremation. An Australian camera crew filmed Sergeant Jim Baker saying in the local language, "You allowed your fighters to be laid down facing west and burned. You are too scared to come down and retrieve the bodies. This proves you are the lady boys we always believed you to be." Another American chimed in, "You attack and run away like women."[33]

Marines view the corps as the most masculine of the branches of the U.S. military and refer to the other branches as "the sister services."[34] Is it a coincidence that the Marine Corps is the branch that has the highest incidence of sexual harassment? When 94 percent of navy specialties were open to women, the Marine Corps only allowed women in 62 percent of their specialties.[35] And when other branches reported a sexual harassment rate of 55 percent, the Marines had a rate of 64 percent.

In 1996, the U.S. Army Senior Review Panel on Sexual Harassment distributed questionnaires to determine the causes of sexual harassment. They found there was a strong statistical correlation between sexual harassment and seven questions on attitudes about gender and sexuality. The data from those questions was destroyed, and personnel who had seen the results of the study were threatened with severe penalties for disclosing the results or releasing copies of the seven questions.[36]

"Patriotism is not enough, I must have no hatred or bitterness for anyone."—The last words of Edith Cavell, a British nurse, before her execution by a German firing squad

HYPERMASCULINITY AND SEXUAL ASSAULT

CERTAIN ATTITUDES RELATED to masculinity have been found to be associated with increased propensity to sexual assault. A view of masculinity that emphasizes dominance, aggression, self-sufficiency, and willingness to take risks, combined with a rejection of compassion and empathy, is correlated with propensity to rape.[37] These are the very values that have been promoted in military training.

Hostility toward women is correlated with sexual aggression. Men with an increased propensity to rape report resentment, anger, and distrust toward women, view them as deceitful flirts who tease men, and believe women take advantage of men who do not stand up to them.[38] Those men believe women "are and should be subordinate to men" and "are to be controlled and manipulated." They also think coercion and aggression are acceptable methods for obtaining sex.[39] Numerous studies have found that men who endorse hypermasculine values are also likely to have a rape-supportive attitude and commit more actual sexual aggression than men who have less extreme masculine values.[40]

The connection between hypermasculinity and sexual abuse is found in other cultures, not just American society. Of 156 societies studied for their attitudes concerning rape, 47 percent were found to have strong taboos against rape, low rates of sexual assault, and a belief that men and women are equals. Eighteen percent of the societies studied were termed "rape-prone," because when rape occurred, it was ignored or even viewed as permissible. In these societies the culture included high rates of "interpersonal violence and male domination and exploitation."[41] Below are the characteristics that have been found to increase the likelihood of sexual abuse.[42] Of these characteristics, one study found that a man's attitude toward feminism was "the most consistent predictor of date rape supportive attitudes."

- Acceptance of interpersonal violence

- Existence of stereotypic gender roles for both men and women (patriarchy)
- Rejection of feminism
- Women viewed as the property of men
- Adversarial and exploitive male-female sexual relationships
- Attraction to sexual aggression (the idea of raping is exciting—women like rough sex)
- Homophobia (anxiety, disgust, anger, aversion, and fear of homosexuals)

Misogyny is simply another word for hate. Psychologist Susan Opotow writes about how hate makes it possible, even easy, to harm another people.

> They [the hated persons] can be seen as expendable, undeserving nonentities who are eligible targets of exploitation or they can be seen as evil enemies who are eligible targets of violence. Whether nonentities or enemies, those outside the scope of justice are morally excluded and seen as less than human. They are not seen as deserving positive social goods, rights, or fair procedure. Distributive or procedural injustice, disadvantage, hardship, exploitation, or harm they experience can seem normal and appropriate and can fail to elicit a sense of injustice, remorse, outrage, or demands for restitution. Instead, for those viewed as evil, harm can be a cause for celebration.[43]

THE FRAGILENESS OF HYPERMASCULINITY

"That warrior mentality will crumble if women are placed in combat positions."
—A First Sergeant testifying before a Presidential Commission[44]

IRONICALLY, DESPITE THE BLUSTER and grandiosity associated with hypermasculinity, it is surprisingly fragile when challenged. One would think that given the gung-ho, can-do attitude associated with the military, there would be very little that military men would find intimidating. However, there are three things that consistently threaten them: competent women; lesbians; and gay men. General John W. Vessey Jr., Chairman of the Joint Chiefs of Staff, testified before a Congressional hearing that increasing the number of women in the military had taken "a male institution" and turned it into "a coed institution," which had been "a traumatic exercise" for military men.[45] His statement was made when only one in ten members of the military were women and they were still restricted to their traditional roles. Major General Jeanne Holm was taken aback at the chairman's reaction to the inclusion of a few more women in the ranks: "That an institution the size of the U.S. armed forces could be so traumatized by a few women speaks volumes about the mind-set of the time. . . . Most disconcerting was the fact that they [women] were demonstrating the ability to perform many military roles previously reserved for men."[46] The first class to include female cadets at West Point contained approximately 100 women. Despite making up a tiny fraction of the student body, the very presence of these women intimidated many of the 4,000 male cadets. If this were a combat setting, imagine how tough a force would have to be to intimidate an enemy forty times their number.

"Until we redefine manhood, we shall not end war."—Paul Fussell[47]

4

HAZING: WHAT GOES AROUND COMES AROUND

ONCE RECRUITS ACCEPT that violence is a legitimate method for obtaining things—security, honor, respect—they may generalize the usefulness of violence beyond the enemy. Hazing is built upon the acceptance of violence among comrades. Periodically, the existence of hazing comes to the attention of the general public, usually due to a death or the release of photographic evidence. Hazing is officially prohibited in the military, but unofficially is widely sanctioned; therefore charges are rarely brought against those involved.* In those rare cases where charges are brought, they are typically dropped. Hazing is often viewed as a harmless ritual; however, there are significant differences between rituals and hazing.

CONTRASTING RITUALS AND HAZING

RITUALS MARK IMPORTANT events. Military academies hold graduation ceremonies in acknowledgment of the graduates' achievements. Such rituals elevate the status of the graduates. In contrast, hazing usually involves submission, humiliation, and physical pain. During hazing, the inductee undergoes a process of being dishonored and debased, all in the name of being allowed to become a member of an honored group or institution. Rituals indicate that someone is willing and able to join a group, and that the group is willing to accept the person as a member, so there is no question as to the outcome of the ritual: The inductee will

---

* There are exceptions. In 2002 a military court found Lt. Cmdr. Jeffery B. Martin guilty of crimes associated with hazing and sentenced him to five days in jail and a $10,000 fine (Nuwer, 2004).

become a member of the group. In hazing, inductees must demonstrate their worth by enduring the hazing. If the inductee fails to properly tolerate the hazing—by protesting, crying, or showing signs of pain—then membership in the group is denied.

Since hazing does not officially exist, it is not regulated; what takes place is up to the imagination of those initiating it. Usually it is a reenactment of what was done to them when they were the targets of hazing. Once the hazing begins, the initiate doesn't know what will occur or for how long and can only hope that his comrades will not do anything that will lead to permanent injury or death.

Some describe hazing as fun and look back on it with affection, and there is a great deal of peer pressure to view it in this manner, otherwise one runs the risk of being seen as a kill-joy, a wimp, or disrespectful of sacred tradition.

For the most part, it is the intent of the person(s) doing the hazing that determines the classification of the hazing more than the specific acts per se. Hazing that occurs once, on the occasion of a special event and with many people present, is more likely to fall under the category of tradition or rite of passage. Hazing that takes place repeatedly over a long period of time, is not paired with a special event, and involves only one person being hazed is more likely to be a form of abuse.

Humiliation

Humiliation is an integral part of hazing. The use of humiliation in hazing is fascinating, since military personnel, particularly men, report that pride and honor are an important aspect of military service, as illustrated by the Marine Corps slogan "The few, the proud, the Marines." A major described the mindset: "In flight school they give you a psychological aptitude test. One of the questions they ask you is, which would you rather do: be violently ill on a public bus with all these people around or slam your hand in a car door? . . . I would rather slam my hand in the car door. Isolated pain [is better than] public humiliation."

Humiliation is induced by treating inductees as members of lower status groups, such as women, homosexuals, and animals, requiring them to dress like women, act as if they are having sex with one another, and crawl around on all fours.

For new cadets the first few weeks at West Point include being ordered by more senior cadets to march while carrying boxes of provisions and chanting, "We are dumb, dumb knuckleheads." Each cadet is provided with his or her own personal "poop," an unflattering statement, which must be recited when a senior cadet demands, "Gimme your poop!" Captain Carol Barkalow recalled one from her time at the Academy: "Sir, I'm the Madwoman of Borneo. I have more hair on my chest than you have on your head."[1]

Pain

Inflicting pain on the enemy is the business of the military, but in hazing the target is one's comrades. Of course, the goals are different: when hurting the enemy it is to disable; when inflicting pain on a comrade the implied goal is to strengthen. Examples of pain induced in the name of hazing include punching, kicking, and applying stinging chemicals such as pepper sauce or edge dressing* to the penis, scrotum, and anus of the initiate.

EXAMPLES OF HAZING

Immersion

THE INITIATE IS IMMERSED in vomit, blood, urine, or feces, or in ice water, creating a risk of hypothermia.

Physical Exertion

Physical training is a normal part of military training; however, the use of painful and even damaging physical exertion is sometimes a part of hazing. When future Army Chief of Staff George C. Marshall attended the Virginia Military Academy, senior cadets ordered him to squat over a bayonet until his knees buckled and he fell on the blade, cutting him and scarring him for life. In 1983, at the Air Force Academy, first-year cadets were ordered to run up and down flights of stairs wearing winter clothing until exhausted, to the point where 139 cadets needed medical treatment for dehydration and some had to be hospitalized.[2] Cadets at West Point easily identified over one hundred forms of hazing, including scalding steam baths, immersion in cold water, forced feeding, beatings

---

* A tar-like shoe polish.

with fists, "dipping" (push-ups), and sliding down a splinter-filled board while naked.

Senior cadets order first-year cadets to perform the eight-count gaze around, which consists of standing at attention, looking up, then straight ahead, then turning the head and eyes to the right, then straight ahead, then to the left, and again straight ahead. These movements are repeated for as long as the senior student desires, sometimes for hundreds of repetitions. When Douglas MacArthur underwent hazing at West Point, he was forced to do calisthenics for over an hour until he fainted and began convulsing. Years later, General MacArthur recalled that "Hazing was practiced with a worthy goal, but with methods that were violent and uncontrolled."[3]

"Sweating to the Wall"

The inductee is required to stand at attention with heels touching a wall, while pressing a dollar bill or other object against the wall with the head. They must keep this posture until they perspire enough that their sweat adheres the object to the wall.

Ingesting Substances

The initiate is forced to ingest massive amounts of water, chili sauce, spices, or food to the point of abdominal pain or vomiting, or substances such as laxatives, dirt, tobacco, blood, urine, or feces. The consumption of alcohol is commonly involved in hazing to reduce inhibitions in both the initiate and those in charge. Forced use of alcohol as a part of the hazing can lead to alcohol overdose, which can cause unconsciousness and death.[4]

Simulated Sex Acts

Since humiliation is a vital aspect of hazing, and hypermasculine men disdain homosexual men, simulation of same-sex acts are common in hazing. As the result of inquiries by Senators Richard Lugar and Dan Quayle, the details of hazing aboard the Coast Guard *Mesquite* became public, including enlisted personnel simulating oral sex on carrots that were then forced into their anuses.[5]

Blood Stripes

A Marine corporal described this form of hazing: "When you pick up rank, they put your new rank on your collar; they don't put the backings on the pins, and with an open palm drive them into your collarbone. A lot of times when you pick up NCO[*] you get 'blood stripes,' [symbolizing] the red stripe on the trousers of your dress blues. . . .[†] you knee the person on the side of the thigh where the blood stripes would be. So you've just had metal pins driven into your collarbone, then you go through a gauntlet, on either side there's guys, and they punch you with their fists, very hard. It's all officially prohibited. You're expected to endure that pain. You're punched or kneed in the leg by half the company...but you're supposed to tolerate this, suck it up, and go on."[6]

Blood Wings

At the graduation celebration for airborne training, each soldier has a metal badge in the shape of wings fastened to their uniform by a family member or military mentor. Once back in the barracks, each soldier is once again awarded the wings, but this time each member of the unit will punch the wings so the uncovered metal pins enter the soldier's flesh—thereby awarding "blood wings."[7]

Final Flight

To mark the occasion of a pilot's final flight before discharge, fellow aviators will meet him by his plane, push him on to the tarmac, and "dog-pile" or "stack," which involves getting as many people as possible on top of him. Newcomers jump onto the bodies already there. The pilot is then taped to a chair, using ordinance tape,[‡] sometimes covering his entire body. Then "tech-pet"[§] is put in his hair, while Speedy Dry[**] is put into his flight suit. Then he is taken to the location where the aircraft are washed and a hose is put down the front of his flight suit.[8]

---

[*] Non-Commissioned Officer
[†] Dress uniform. The stripe is said to commemorate the bloodshed at Chapultepec and the Halls of Montezuma in 1847 mentioned in "The Marines' Hymn" (Woulfe, 1998).
[‡] Four-inch-wide very sticky tape, similar to duct tape.
[§] Technical petrolatum.
[**] A product similar to cat litter used to clean up spilled oil and other fluids.

Crossing the Line

Sailors and marines who are crossing the equator on a ship for the first time undergo an initiation in which they are required to dress like women, act as if they are having sex with one another, and crawl around on all fours. They simulate oral sex by sucking on a section of rubber hose that hangs out the front of the pants of one of the veteran sailors, who is dressed as King Neptune. There is also the "elephant walk," which involves each man holding the genitals of the man in front of him as they parade in front of the other members of the crew.[9]

EXPLANATIONS FOR HAZING

Tradition

THE MOST COMMON EXPLANATION for the continuation of hazing is that it has been a part of the military for so long, it has become an unofficial tradition. John Lenny wrote of the power of tradition, "Hazing is tolerated by the military authorities at West Point—not infrequently approved, openly or covertly. It is not one whit less binding upon the Academic Board, other military officials and the cadets of the military academy than the enactments of Congress."[10] Once a tradition is established, there is little motivation to question it.

Rite of Passage

Another explanation for hazing is that it is a rite of passage and serves to build group unity. This explanation fails to address the reasons that pain, submission, and humiliation are components of the rite. Strengthening the individual's commitment to the cause and developing group cohesion need not involve the three characteristics associated with hazing. The ordination of clergy is a rite of passage that seeks to increase the individual's sense of being a full member of a religious order, but it doesn't involve physical pain or humiliation.

Motivation

In some cases, hazing is committed with the intent of improving the initiate's performance.[11] When people publicly defend hazing, this is the most common defense.

Punishment

This type of hazing is ostensibly used to improve the inductee's sub-standard performance with aversive stimuli. Inductees are supposed to improve to avoid further punishment.[12] "Blanket parties" or "code reds" are examples of this type of hazing, in which an individual who is functioning poorly and thereby bringing extra duties to the entire unit is targeted for punishment. Several comrades restrain the victim with a blanket, while other members of the unit punch, kick, or strike the victim with objects (e.g., bars of soap in the ends of socks).

Teaching Respect for Authority

The military relies on compliance with authority, and hazing has been justified on the grounds that it teaches the inductee respect for author-ity.[13] This result may not be the case, depending on how brutal the hazing. Unfortunately, hazing often merely induces fear of authority and the desire to avoid displeasing superiors. Given the high number of military personnel who experienced domestic violence as children, instead of "inducing" fear of authority it might be more accurate to say hazing "reinforces" the fear of authority.* Unfortunately, those who fear authority are much less likely to be creative in their problem-solving, since they are more interested in avoiding getting in trouble than in getting the job done right.

Desensitization: "Makes 'Em Tough"

Military personnel, particularly those who volunteer for combat and elite units, are consciously putting themselves in situations where they are likely to experience cold, hunger, lack of sleep, and threat to life and limb, aspects of life that most people avoid and even fear. Hazing can be viewed as a method of seeking to desensitize oneself to these unpleas-ant conditions. Rear Admiral James B. Stockdale, who endured eight years in North Vietnam as a prisoner of war, believed the hazing he had undergone while a cadet at the Naval Academy prepared him to cope with his imprisonment. "You have to learn to take a bunch of junk and accept it with a sense of humor."[14] James Webb also believes that hazing is useful in preparing personnel for a military career.

---

* One study found that 48 percent of the female soldiers and 50 percent of the male soldiers reported they had been physically abused before the age of 18 years.

So how do you teach combat leadership? You don't do it with a textbook; you do it by creating a stress environment. My academic education at the Naval Academy always took a back seat to my military education. During our first year, my classmates and I were regularly tested and abused inside Bancroft Hall, our living spaces. We were pushed deep inside ourselves for that entire year, punished physically and mentally stressed to the point that virtually every one of us completely broke down at least once. And when we finished our first year we carried out the same form of abuse on other entering classes. That was the plebe system.* It was harsh and cruel. It was designed to produce a man who would be able to be an effective leader in combat, to endure prisoner-of-war camps, to fight this country's wars with skill and tenacity.[15]

Although these men insist that "abuse" and "harsh and cruel" treatment is a useful way to treat young men, neither of them suggest that older, more high ranking men periodically undergo such treatment to make certain they remain able to endure capture and have what it takes to be effective leaders.

Not everyone who has endured hazing while a cadet at a military academy found it to be useful in preparing him for the experience of being a prisoner of war. A veteran of three and a half years in a World War II Japanese POW camp noted that, although he had suffered at the hands of his captors, he bore "no animosity" against them, because they were enemies at war. But even years after being liberated from the camp, he still "bitterly resented" what had been done to him by his comrades while he was a cadet.[16]

Eliminating the Weak

Captain (later Senator) John McCain explained the purpose of hazing at West Point. "Service academies are not just colleges with a uniform dress code. Their purpose is to prepare you for one profession alone, and that profession's ultimate aspiration is combat command. The Academy experience is intended to determine whether you are fit for such work, and if you are, to mold your natural ability into the attributes of a capable

---

* "Plebe came from the Latin word meaning common people, but plebe at the Academy could best be translated as 'lowest form of life.'" Knudson, 1981, p. 11.

officer. If you aren't, the Academy wants to discover your inaptitude as quickly as possible. The period of discovery is your plebe year, when you are subjected to as much stress as the law and civilized society will allow." He noted that one quarter of the cadets who entered the academy with him were "driven out" by upperclassmen.[17] "Driven out" may mean merely dropping out, but in any given year at West Point an average of nine "plebes" (first-year cadets) attempt suicide.

Dr. Donna Dean, a navy veteran disabled by PTSD brought on by sexual assault, also questions the usefulness of hazing.

> It seems quite odd that the leaders of these institutions and the public in general seem to display an appalling lack of understanding of the inevitable results of such systematic abuses for both the abused and abuser. In fact, many of the 'hallowed traditions' so integral to the military are nothing more than gross violations of human dignity, with the payoff being the promise that the victim can ultimately get even by inflicting abuse on those who follow . . . . How, one must ask, can an abusive, arrogant, insensitive monster of an upperclassman created in a service academy be expected to suddenly transform into an aware, honorable, sensitive leader upon graduation?

Eliminating Undesirables

This form of hazing is done to drive out those considered unfit for military service.[18] Examples of this form of hazing include acts at the military academies directed toward African Americans, women, and gays, in an attempt to drive them out of the armed forces.

Displaying Power

Sometimes there is no pretext that the hazing is being done to benefit either the inductee or the military as a whole. The hazing is done solely for the personal pleasure of the hazer. When asked why they do it, they respond, "Because its fun," "Because I can," or "Because I like the way I feel when I do it." Since there is little or no concern for the inductee, if it becomes out of control, it can lead to serious injury or even death.

"There's no place for humiliation or degradation within the system. And yet there are cadets—little weenies—who go through West Point with a stick up their ass and get their jollies out of picking on people. And we tolerate that."—Captain Kevin Lang[19]

Repetition Compulsion: "It's My Turn Now!"

People who have experienced trauma sometimes have a powerful urge to recreate the traumatic event, but to be in the role of perpetrator rather than victim. The classic example is the people who were sexually abused as children becoming adults who sexually abuse children in turn. One has to wonder if, in some cases, hazing is little more than repetition compulsion passed on from one "generation" to the next. However, given the high rate of military personnel who experienced childhood physical and/or sexual abuse, the compulsion to engage in hazing may stem from childhood experiences rather than hazing experienced as an adult. In any case, for those who, as children, were physically or sexually abused, hazing that involves physical pain and sexual acts can be terrifying.

Sadism

Dr. Arthur Reber defines sadism as "The association of sexual pleasure from the inflicting of pain upon another. Note that pain here may take many forms other than the purely physical. As the term is used, psychic pain, humiliation, debasement, exploitation, etc. may all be regarded as sadistic acts…"[20] It may be that some military members experience great personal satisfaction, and even erotic responses, from humiliating and causing pain to their comrades. These people engage in hazing as a way to indulge themselves.

OBJECTIONS TO MILITARY HAZING

GIVEN THE LONG TRADITION of hazing in the military, some service members are puzzled by the reactions of civilians when a new case of hazing becomes public. They discount civilians' outrage as merely another indication that civilians do not understand military culture. However, not all American military personnel endorse hazing as a desirable aspect of the military. Marine Sergeant Joe Jansen commented, "I don't think that society has a natural aversion to rites of passage and ritual. But I think that society does have an aversion to senseless brutality."[21]

"The discipline which makes the soldiers of a free country reliable in battle is not to be gained by harsh or tyrannical treatment. On the contrary, such treatment is far more likely to destroy than to make an army."—Schofiel's Definition of Discipline, which West Point cadets are required to memorize.[22]

HAZING, HIGHLY COERCIVE INTERROGATION, PRISONER ABUSE, OR CRUEL, INHUMAN, AND DEGRADING TREATMENT?*

"Soldier No. 25, an interrogator with the 321st Military Intelligence Battalion, 'thought it was funny' to see detainees flee from dogs and failed to report prisoners handcuffed together in contorted positions, making it look as though they were having sex with each other."—Abu Ghraib Report

NIGHT AFTER NIGHT the news reports in America and around the world displayed the now infamous image of a man, naked except for a black hood over his head, with electric wires hanging from his body. It is a scandal that damaged the image of America's military and will continue to haunt our foreign and domestic polices for years to come. Most Americans want to believe the acts at Abu Ghraib, Iraq, and Guantanamo Bay, Cuba, were done in the name of national security in order to gain useful information. Unfortunately, according to General Kern there was no noble purpose to these acts. "Most, though not all of the violent or sexual abuses occurred separately from scheduled interrogations and did not focus on persons held for intelligence purposes."[23] A former marine who was stationed at Guantanamo Bay, Cuba, admitted, "The prisoners would talk, but we didn't know what they were saying. I wasn't trying to get information. I was just having a little fun—playing mind control." Sgt. Michael J. Smith appeared in photographs that showed him with his unmuzzled black Belgian shepherd, Marco, barking, lunging, and straining on its leash just inches from the face of a cowering prisoner. He admitted he engaged in these acts for his own amusement and explained his action

---

* H.C.I. & C.I.D. are points along a continuum of physical and mental techniques utilized to obtain information from prisoners. Some people refer to H.C.I. as torture lite (Lelyveld, 2005).

by testifying, "Soldiers are not supposed to be soft and cuddly." He was eventually charged with thirteen crimes and was convicted on six.

The contents of Major General Antonio Taguba's fifty-three-page report on the events at Abu Ghraib prison can be summed up in one word: "sadistic."[24] General Paul Kern described the treatment of prisoners as ranging from "inhumane to sadistic."[25] Former Defense Secretary James Schlesinger characterized the events as "sadism on the night shift."[26] Lieutenant Anthony R. Jones wrote, "No Soldier or contractor believed that these abuses were permitted by any policy or guidance. If proven, these actions would be criminal acts. The primary causes of the violent and sexual abuses were relatively straight-forward individual criminal misconduct, clearly in violation of law, policy, and doctrine and contrary to Army values."

It would be easy and comforting to explain away the events at the American prisons in Iraq and Cuba as being perpetrated by sadistic criminals who somehow managed to make their way into the ranks without being identified. Unfortunately, it was not that simple. Take for example SPC Armin J. Cruz. Prior to being accused of prisoner abuse he had been awarded the Purple Heart for multiple shrapnel wounds as the result of enemy mortar fire, and the Bronze Star for bravery. In preparing his defense, Cruz's attorney sent a package to Lt. General Thomas F. Metz, the commander at Victory Base, Iraq.

> This packet catalogues the evidence for SPC Cruz's superlative moral character. There are over forty letters, military and civilian, from people attesting to the values that SPC Cruz has demonstrated to them though his actions—generosity, bravery, loyalty, integrity, humility, work ethic, professionalism, discipline, and superior competence.... To be plain, SPC Cruz is the 'real deal.' He is the friend that never lets you down, the son that parent's [sic] dream to have, and the Soldier [sic] that personifies the mission and values of the United States Army.

What drives otherwise outstanding personnel to engage in apparently illegal treatment of prisoners for whom they were responsible? When President George W. Bush said he was deeply disgusted by the way an Iraqi prisoner had been treated by American guards at the Abu Ghraib prison in Baghdad, and insisted, "That's not the way we do things in America," he was mistaken. These events do represent the American military. They take place on U.S. military bases and ships throughout the world, and the people being dominated, humiliated, and hurt are not foreigners but Americans. The treatment of foreigners in military prisons is quite similar to the hazing that Americans experience. Hazing and prisoner abuse both include the use of degrading names. Major General Antonio Tagub's report noted prisoners were referred to as "animals," and in at least one photo a prisoner appeared with a blindfold with "shithead" written across it. Major General Tagub indicated male prisoners were subjected to threats of rape, were made to wear women's underwear, and were sodomized with a chemical light and a broomstick. They were forced to masturbate and to kneel in front of other naked prisoners to make it appear they were having oral sex, while photographs and videotapes were made. This sounds nearly identical to the hazing that took place on the *Mesquite*, where enlisted personnel were told to simulate performing oral sex on carrots that were then forced into their anuses. Hazing rituals at West Point have included deprivation of food and black hoods being placed over people's heads, both of which were a part of the acts investigated at Abu Ghraib as crimes.

Sergeant Kayla Williams took part in interrogations in Iraq. She described how male prisoners were brought in blindfolded and naked and how she was directed to embarrass, humiliate, mock, and degrade them. She was told to ridicule their manhood and the size of their genitals.[28] How is it that these acts are considered torture when done to prisoners to break their will, but when done to comrades as hazing they are thought to be useful? The photos of naked prisoners being paraded about on a dog leash, forced to masturbate and to simulate fellatio in front of guards are reminiscent of the descriptions of hazing. Why would we expect U.S. military personnel to treat enemy prisoners better than they themselves were treated when being hazed?

Even the initial explanations given for the events at Abu Ghraib sound like the usual justifications for hazing: "That kind of behavior is not official policy"; "They were only joking around"; "They wouldn't have really seriously hurt anyone."

When the scandal about the Iraqi detainees in Abu Ghraib was front page news, John Kojac, a member of President Bush's nation security staff and a former Marine, complained that human rights activists were using the incidences at the prison to push through their agenda, which was, in his words, "if you're holding somebody captive, you cannot cause them pain." In his protest he noted, "Painful and humiliating tactics are routinely used against Marine recruits in boot camp, against people trying to get into fraternities and against boys trying out for sports teams."[29] In other words, of course we treat our enemies this way; it's the way we treat our comrades and children.

The use of nudity and other forms of sexual humiliation did not begin at Abu Ghraib. One report noted that:

> The use of nudity as an interrogation technique or incentive to maintain the cooperation of detainees was not a technique developed at Abu Ghraib, but rather a technique which was imported and can be traced through Afghanistan and GTMO [The American military facility at Guantanamo Bay, Cuba]. As interrogation operations in Iraq began to take form, it was often the same personnel who had operated and deployed in other theaters who were called upon to establish and conduct interrogation operations in Abu Ghraib. The lines of authority and the prior legal opinions blurred. They simply carried forward the use of nudity into the Iraqi theater of operations. The use of clothing as an incentive (nudity) is significant in that it likely contributes to an escalating 'de-humanization' of the detainees and set the stage for additional and more severe abuses to occur.[30]

What this report failed to mention is that nudity and sexual humiliation was introduced to some American personnel when they themselves were the targets of the behavior as a form of hazing.

In the mid-1990s, as a part of training at the Air Force Academy cadets, both male and female, were assigned the role of "prisoner." They were slapped, punched, and shaken by other cadets who were in the role of "guard." Their pants were unbuttoned, and guards climbed on top of the prisoners to simulate raping them.[31] In Abu Ghraib prison, sexual assault and humiliation were utilized against actual prisoners, and the events were photographed. The justification for the treatment of the American "prisoners" had been that it would toughen them up, yet the explanation for the same type of treatment of actual prisoners was to soften them up. Lieutenant Anthony R. Jones described the events at Abu Ghraib as "straightforward criminal misconduct that are clearly in violation of military law, policy, and doctrine." Yet nearly identical acts are done to Americans by their comrades.[32]

In February 2005, the U.S. State Department issued its annual report on human rights that criticized a number of countries, including Egypt and Syria, for engaging in "torture." Among the methods listed as forms of torture were sleep deprivation and stripping prisoners, two actions that are frequently a part of American military hazing rituals.[33] International law, which has been agreed to by the United States, forbids "Outrages upon personal dignity, in particular humiliating and degrading treatment, enforced prostitution and any form of indecent assault.... at any time and in any place whatsoever, whether committed by civilians or military personnel."[34] One must wonder how acts that are described as torture by the U.S. government and outlawed by international law are believed to be acceptable when done to Americans by Americans in the name of hazing.

The Geneva Convention, Relative to the Treatment of Prisoners of War is an international treaty designed to encourage soldiers to surrender rather than fight to the death, since they believe their captors will not abuse them. The United States of America has agreed to the terms of this document in the hope that when Americans are prisoners of war they will not be tortured. The events at Abu Ghraib prison in Iraq violated three of the Articles of the *Convention*.[35]

Article 13: "Likewise, prisoners of war must at all times be protected, particularly against acts of violence or intimidation and against insults and public curiosity."

Article 17: "No physical or mental torture, nor any other form of coercion, may be inflicted on prisoners of war to secure from them information of any kind whatever. Prisoners of war who refuse to answer may not be threatened, insulted, or exposed to any unpleasant or disadvantageous treatment of any kind."

Article 99: "No moral or physical coercion may be exerted on a prisoner of war in order to induce him to admit himself guilty of the act of which he is accused."

"Intimidation and insults" and "unpleasant treatment" are classic aspects of the hazing experience. How is it that international law forbids this type of treatment of enemy combatants, yet so many in the American military continue to defend hazing as a benign form of behavior?

For those who think that American military prohibitions against humiliating prisoners are new policies and a result of the "feminization of the military," some liberal "activist" judge, political civilians who don't understand the military, or the United Nations, I refer them to General Orders No. 100 released in April 24, 1863: "A prisoner of war is subject to no punishment for being a public enemy, nor is any revenge wreaked upon him by the intentional infliction of any suffering, or disgrace, by cruel imprisonment, want of food, by mutilation, death, or any other barbarity."[36]

The American military is not alone in its practice of hazing nor in prisoner abuse. The elite members of the Canadian Airborne Regiment engaged in hazing that was videotaped and later became public when it was broadcast over Canadian television. The tape showed twenty-three young men lined in a row drinking beer until intoxicated. Then they began to chew on wads of bread with chewing tobacco. The first one to vomit was required to urinate on the masticated wad, put it back in his mouth, and then pass it on to the soldier next to him, so he could place it in his mouth. One man performed push-ups in excrement while his comrades urinated on him. Meanwhile, others were simulating sodomy and masturbation. The one and only black member of the group was led around by a leash while he crawled on all fours. On his back was painted "I love the KKK." Several of his comrades had "bearded" him, which involved smearing feces on his face.

Meanwhile, the remainder of the unit watched, shouting, "We're not racist—we just don't want niggers in the Airborne." The commanders could not claim these were the actions of renegades, because the tape showed the unit's officers standing by, watching the proceedings. One year later, when this unit was serving as United Nations peacekeepers in Somalia, a sixteen year-old (black) boy mysteriously died while in their custody. Was the death of this "nigger" just another case of the harmful effects of hazing on military personnel? Eight soldiers were tried, and one was convicted of torture and manslaughter and given a five-year sentence. The other charged, enlisted men were freed of charges or rebuked with charges of negligence. The commanding officer was cleared of all charges.[37]

As of March 2006, ten-low ranking Americans had been convicted of charges related to their treatment of prisoners at Abu Ghraib prison. No one above the rank of staff sergeant was convicted. Former Corporal Charles Graner Jr. received the longest sentence—ten years in prison. Lynndie England, a twenty-three-year-old reservist who appeared in an infamous photograph giving a thumbs-up in front of naked prisoners, was sentenced to three years behind bars.

Although punishing a few low-ranking Americans served to get the Abu Ghraib prison scandal out of the media spotlight, ignoring the widespread acceptance and encouragement of hazing within the U.S. military only insures that within a matter of time a new batch of Americans will be in the headlines for treating prisoners in similar fashion. I can write that with confidence because, as of October 2005, the Army alone had investigated 400 allegations of detainee abuse that took place after the Abu Ghraib scandal, leading to more than 230 cases of nonjudicial punishments and courts-martial. As before, none of those punished were senior officers.[38]

Hazing is one step along a continuum that normalizes violence as a form of fun and can lead to what Joseph Harry referred as "recreational violence." But providing an environment in which to indulge in personal fantasies of power is not the purpose of the military. The truly professional soldier has a higher calling. As Paul Woodruff noted in his book *Reverence: Renewing a Forgotten Virtue*, "The ceremony with which we surround ourselves in war is part of what makes warriors warriors and not bandits. It's part of what expresses the attitude that is essential to any orderly military force: that the violence they use is not in their own service, but in the service of something larger than themselves—even, in the end, larger than nations."[39]

"Nearly all men can stand adversity, but if you want to test a man's character, give him power."—Abraham Lincoln

5

PROSTITUTION:
THE NECESSARY EVIL?

WHEN SURVEYED, 84 PERCENT of American servicemen said they had been sexual with at least one prostitute during their time in the military.[1] Unlike most civilian agencies, the military has viewed prostitution as necessary to the welfare of its men and has ensured that they have access to prostitutes. In order to maintain friendly relationships back home (including with the religious right), the U.S. military and its allies have long used euphemisms, such as bar girls, hostesses, and special entertainers, for prostitutes.[2] The military views prostitution in terms of combat readiness and foreign relations, not as a moral issue or a women's welfare issue.

PROSTITUTION AS A PERK

SOME HOST NATIONS ACTIVELY provide prostitutes to U.S. military personnel as a sign of friendship. In return, the host country receives military protection and the economic benefits of having military personnel stationed on their soil. This source of income can be significant. At one point, an estimated 25 percent of South Korea's gross national product came from general spending by American troops, and the South Korean government actively promoted selling sex to U.S. military personnel.[3] South Korea's Minister of Education publicly praised how much prostitutes contributed to the gross national product.[4] The Korea International Tourism Association not only licensed, but also trained, women to function as sex workers for foreign men.

The hypermasculine view of manhood holds that men must have, and are entitled to, sex on a regular basis. Since military men are often away from their wives and girlfriends for extended periods of time, they must therefore have access to prostitutes. However, this attitude does not apply to women. Meredith Lehr, herself a military wife, wrote that "model military wives" are expected to be sexually faithful to their husbands regardless of how often or how long they are away on military business, and are expected to accept that husbands will not reveal covert military missions or sexual activity they might engage in while away from home.[5]

PROSTITUTION AS IMPULSE CONTROL

"Prostitutes are a necessity. Without them men would attack respectable women in the streets."—General Napoleon Bonaparte

THE HYPERMASCULINE VIEW maintains that if men are "deprived" of sex, they are more likely to engage in sexual assault. Therefore, in order to protect the good women of the host nation from sexual assault, American men must have access to prostitutes. When several U.S. servicemen rented a car in Okinawa and used it to rape a twelve-year-old girl, the Chief of Pacific Command, Admiral Richard Macke, thought their actions showed poor economic judgment. "I think it was absolutely stupid, as I've said several times. For the price they paid to rent the car, they could have had a girl [prostitute]."[6]

"WE CAN'T DO ANYTHING ABOUT IT"

NONINTERFERENCE IN THE INTERNAL affairs of another nation is a widely used justification for not pressuring a host nation to curtail prostitution near U.S. military bases. The rationale is that prostitution existed in the host country before the American military arrived, and Americans should not impose their values on the citizens of another nation. However, history shows that when the military wants to have an impact on prostitution, it can. In Korea during the 1960s and early 1970s, it was common practice for Korean bars that served Americans to be racially segregated. The prostitutes also restricted themselves to servicing only blacks or whites. As the American civil rights movement began to influence African–American military personnel, they became less tolerant of this segregated system and began demanding access to more bars and prostitutes, demands that sometimes led to violent conflicts between black and white servicemen. The military became concerned that this conflict would reduce morale and be exploited by North Korea.[7] U.S. military officers held meetings with club managers to demand that both black and white Americans be given equal access to both club facilities and women, and threatened that those bars which did not comply would be placed off-limits to military personnel and that the ban would be enforced by military police. When these demands were not met, the commanding general of the 2nd Infantry Division placed whole sections of a town off-limits and indicated the ban would not be lifted until businesses catering to military personnel were transferred to the main streets and street lighting was installed. The town quickly complied. The American military then endorsed certain off-base clubs by placing signs at the entrances indicating that they met acceptable standards for patronage by service personnel. Such actions usually succeed in persuading the club owners to comply with the military's standards.

During the First Gulf War, the military feared that, if U.S. military personnel tried to purchase sex while stationed in Islamic host nations such as Saudi Arabia, the host nations would withdraw their permission to house U.S. troops, endangering the mission. Therefore, U.S. military commanders implemented and enforced strict policies prohibiting personnel from patronizing prostitutes.[8]

"IF YOU CAN'T BEAT THEM, JOIN THEM"

"In Vietnam, all the woman either have TB or VD. If you want to screw someone, make sure she's coughing."—Latrine graffiti[9]

IN MANY CASES the American military has not only tolerated prostitution, but also actively participated in it. In World War II, Army personnel toured brothels and then designated them for officers, white enlisted men, or nonwhite enlisted men. Prices for sexual services were listed on bulletin boards at military posts and military trucks transported men to and from brothels.[10] During the Vietnam War, U.S. military personnel tested and treated prostitutes for sexually transmitted diseases (Sidebar

5-1). Prostitutes were issued "VD" cards to show potential customers that they had been determined to be disease free within the previous two weeks. Other commands adopted a "contact slip" system, whereby a GI who purchased sex was expected to obtain a preprinted form to record the name and VD registration number of the woman, and retain it for at least two weeks so he could accurately report who had infected him if he developed a sexually transmitted disease. This system was abandoned, because personnel were often so intoxicated when they solicited the prostitute that they forgot to complete the slips. Furthermore, over half of the cases contracted by military personnel were the result of sex with unlicensed prostitutes. Since they didn't have to pay for medical examinations, these prostitutes were able to charge less than their licensed counterparts.[11]

Officers made announcements or "conscience calls" to inform those who were scheduled to return to America of their PCOD (Pussy Cut Off Date), which allowed for thirty days of medical treatment for sexually transmitted diseases.[12] As with all things, military rank had its privileges. While draftees stood in public lines at clinics to receive injections for VD, senior officers obtained treatment during individual appointments with physicians and had their diagnosis recorded as "nonspecific urethritis," sparing them any embarrassment with their wives stateside.[13]

The U.S. military has even provided brothels on many bases. The 1st Infantry Division's "recreation area" consisted of a one-acre compound within barbed wire that was guarded by U.S. military police. Within this compound, off-duty personnel could purchase hot dogs, hamburgers, soda, liquor, and enter one of the sixty cubicles that held the Vietnamese women who sexually serviced the 4,000-man brigade. At Camp Casey, an American base in Korea during the 1970s, GIs didn't have to leave the base to obtain sexual services: U.S. military personnel in government vehicles transported two hundred prostitutes to and from the compound each day.[14]

When calling on Australian ports, it has been common for American officers to remind their crews that the age of consent for females in that country is fourteen. Military newspapers carry advertisements for nude dancing shows and "massage" parlors.[15]

Sidebar 5-1

FIGHTING COMMUNISM ONE PROSTITUTE AT A TIME

Once we got settled in our hooch (Army lingo for bunkhouse), we were given our orientation to life in Vietnam. First on the orientation agenda was the "dental hygienist" who gave us a field dental kit and explained how to brush your teeth out in the boonies. "Do it just like you're jerking off. Back and forth, up and down. Don't worry about flossing." Next came the orientation on sex with the Vietnamese prostitutes, "Use condoms and wash with antibacterial soap when you're finished and then pee." If the GIs had done this consistently there wouldn't have been the huge number of soldiers coming into the clinic with gonorrhea. But they came not just once, but many times. Obviously that message didn't get through.

I was assigned to the 3rd Field Hospital, the 218th Dispensary in Saigon. Among other things it was my job and that of a few others in my unit to identify all the prostitutes in Vietnam who were carriers of the gonococcus bacillus and then if they were infected to treat them with antibiotics. If we could clean up the prostitutes, they wouldn't infect the soldiers. We knew from the beginning that this was an impossible task. If we could have isolated all the soldiers and prevented them from having sex while we were treating both groups, it might have had a slim chance of success, but how do you stop a GI who is coming to Saigon from the field to spend a weekend partying and fucking from having intercourse with the myriad of young Vietnamese women who were eager to make a couple of bucks? So it was a dumb idea, but we did it anyway. I'm sure some enlightened officer knew better than I so I was just following orders.

We went to just about every bar in Saigon and set up an assembly line. The prostitutes lined up outside the room and one by one came in, dropped their underpants, and I used a long Q-Tip to swab their cervix. I wiped it on a slide and gave it to the lab tech that looked at it under the microscope. If she was positive, she went into another room and received her antibiotic injection. Most were positive, but not all. I'm sure they were only following orders also, and didn't really have a choice if they wanted to work. It seems degrading now as I look back on the experience. No one gave these young women an explanation or the choice to opt out that I knew. They were embarrassed and yet did what they were told as I did. In some ways we were both victims of the war. I'm not certain how long we continued that campaign, but I think someone in his right mind must have realized how useless a project it was and gave it up. The fallout for me was that I was recognized by just about every prostitute in town so anytime I went into a bar, the chatter began and the girls looked embarrassed.

—Peter T. Dimock, U.S. Army,
Preventive Medicine Specialist

MILITARY CONCERNS ABOUT THE EXISTENCE OF PROSTITUTION
Disease

PROSTITUTION IS A DOUBLE-EDGED sword; having easy access to prostitutes may increase morale, but it also increases the rate of illness among the troops. Troops infected with serious venereal diseases reduce combat readiness. During World War I, it was estimated that seven million days of active duty were lost due to venereal disease. The only illness more common among the troops than venereal disease was influenza. The cost to the government to treat sexually transmitted diseases during that war was fifty million dollars.[16]

Loose Lips Sink Ships

Military leaders are often anxious that prostitutes may be acting as spies. When servicemen are in the company of prostitutes, they are often intoxicated and are therefore more likely to disclose sensitive military information. This is one reason military leaders prefer their men seek the services of prostitutes who do not speak English.

Here Come the Brides

"Picture having three or four of the loveliest creatures God ever created hovering around you, singing, dancing, feeding you, washing what they feed you down with rice wine or beer, all saying at once, 'You are the greatest.' This is the Asia you heard about and came to find."—Stars and Stripes, American military newspaper[17]

Another major problem is the risk of servicemen marrying prostitutes and making them dependents of the military. According to a social worker who specializes in helping Asian prostitutes who became wives of U.S. servicemen, "Many of these men discovered that in their relationships to Asian women, their feelings, comfort and welfare were given precedence. Thus for the first time they felt accepted by solicitous, unquestioning women who respected them. . ." Certainly not all foreign women who marry servicemen are prostitutes, but those women who are have even greater motivation than other women to leave their country of origin and start a new life in America. This is enough of a problem that military regulations address it directly. The regulations on military personnel marrying under the section titled "Problems to Be Considered" address the morals of the foreigner as a potential spouse.

> Mental and physical health of the foreign spouse, as well as character, morals, and political beliefs and affiliations, are matters of primary importance since individuals in certain categories may be inadmissible to the United States for permanent residence. These categories include, but are not limited to, foreigners who:
> (5) Are prostitutes, or have engaged in or profited from prostitution.[18]

THE ACCEPTANCE OF PROSTITUTION DAMAGES AMERICANS' VIEW OF OTHER NATIONS

BARS, TATTOO SHOPS, and "massage" parlors often surround American military bases. This is true in America, but even more so in foreign countries, particularly in the Pacific nations. Many military personnel never venture beyond this pseudo-city that has been set up to service them, and as a result, they never really see the host country. They return from overseas with the impression that the host country is "populated solely with poor, thieving people, groveling for U.S. dollars, and lacking in national culture and pride." [19]

THE ACCEPTANCE OF PROSTITUTION DAMAGES AMERICA'S STANDING IN THE WORLD

"We are here to fuck your women!"—Sailors yelling to Australian civilians from the deck of a U.S. Navy ship[20]

U.S. MILITARY PERSONNEL and Koreans had very different views of their relationship. A majority of the Americans said they liked Koreans. When asked, "Do you think Americans like Koreans?" a majority of Koreans responded "no," reported resenting American ignorance of Korean culture and values, and thought Americans were arrogant because they thought themselves superior to Koreans. While an overwhelming majority of Koreans thought that prostitution hurt Korean-American relations, most GIs thought it helped to improve the relationship between the two countries, and believed that prostitutes endeared American troops to the host country and made them "more willing to fight." [21]

THE ACCEPTANCE OF PROSTITUTION NEGATIVELY AFFECTS MALE MILITARY PERSONNEL

WHAT IS THE IMPACT on American society when young men return to civilian life after being part of a subculture in which women selling their bodies to strangers is a common and widely accepted practice? Some males enlist in the military immediately after graduating from high school. They spend their late adolescence and young adulthood in military service, not forming lasting intimate relationships with female peers but engaging in sex for hire with strangers.

Prostitution and Power

Many people view prostitution as merely a business, an exchange of services for money, taking place between equals. However, when the customer is a member of the American military and the prostitute is a citizen of a much less developed country, there is a profound difference in the power between the two parties. Those who have researched sex workers point out, "The overwhelming majority of the prostitutes have experienced a combination of poverty, low class status, physical, sexual and emotional abuse" even before beginning prostitution.[22] One study of prostitutes found that two-thirds of them met the diagnostic criteria for Post-Traumatic Stress Disorder from the numerous physical and sexual assaults they had endured. This rate of PTSD is higher than the rate for combat veterans.[23]

Women involved in prostitution typically have little education; only 9 percent have graduated from high school, and 46 percent have six or fewer years of education. At the time of their enlistment, 91 percent of American recruits have a high school diploma or some college experience.[24] In addition to having more general education, GIs are given lectures on sexually transmitted diseases by the U.S. military, so they understand how HIV and other diseases are contracted.

U.S. personnel have access to clergy, social workers, psychologists, and medical services. Prostitutes are unlikely to have access to these support systems. Military personnel will eventually return to their native land,

and once the obligations of enlistment are met, they are free to choose another line of work. The prostitutes have no other place to go and may be considered tainted for having sexual relations with foreigners. If a prostitute has the misfortune to have given birth to a child whose father is of another race, her past deeds will be obvious to those around her; she can never be "normal" again.

The dynamics mentioned above involve sex between two adults; the power difference is still greater when the prostitute is a child. It is disturbing to imagine members of the U.S. military exploiting children for sexual gratification, but it is common enough that, in 1997, the Army announced that it would attempt to curtail sex between child prostitutes and American personnel in order to "protect soldiers, our national interest, and in the process save the lives of children."[25] The assistant secretary of defense also distributed a memo officially declaring that "any use of child prostitutes is not only an egregious exploitation of children, but, to the extent that there is potential for involvement of US service members, is detrimental to the health and welfare of service members and the ability of US forces to carry out their mission."[26]

Many of the mothers of these child prostitutes were themselves prostitutes who were impregnated by Americans. In the Philippines alone there are 30,000 children fathered, and abandoned, by American servicemen. One-third of these children are homeless and make their living as beggars, thieves, and child prostitutes. There are also untold numbers of abortions performed on pregnant prostitutes.[27]

THE ACCEPTANCE OF PROSTITUTION NEGATIVELY AFFECTS HOW FEMALE MILITARY PERSONNEL ARE VIEWED

"Man should be trained as a warrior and woman as recreation for the warrior."
—Joseph Goebbsel, Minister of Propaganda for Nazi Germany[28]

"Little Brown Fucking Machines Powered with Rice"—Description of Japanese and Filipino prostitutes available on T-shirts near U.S. bases[29]

SETTINGS IN WHICH MEN'S primary social contact with women is interacting with prostitutes is a training ground for sexual harassment and abuse. Men who obtain sex from downtrodden women learn they can do whatever they wish to women with impunity. When servicemen view females first and foremost as sex machines, they are likely to apply these same attitudes to the American military women with whom they serve, negatively affecting the ability of males and females to serve together.

6

A MAN'S HOME IS HIS CASTLE: ACCEPTANCE OF DOMESTIC VIOLENCE

THE PRACTICE OF OVERLOOKING physical abuse within military families contributes to the ability and willingness to ignore sexual abuse that takes place between comrades. Although the permanent bachelor who is "married to the military" has long been the stereotype of the military man, over half of the Army's personnel are currently married.[1]

DOMESTIC VIOLENCE IN MILITARY FAMILIES

IN 2001, THE REPORTED rate of domestic violence in the military was five times greater than the rate in civilian families (if the military had accounted for unmarried couples, the rate would have been much higher). Investigations substantiated 61 percent of the reports of domestic violence, and rated 57 percent as mild, 36 percent as moderate, and 7 percent as severe. In some cases, "severe" meant fatal.

Forty percent of female patients at VA medical clinics acknowledged having been in emotionally or physically abusive relations as adults, and 7 percent stated their current partner was actively abusive. Of the women who reported they had been abused, over 50 percent stated the abuse included being punched, kicked, or beaten up; 22 percent had survived life-threatening violence, including being stabbed or shot. Three percent of the women admitted their partner had "forced" them to have sex within the last twelve months. In addition to dependents, nearly 22 percent of female active duty personnel reported being physically or sexually abused by their partners. Although 68 percent of the women thought they would be willing to discuss the abuse with medical staff, only 12 percent had ever been asked about it. When women informed their physicians they were being abused, 20 percent of the doctors did nothing. The physicians who did not take action gave four reasons: domestic violence is a private matter to be resolved privately by the couple (68 percent); intervening requires too much time or effort (65 percent); women are responsible for causing the violence (40 percent); or fear for their own safety if they did something that angered the perpetrator (46 percent).[2]

THE COSTS OF DOMESTIC ABUSE

DOMESTIC VIOLENCE IS an expensive problem for the Department of Defense. There are costs associated with replacing personnel who are separated from active duty, costs of transitional compensation, and expenses to cover intervention for victims and perpetrators, which includes the efforts of law enforcement, command, psychological, and medical personnel. Domestic violence costs the military $273 million dollars each year.[3]

These are merely the financial costs; the costs in terms of human suffering are more difficult to measure. There is a link between domestic violence and increased rate of error, indifference toward work, increased absenteeism, and increased utilization of health care services. A majority (64 percent) of physically abused women were regularly late to work, half of them missed three days of work per month, and 75 percent used company time to contact lawyers, doctors, shelters, or counselors because they were afraid to make these calls at home.[4]

Of course, the ultimate price for ignoring domestic violence is the deaths of the victims. During an average week in the 1990s, an active member of the U.S. military killed a spouse or child. During that decade, the Federal Government spent $794 per year on research for every person who died from cancer, but only $31 per year for each life lost due to violence.[5]

The most widely reported recent episodes of military domestic violence occurred in 2002, when, in a period of six weeks, four Fort Bragg soldiers murdered their wives. The death rate at the base exceeded the casualty rate for those serving in the combat zone of Afghanistan. That summer, there was a fifth domestic killing at the same base when the wife of a Special Forces major allegedly shot him while he slept. In the three days following national media reports of these murders, the Miles Foundations Helpline received 300 calls from military family members who were being physically or sexually abused.[6]

A high percentage of physically abused women are also being sexually abused. Of women who sought an order for protection from a judge, 15 percent were infected with one or more sexually transmitted diseases as the result of being sexually assaulted, and 20 percent experienced rape-related pregnancy. Some of these women had already undergone several abortions to end unwanted pregnancies resulting from their partners' previous assaults.[7]

However, the risk of being re-assaulted after the initial sexual assault decreased by 32 percent if the woman obtained rapid medical care, by 59 percent if the police were contacted, and 70 percent for those who applied for a protection order. In other words, if the existence of the violence is suppressed, the abuse is much more likely to continue.[8]

It seems likely that high rates of physical abuse will continue to be a part of military life until meaningful action is taken. One third of Army recruits came from families in which there was violence. Between 42 percent and 60 percent of parents who abuse their children also abuse—or are abused by—their partners.[9] Experiencing or witnessing violence as a child puts a person at greater risk of being involved in abusive relationships as an adult. Persons who commit sex crimes as adults are more likely to have a history of physical abuse from one or both of their parents than are those criminals who commit violent acts of a nonsexual nature.

ASPECTS OF MILITARY CULTURE THAT CONTRIBUTE TO DOMESTIC VIOLENCE

According to the Inspector General's office, "military service is probably more conductive to violence at home than any other occupation because of the military's authoritarianism, its use of physical force in training, and the stress produced by perpetual moves and separations."[10]

Age of Marriage

Currently, the rate at which military personnel marry before the age of twenty-one is 31 percent, compared to a much lower 7.5 percent for civilians. Since only 4 percent of recruits are married when they enlist, the majority of these marriages take place during the recruit's first enlistment. Problems related to marriage and finances are a major reason 30 percent of personnel fail to finish their first enlistment and are discharged.[11]

It would be almost comforting to believe that domestic violence only occurred in the marriages of young, inexperienced couples, and that once they had grown accustomed to military life, the violence would cease. Unfortunately, this is not the case. Violence occurs in military families in every branch and at all levels of rank.

Frequent Transfers

"Home is where the Army sends you."—Sign hung in the kitchens of Alana Blatt's eleven childhood homes[12]

Historically, the military has shown little regard for family stability when making military assignments. In the 1980s, 80 percent of Army personnel were relocated at least once a year. Currently, Army families relocate every two years on average, and Air Force families are transferred every three to four years.[13]

In 2004, an experimental program called "Force Stabilization" was introduced. In this program, units trained, deployed, and redeployed together so that families remained in one location for up to seven years, making it easier to develop and maintain social relationships. Frequent relocations disrupt social support and contribute to a sense of isolation for family members, who then rely on one another to an increasing degree until the family becomes an island unto itself, further reducing the likelihood that domestic violence will be reported.

Spousal Absence

Military life often requires extended deployments away from family. Only 21 percent of captains surveyed said that the Army allowed for a good balance between work and family life.

Social Isolation

On many bases, the hierarchy of rank guides relationships, or lack thereof, between families. The family members of enlisted personnel socialize with the families of other enlisted personnel, while the family members of officers restrict their relationships to the families of other officers.

A family housed off-base may be surrounded by people who speak another language. Even when housed among English speakers, some military families do not interact with their civilian neighbors, because many military families view themselves as different from civilian families.

Unfamiliarity with the System

Although counseling and other services are available to military family members, they may not be aware of their existence or what is required to obtain them. This is particularly a problem for spouses from another culture who may have a limited ability to speak or read English.

Transportation Difficulties

Some military families are unable to afford an automobile, and most American cities do not provide convenient mass transit. For a wife who seeks counseling at a civilian agency rather than at military services, for fear of damaging her husband's career, difficulty getting to the counselor's office can be a barrier to getting help.

Strained Finances and Gender Role Expectations: A Woman's Place Is In the Home

Despite the frequent problem of strained finances, military wives are less likely than civilian wives to work outside of the home. Only 49 percent of military wives with high school diplomas have paid employment, compared to 62 percent of civilian wives. The pattern is the same when comparing women with a college degree: Only 56 percent of military wives are employed, compared to 70 percent of civilian wives. This is the result of the gender role expectation that a woman's place is in the home, while a man should be the sole provider of household income.[14]

Wives who do work outside the home often have difficulty obtaining high-paying employment; their sporadic work history, a result of their military spouse being transferred, does not appeal to employers. Jobs that require licenses, such as teaching and nursing, necessitate obtaining a new license each time a move is made. The Army's Community and Family Support Center found that 37 percent of the wives surveyed stated they were dissatisfied with the employment opportunities open to them.[15]

In some marriages, the wife becomes so vested in the husband's career that it becomes apparent in her style of speech; she will say "We got orders," and "We got promoted." This attitude, combined with the dependence on the spouse for income, contributes to the reluctance of the battered wife to take action to protect herself, as she fears damaging "their" chances for career advancement.[16] Wives of career servicemen who divorced their spouses were ineligible to collect alimony because the U.S. Supreme Court had declared that military retirement benefits, including pensions, PX privileges, and health care services were the sole property of the individual who had served.[17]

Image Maintenance

The military has long viewed spouses as a liability. They make it more difficult to relocate personnel and can distract from duties. Spouses have to be cared for enough by the military so that they won't object to personnel reenlisting, but that means spending funds that otherwise could be used for purchasing weapons. Historically, the military has tolerated the existence of spouses and families. Military families recognize this precarious relationship, and all members are expected to understand and live by the values and expectations of military culture. The primary rule is never to do anything that might embarrass the family or the military; to do so can lead to a stagnated career with no increase in pay and posting to undesirable locations, affecting the future of the entire family.

Dr. Doreen Lehr provided "a list of risky behaviors" based on her experience as a military wife: "A military wife's refusal to comply with the military system; their housekeeping ability; their appearance; their civilian employment; reporting domestic abuse; offending a senior officer or his wife; or living by their own rather than military standards."[18] Though the rate of reported spousal abuse in the military declined from 1997 to 2001, these unwritten rules help explain why officials suspected there was no actual reduction in abuse, but merely a decline in the reporting of abuse—an effort to avoid harming the careers of the abusers and their base commanders.[19]

Authoritarianism

Authoritarianism is a professional hazard for military personnel, particularly officers. In the hierarchy of the military, orders are given and followed without question. Many service members expect their family members to respond as subordinates. In her book on military marriages, Karen Houppert observed, "When husbands spend all day doing what they've been told, even when they might think it's stupid, there is a way in which blind faith becomes virtuous. Doubt is for the lazy and faint of heart; it's for those who can't hack it the way it is. Questioning equals complaining."[20] When a spouse or child does not immediately react as expected, it is viewed as an act of disrespect and insubordination, leading to frustration and violence in an attempt to restore proper order.

When a parent has been deployed overseas for months at a time, the family must reorganize to compensate for the absence of that member. Family members, other than the absent one, get used to doing things a certain way. When the military member returns to the family, things have changed. Children are older, more mature, and used to more privileges. The spouse who stayed home is used to being the head of the household, making financial decisions, and setting rules about child behavior. All these changes can be overwhelming to the returning spouse, who may disapprove of how the family is run and wonder what place is left for him or her.

Combat Values

In the chapter on the culture of the military, I described combat values, the acceptance of violence, the ability to objectify others, reduction of empathy, and protecting the larger group even at the expense of individuals. All these values are assets in battle, but become liabilities in the family home and contribute to domestic violence, not only in active military families, but also in families in which the veteran is no longer on active duty. In other words, men who served in the military are more likely to be violent toward their family members than are men who never served in the military.[21]

Excessive Devotion to Honor

Professor Judith Hicks Stiehm described the effects of excessive devotion to honor, "It leads husbands to slay wives; it leads young men to serve as kamikaze pilots or self-sacrificing truck bombers. How are we to determine when honor is blind and when it is admirable, when it should be paid tribute and when it is shameful?"[22]

Cultural Differences

"Service members should be advised of the desirability of pastoral counseling by a military chaplain with reference to spiritual and religious matters, adjustments which may be required as a result of language and environmental background differences, and the moral and financial obligations of marriage and family life."—Army Regulation #600-240; Air Force Regulation #211-18

From 1950 to the early 1990s, over 100,000 Korean women immigrated to the U.S. as wives of servicemen. Unfortunately, 80 percent of these marriages would end in divorce. This rate is 30 percent higher than the rate of civilian divorce. This usual rate of military divorce may be due in part to the high incidence of violence in these marriages. When Asian wives are exposed to American culture, they often become more assertive, a change that is met with resistance from the husbands who preferred submissiveness. These men respond with violence to what they see as betrayal and lack of gratitude. The level of violence in these marriages was so great that the military Chaplain's Office, the American Red Cross, and various women's groups came together to form the National Committee Concerned with Asian Wives of U.S. Servicemen.[23]

THE RESPONSE TO DOMESTIC VIOLENCE

THE MILITARY HAS LONG known of the existence of abuse within the ranks, but has not taken effective action. Carol Enloe described the situation: "Until recently, however, military officials refused to admit that widespread wife battering occurred under their commands or to take responsibility for the 'exceptional' incidents that did get reported. Military social workers, chaplains, police, psychiatrists, and doctors joined together with base commanders to weave a curtain of silence around military wife battering."[24]

In 1975, the Department of Defense created the Child Advocacy Program in response to an increased awareness of child abuse and neglect. This was a multidisciplinary interagency program to address issues related to child abuse perpetrated by military personnel. In 1980, the program was expanded to include spousal abuse and was renamed the Family Advocacy Program.[25] However, according to the General Accounting Office, leaders viewed these programs as low priorities; they were not directly funded, and staff members were unable to devote all of their time to identifying and responding to cases of abuse because they were assigned additional duties. The program was so understaffed and inconsistent that the GAO's report was titled *Military Child Advocacy Programs: Victims of Neglect*.[26]

In 2000, it was discovered the military did not even have a definition of domestic violence! Eventually, a task force came to define it as

> The use, attempted use, or threatened use of physical force, violence, a deadly weapon, sexual assault, or the intentional destruction of property; or behavior that has the intent or impact of placing a victim in fear of physical injury; or a pattern of behavior resulting in emotional/psychological abuse, economic control, and/or interference with personal liberty that is directed toward the following: (1) a current or former spouse, (2) a person with whom the abuser shares a child in common, or (3) a current or former intimate partner.[27]

By 2004, the Army had expanded their definition to include

> Verbally abusive behaviors such as berating; coercive acts such as threats to children, pets, or personal property; restriction of economic resources; isolation; intentional interference with cultural adaptation; physical assault or threat of violence; stalking; sexual coercion, sexual assault or threat of sexual assault, and; obstruction of appropriate social, mental, or medical services.[28]

Even when domestic violence is reported, the military has been hesitant to take meaningful action against perpetrators. Less than 5 percent of soldiers who beat their wives or girlfriends ever face court-martial, and those who do usually evade jail. During years when 65 percent of all military personnel obtained promotions, 54 percent of known perpetrators of domestic violence were given promotions. Of the known abusers who left the military between 1988 and 1993, at least 84 percent received honorable discharges. They reentered the civilian world with no record of criminal behavior and the stamp of approval of the military in the form of an honorable discharge.[29]

The lack of response on the part of military leaders is important in a number of ways. Perpetrators of domestic violence seek to control their victims. They restrict their victims' social relationships so as to keep the abuse secret. When the military doesn't demand that offenders get treatment, it all but guarantees that the victims will not have access to psychological services. The services are available on base, but the victims will not be permitted by the offender to utilize them. When perpetrators are not held responsible for their violent acts, they have little motivation to stop, nor are they likely to obtain treatment. Of all employers, the military is in the best position to demand that its personnel receive psychological treatment related to domestic violence. When perpetrators are not held accountable for their violent action towards their family members, it gives tacit permission for offenders to harass or assault their military comrades.

LOOKING TO THE FUTURE

THE PROBLEM OF DOMESTIC violence in military families is not going to go away. One in nine personnel returning from Afghanistan, and one in six of those returning from Iraq, report symptoms consistent with major depression, generalized anxiety, or PTSD.[30] Mental health providers in the military have found that "a substantial proportion of veterans" with PTSD have "persistent and pervasive disruptions and dysfunction" in their intimate relationships. Enlisted personnel of the first Gulf War were five times more likely to develop PTSD than were officers, and National Guard and reservists were three times more likely to develop the disorder than were enlisted personnel. The veterans returning from Iraq appear to have even higher rates of PTSD than those who returned from the Persian Gulf in 1991.[31]

As with sexual abuse, family violence doesn't take place in a vacuum; it occurs within a context, a community. What the community does or does not do will greatly influence whether the violence continues or abates. Historically, violence within the family was viewed as a normal part of daily life. The saying "rule of thumb" comes from the English law that limited the size of the stick with which a man could beat his children and wife to the width of his thumb. Another law forbade wife-beating after nine o'clock in the evening, to insure that the noise associated with the violence would not disturb people's sleep. Contemporary society now sees these laws as barbaric. When civilian police departments began to remove the man from the house following an episode of domestic violence, more men began to think twice about using violence against family members. Simply put, communities that turn a blind eye to violence have higher rates of abuse than communities that not only condemn the use of violence in the home but also provide assistance to the victims and punishment and/or treatment for the perpetrator. Unfortunately, domestic violence is viewed as a family problem rather than a criminal act, even though, if the same violence were perpetrated against someone other than a family member, charges of assault and battery would likely be filed.

7

WHEN JANIE COMES MARCHING HOME AGAIN: WOMEN IN THE MILITARY

"With the exception of their disparate roles in the physical acts of procreation, childbearing, and nursing, nothing has ever been more characteristic of the relationship between men and women than men's unwillingness to allow women to take part in war and combat. One suspects that, should they ever be faced with such a choice, men might well give up women before they give up war."—Martin Van Creveld[1]

AS OF THE EARLY MONTHS of 2005, 91 percent of all Army career fields were open to women, and females could sign up for 87 percent of military occupational specialties; however, women were not allowed to serve in artillery, drive tanks, or apply for Rangers or Special Forces.[2] In 2006, after the Army announced it needed to spend $1.35 billion on recruitment efforts, Representative Duncan Hunter (R–CA), chair of the House Armed Services Committee, sought to bar women from 22,000 military jobs.[3]

What cultural/psychological factors keep women from serving in all aspects of the military? According to Francine D'Amico it is simple: "War has been perceived as men's domain, a masculine endeavor for which women may serve as victim, spectator, or prize."[4] But throughout history, women also have fought, killed, and died in combat. During World War II, the Russian "Battalions of Death" consisted entirely of female warriors and were highly effective in killing those invading their country.[5] North Vietnamese forces trained women and sent them into combat against American soldiers.

Women have been involved with the American military in various official and unofficial roles at home and in the field since the creation of the country, and their services have been vital. During World War II, newspaper editorials suggested that women were "shirking their duty" by avoiding military service. In response to a shortage of nurses, the House of Representatives passed the Nurse Draft Bill. Had not the war ended before the Senate could pass it, America would have had its first involuntary conscription of nonmarried women into the military.[6]

OBJECTIONS TO WOMEN IN THE AMERICAN MILITARY

Male Cadet: "Excuse me, miss, but why do you want to come here?"
Female Cadet: "Because I want to become the best Army officer I can be."
Male Cadet: "That's fine, but couldn't you do it someplace else?"
—Captain Carol Barkalow's memory of her first day at West Point[7]

UNTIL VERY RECENTLY, the fighting forces of the American military have officially been exclusively male. Females were seen only as support personnel. The military was "looking for a few good *men*," not a few good people. For the hypermasculine, this separation of the sexes is part of the appeal of the military; the exclusion of women as fighters proved that any male who could successfully complete boot camp was a "real man." Once women were allowed to take part in combat, the perceived value of being a warrior diminished. This explains the resistance to women becoming fighter pilots and other high status ("real man") positions.

Historically, many Americans have objected to the inclusion of women anywhere in the military. Half of the women who volunteered as nurses in World War II reported that they had to overcome opposition from their families.[8] A 2005 report released by the Department of Defense on sexual abuse at U.S. military academies found, "Although progress has been made, hostile attitudes and inappropriate actions toward women, and the toleration of these by some cadets and midshipmen, continue to hinder the establishment of a safe and professional environment in which to prepare future military officers."[9] These attitudes continue to exist even though women have been successful students for over twenty-five years.

Physical Abilities or "All Women Are Unfit"

"There is no question, but that women could do a lot of things in the military. So could men in wheelchairs. But you couldn't expect the services to want a whole company of people in wheelchairs."—General Lewis B. Hershey, Director, Selective Service System, 1978[10]

One of the main objections to including women in certain military roles is the argument that they lack the physical strength necessary to be warriors. Forbidding all women regardless of individual strength, because women on average have less upper body strength than men, is blatant discrimination. If the actual issue is level physical strength, why not simply set a standard for physical strength and require that anyone, female or male, meet that standard? When asked that very question, the head of the Marine Corps, General Charles Krulak, balked. He expressed concern that, if a woman met the standard and was allowed combat duty, it would be a blow to any man's ego who had not met the standard, because he would have been bested by a female. Apparently, he was more concerned about the male self-image than about getting the most qualified personnel.[11]

Some male soldiers complain the standards for women on the Army Physical Fitness Test are "too low" and that the test is "biased."[12] On the surface this appears to be a reasonable complaint. However, it has long been the Army's practice to have different standards that reflect physiological differences between younger and older soldiers. Other than sexism, why do soldiers understand and accept the different standards based on age, but protest different standards based on sex? When a West Point alumnus visited the campus, he expressed some concern about "the feminization of the military now that women had forced their way into the Academy." The Commandant of Cadets showed him the physical training performances of the current cadets, noting they were doing more push-ups and sit-ups in two minutes and running two miles faster than had the cadets in the days the alumnus was a cadet. After the alumnus expressed his approval, the commandant added, "And those are just the women."[13] How does one justify discriminating against women who meet not only the women's standards but also the male standards? West Point graduate Major Lillian Pfluke had the maximum score on *every* Army physical fitness test for fifteen years, a first-class score on the Marine Corps *men's* physical fitness test, won the Military Triathlon Champion, and was two-time winner of both the Interservice European Ski Championship and the National Military Cycling Championship.[14]

Opponents of women in the military claim women's menstrual periods and risk of pregnancy make them unfit to serve. When women became crewmembers of Navy ships deployed on six-month deployments, there were dire predictions of rampant pregnancy on board. In reality, the rate of pregnancy on ships is lower than that of female sailors stationed on shore.[15] During the first Gulf War, women in combat zones were encouraged by military medical personnel to take contraceptive pills for six months without a break in order to suppress menstrual periods.[16] This was done to insure that they would not lose time from their duties. Even without these measures, when all causes of lost time are taken into account (pregnancy, absence without leave, desertion, substance abuse, etc.), male personnel lose more time away from duties than do female personnel.[17]

After the plane crash death of Navy pilot Kara Hultgreen, opponents of women in combat aviation cited the incident as evidence that women were substandard pilots and were in the Navy only for political reasons. These critics failed to mentioned that in the three years preceding the accident, nine male pilots had also died while flying the F-14A, and when in-flight simulators were presented with the situation Hultgreen had faced, eight of nine male pilots failed to land safely.[18]

Is it possible that some women are physically superior to some men? On average, women can take more "G forces" than men. In tests for potential astronauts several women outperformed men on tests for tolerating stress, vertigo, and isolation, and on lung power.[19] Women as a group also perform better than men as a group in academics. In 1999, over 60 percent of the female seniors at the Air Force Academy made the dean's list, while only 48 percent of the male cadets did, and the women out-performed the men on scores of military performance (39 percent vs. 32 percent).[20]

Psychological Weakness: Women Lack "The Right Stuff"

"They [women] want to be in the military until it becomes dangerous, then they shirk their duty. "—Captain Marie de Young, U.S. Army [21]

Given the stereotype of women as emotionally fragile, one would predict that they would be overwhelmed by war. In 1995, researchers followed up on women and men who had been POWs during World War II, to see how they had been impacted by their ordeal, and found that over half (54 percent) of these women had some degree of service-connected disability, which was virtually the same percentage as male ex-POWs who had service-disconnected disabilities (50.6 percent). Among the women who had a service-connected disability, the average degree of that disability was 37 percent, nearly the same as that of male ex-POW's (40 percent).[22] More recently, the personnel returning from Afghanistan and Iraq experienced symptoms of Post Traumatic Stress Disorder at approximately the same rate regardless of race, age, or sex.[23]

Women Lack the "Killer Instinct"

In 1991, while testifying before the Senate General, Marine Corps Commandant Robert Barrows insisted, "Combat is uncivilized and women cannot do it. I think the very nature of women disqualifies them from doing it. Women give life, sustain life, nurture life; they do not take it."[24] Apparently, General Barrows has not noticed what Gwynne Dyer has observed: "Women have almost always fought side by side with men in guerrilla or revolutionary wars, and there isn't any evidence they are significantly worse at killing people—which may or many not be comforting, depending on whether you see war as a male problem or a human one."[25] The historical evidence does not support the claim that women are incapable of being effective killers. Anyone, male or female, who is squeamish about seeing the face of the person he or she is about to kill will never succeed as a sniper. Unlike with bombers and artillery, the enemy is not an anonymous, faceless enemy. If women truly lack the ability to kill, then they would be failures as snipers. But history shows that women make excellent snipers. During World War II, Russian female snipers were credited with 10,000 kills. One female sniper took out an entire company of enemy soldiers, and another was credited with killing 300 German soldiers.[26] Currently, American women are being trained in sniper school and are proving to be excellent students. Sergeant First Class Dolan, the school's head instructor, stated, "women can shoot better, by and large, and they're easier to train because they don't have the inflated egos that a lot of men bring to these programs."[27]

Some acknowledge that although women can kill, they shouldn't. In 1992, Air Force Chief of Staff General Merrill McPeak stated, "Combat is about killing people. Even though logic tells us that women can do that as well as men, I have a traditional attitude about wives and mothers and daughters being ordered to kill people."[28]

For years, female police officers have been "on the front line," where they put themselves in harm's way. They face armed opponents who are often physically larger and stronger than they are, and yet the officers prevail. It appears that hand-to-hand combat is the last remnant of the male-only military. With the number of women who are in the military, and the frequency with which the American military is deployed, it is only a matter of time, if it hasn't already occurred, that an American woman will be involved in "whites of their eyes," hand-to-hand combat.

Women are Distracting Sex Objects

"It's tough to discipline a soldier when she blinks her baby-blue eyes or slips you a dimple."—Army colonel[29]

"Nothing has done more to cheapen rank and diminish respect for authority than cute little female lieutenants and privates."—Brian Mitchell, *Women in the Military: Flirting with Disaster*[30]

Historically, the American military has long feared that the very presence of women is such a distraction to men that they would be unable to perform their duties. It was this very fear that prompted the War Department to order that the first official military nurses were to be healthy, thirty-five to fifty years old, and "matronly" in appearance.[31] Although the purpose of uniforms is to reduce the individual differences between persons and increase group identity, the military has historically been resistant to dressing men and women in the same style clothing.

In the 1940s, the military faced the decision of whether uniforms ought to be just that—uniform. It was determined that breast pockets on women's uniforms might be too distracting to male personnel, since they might be reminded that women have breasts, so these pockets were eliminated.[32] In the early 1980s, male personnel were ordered to wear the shirts of their work uniforms tucked into their pants, but female personnel were ordered to wear their shirts outside of the pants in order to cover their waist, hips, and buttocks.[33] When women entered West Point, their uniforms did not include pockets on the seat of the slacks, nor did the jackets have the traditional tails, for fear that their buttocks would be too prominent.[34] The fear that the presence of female bodies will be too distracting to male personnel continues to this day.

It would seem that men who pride themselves on their ability to overcome fear and face enemy fire would be able exert some control over their sexual urges. Erin Solaro wrote, "I find it quite interesting that many of those who talk about the need for the military to remain 'morally' pure by excluding gay, bisexual and lesbian citizens, and protecting men from the sexual rapacity of women troops—all in the interests of readiness, of course, and combat efficiency are often also most vociferously against the idea of requiring male troops to exercise their sexuality in a civilized manner."[35] Kathryn McCreery at the U.S. Naval Academy put it even more bluntly: "If men can't control their penises, how can we trust them with guns?"[36]

"Some of the best soldiers wear lipstick."—Army recruiting brochure

Although one of the primary objections to women serving in the military has been the fear that they will distract men, it has occasionally been in the military's interests to actively promote sexual interest between male and female personnel. During World War II, the military told women, "Many service women say they receive more masculine attention—have more dates, a better time—than they ever had in civilian life. Their uniforms have been styled by some of the world's greatest designers to flatter face and figure."[37]

As late as 1987, Women Marines* were given additional training that was not offered to Marines: the Professional Development Package.* A

---

* I capitalize "women" because that is the term by which they were referred. There are two types of Marines: Marines (males) and Women Marines (females).

special instructor and a representative of a cosmetics company taught this six-hour mandatory course on the proper way to apply lipstick, eyeliner, and blush.[38] When the first women were admitted to West Point and the Air Force Academy, the leadership had consultants brought in to instruct the female cadets in the proper use of makeup, but some of the women so resented it they used the makeup to "war-paint" their faces in protest.[39] More recently, a recruitment poster showed a woman beside a helicopter with the words "There's something about a soldier." In addition to her flight suit she wears lipstick and eye makeup. The subtext reads, "The point is, a woman in the Army is still a woman."[40]

Women Need to be Protected by Men

Opponents to women in combat fear that male personnel will needlessly put themselves in danger in order to protect female comrades. According to the Center for Military Readiness, women should not be permitted in combat roles.

Assigning female soldiers to close combat units would be tantamount to acceptance of deliberate violence against women, as long as it occurs at the hands of the enemy. The 1992 Presidential Commission on the Assignment of Women in the Armed Forces saw this as an unnecessary and unacceptable setback for American cultural values. The Executive Summary of the Commission's Report explains why: Those skeptical about assigning women to combat, however, primarily have focused on the needs of the military and combat effectiveness, as well as deep-seated cultural and family values millions of Americans hold and are still teaching their children. As one Commissioner put it, those values can be summed up in one simple phrase: "Good men respect and defend women."[41]

"An attitude of romantic paternalism puts women, not on a pedestal, but in a cage."—Jeanne Lieberman.[42]

Women Need to be Protected From Men

Contemporary society is now comfortable with the idea of women serving as nurses, but this has not always been the case. During the American

Civil War women, particularly Southern women, were thought to be too fragile to function as nurses. It was believed wounded men would rather suffer than ask a woman to do the unladylike tasks of nursing. A male military surgeon wrote in the *American Medical Times*:

> Imagine a delicate refined woman assisting a rough soldier to the close-stool, or supplying him with a bed pan, or adjusting the knots in a T-bandage employed in retaining a catheter in position, or a dozen offices of a like character which one would hesitate long before asking a female nurse to perform, but which are frequently and continually necessary in a military hospital...[43]

A contemporary example of the need to protect women from unladylike circumstances is that men don't feel as free to behave crudely if women are nearby. When a Marine Corps Major was asked why he opposed women in the military he replied, "You can no longer be foul-mouthed, and tell degrading jokes and stories about women, and use derogatory female terms to abuse men good-humoredly."[44] If impolite words were all servicewomen had to fear from their male comrades, there would be no need for this book.

To those who endorse hyper-masculinity and hyper-femininity, the worst thing that can happen to a woman is being raped after falling into the hands of the enemy.* This is a fate worse than death and cannot be allowed to happen. Nurse Wendy Weller wrote of her experiences in Vietnam. During a time when she and other nurses were in a compound that came under attack, they were given flak jackets and helmets, but not weapons. During the battle, a solitary soldier remained in the room with them. When the battle was over, they thanked the young man for guarding them. To their shock and dismay they were informed that his orders, in the event that the hospital was overrun, had been to kill them rather than let them be captured. No one had bothered to consult with the women when formulating this plan.[45]

Conservative activist Elaine Donnelly feared female prisoners of war would be a public relations nightmare because the enemy would use

---

* An American woman being raped by an enemy soldier is considered to be much greater affront to her and the honor of her country than were she to be raped by a fellow American (Herbert, 1988).

them for propaganda purposes: "Advocates of women in combat often talk about 'sharing the risk' of war, but the truth is that women face unequal and greater risks. The vulnerabilities unique to women can and probably will be exploited by enemy captors."[46] (If by "vulnerabilities unique to women" she means rape, the stories in the latter part of this book illustrate that vulnerability to rape is not unique to women.) American women were taken prisoner by both Germany and Japan during World War II and by the Iraqi military in the Gulf War, but none were used for propaganda purposes.

During the first Gulf War, Colonel Rhonda Cornum was captured and taken prisoner. When describing her experience she stated, "It's just another bad thing that can happen to you. While I was subjected to an unpleasant episode of sexual abuse during my captivity, it did not represent a threat to life, limb, or chance of being released, and therefore occupied a much lower level of concern than it might have under other circumstances." Colonel Cornum noted her main concern when an Iraqi soldier began to unzip her pants in the truck that was transporting her was whether the pending assault would aggravate her injuries that included a shattered knee, two broken arms, and a bullet in her shoulder.[47] Colonel Cornum, who has both a medical degree and a Ph.D., wrote after her release, "It is my opinion that sexual abuse should be considered just one of many potential physical and psychological torture techniques, whether the subject is male or female."[48]

History supports her opinion. In 1996, rebellious Iraqi officers were forced by their former comrades to rape each other before "execution by slow mutilation."[49] That same year the Zagreb Medical Centre [sic] for Human Rights estimated that 4,000 Croatian male prisoners were sexually tortured in Serb detention camps. Twenty percent were forced to fellate their fellow prisoners, and 11 percent were partially or completely castrated (sometimes by women). Seventy percent were left with permanent disabilities as the result of anal penetration from penises, barrels of weapons, blunt objects, or knives.[50] Since both women and men can be tortured, sexually assaulted, and used for propaganda purposes, it appears the only risk unique to women is the risk of pregnancy, which can be reduced through birth control drugs.

Women Combatants Would Be an Embarrassment to the Image of America

"When you get right down to it, you have to protect the manliness of war."
—General Robert Barrow, Marine Corps Commandant[51]

The idea of women being an official part of the U.S. military, even in support roles, has long been viewed as an embarrassment. When a proposal to create the Women's Auxiliary Army Corps was brought before Congress in 1942, one Congressman exclaimed, "Think of the humiliation! What has become of the manhood of America?"[52] In 1991, when the discussion of women in combat roles began in earnest, conservative activist Phyllis Schlafly had an identical reaction: "It's absolutely ridiculous to have women in combat. It's an embarrassment to our country."[53] Some insist America's security would be endangered by the presence of women fighters, since our enemies would perceive our military as weak and ineffective.

"No man with gumption wants a woman to fight his battles."—General William Westmoreland[54]

Women Shouldn't Be Powerful

Historically, being a soldier has been so fundamental to the achievement of masculinity that it seems in order to be a soldier one must be male.[55] The presence of women in the military, particularly in combat roles, conflicts with this belief and is very disturbing to many people. A 1945 survey of males in the Army found that many of the men thought women serving in the Women's Auxiliary Corps could lead to women becoming "too powerful" when they returned to civilian life.[56] More recently, the 1998 Southern Baptist Convention passed a resolution that women serving in combat "rejects gender-based distinctions established by God."[57]

"God did not make women to be soldiers."—Male West Point squad leader to his female subordinates[58]

Dr. Melissa Embser-Herbert theorized, that for the general public, one of the most shocking aspects of the scandal at Abu Ghraib prison was the fact that several of those accused of prisoner abuse were women.

Women at the receiving end of degradation and abuse are everywhere in the media. And while women may also be seen in powerful roles, rarely are they seen wielding power in a way that's intended to degrade or abuse, and even more rarely is it directed at men. When women are seen in that light, their victims are children, usually their own. . . . Ultimately, the distinction between seeing men as aggressors and seeing women as aggressors is that the women are usually acting as individuals, not as part of a larger, structural arrangement of discrimination or abuse. . . . We're somewhat desensitized to women being on the receiving end of violence. And we are, all too unfortunately, just as desensitized to men being on the aggressor's end. In Abu Ghraib the tables are turned. Men—men who have been characterized by many as evil, or at the least not to be trusted—are on the receiving end. And women, long held up by our society as a "kinder, gentler" class of persons, are engaging in abuse and humiliation. As a society that has—albeit misguidedly—arranged itself around perceptions of women and men as fundamentally different creatures, we are simply at a loss to understand this role inversion.[59]

The Specter of Motherhood

"If for no other reason than because women are the bearer of children, they should not be in combat."—General Jacqueline Cochran, USAF[60]

The fact that many servicemen are fathers has not been seen as a liability to military readiness. It has been assumed that men will have little difficulty leaving their children in order to fulfill their military duties. When it comes to female personnel, the opposite has been assumed: the role of mother will trump the role of soldier, and will resist deployment. With overseas deployment of reserve and National Guard troops, many mothers have fulfilled their duties despite having to be separated from their children for long periods of time. During the first Gulf War, America utilized the highest percentage of female military personnel of any of the coalition forces (USA 11 percent, Canada 9.2 percent, United Kingdom 5 percent, France 2.7 percent).[61]

The American Public's Lack of Acceptance of Women Killed in Action
More disturbing than scenes of uniformed mothers bidding their babies

goodbye as they go to war would be images of those mothers returning home in flag-draped coffins. Planners in the Pentagon have been
concerned that the American people would not tolerate women being
killed in action, and as a result, the military's mission will be terminated
prematurely. However, the deaths of eleven female military personnel
during the first Gulf War were taken in stride by the general public.[62]
By September 2006, sixty-eight female American military personnel
had been killed in Afghanistan and Iraq, the majority of them by enemy
fire, and hundreds of servicewomen had been wounded, which included
losing their limbs and other forms of mutilation, yet there was no mass
public outcry.[63] It seems clear that Americans are willing to sacrifice both
male and female bodies in order to wage war.

Being Shot At

The American military has been resistant to admitting that women are,
and long have been, in combat situations. General George Washington
and other commanders utilized women, nicknamed "Molly Pitchers,"
to carry water onto the battlefields to pour over cannon barrels to keep
them from overheating during repeated firing.[64] In 1942, the U.S. Army
created Mobile Army Surgical Hospital Units (MASH units), which
were designed to be close to the battle lines so that wounded soldiers
could obtain medical care rapidly. Female nurses were assigned to these
units in World War II and the Korean War. These units were regularly
subjected to artillery and mortar fire from the enemy. In fact, the first
female nurse wounded in Italy during World War II was a member of a
MASH unit.

With the advent of long-range missiles, particularly those with nuclear
warheads, and the increased use of terrorist tactics, the notion of a front
(dangerous) and a rear (safe) is obsolete. No matter where military personnel, female or male, are stationed, they can be attacked and killed.
Professor Judith Hicks Stiehm made this point when she wrote, "One
of the myths is that there is a battlefield. This concept permits one to
think of war as something that is fought in a location like a football
stadium or a great unoccupied desert where trained, declared antago-
nists fight according to an agreed-on set of rules and in an agreed-on
physical space. The fact is that a nuclear battlefield can be everywhere,

and that somewhere is not agreed-on in advance, is not 'distant,' and is not uninhabited."[65]

Shooting Back

"Exposure to danger is not combat. Being shot at, even being killed, is not combat. Combat is finding…closing with…and killing or capturing the enemy. It's killing."—General Robert H. Barrow, Commandant of the Marine Corps[66]

By the beginning of the twenty-first century, more than a dozen of America's allied countries officially allowed women into roles where they are expected to engage in combat.[67] However, the American military has continued to resist officially placing women in combat roles. Despite the official ban on women in combat roles, American females have taken up arms in the defense of their country's interests. In 1979, when the American consulate in Karachi, Pakistan, was rushed by thousands of protesters, two female members of the Marine Security Battalion, armed with shotguns and pistols, defended the consulate.[68, 69] Female Naval aviators flew combat missions in Iraq starting in 1998 and in Serbia in 1999.

Question: When is a combat zone not a combat zone?
Answer: When female personnel are present.

One simple way to maintain the appearance of keeping women out of combat is to redefine what constitutes combat. Prior to 1986, male pilots who flew air tanker missions were considered to be flying in a combat setting and were eligible for medals. When women pilots were needed to fly air tankers in air strikes against Libya in 1986, these flights were suddenly redefined as noncombat missions.[70] Although the American military did not consider female Americans capable of flying combat missions, they were competent enough to train male and female pilots of other NATO nations to fly such missions.[71, 72] Until 1994, women service members were not allowed on Navy destroyers, but were permitted to serve on the other ships (the ones without the big guns) that sailed in the same waters. To add to the hypocrisy of this policy, it was common practice to allow, even encourage, female journalists, politicians, and dependents aboard ships on which servicewomen were not permitted.[73]

When two American female military personnel were taken prisoner during the Gulf War, the "combat/not combat" word game continued. Lieutenant Colonel Rhonda Cornum took part in capturing, guarding, and transporting Iraqi soldiers. While on a rescue mission, she was taken prisoner after the helicopter in which she was traveling was shot down. She sustained two broken arms and a bullet wound in her back from enemy fire.[74] Although all the male members of the mission were awarded the Distinguished Flying Cross, she was not. The other female prisoner of that war, Melissa Rathbun-Nealy, was not listed as a POW or even missing in action, but merely as "missing."[75]

"In modern warfare, geography and circumstances, not policy, good intensions, or misplaced chivalry, dictate who will face hostilities in war."—Major General Jeanne Holm[76]

Women Are More Difficult to Recruit Than Men

Some authors have argued that women are more difficult to recruit than men and proposed ending recruitment efforts toward women.[77] This argument has no validity, since women are currently enlisting at a faster rate than are males, and if the rate of sexual abuse were reduced, even more would be enlisting.[78] Furthermore, more women have sought to enlist than the military wanted. Even when there have been personnel shortages, the military has seen this as a manpower shortage; therefore, recruiting women wouldn't resolve the issue. In the 1980s, the Army had a policy to limit the number of female enlisted personnel to 65,000.[79] The Marine Corps not only restricted women from combat roles, but also placed a limit on the percentage of women who could enter any occupation in the Corps.[80]

Women Have Higher Rates of Attrition

Some have argued that because women as a group have had a higher rate of attrition than men as a group no women should be allowed to enlist.[81] One reason for the higher attrition rate was the military's policy of automatically discharging female personnel as soon as pregnancy was discovered. This policy lasted until 1975.[82] Servicewomen could also be discharged if they married men with children from a previous marriage. Servicemen could have dependents, but servicewomen were forbidden to have a family.[83]

In the 1990s, female cadets dropped out of the Air Force Academy at a higher rate than male cadets (33 percent vs. 28 percent), even though they were routinely performing better academically than men.[84] This has prompted the argument that only those whom the military can guarantee will be career officers should be trained, since the training is so costly. Opponents of women in the military view women resigning as a sign that they are unable to adjust to military life, rather than an indication of shortcomings in the military itself. As long as women are prevented from serving in high-status roles, their motivation to make the military a long-term career will be reduced. In the 1980s, women pilots were leaving the Air Force in droves because of the limitations Air Force policies placed on them. Captain Theresa Claiborne spent seven years flying KC0135 tankers to refuel B-52s, but was forbidden to fly a B-52. She decided that within the restrictions of the military she could no longer advance her career and resigned to become a civilian airline pilot. Captain Stephanie Well also grew tired of what is called the "glass ceiling" by civilians, and the "camouflage ceiling" in the military, and did not reenlist. Instead, she became a research pilot and flight instructor for NASA, where she trained astronauts.[85] General Omar Bradley noted that infantry is the branch of the Army in which, "more than any other. . . a soldier learns the art of leadership and command and, ultimately, has the best chance of reaching the topmost positions."[86] Women soon learn that unless they obtain infantry commands, advancement is stymied.

Even as more roles in the military are opened to women, they still face discrimination, harassment, and abuse. When there is less abuse directed toward servicewomen, they will be more motivated to remain in the military.

Intent or Character

"Many Americans could believe only that the kind of women who would join the Army were not the kind to take home to mother."—Brian Mitchell[87]

As early as the Civil War the military was suspect of the intent of women who would be willing to put themselves in a setting that consisted of mostly male bodies. For many, the role of nurse was a bit too similar to that of prostitute, since both roles required the woman to perform the "physical work of tending to strange men's bodies," so the War Department required that any nurse during the Civil War have "good character."[88] By 1945, not much had changed; a survey of servicemen found that 50 percent thought it was bad for a girl's reputation [read: slut] to be a member of the Women's Auxiliary Corps.[89] In *War And Gender*, J. S. Goldstein claimed, "The moral character of [military] nurses has traditionally mattered more to the military men than professional ability."[90]

In Vietnam the image of women in the military had changed little. Nurse Lynda Van Devanter described her experience: "People figure you were either a hooker or a lesbian if you were a woman in the Army in Vietnam. Why else would a woman want to be with 500,000 men unless she was [sexually] servicing them?"[91]

In 1979 Marine James Webb wrote an article "Women Can't Fight" in which he described the dormitories of military academies as "a horny woman's dream."[92] With this attitude prevalent, it ought to be no surprise that the first women at the Naval Academy were officially known as WUBAs, an acronym for the name of their uniform, "Working Uniform Blue Alpha." But unofficially it meant "Women Used By All."[93]

Many people still believe any woman that would purposely place herself with most male coworkers must either be looking for a husband or be promiscuous. In the former case, she won't be an asset to the service because she will leave the service as soon as she snags a husband, thereby rendering all of the training she received at taxpayer expense worthless to her as well as to the military. If she is just a "slut" looking for a good time, she will be a distraction to the males in the unit, putting them in unnecessary danger.

When Donna Dean decided to join the Navy, her mother was "horrified at the thought of her daughter becoming one of the 'drunken whores' she was positive abound in the military."[94] Her father, who had served in both the Army and the Marines, objected for the same reason.

Sergeant Kayla Williams's book on her tour of duty in Iraq summarized her experience of the way women continue to be viewed by many military men.

Sometimes, even now, I wake up before dawn and forget I am not a slut. The air is not quite dark, not quite light, and I lie absolutely still, trying to will myself to remember that that is not what I am. Sometimes, on better mornings, it comes to me right away. And then there are all those other times. Slut. The other choice is bitch. If you're a woman and a soldier, those are the choices you get."[95]

In her experience the difference between a slut and a bitch is a slut will have sex with anyone, while a bitch will have sex with anyone but you. A woman who is friendly and outgoing is a slut. A woman who is revered or maintains professional distance is a bitch.[96]

Sexual Orientation, or "These Women are Misfits"

"Welcome to the fleet. In the Navy's eyes you're either dykes or whores—get used to it."—Company Commander's welcome to female sailors at the beginning of basic training[97]

Although Sergeant Williams claimed there were only two choices for women in the military, slut and bitch, there is another choice: lesbian. A female drill instructor at Parris Island complained, "The qualities and traits that we demand and are supposed to be training our recruits are the same traits that make us look homosexual."[98] The most common form of harassment of women in the military is being accused of being a lesbian and demanding that she prove she is not by having sex with the man making the accusation. Both heterosexual and homosexual women fear being labeled as lesbian since it can lead to an intrusive investigation and possible discharge. Women who are homosexual face double discrimination: being female and lesbian. Women have disproportionately been discharged on charges of homosexuality. When women made up only 13 percent of the armed forces they accounted for 29 percent of discharges due to charges of homosexuality.

METHODS WOMEN USE IN RESPONSE TO MILITARY CULTURE

"If you're too feminine, then you're not strong enough to command respect and lead men into battle, but if you're strong and aggressive you're not being

a woman. "—U.S. Air Force Captain [99]

Female military personnel are expected to find a balance between being feminine enough to be seen as heterosexual women, while not misusing their sexuality to an unfair advantage, and being masculine enough to be good soldiers and leaders. Dr. Melissa Herbert found that 42 percent of women surveyed consciously engaged in "gender image management." She used the phrase "consciously engaged" because the respondents were aware of taking these actions. She suggested that there are many more women who engage in these behaviors but are not fully aware it, or their motivation for doing so.[100]

Assuming the Masculine Role

One would think that with all the nontraditional tasks and roles military woman strive to undertake they would think of themselves as feminists. However, the opposite is true; most military women do not identify themselves as feminists.[101] Since the military is basically a masculine culture, many women believe if they behave in accordance with masculine values they will prosper and advance. The female identifies with the hypermasculine attitudes, language, and behavior, including how they socialize with men. Anything considered feminine is eliminated. In simple language, "I'm just one of the guys." One of the methods for appearing more masculine, the use of alcohol, puts women at greater risk of being sexually assaulted and being viewed as at least partially responsible for any assault that takes place.

One study found 75 percent of female subjects consciously utilized at least one strategy to appear more masculine. These tactics included rarely wearing makeup, keeping their hair cut short, wearing uniform pants instead of skirts, and becoming highly aggressive. Unfortunately for many of these women, the strategy backfired, because they were then penalized for being "too masculine." When Captain Carol Barkalow took second place in a civilian bodybuilding contest, she was informed by her military supervisor it was "dumb" and had damaged her career. Which raises two questions: would a male officer damage his career by being involved in a body building competition, and can *male* military personnel be too masculine?

In three of the four branches, half or more women reported being penalized for being too masculine. Only in the Marine Corps, the branch that is most highly associated with hypermasculinity, did fewer than half the women report negative consequences for assuming the masculine role. But even in the Marines a significant percentage of the women reported being penalized. Women who expressed interests in aggression and violence, the core of military culture, were viewed as "not normal" and therefore "not trustworthy."[102] Misogynistic men resent women who assume the masculine role and view them as uppity. Sexual abuse is used as a form of punishment to put women in their rightful place and to warn other women not to stray into roles where they don't belong.

Assuming the Feminine Role

In this strategy, femininity is considered a useful resource, so wearing makeup, perfume, heels, and a skirt while on duty emphasizes it. Social relationships, and even flirting, are used to develop and maintain influence. Lt. General Kennedy described the "Little Sexy Doll file," an unofficial file of photographs circulated by female officers in hopes their physical appearance would help them obtain prestigious positions working as aides to male senior officers.[103]

> *"In essence, it is probably better to be perceived as an 'incompetent, heterosexual slut' than a lesbian, competent or not."*—Dr. Melissa S. Herbert [104]

Fear of being labeled a lesbian, and therefore risking being discharged, sometimes plays a role in women, both heterosexual and lesbian, emphasizing stereotypical feminine attributes. But then that brings on unwanted sexual attention from some men.[105] In all branches of the military, over half of the women surveyed reported having been penalized for appearing too feminine. Both males and other females inflicted these penalties. Examples of these penalties include being prevented from career mobility, not being assigned to the specialty in which one has already trained, not being promoted in rank, not getting choice assignments, and not being offered specialized training opportunities.

The stereotypic feminine role is problematic for women not only in military settings, but also in other organizational settings. When studying human behavior in civilian businesses, one researcher found over 100 things woman do that reduce their chances of career advancement and success.[106] A number of these behaviors also make them easier targets for sexual harassment and assault. Among these are acquiescing to bullies, allowing themselves to be scapegoated, being overly concerned with not offending others, and tolerating inappropriate behavior. Women who assume primarily feminine behaviors may be targeted for sexual abuse because, in the view of misogynistic males, all women are good for nothing other than to serve as sexual objects for the pleasure of men.

Attempting Balance

A third strategy seeks to avoid all stereotypic gender role behaviors. Servicewomen utilizing this approach remain as aloof as possible from males through the use of bureaucratic and procedural methods. Every interaction is all business. There is no attempt on the part of the servicewoman to form social relationships with her comrades. This is sometimes referred to as the neutered strategy, because the servicewoman strives to minimize both stereotypic feminine and masculine behaviors.

The fourth strategy, and the most psychologically healthy, is the balanced approach, in which servicewomen utilize both stereotypical feminine and masculine behaviors in a spontaneous, nonrigid, authentic manner.[107] This strategy requires a high level of self-confidence. Hopefully, as more and more women make the military their career, they will develop this strategy and serve as examples to both women and men that a good military leader need not rigidly adhere to gender stereotypes to be successful.

The Good Old Days (Ain't What They Used To Be)

The roles within the military in which women have been permitted to serve have changed back and forth over the years. For a while a role is open to women, but then females are forbidden to serve in that capacity. During the Clinton Administration the number of billets open to women once again increased, although not every branch was as equally compliant with these changes. At the behest of the administration, the Army opened approximately 40,000 jobs to women. Similarly, the Navy was pressured to end its restrictions on placing women aboard combat ships.[108] Women were integrated into basic training groups with men rather than trained separately, so some of their drill sergeants were men. Those who sought to restrict the role of women in the military referred to these changes as the feminization of the military. Let us examine the so-called feminization of the military.

> *"They took away from the DI the one big weapon he had: fear. He could not harass them anymore."*—Staff Sergeant Matthew C. McKeon, who marched six recruits to their deaths by drowning[109]

Media portrayals of basic training entail a screaming, foul-mouthed sergeant kicking hapless recruits through their paces, until he forges them into the fighting men he always knew they could be. In the newspaper comic strip *Beetle Bailey* the sergeant is beating poor old Beetle Bailey into a bloody pulp. Many male veterans look back on their boot camp experience with nostalgia, seeing it as a rite of passage, a test of endurance, and initiation into manhood. They are convinced the presence of women degraded the standards of the training and bemoan the passing of the good old days.

Swearing Like a Drunken Sailor

Opponents of women in the military complain that when more women began to enlist, drill instructors suddenly were forbidden to curse or refer to recruits by degrading names, an indication that the military was getting soft. If someone couldn't tolerate being cursed at, how are they going to be able to function when the enemy takes a shot at them? However, foul language has not been a part of approved training techniques for decades, long before women and men began to train together. In the Marine Corps, the standard operating policies as far back as the 1940s forbade the use of vulgar language from drill instructors toward recruits (Sidebar 7-1).[110] Furthermore, given the type of language commonly heard in movies, it seems unlikely that vulgar language would have much shock value to contemporary recruits. Nowadays, a person who is able to command respect without the use of foul language is probably more shocking than someone who can swear "like a drunken sailor."

Sidebar 7-1

USE OF PROFANITY AND OBSCENE LANGUAGE

"A practice to be eliminated is that of directing vulgarity and profanity toward recruits. A Drill Instructor who must interlace his remarks to a recruit with a constant stream of vulgarity and verbal filth will not be tolerated. Such a Drill Instructor demonstrates his own lack of self-confidence when he has to assert himself against a defenseless recruit by profane language. A Drill Instructor who must bury his words of instruction in a stream of senseless profanity is at a loss for words to express himself; he reduces the value of his instruction and mars the image of the noncommissioned officer which he projects to his recruits; and he teaches recruits that profanity is expected and accepted in the Marine Corps. Drill Instructors will not direct toward recruits vulgar, obscene, or profane language."

"Bitch Slap That Punk"

Women are also blamed for eliminating the practice of drill instructors slapping, punching, and kicking recruits.[111] These techniques were supposedly used to ensure that recruits were tough enough to be effective fighters. Not all veterans grieve over the loss of violence as a teaching technique; in fact, some military personnel report that, even in the days before women and men trained together, violence from superiors was absent. Brig. General Samuel R. Shaw claimed, "I went through Parris Island when it was supposed to be the old tough Marine Corps. Nobody ever laid a hand on anybody in my platoon. We didn't have those things happen to us. Most were young men, and were treated like men. We weren't no-account people who were slapped and kicked."[112] Col. M. F. McLane, USMC, completed boot camp a decade later and noted, "Drill instructors put my platoon through vigorous training without laying a hand on any of us."[113] In 1980, Private First Class Eugene Sledge, USMC, wrote, "My drill instructor was a small man. He didn't have a big mouth. He was neither cruel nor sadistic. He was not a bully. But he was a strict disciplinarian, a total realist about our future and an absolute perfectionist dedicated to excellence."[114]

Although the above servicemen's personal experiences did not include the use of humiliation or violence from their superiors, other personnel were not so fortunate.

Private Abrahamson stood rigidly at attention in the DI squad room, waiting, as Sergeant Styles ambled slowly inside, kicking the door closed behind him. . . . "Tell me something, Abra-*ham*-son, are you a Jew?"

"Yes, sir," Abrahamson said. Styles nodded.

"I figured you were a Jew-boy," he said. . . . Slapping the swagger stick in his palm as he returned, the DI asked, "Jews like to eat a thing called a bagel, right, Abra-*ham*-son?"

"Yes, sir," Private Abrahamson said.

"I never did have one of those bagel things, and I don't think I ever will. I prefer American food. Tell me Bagel Boy, are you an old-fashioned Jew?"

"N–no sir," Abrahamson said. The DI nodded, slapped the swagger stick in his palm. "No, I guess all the old-fashioned Jews were wiped out by the Germans, eh?" He raised the swagger stick, tapping it lightly against Abrahamson's cheek, then a little harder at the side of the private's head. "Did you know Sergeant Richards is of German extraction, Abra-hamson? You know what Germans think of Jews, don't you, Abra-*ham*-son?" The sergeant rapped the swagger stick against the private's head once more. . . . "Get with it, Jew-boy," the sergeant growled, "this ain't no fuckin' synagogue. This is the United States Marine Corps."[115]

R. Wayne Eisenhart, a veteran of the Vietnam era, wrote about his boot camp experience.

While in basic training we were issued M-14 rifles. The breech of the weapon is closed by a bolt which is continually pushed forward by a large spring with considerable force. One night three men who had been censured for ineffectiveness in their assigned tasks were called forward in front of the assembled platoon, ordered to insert their penises into the breeches of their weapons, close the bolt, and run the length of the squad bay singing "The Marine Corps Hymn." This violent ritual ended as the drill instructor left and the three men sank to the floor, penises still clamped into their weapons. We helped them remove the rifles and guided them to their beds. There was considerable bleeding as the men cupped their wounded penises with their hands, curled into balls, and cried.[116]

As someone who has extensive training in motivating humans to undertake unpleasant tasks and face challenging situations, I fail to see how this type of treatment would lead to the creation of a disciplined, honor-bound individual who respects authority and is committed to excellence in the performance of his duties. However, I do see that it would lead to the creation of a humiliated, resentful person bent on revenge. I have to agree with Congressman Mario A. Biaggi, who said, "Brutality and death on the battlefield are unavoidable results of war and are intricately interwoven into the legend of the Marines. . . . But brutality and death on the training ground and in the barracks can only tarnish the nation's pride in its Marines."[117]

Feminization: An Alternative Explanation

Those who mourn over the "feminization" of their cherished institution apparently have short memories or are ignorant of military history. Changes in training in the Marine Corps were motivated by a number of incidents in the 1960s and 1970s long before large numbers of women were enlisting. In 1975 Marine recruits beat a fellow recruit to death while learning hand-to-hand combat techniques. Two weeks later a recruit died of heat stroke. A few months later a drill instructor shot a recruit in an attempt to frighten him. In a sixteen-month period seventeen recruits died at Parris Island. The causes of death were listed as drowning, suicide, accidental choking, and "natural." However, some of those whose deaths were listed as natural died as the result of heart failure, brain abscess, and kidney failure brought on by maltreatment and violence, including beatings.[118] In another forty-five-month period, fifty-eight Parris Island DIs were court-martialed on charges of maltreatment of recruits, and 58 percent of them were convicted.[119] One DI was convicted of assaulting a number of recruits, including breaking the nose and jaw of one recruit and choking him.[120]

When the Senate Armed Services Committee investigated, they found that the attrition rate for males had gone from 11 percent in 1972 to 18 percent in 1975. They also found that the number of recorded incidents of abuse in the Marine Corps was three times higher than in the other services.[121] According to Lt. General Bernard Trainer, "In the seventies, the process (of abuse) became institutionalized."[122]

Those who complain of women "forcing" their way into the military tend to overlook that military planners purposely sought to increase the number of women in the military. According to the office of the Secretary of the Army:

> Change began in 1973 with the end of the draft and the beginning of the all-volunteer Army. A policy decision was made to expand the number of Army women and to integrate them more widely into Army career fields. This decision was made in part to sustain a quality force in the post-draft era and to ensure the viability of the all-volunteer Army.[123]

In 1973, when the draft was eliminated, some military leaders feared that, since they could no longer force white men into serving, the void in the ranks would be filled by unemployed, under-educated African-American males. This was referred to as the "economic draft," because those who couldn't find employment would enlist. For some military leaders and members of Congress, it was better to have an American military that included women, black or white, than to have a military made up primarily of well-armed black men.[124] In other words, the increase in the recruitment of women was not because the civilian government demanded it, but because the military couldn't attract enough white male recruits to fulfill personnel needs. By 1993 fewer than eight in 1,000 eighteen-to-twenty-four-year-olds were enlisting.[125] By 1999 nearly one-third of young Americans males were ineligible for any form of military service, mostly due to their low educational achievement.[126] The increase in the number of women serving in the military says at least as much about men as it does about women. Instead of demanding to know why so many women enlist, perhaps we ought to ask why so many men don't enlist.

Likewise, the admission of women at the military academies was not the result of forced integration by civilian courts but of active recruitment by the military. In the early 1970s the Army began Project Athena, to study the process and impact of admission of women to West Point. In the pamphlet *Information for Women Cadets*, readers were informed, "West Point is embarking on a new chapter in its history of service to the country—the education of women as well as men officers for the United States Army. The Academy and the Army offer remarkable opportunities for meaningful service and personal satisfaction. West Point is resolved to challenge all cadets to their best efforts and to graduate quality young leaders for the Army."[127]

Some believe the old culture of the military is becoming obsolete solely because of the increase in the number of women enlisting.

> The old and almost always unofficial rites that cement ties among post adolescent males don't work their bonding magic with women in the same company or platoon. The old jokes and songs that celebrate the sexual exploits of predatory males whose warrior skills are visited not upon the enemy in the battlefield but upon the women in port don't voice a fantasy shared by gender integrated troops.[128]

What he fails to note is that there is more to the new military than men and women training and serving together: The men who are serving are different. By the early 1990s over half of military personnel were married. The military was supporting nearly three million spouses and children. There were more Marine dependents than Marines. In the Gulf War, two-thirds of those employed overseas left a family behind, which was four times the rate during the Vietnam War.[129] Men with wives and daughters at home just aren't going to react to Jody calls that celebrate rape, incest, or killing children the way unmarried eighteen year olds do.

THE NEGATIVE EFFECTS OF DISCRIMINATION AGAINST WOMEN IN THE MILITARY

DISCRIMINATING AGAINST WOMEN by limiting the roles in which they can serve reduces the effectiveness and efficiency of the military in numerous ways.

Increases Difficulty of Recruitment

Personnel who know that they will not be allowed to reach their full potential in an organization are much less likely to volunteer to join that organization. This means the military will have difficulty attracting the best and brightest citizens.

Reduction in Retention

Even when the military succeeds in getting intelligent motivated women to enlist, eventually they discover that they are considered second-class members of the organization. They realize they can make more money and have higher status in civilian organizations. The military loses a highly trained, desirable employee due to its own discriminatory policies.

Promotes Sexual Abuse

In any organization, when one group is treated as less capable than another, the discriminated group becomes a likely target for abuse.

Decreases Mission Readiness

As long as service women are not allowed to function in the roles for which they are trained, the military's mission will be at risk. In 1983, when integrated Army units were deployed to Grenada on Operation Urgent Fury, military police women were returned to their stateside base because they might be exposed to enemy fire. Not only was this an insult to the women who were fully trained and motivated, but also the unit lost members of the team with whom they had trained. In 1989, when troops were deployed on Operation Just Cause in Panama, a female Army intelligence analyst with expertise was replaced by a male analyst who had no knowledge of the area, because Panama was considered a combat zone and inappropriate for a woman. That action put the mission and many lives at stake in order to maintain the illusion that woman can't be involved in combat zones.[130]

MIGHT THE MILITARY BE IMPROVED BY HAVING MORE WOMEN PERSONNEL?

Nearly all the debate about women in the military has focused not on "if," but "how" damaging it is to have women in the military. Almost no attention has been given to the concept that having more women serve might improve the military.

Not all armed forces have demanded only hypermasculine traits in their warriors. Some have encouraged their warriors to engage in practices that many Americans would see as stereotypically feminine. Japan's warrior class, the samurai, and the ninjas, were trained not only in hand-to-hand combat but also in flute playing, flower arranging, and writing poetry. They did this to cultivate calm and increase concentration skills, which were viewed as essential assets for fighting men.[131]

In writing about women in the military, Judith Hicks Stiehm wondered if the existence of women fully integrated into the military would demonstrate to America's enemies that every citizen, male and female, would have to be defeated before the country could be occupied.[132]

In 1995, when women shipped out on the U.S.S. *Eisenhower*, many Naval personnel and civilians predicted failure. They were disappointed when, six months later the ship returned to port and the executive officer, Captain Doug Roulstone, declared the cruise "a resounding success," since the crew had performed "as well, if not better than before women were aboard." The number of disciplinary cases was lower than on previously all-male cruises, and the ship's overall performance showed improvement.[133] The Presidential Commission on the Assignment of Women in the Armed Forces found that "mixed-gender units seemed to communicate and work better than single-gender units performing similar tasks."[134] According to National Defense Research Institute personnel who trained in mixed-sex units exerted greater effort than those in single-sex units. "The women worked harder to gain male approval and the men worker harder not to be outdone by the women."[135]

In the past, wives were viewed as a liability to readiness and retention, because marriage might dilute the loyalty of personnel to the military way of life. Now there are many marriages in which both the husband and the wife are enlisted. As early as 1981, 25 percent of the married women in the military had a husband who was also enlisted.[136] In these marriages both of the spouses understand and are committed to the military culture. They tolerate reassignments that require relocation and long separations due to deployment that nonmilitary spouses find unacceptable. Of course, the down side of the two-military-career marriage is, if the military doesn't keep one of the members satisfied, to the point where he or she doesn't want to reenlist, the other spouse may also leave the service. With half of all enlisted women and more than a third of all female officers having husbands who are also in the military, this has become an issue worthy of the military's attention.[137]

"We know more about war than we do about peace—more about killing than we do about living."—General Omar Bradley[*]

In the twenty-first century, America's military faces a very different type of war than it did in the previous century. It is inappropriate to use the strategies of previous wars, no matter how effective they were, and no matter how much nostalgia is associated with them, to fight current battles. The military must meet contemporary challenges with contemporary methods. Former commandant of the Marine Corps, General Chuck Krulak, describes the type of conflicts the American military now face: "In one moment in time our service members will be feeding and clothing displaced refugees—providing humanitarian assistance. In the next moment, they will be holding two warring tribes apart—conducting peacekeeping operations. And finally, they will be fighting a highly lethal mid-intensity battle—all on the same day.... all within three city blocks."[138] Perhaps such missions benefit from female personnel. Other armies seem to think so.

The leaders of FARC, the guerrilla fighters that control much of southern Colombia, make it a practice to assign a female commander to each town. They do this because they believe that females relate more warmly to the local citizens than do male commanders and therefore are able to obtain a greater level of cooperation from the population.[139] In the U.S. Army, nearly one-third of the Military Intelligence personnel, the ones that negotiate with the Iraqi citizens, are female.[140] Some male leaders are learning that the old-style stand-off, like gunslingers in the Wild West approach, is counter-productive in the warfare of the twenty-first century. Although when faced with direct attack they respond with their usual tactics, when dealing with counterinsurgency they emphasize community relations over violence, an approach that hypermasculine men scorn as soft and unwarrior-like.[141] Despite these objections the new

[*] The man for which Bradley M2/M3 fighting vehicles were named.

stance appears to be effective. Captain Max Barela, who commanded Lim Company in Ramadi, Iraq, stopped kicking down doors and began to knock and ask to come in. Once inside he sometimes spent hours "chit-chatting."[142] He found he gained not only a great deal of useful intelligence but also increased cooperation. In the first three months in which this kinder, gentler approach to nation building was tried, violent incidents in Lima Company's area of operation decreased 70 percent, IED[*] attacks were almost nonexistent, and children once again were playing in the streets.

In addition to cooperating with civilian populations, peacekeeping forces increasingly have to work together with the armed services of other countries to form and maintain coalitions. Professor Teresa Amabile, who heads the Entrepreneurial Management Unit at Harvard Business School, has been studying the effects of competition and collaboration on the success of organizations for thirty years. Her research has consistently found that although there is a widespread belief that internal competition fosters innovation, in fact creativity is greatly reduced when people in a work group compete instead of collaborate. When people compete for recognition, they stop sharing information. This is destructive, because nobody in an organization has all the information required to put all the pieces of the puzzle together. In other words, the big picture is never seen. The most creative teams are those that have the confidence to share and debate ideas.

From an early age boys are more competitive than girls. A study of fourth- and sixth-graders found 50 percent of boys' interactions were direct competition, while girls spent only 1 percent of their time being competitive.[143] The inclusion of women, particularly if they do not endorse hypermasculine ideals, is likely to improve a unit's ability to function as a team, foster cooperation, and develop useful alliances with others.

A SIMPLE CONCLUSION

IT WOULD SEEM THAT the military would be delighted to have brave, motivated, patriotic citizens volunteer for dangerous jobs with low pay,

---

[*] Improvised explosive devices.

but as we have seen this is not the case when those volunteers are female. Instead of being welcomed they are viewed as being sluts and lesbians, as emasculating men, and concurrently driving them to rape.[144] One has to wonder, with all the hostility and barriers women who have wanted to enlist have faced and continue to face, why they continue to even consider being part of the military. According to a wounded veteran of the first Iraqi War, Lieutenant Colonel Rhonda Cornum, women are motivated to be a part of the military by the same factors as are men: "The things that are really important are loyalty and integrity, moral courage, a sense of humor, dedication, and commitment." She also noted, "I don't think those things are any better represented in either sex."[145] When all the facts are examined, it becomes clear that the objections to women serving in the military are obsolete, irrational, and nothing more than blatant sexism.

"Do women really contribute to mission readiness? Anyone who asks that question seriously, man or woman, needs to question his or her assumptions and prejudices, and instead face the facts."—Major General Mary Clarke[146]

8

THE FAG OF WAR:
HOMOPHOBIA IN THE MILITARY

ALTHOUGH THE FOLLOWING directive was written during World War II, it still sounds quite contemporary: "The interests of the war effort, military discipline, and the protection of youth, as well as considerations to do with population policy, absolutely require the prevention of all same-sex acts, the identification of homosexuals, their punishment, and their removal from the armed forces (*Instruction for Medical Officers of the Luftwaffe*, 1944)."[1]

DEFINING HOMOPHOBIA

THE AMERICAN PSYCHIATRIC ASSOCIATION defines a phobia as "A persistent, irrational fear of a specific object, activity, or situation (the phobic stimulus) that results in a compelling desire to avoid it. This often leads either to avoidance of the phobic stimulation or enduring it with dread."[2] In the case of homophobic military personnel, avoiding or enduring homosexuals (or those perceived to display homosexual tendencies) may be replaced by threats of violence. Homophobia by definition is an overreaction. When female cadets began attending dances at West Point, they were ordered to wear their uniform skirts instead of their uniform slacks, because the sight of two cadets both wearing slacks and dancing together disturbed a senior officer.[3] The Navy has penalized consensual same-sex behavior between adults more harshly than it punished those who engaged in child molesting, sexual assault, or incest. A

Navy dentist who had pleaded guilty to sodomizing his sixteen-year-old son was not charged with a crime, was kept on duty, and was provided with a rehabilitation program. At the same base, more than a half-dozen officers and enlisted personnel were being discharged against their will merely for declaring they were gay.[4]

Dr. Gregory Lehne's studies of homophobia lead him to conclude "Homophobia is irrational because it generally embodies misconceptions and false stereotypes of male homosexuality. These belief systems, or prejudices, are rationalizations supporting homophobia, not causes of homophobia."[5] One of these common false beliefs is that homosexuals are afraid of the other sex. However, approximately 50 percent of men who identified themselves as homosexual had at one time or another been involved in a sexual relationship with a woman for at least one year.[6]

Another commonly held false belief is that homosexuals molest children as a way to "recruit into the gay lifestyle." Research disputes this; when interviewed, only 4 percent of male homosexuals reported they were forced into their first same-sex experience. On the other hand, 6 percent of heterosexual adolescent girls reported sexual assault from a male as their first sexual experience.[7]

"DON'T ASK, DON'T TELL": THE CLINTON LEGACY

Most Americans had not given any thought to homosexuals serving in the military until presidential candidate Bill Clinton pledged to end the exclusion of homosexuals.[8] Once elected president, he sent a memorandum to the Secretary of Defense ordering him to "end discrimination on the basis of sexual orientation in determining who may serve in the Armed Forces."[9] There was immediate opposition from the military, Congress, and the general public. After six months of controversy, a new policy, popularly referred to as "Don't Ask, Don't Tell," was announced, under which homosexual personnel were allowed to continue serving as long as they were not open about their orientation and did not engage in any prohibited behavior. According to the policy, homosexual conduct is forbidden both on and off base and includes not only same-sex intercourse, but also public acknowledgement of homosexuality, attempting same-sex marriage, and same-sex hand-holding or kissing.* It was made

---

* Commander-in-Chief President George W. Bush was not held to these standards. He was filmed on more than one occasion walking hand-in-hand with other men. He explained it was a sign of friendship between the American government and its Arab allies. He also publicly kissed Senator Joseph Lieberman.

into law four months later as the Defense Authorization Act of 1994. In 1999, a "Don't Pursue, Don't Harass" clause was added to "Don't Ask, Don't Tell" (DADTDPDH). The Servicemembers Legal Defense Network was less than pleased.

> DADTDPDH is the only law in the land that authorizes the firing of an American for being gay. There is no other federal, state, or local law like it. Indeed, DADTDPDH is the only law that punishes gays, lesbians, and bisexuals for coming out. Many Americans view DADTDPDH as a benign gentlemen's agreement with discretion as the key to job security. That is simply not the case. An honest statement of one's sexual orientation to anyone, anywhere, anytime may lead to being fired.[10]

Ironically, the media attention generated in the 1990s by these policies made the military a more attractive career option for both homosexuals and heterosexuals, since much of the debate revolved around gays and lesbians being patriotic citizens who wanted to serve their country. The military was presented as a highly desirable organization worth fighting over.[11]

> "Are you a homosexual or bisexual?"—Question 36d, Enlistment/Reenlistment Document of the Armed Forces

As the result of the "Don't Ask, Don't Tell" policy, question 36d was supposed to be dropped. In the civilian world, such questions had been eliminated two decades earlier. In the 1970s, the employment application for Northwestern Bell included the question "Are you a homosexual?" Those who checked the "yes" box were not hired. When this was brought to the attention of the Minneapolis City Council, they determined this was discrimination based on freedom of association and violated the U.S. Constitution. They unanimously amended the existing Civil Rights Ordinance to make such questions on job applications illegal.[12]

Witch Hunts: What Part of "Don't Pursue, Don't Harass" Don't You Understand?

Despite the official policy forbidding the harassment of people suspected of being homosexual, the military has a much higher rate of antihomosexual acts than the civilian world. A study from thirty-eight randomly selected bases found that 80 percent of the subjects had heard hostile antigay speech and 5 percent had witnessed at least one violent antigay assault. Furthermore, 25 percent of the military respondents reported a person of authority observed the offense, which was nearly three times higher than was reported by civilians. Even more disturbing was the finding that the abuser in the military setting was a person of authority, a rate over two times higher than civilians reported.[13]

Despite the directive to stop pursuing suspected homosexuals, the military has continued to expend time and resources searching the ranks for them. Every day, the U.S. government fires two people simply for being homosexual.[14] Many people believe that anyone determined to be a homosexual is merely discharged; in fact, the individual receives a dishonorable discharge, which prohibits future employment with any branch of the federal government and denies veterans' benefits.[15] Lt. Paul Starr was court-martialed for acts with other consenting adults while in the military. The prosecutor described Starr as "despicable" and sought to have him incarcerated for twenty-one years. Those who testified against Starr were given honorable discharges in exchange for their testimony; he was dismissed, forfeited all pay allowances, and was sentenced to eighteen months in prison.[16]

Lack of evidence of same-sex sexual activity hasn't stopped the military from harassing women suspected of being lesbians. Military police Captain Judy Meade was accused of being a lesbian by another servicewoman, who was under investigation for suspected homosexuality and had undergone fourteen continuous hours of questioning during which she was pressured to name other lesbians. Even though an investigation found no evidence to substantiate the accuser's claim, Meade was charged with conduct unbecoming an officer. Her crime? She had a friendship with a civilian who was believed to be a lesbian. The punishment recommended for this "crime" was a less-than-honorable discharge. During the administrative board proceedings Meade was asked why she did not suspect certain female comrades were lesbian and avoid them. The board members wondered why her "antenna did not go up," because in their opinion these women "looked like homosexuals" and engaged in "homosexual activities such as softball."[17]

SAME-SEX PHYSICAL CONTACT

IT HAS ONLY BEEN since the late 1800s that physical contact between men has been viewed as abnormal or an indication of homosexuality. In the military, soldiers have long slept huddled up against one another for warmth. Civil War diaries are full of references to soldiers cuddling together for warmth.

> The "A" or wedge tent covered an area of about seven feet by seven feet and was made to house about four men, although often six men occupied them. In this case, the men would "spoon" together when sleeping. This meant that they would all sleep in the same direction and turn over together at the same time, when one of the men would say to do so.[18]

SAME-SEX SEXUAL CONTACT

NOT ALL ARMIES have feared same-sex sexual contact. Some have even encouraged it, believing that it promoted morale, bonded soldiers to one another, and made them more willing to fight the enemy in order to protect one another. Sex acts between men were considered to be a vital form of bonding between warriors in military societies such as Sparta, Crete, and feudal Japan.[19]

The ban on same-sex sexual contact between American military personnel was copied from the laws that governed the British navy.[20] The first recorded court martial in the U.S. military related to same-sex behavior took place in 1778, when Lieutenant General Gotthold Fredrick Enslin was discovered in bed with Private John Monhart. General Enslin was found guilty of sodomy and discharged.[21]

The 1917 *Articles of War* made explicit for the first time in American military law that "assault with intent to commit sodomy" was grounds for court martial. At this point in history the focus was on the behavior of assault, not on one's sexual identity as homosexual or heterosexual. By 1920 the *Articles of War* firmly established that even consensual same-sex sexual contact was grounds for discharge.[22]

OTHER SEXUAL ACTS

ACCORDING TO THE *Manual of Instruction for Military Surgeons*, men who engaged in "solitary vice" (masturbation) ought to be kept from enlisting, or discharged if they were already in the ranks.[23] At the end of World War II, the military replaced the *Articles of War* with the *Uniform Code of Military Justice*, which is still in effect today. Consensual oral or anal contact became not only grounds for discharge but also punishable by five years at hard labor, and forfeiture of pay and allowances. If the sexual contact was the result of assault, then the penalty can be increased by an additional five years. The article treats oral or anal sex with a willing human partner as the same as sex with an animal. Both anal and oral sex between willing homosexual partners, as well as between willing heterosexual partners, even if married, are illegal—despite the research indicating that anal sex is engaged in by at least 11 percent of married heterosexual couples and oral sex is engaged in by nearly 50 percent of the general population. In 2003, the U.S. Supreme Court rejected antisodomy laws for civilians as unconstitutional, but such laws are still considered essential in the military.

DREAD OF HOMOSEXUALS

IN 1981, THE STANDARD for discharge became even more restrictive. Department of Defense Directive 1332.14 clarified that one no longer needed to engage in same-sex sexual contact in order to be discharged— one need only have a "propensity to or intent to engage in" same-sex acts.[24] This meant that not only was same-sex sexual behavior a crime, but also simply being homosexual or bisexual had become criminalized. In civilian courts this is referred to as a *status crime*, one in which a person is guilty merely by being in a certain condition (for example, being homeless).[25] In a decision handed down nearly two decades before Directive 1332.14 made the status of homosexuality or bisexuality a crime, the justices ruled that, at least in civilian society, status laws are unconstitutional.[26]

> *"In no other area of American life is discrimination against gay men and women so clearly stated and institutionally supported [than in the military]."*—Rhonda R. Rivera, Professor of Law[27]

An excellent example of the effect of Directive 1332.14 is the case of Lt. Richard P. Watson, assistant professor of Naval Science. Watson disclosed his sexual orientation to his supervisor because of his "commitment to honesty and desire to eliminate any potential for blackmail attempts in the future."[28] In his disclosure he wrote,"I expressly deny that I have engaged in any homosexual conduct with any military student or service member. I expressly deny that I engaged in any homosexual conduct during the performance of military duty, or while on any military installation. I expressly deny that I have any intent or propensity to engage in any conduct described above."[29] Navy authorities determined that, since Watson's statement failed to address whether he had any intent or propensity to engage in off-base, off-duty sexual conduct with nonmilitary personnel, he be discharged.

COMMON OBJECTIONS TO HOMOSEXUALS SERVING IN THE MILITARY

THE OFFICE OF THE SECRETARY of Defense in 1982 provided a summary of the most common objections.

> Homosexuality is incompatible with military service. The presence of such members adversely affects the ability of the Armed Forces to maintain discipline, good order, and morale; to foster mutual trust and confidence among the members; to ensure the integrity of the system of rank and command; to facilitate assignment and worldwide deployment of members who frequently must live and work under close conditions affording minimal privacy; to recruit and retrain members of the military services; to maintain the public acceptability of military services; and, in certain circumstances, to prevent breaches of security.[30]

It Would Be Embarrassing

General "Stormin' Norman" Schwarzkopf explained that the U.S. military could not afford to acknowledge homosexuals in the military: "Because of the prevailing aversion to homosexuals in our society, the Army would suffer in esteem if known homosexuals were allowed to serve."[31] Of course, as more of our military allies eliminate their bans on homosexuals and more civilians become accepting of homosexuals, this objection will lose any credibility.

Male Homosexuals Are Not "Real Men"; Therefore, They Make Poor Warriors

"From a military viewpoint, the homosexual is not only dangerous, but ineffective as a fighter."—Dr. Albert Abrams, *"Homosexuality: A Military Menace,"* 1918

Many persons, particularly those who endorse hypermasculinity, view homosexual men as not being "real men." They believe that all homosexual men are effeminate, so they could easily identify a homosexual man by his appearance. Although 37 percent of Americans believe "it is easy to tell homosexuals by how they look," studies have found less than 20 percent of male homosexuals are suspected of being gay by their coworkers or other social relationships.[32]

In modern times not all countries' militaries believe that having homosexuals serve will destroy the effectiveness of their armed forces. Israel—a country that has fought and won five major wars in less than fifty years, continues to occupy hostile territories, and faces ongoing guerilla warfare—does not officially discriminate against gays or lesbians. The Israeli Defense Force is made up of men and women who begin mandatory military service starting at the age of eighteen years. Conscripts are not asked about their sexual orientation, and even openly homosexual men and women are not exempted from service. Perhaps because Israel is only the size of New Jersey and is surrounded on all sides by enemies, it can't afford to reject potential fighters because of their sexual orientation. Homosexual soldiers have served in the Israel Defense Force in combat units, even elite combat units, since the founding of the State of Israel in 1948. The highest-ranking openly gay officer is a colonel.[33] The Israeli media doesn't cover gays in the military, because the general public and, more importantly, service members show little interest in the topic.[34] Contrast this with the uproar that followed President Clinton's efforts to reduce discrimination toward homosexuals in our armed forces.

High-ranking officials admit that many homosexual personnel conduct themselves in an outstanding manner. In 1990 Vice Admiral Joseph Donnell sent a memo to Navy commanders in which he described lesbian military personnel as "hard-working, career-oriented, willing to put in long hours on the job, and among the command's top performers." Despite his positive description of lesbian personnel, the purpose of his directive was to demand that commanders more vigorously discourage lesbian enlistment. He was concerned that current investigations were being pursued "halfheartedly" because commanders were reluctant to lose such valuable personnel.[35] Many effective high-ranking officers are homosexual. In 2003 Admiral Alan Steinman and Generals Keith Kerr and Virgil Richard come out as gay.[36] They waited until retired before going public, for obvious reasons.

The Presence of Known Homosexuals Is Damaging to Morale

"Tolerating homosexuals in the armed forces is contrary to good order and discipline." —Major Randel Webb, USMC[37]

Research by the British military found that 66 percent of their male service members stated they would not serve with gays if their country lifted its ban on homosexuals serving. However, when the ban was eliminated, it proved "unproblematic."[38] Rolf Kurth joined the Royal Navy in 1990 and served honorably until 1997, when he was discharged against his will for being a homosexual. After nearly four years in civilian life, Lieutenant Kurth was officially invited to rejoin the Navy after the British government lifted its gay ban to comply with a ruling of the European Court of Human Rights. Kurth reenlisted in 2001, graduated in the top of his class at the Principle Warfare Officers' course, served on the Royal Navy's largest amphibious ship in the Persian Gulf throughout the first war against Iraq, and served effectively—despite his sexual orientation being common knowledge.[39]

Privacy Issues

"We've got to consider not only the rights of homosexuals but also the rights of those who are not homosexual and who give up a great deal of privacy when they go into the military."—Sam Nunn on *Face the Nation*

One of the major concerns heterosexuals express about serving with homosexuals is their discomfort disrobing or showering with them.

Professional sports teams have managed to function for their entire existence with heterosexual and homosexual men dressing and showering in the same location. Heterosexual military men seem much more intimidated than professional athletes by the presence of homosexual men in their showers. When interviewed about his experience in the military, a gay Marine Corps major described showering with other men when one of them started "spouting off that he would never allow gays in the military, because he would never shower next to a homosexual." The major simply quipped, "Too late."[40]

Women are routinely subjected to leering and sexual taunting, and most heterosexual men consider it a birthright of males to view women as sexual objects, but they find it very disturbing if they are the targets of unwanted sexual attention. Steven Zeeland asked, "How can the American fighting man, aggressive and predatory, be expected to stand naked in the shower before a man known to *penetrate other men* without that macho soldier being made to *feel like a woman?*"[41] Sergeant Kayla Williams described the leering she endured while stationed in Iraq: "I remember walking through the chow hall at the airfield was like running a gauntlet of eyes. Guys stared and stared and stared. Sometimes it felt like I was some fucking zoo animal."[42]

One topic that rarely gets mentioned during discussions of privacy is the loss of privacy experienced by heterosexuals because of the military's zeal in investigating alleged homosexuals. When military investigators look into the personal lives of suspected homosexuals, they also actively inquire into the private lives of the suspect's coworkers, friends, and family.[43] If sexual orientation was not an issue, then everyone would be free of these intrusions into private matters.

Homosexuals Are Dangerous

"A convenient way of excluding an unwanted group is to maintain that they pose a physical threat, and any discrimination is simply self-defense."—Dr. David Ari Bianco[44]

In 1993, Petty Officer Albert Ruggiero was sentenced to seven years in prison after being convicted of two counts of rape for sexually assaulting another male.[45] Admiral John Dalrymple proclaimed, "What this shows is that homosexuals cannot be expected to remain celibate while on active duty in the military."[46] However, three years later, when the numerous sexual assaults of women by men at the 1991 Tailhook convention became public, Dalrymple did not perceive these events as evidence that *hetero*sexuals are dangerous, that heterosexuality is not compatible with military service, or that heterosexuals should not be allowed to remain in the ranks.

Not only are heterosexual men homophobic, but so, too, are many heterosexual women. Captain Rosemary Mariner expressed concern that, if the sleeping quarters of male and female personnel were separate, women would be subject to sexual attacks by lesbians during the night. She was not only invoking the stereotype that homosexuals cannot control their sexual urges and are dangerous, but also that women need the protection of men.[47] The view that all homosexuals are dangerous has been enshrined in military justice through a legal opinion handed down by a 1953 Court of Military Appeals which found, "[A] person who practices homosexuality is likely to assault for the purpose of satisfying his perverted sexual cravings."[48] Actually, it is more common for homosexuals to be the target of attacks than to commit them. In 1992 Allen Schindler was stomped to death in a bathroom by his comrades because they believed he was gay. Following an autopsy the Navy pathologist reported that death could have resulted from at least four different wounds to the head, chest, and abdomen. The sailor had eight broken ribs, a broken nose, a broken jaw, a skull fracture, and the front of his face was detached. The physician likened the condition of the body to that of someone who had been kicked to death by a horse, hit by a speeding car, or in an airplane crash.[49] In 1999, Private First Class Barry Winchell was murdered in his sleep because his comrades suspected he was gay. In the year following this murder the authorities at Fort Campbell increased the number of discharges based on charges of homosexuality at a rate eleven times that of the previous year.[50]

Homosexuals Are a Security Risk

Both General Colin Powell and Vice President Dick Cheney have dismissed the danger of homosexuals being a security risk due to blackmail. As early as 1957, the military's own research rejected the argument that homosexual personnel were a security risk.

The concept that homosexuals pose a security risk is unsupported by any factual data. Homosexuals are no more a security risk, and in many case are much less of a security risk, than alcoholics and those people with marked feelings of inferiority who must brag of their knowledge of secret information and disclose it to gain stature. Promiscuous heterosexual activity also provides serious security implications. Some intelligence officers consider a senior officer having illicit heterosexual activity with the wife of a junior officer or enlisted man is much more of a security risk than the ordinary homosexual. . . . No factual data exist to support the contention that homosexuals are a greater risk than heterosexuals. [51]

Two more recent studies have found no evidence that gay men pose any particular risk to national security. In fact, one study determined gay men are "as good or better than the average heterosexual" for military roles involving security clearance.[52] Perhaps this is because, in order to serve in the U.S. military, a gay man must be skilled at keeping his orientation a secret, and this competence transfers to his work duties.

Fear of HIV/AIDS

"These diseases don't spread through sharing ammunition."—Dr. David Ari Bianco[53]

Major Edward Proskie objected to known homosexuals serving in the military because, "In the event soldiers are wounded and blood is spilled, if the person is suspected of being infected with AIDS, there could be some apprehension in responding to his aid."[54] As the AIDS epidemic in Africa proves all too well, *hetero*sexuals can be infected with HIV due to their sexual behavior; therefore, military personnel ought to be trained to protect themselves from blood-borne illnesses regardless of the sexual orientation of the wounded individual—just as civilian emergency responders have done for years.

Opponents of homosexuals serving in the military warn that homosexuals would overwhelm the military's medical system because they would require treatment for HIV/AIDS or other sexually transmitted diseases. Of the twenty-four foreign militaries that removed their bans on homosexuals serving, none has suffered a strain on their medical systems.[55] A study of the militaries of Australia, Britain, Canada, and Israel found that, when they lifted their ban on gays serving, there was no increase in the rate of HIV infection among their troops.[56]

Those who worry that the health care system of the military will be overwhelmed by risky behaviors of homosexuals could save vastly more money if they put their efforts into combating a health problem that actually exists: alcohol abuse. The Department of Defense determined that alcohol use costs the military more than $600 million in medical care and lost productivity each year.[57] The rate of alcohol consumption for eighteen-to-twenty-five-year-olds in the military is more than two-and-a-half times higher than in civilians of the same age group, and that 21 percent of military personnel admit to heavy drinking, which is 5 or more drinks a night at least once a week. The American Medical Association's guideline for the consumption of alcohol without risking damage to the body is 5 or less drinks per week. Another Pentagon study found 41.8 percent of U.S. military personnel engage in binge drinking.[58]

Homosexuality Is a Mental Illness

In the 1990s nearly half of the recruits enlisting in the Marine Corps did so under a waiver for psychological problems, medical problems, illegal drug use or other crimes.[59] Opponents to gays serving in the military insist that homosexuality is a mental disorder that renders a person unfit for military service—this, despite that since 1975 both the American Psychiatric Association and the American Psychological Association have publicly stated that homosexuality is not a mental disorder. Psychologist Dr. John Gonsiorek compared psychological testing of homosexuals to heterosexuals. He concluded, "Testing results overwhelmingly suggest that there are few, if any, consistent, measurable differences between heterosexuals and homosexual populations." He added, "Does the statement that homosexuality per se is not a sign of psychological disturbance mean that there are no disturbed homosexuals? No. It means that the proportion, or base rate, of disturbed individuals in homosexual and heterosexual populations is roughly equivalent."[60]

Research conducted by the Pentagon in the 1980s found that the military's discrimination against homosexuals had no rational basis, and a review of the service records of known homosexual personnel found their performance to be "superior on the average to comparable records of heterosexual military personnel."[61] Despite this finding, the 1996 Department of Defense form on physical disability evaluation for the purpose of retirement or other discharges included homosexuality under a list of mental disorders that included alcoholism and mental retardation. When asked ten years later about this document, Pentagon spokesperson Lt. Col. Jeremy M. Martin said the policy was still under review.[62]

Homosexuality Is Unnatural

"Recruiting and retention of homosexuals would force upon others tolerance of a lifestyle many consider abnormal and totally unacceptable."—Charles R. Jackson, Executive Vice President of the Non Commissioned Officers Association[63]

The contention that homosexuality is unnatural is undermined when one looks at cross-cultural studies. In forty-nine out of seventy-seven societies studied, not only did homosexuality exist, it was socially sanctioned.[64] In America 37 percent of men acknowledge engaging in sexual acts to orgasm with another man.[65] Robert Brannon summarized the current scientific view of the "naturalness" of homosexuality:

Every human society in the world today, from vast industrial nations to the smallest and simplest tribes in remote parts of the world, has some degree of homosexuality. Every society in the history of the Earth, for which we have records, going back to the beginning of recorded history, had some degree of homosexuality. Some of these societies accepted homosexuality readily while others severely condemned it, but *all* human societies have been aware of it because homosexuality has always existed wherever human beings have existed. . . . There is no more objective reason to consider homosexuality unnatural than there is to consider left-handedness unnatural.[66]

Homosexuality Is Nothing More Than a Sin

"For some in uniform, opposition to demands for acceptance of homosexuals includes a moral component—the religious belief that homosexual relations are sinful—encouraging admirers to see the armed forces as bastions of self-restraint

and traditional virtue in a society otherwise gone 'bonkers' over sex."—A. J. Bacevich [67]

Two Bible passages are often referenced when discussing homosexuality: "You shall not lie with a male as with a woman" (Leviticus 18:22) and "If a man lies with a male as with a woman, both of them have committed an abomination; they shall be put to death, their blood is upon them" (20:13).[68] The remainder of Leviticus is infrequently cited, perhaps because it includes acts in which most modern Americans, Christians included, frequently engage, such as eating rare meat and wearing clothes made of more than one fabric. Some actions expressly forbidden by Leviticus, such as shaving one's beard, are required by the military.

Regardless of the views on the sinfulness of homosexuality held by some individuals or organized religions, the U.S. military is not a religious institution—it is an arm of the secular government. Therefore it cannot base its regulations on religious teachings. If it were to do so, it would seem that the commandment "Thou shalt not kill" would seem to put the military completely out of business. Nor does the U.S. military make any effort whatsoever to comply with the biblical teachings found in Numbers chapter 19, which directs that "Whoever touches the dead body of anyone will be unclean for seven days. He must purify himself and on the seventh day he will be clean. Whoever touches the dead body of anyone and fails to purify himself defiles the Lord's tabernacle."

The federal courts have already ruled that when military regulations conflict with religious teachings the regulations prevail. When a Jewish serviceman sued to be permitted to wear a yarmulke while in uniform, the court sided with the military and its claim that maintaining uniform dress was critical to military order.[69] In 1995, a board of Naval captains recommended that a lieutenant commander be discharged because he claimed his understanding of his religion (Episcopalian) made it impossible for him to lead women into combat.[70]

When the federal courts examine cases that involve the overlap of legislation and religion it uses three criteria.[71] First, the law must reflect a clearly secular purpose. Secondly, its primary effect must be neither to advance nor inhibit religion. Finally, it must avoid excessive government entanglement with religion. The military's ban on certain types of consensual sexual contact between heterosexuals, and the discrimination against homosexuals, do not pass any of these three criteria.

Heterosexuals Will Refuse to Obey Orders from Known Homosexuals

Military personnel constantly respond to orders from people they don't respect, dislike, or even hate. Racists take orders from the members of the race they despise. Misogynists take orders from women. Members of one religion take orders from those they are convinced will burn in hell for heretical beliefs. Fundamentalists take orders from atheists. It is absurd to think that military personnel would actually risk court martial by disobeying a direct order merely because they disapprove of the superiors' sexual behavior. If everyone who disapproved of their superior's behavior refused to follow orders, the military would have fallen apart decades ago. When the military began to be racially integrated, it was argued that whites would not take orders from African-American officers, yet forty years later the highest ranking officer in the U.S. military was Colin Powell, an African American.

Exceptions to the Objections

When the country is in desperate need for personnel, such as in times of war, the military tolerates the services of homosexuals (Sidebar 8-1). During periods of actual combat, when one would think the concept of unit readiness would be of utmost importance, the supposed danger of homosexuals serving ceases to be an issue. In 2001, following the invasion of Afghanistan, discharges for reasons of homosexuality decreased almost 30 percent.[72] In 2003, when Operation Iraqi Freedom began, discharges for homosexuality decreased another 40 percent from the rates of 2001, through the use of stop-loss orders.[73] According to the Servicemembers Legal Defense Network, this is standard operating procedure: "The number of gays discharged from the military service because of homosexuality has dropped every time America has entered a war."[74]

Sidebar 8-1

IKE AND DYKES

Second Lieutenant Johnnie Phelps was one of the first women to enlist in the Women's Army Corps when it was created.* She served overseas under the direct command of Five-Star General Dwight D. "Ike" Eisenhower, Supreme Commander of the Allied Expeditionary Force in Europe. Toward the end of the war she was summoned to his office. The General informed her, "It's been reported to me that there are lesbians in the WAC battalion. I want you to find them and give me a list. We've got to get rid of them."

"Sir, if the General pleases, I'll be happy to check into this and make you a list. But you've got to know, when you get the list back, my name's going to be the first," responded Lt. Phelps.

Before the General could respond his long-time secretary who was present announced, "Sir, if the General pleases, Lieutenant Phelps will have to be second on the list because mine will be first. You see because I'm going to type it." The General sat back in silence.

Lt. Phelps plunged on, "You have the highest-ranking WAC battalion assembled anywhere in the world. Most decorated. If you want to get rid of your file clerks, typists, section commanders, and your most key personnel, then I'll make that list. But when I make the list, I want you to remember that we haven't had any illegal pregnancies, we do not have any venereal disease, we have never had any negative reports, and we have always served and done our duty, just like we're supposed to. As a matter of fact, since this unit has been here, it has received Meritorious Commendations on a regular, six-month basis. Now, if you want me to get rid of these women, I'll get rid of them, but I'll go with them."

"Forget that order," the General responded.[75]

MILITARY PERSONNEL HAVE ALWAYS SERVED WITH HOMOSEXUAL COMRADES

Multinational Forces

SINCE THE FIRST GULF WAR and up through the end of the century, Western militaries were involved in fifty-four military actions, including North Atlantic Treaty Organization mandated actions and UN peacekeeping operations. The United States participated in forty of these actions, and nineteen of them involved U.S. forces deploying with military personnel from other nations.[76] Therefore, U.S. personnel have been training with

---

* Lt. Phelps served from 1943–1946 and was honorably discharged.

and fighting alongside known homosexuals for years, because by 1995 all the members of NATO (except for Greece, Turkey, and America) had eliminated discriminatory policies toward homosexuals.[77]

In a 2003 issue of *Parameters*, the official journal of the U.S. Army War College, a study was published that examined the integration of acknowledged gay and lesbian military personnel in the militaries of Australia, Britain, Canada, and Israel. It concluded that, in all these countries, the lifting of the ban had no impact on military recruitment, cohesion, readiness, or performance, disputing the claims that gay and lesbian personnel receive special treatment in foreign militaries, that no known homosexuals serve in combat units, and that cultural differences between the militaries studied and the U.S. make their experiences inapplicable to America's military.[78] The experiences of America's allies clearly indicate that homosexuality is compatible with military service. As ever-increasing numbers of armed forces eliminate their bans on homosexuals, America will be in the minority in maintaining a ban on homosexual service members.

American Forces

As distasteful as it may be for some military personnel to realize, the fact is that, as long as there has been an American military, there have been homosexuals serving in it. The question isn't, "Should homosexual Americans serve in the military?" They do and always have. A more relevant question would be, "Should homosexual Americans serving in the our military be discriminated against?"

Those opposed to lifting the ban might grudgingly acknowledge that even though there are some homosexuals that serve in the military—even some in positions of great responsibility or rank—they are still not open about their orientation, and were they to serve openly, then the real trouble would begin. Unfortunately, at least for those who make such a claim, there are already Americans who serve in the armed forces who are open about being homosexual, and the sky has not fallen.

Out and About

In 2003, Rhonda Evans interviewed some "high profile" cases of homosexuals who served in the U.S. military while their sexual orientation was widely known, including Petty Officer Keith Meinhold, who was an exceptional sailor.[79] He consistently graduated at the top of his classes and had been certified as a Master Training Specialist, an honor bestowed on only the top 10 percent of instructors. He supervised a team of thirty-two Navy instructors and was recognized as "Aircrew Instructor of the Year." He logged over 3,500 flight hours in P-3 Orion antisubmarine warfare planes, on missions throughout the Pacific, the Indian Ocean, and the Persian Gulf. He consistently received high performance evaluations throughout his career.

In 1992, after having served for twelve years, he disclosed that he was gay on the *ABC Nightly News* as a form of protest. As a result of his public statement, Meinhold's commanding officer initiated discharge proceedings. During the discharge hearing, several comrades testified that Meinhold was an "outstanding sailor," that his sexual orientation was not a problem for them, and they expressed their willingness to continue to work alongside him. It became clear that many of his coworkers—superior officers as well as his base commander—knew he was gay before his public announcement, and some had even made efforts to shield him from harassment.[80] One officer admitted that previously he had been prejudiced against gays, but had changed his mind after working with Meinhold. The administrative board unanimously agreed that Meinhold should be discharged under honorable conditions.

Three months after appearing on television he was separated from the Navy against his will. But Meinhold was too feisty to go quietly into the night. He filed suit in federal court, arguing among other things that the ban on homosexual service members violated the U.S. Constitution. He obtained a court order allowing him to return to work with his squadron while the government decided whether to appeal the case. During this time, whenever Meinhold was to teach a class or take to the air the executive officer would ask the class or crew if they were comfortable working with "an avowed homosexual." This went on for a month until *the students* asked the commanding officer to put a stop to the questioning. The government decided not to appeal the decision, and Meinhold re-enlisted in the Navy in 1993. In his final Navy tour, when his sexual orientation was public knowledge, Meinhold was recognized with two awards for the quality of his photographic intelligence, and his crew was cited as the most combat-effective P-3 crew in the Pacific Fleet with both the "Crew of the Quarter" and "Crew of the Year" awards. Meinhold retired from the Navy after sixteen years of service. He retired with full military honors and was awarded the Navy Achievement Medal for his service.[81] In summing up his experience as an openly gay petty officer he stated, "I think a lot of people underestimated the professionalism of sailors in the Navy. The majority are much more tolerant than they're given credit for."

HOMOPHOBIA REDUCES THE MISSION READINESS OF THE MILITARY

DISCHARGING PERSONNEL ON GROUNDS of homosexuality has a profound effect on the mission readiness of our military. From 2002 to 2003, during the war on terrorism and despite an admitted, severe shortage of linguists, thirty-seven trained linguists, many of whom spoke Arabic, Farsi, and Korean, were discharged for allegedly being homosexuals. Alistair Gamble successfully completed more than thirty weeks of Arabic language training at the Defense Language Institute and received a commendation for distinguished service, but was then discharged when it was discovered that he was a homosexual.[82] It's not like it is easy to replace Arabic speakers—40 percent of those who enroll in the program don't complete it. The military resorted to hiring civilians at up to $170,000 a year and sending them to Iraq.[83]

Homophobia negatively affected the mission readiness of all personnel, both homosexual and heterosexual. Professor Sheridan Embser-Herbert described the problem: "Because the ban on lesbians and gay men compels military personnel to constantly prove their heterosexuality, the military is, in fact, a highly sexualized workplace. And, gender remains salient because of its relationship to expectations surrounding sexuality. In our culture, the way in which gender and sexuality are embedded within one another means that as long as sexuality is at the core of what it means to participate in the military, so, too, will masculinity—and, indirectly, femininity—remain at that core."[84]

Homophobia Reduces the Effectiveness of Male Personnel

The military culture's focus on gender role image management—not appearing homosexual by acting hypermasculine—is a waste of personnel energy, increases stress, and lowers efficiency. Even the most benign acts can, and are, seen as evidence of possible homosexual tendencies. When Keith Meinhold announced on ABC's *World News Tonight* that he was gay, one of his coworkers, Tom Paulson, stated he had long suspected that Meinhold was gay because the in-box on his desk was not black but "colorful."[85]

Homophobia Reduces the Effectiveness of Female Personnel

Regardless of their own sexual orientation, homophobia negatively affects all women in the military. Researchers have found that threatening to denounce a woman as homosexual is the most prevalent form of sexual harassment in the military.[86] Women are under constant pressure not to exhibit lesbian tendencies. Unfortunately, normal behaviors are taken as indications of homosexuality in the military.

> "Lesbian tendencies" may be seen in behavior that seems perfectly conventional—even puritanical—to civilian women. We see [First Lady] Mrs. Reagan on the evening news hug and kiss friends she greets. Born-again Christians speak approvingly of chastity for unmarried women. Yet military women, tired of fighting off sexual advances from the only available men, who choose instead to spend their free time with women friends, drinking Diet Coke and playing board games, find themselves branded as "Lezzies."[87]

Sexual harassers prey on women's fears that they will be discharged as homosexuals by demanding that they provide sexual services as a way to "prove" they are not lesbians. Such threats mean that females are much less free to reach their potential, particularly in behaviors traditionally thought of as masculine.

If women did not think they were compelled to be seen as heterosexual, there would be less pressure to act in ways historically viewed as feminine. By having to prove their heterosexuality through stereotypical femininity, they are perceived as less capable than their male counterparts.

The Financial Costs of Homophobia

The two primary methods for attempting to eliminate homosexuals in the military have been to ask recruits about their sexual conduct and their sexual orientation on their application and to investigate, prosecute, and discharge those determined to be homosexuals. It has proven financially expensive to attempt to eliminate homosexuals from the ranks. In 1992, a Congressional study found that the ban on homosexuals in the armed forces was costing the Pentagon at least $27 million a year.[88] Even after the "Don't Ask, Don't Tell" policy had been in effect for two years the annual expense of discharging homosexuals was over $25 million.[89] A more recent study released in 2006 found that during the years 1994 to 2003 the cost of implementing the policy was $363.8 million.[90] Of course that is just the financial costs of discharging members of the military, and of recruiting and training their replacements. These figures do not measure how the loss of highly trained personnel affects overall mission readiness. In the first ten years of the policy, two professors at the U.S. Military Academy at West Point, two professors at the Naval Postgraduate School, and 244 surgeons, nurses, dentists, and other medical personnel were discharged. According to Senators Christopher Bond and Patrick Leahy, the loss of these service members led to wounded guard and Army Reserve soldiers "receiving inadequate medical attention," because of "an insufficient number of medical clinicians and specialists which has caused excessive delays in the delivery of care."[91]

HOMOPHOBIA CONTRIBUTES TO SEXUAL ABUSE

Harassment

DURING HIS FIRST NIGHT in boot camp a new recruit admitted he was nervous:

> I was shaking. The junior DI, he says, "you're shaking so bad you're making me *hard*. I'm gonna bend you over and fuck you right now." I was really scared. He's saying that right in front of God and everybody. And from then on he called me a faggot...."[92]

This is a fascinating story, because the drill instructor first associates fear with being homosexual. Secondly, he finds evidence of fear sexually arousing. Finally, he threatens to sexually assault the recruit anally, yet views the recruit as a "faggot." All the behaviors engaged in by the drill instructor constitute sexual harassment. His behavior is discrimination against homosexuals and harassment of the recruit. It matters not whether the recruit himself is homosexual or heterosexual; he is still being harassed.

Sexual Assault

Other than threats of death, the fear of being labeled homosexual is the most powerful psychological dynamic that prevent males who have been sexually abused from reporting it to military authorities. Since male victims of sexual assault, whether heterosexual or homosexual, are even less likely to report it than female victims, perpetrators can be confident they can get by with little fear of punishment or even investigation.

METHODS FOR REDUCING HOMOPHOBIA IN THE MILITARY.

AS HAS ALREADY BEEN pointed out, homosexuals have always served in the military; instead of speaking about integrating them into the military it would be more accurate to describe the ongoing changes as a process of recognition, tolerance, and eventual acceptance. Foreign militaries that have eliminated their ban on gays have found there was not a substantial increase in the number of personnel who revealed their orientation, and problems associated with homophobia went down.

Many members of the American military have already changed their attitude about gays serving in the military. Major John W. Bicknell of the Naval Postgraduate School found that between 1994 and 1999 the percentage of U.S. Navy officers who "feel uncomfortable in the presence of homosexuals" decreased from 57 percent to 36 percent.[93] General Wesley Clark confirmed in 2003 that the "temperature of the issue has changed over the decade," saying that "people were much more irate about this issue in the early '90s than I found in the late '90s."[94] The General's observation was confirmed by a 2004 poll, which found 50 percent of junior enlisted service members believed that gays and lesbians should serve openly in the military, though senior officers and NCOs continued to resist the idea.

In 2005 West Point, usually perceived as a bastion of hypermasculinity, honored a cadet for authoring a senior thesis titled, *Don't Ask, Don't*

Tell, Don't Be: A Philosophical Analysis of the Gay Ban in the U.S. Military, which argued that the military's gay ban should be eliminated because it violates military values. Cadet Alexander Raggio, a *hetero*sexual, was presented the BG Carroll E. Adams Award for the best dissertation in art, philosophy, or literature, and also earned special recognition from the vice dean for education. In addition, Congressman Marty Meehan of Massachusetts, a senior member of the House Armed Services Committee, issued a letter of commendation to Raggio for taking a morally courageous position on a controversial topic. One year after graduation, Raggio held the rank of lieutenant and was leading a platoon of thirty-five to forty soldiers. He noted many of his comrades who had opposed openly gay personnel had moderated their position once they were provided with more complete information.[95]

There are a number of simple things that could be done to reduce homophobia in the military.[96] Not only would these not require funds, they would also save American taxpayers millions of dollars each year, because the military would not be wasting time and money investigating allegations of homosexuality, and the unnecessary loss of valuable, expensively trained personnel would be reduced.[*]

- Provide personnel with a method to report antigay harassment, such as death threats and hate crimes, without fear of retribution or discharge.
- Exclude wrongly obtained evidence from administrative discharge boards. The Advisory Board on Department of Defense Investigative Capability suggested this as early as 1995.
- Eliminate penalties for consensual sexual behavior between adults while retaining those regulations that address sex with a minor, sexual assault, and antifraternization. Cease the selective criminal prosecution of personnel for allegations of adult, consensual, homosexual relationships in circumstances where heterosexuals would not be prosecuted as required by current regulations. In other words, be consistent.

---

[*] I am not the first to propose such changes. The RAND Sexual Orientation study made similar recommendations in 1993.

- Make it clear to all commands that inquiries and investigations can only be initiated based on credible information. Commanders cannot start inquiries solely on rumors or retaliatory accusations, hoping they will eventually discover credible information if they investigate long enough. In other words, no more fishing expeditions.
- If homosexuality is going to remain a reason for discharge, then removal from the military ought to take place rapidly and simply. Individuals who disclose their homosexual orientation to commanders ought to be immediately discharged without costly, wide-ranging investigations to establish criminal charges or reduce the military benefits of the individual, or to pressure them to identify other homosexual personnel.

Of course, the simplest way to deal with the existence of homosexuals in the military is to do what other civilized nations have done: stop making it an issue and focus on the primary mission of the military. Harassing, discharging, and even murdering fellow Americans does nothing to make America safer. The "Don't Ask, Don't Tell Policy" has not benefited anyone in the military. I agree with Judge Stephen Reinhardt of the U.S. 9th Circuit Court of Appeals, who wrote in a dissenting opinion that

> [T]he military now purports to welcome into the service individuals who are homosexuals—but only so long as they don't engage in homosexual conduct. This might appropriately be analogized to welcoming Jews to be a part of society so long as they do not attend synagogue or pray publicly or privately to G-d. . . .* Hypocrisy about sexual conduct will undoubtedly continue to plague the military and disqualify some of its finest members from completing their careers, until some fundamental policy changes are adopted, and its sexual codes are made more realistic. From General Eisenhower on, up and down the ranks, even to Commander-in-Chief, there are many who would have had to forfeit their positions had the military's code of sexual conduct been strictly and honestly enforced. Instead, it is applied selectively, and frequently only when public whim or political pressures so dictate.[97]

---

* Jews do not spell out the word God.

Will the military ever stop wasting resources probing for homosexuals? I predict they will and I am not alone. An Air Force colonel predicted, "It's the military tradition. We resist it, and then we do it. We did it with [racial] integration, and now we're doing it with women. It's the same as the other things. We'll find a way."[98] Perhaps Republican Senator Barry Goldwater said it best, "You don't need to be straight to fight and die for your country. You just need to shoot straight."[99]

"Hate I consider is an internal sin and hate is closely associated with fear. I think fear breeds defeatism and that is a disease that we cannot afford in this country if we are going to maintain our position in the family of freedom-loving people."
—General David M. Shoup, Commandant of the Marine Corps[100]

9

DÉJÀ VU: CHARACTERISTICS FOUND BOTH IN ABUSIVE FAMILIES AND IN THE MILITARY

TRAUMA PRIOR TO ENLISTMENT

MANY PERSONNEL ENTER the military already having experienced trauma. A majority of female veterans who developed PTSD after combat had previous trauma: 80 percent had been raped; 74 percent had been attacked with a weapon outside of combat; and 67 percent reported at least one of their family had been murdered. The male veterans of combat with PTSD reported similar histories of trauma; 73 percent had been attacked with a weapon outside of combat; 71 percent had a loved one murdered.[1] For both sexes, the more types of trauma experienced, the worse the symptoms.[2]

Sexual Abuse

"Assuming that 1 in 6 men are survivors of sexual abuse, there could be 7 on every NFL football team, over 50,000 fought in the Persian Gulf…"—Fred Tolson[3]

The rate of reported childhood sexual abuse for male civilians and servicemen is identical (15 percent), while servicewomen have much higher rates of childhood sexual abuse than the general public (49 percent vs. 27 percent).[4] Both men and women who experienced childhood sexual abuse have an increased risk of being sexually assaulted as adults. Women who were sexually abused as children are twice as likely as nonvictims to be raped as adults.[5] A majority (61 percent) of men sexually assaulted as adults have been sexually abused as children.[6]

In addition to being at risk for revictimization, they are at greater risk for offending. Persons who commit sex crimes are more likely to have been sexually abused as children than persons charged with other violent crimes.[7]

Violence

Personnel with histories of physical abuse are more likely to develop Post Traumatic Stress Disorder (PTSD) when exposed to combat.[8] Military personnel have high rates of physical abuse in their pasts: 48 percent of female soldiers and 50 percent of male soldiers reported they had been physically abused as children. One of the effects of being physically abused is an increased risk of perpetrating violence. The high rates of childhood abuse may help explain the high rate of domestic violence in military families.

SIMILARITIES BETWEEN ABUSIVE FAMILIES AND THE MILITARY CULTURE

TO BE IN THE MILITARY is to be surrounded by persons who endorse the use of violence and access to weapons. For someone who has been physically or sexually abused as a child by an authority figure, this can be a very threatening environment. A number of characteristics commonly found in families in which there was incest or physical abuse are also found in a military setting.[9] By pointing out these parallels I am not suggesting that the military is inherently an abusive system, but that these similarities help explain the reactions of personnel who enter the military with a history of abuse. A history of abuse makes adjusting to military life more difficult, puts the individual at greater risk of being sexually harassed or assaulted, and makes him or her less likely to report abuse.

Relationships Based on Rigid Hierarchy and Control

Families in which there is abuse tend to have rigid gender role expectations, including that the women and children be subservient to the unchallenged authority of the man. Children are not asked to do something; they are told. Being raised in such a family trains individuals to follow orders, even inappropriate orders, and to keep silent about abuse. In both the military and abusive families, those who have power can wield it with few limits.

Demands for Obedience and Recognition of Authority

In abusive families, children are constantly required to prove their obedience to the parents. If they ask the reasoning behind a directive, they are told, "Because I said so, that's why." In the military, every day is filled with rituals to demonstrate obedience and recognition of authority, from saluting to the ever-present "Yes, Sir."

Barriers to Escape

One of the most powerful forms of control is freedom of movement. Neither children nor military personnel have freedom of movement. They are told where to be and when to be there. The fences and guards that prevent outsiders from coming on base also prevent personnel from easily leaving. Just as the child who runs away can be reported to civilian law enforcement, military personal who go absent without leave are subject to detention by military police. If a civilian leaves the workplace or fails to fulfill a directive from a higher up, the worst that can happen is termination of employment. When military personnel are being harassed or otherwise abused, they cannot merely walk away without facing charges.

Sleeping

Adults tell children when and where to sleep. Being a member of the military is not a nine-to-five job. Military personnel are told to sleep in a room with strangers, when to rise, what watch to take, and when to go without sleep for extended periods of time.

Privacy

In sexually abusive families, privacy is one of the personal boundaries that is violated. Parents enter bathrooms with out knocking, watch adolescents bathing and dressing, and doors are sometimes removed so there is no place the child can obtain any privacy.

In the military, personnel—particularly those low in rank—undress and shower with others. In some facilities, toilet stalls do not have doors on them. Male personnel become accustomed to hearing or seeing other men masturbating.

Personal Space

A child in an abusive family lives with the abuser. Imagine someone who daily has to eat breakfast with the person who raped her. This is exactly the situation for children who live in incestuous families and for military personnel who have been assaulted by comrades.

Personal Belongings

In abusive families, adults use material goods to demonstrate power as well as to punish or reward behavior. A gift may be given out of guilt for a beating or sexual act, or as a reward for the child keeping quiet.

To enter the military is to surrender one's belongings. From the moment one arrives at basic training, the recruit has no personal belongings. This is quite a change from the materialistic civilian society: "'Now, get off my bus,' shouts Staff Sergeant Bichl. They hadn't known it was his bus—but they soon will realize that they are on his island, in *his* Corps, and playing by *his* rules. Every drill instructor they meet will talk to them the same way. Nothing here is theirs. . . . "[10]

Appearance

Of course, all parents ought to have limits on how a child will dress and appear, but in a sexually abusive family the child's appearance can be a battle ground. One parent demands the child wear revealing clothing because it is sexually arousing, the other parent attempts to keep the child's body completely covered.

In civilian life, clothing is used to differentiate individuals, while in the military it has the opposite function. Personnel are told what to wear and how that clothing will appear. Upon entering the military, one of the first changes in appearance, at least for males, is a military haircut. Whether fiction or documentary, films on the military include the classical scene of recruits getting shorn and their dismay at the loss of their hair. The military is one of the few organizations that can, and does, demand certain a body weight and level of physical fitness.

Monopolization of Communications

One of the classic signs of an abusive relationship is that the perpetrator isolates the victim from social support. The victim is cut off from friends and family so that the victim cannot disclose the abuse or seek help. During boot camp, overseas deployment, and while on board ship, military personnel's ability to communicate with others is controlled by the military system, which can limit the amount, timing, and even the content of interactions.

Secrecy Regarding Activities and Events

In abusive families, there are many secrets. Children learn not to disclose what takes place within the household. Military personnel are required to keep silent about locations, functions, tactics, and events. They are required to sign documents that forbid them from talking about their experiences, even after they are discharged.

10

"CAN'T YA TAKE A JOKE?": SEXUAL HARASSMENT

"We have committed ourselves to providing an environment that is free of sexual harassment and free of the conditions that would spawn sexual misconduct." —General Reimer, 1997[1]

"Sexual harassment exists throughout the Army, crossing gender, rank, and racial lines."—Secretary of the Army, 1997[2]

ALTHOUGH THE BEHAVIORS that constitute sexual harassment have been around forever, the term of "sexual harassment" is relatively new. The concept of sexual discrimination was first introduced into legislation when the Civil Rights Act of 1964 (Title VII) was passed in Congress. Ironically, those who opposed the bill on racial grounds, and expected that including sexual discrimination would guarantee its defeat, introduced the inclusion of sex as a protected category.[3] Catherine MacKinnon, a professor of law, coined the term "sexual harassment" in the 1970s.[4] The first case testing the concept of sexual harassment made it to the U.S. Supreme Court in 1986.[5] Twelve years later, the court determined that it was legally possible for a man to sexually harass another man.[6]

HOW IS SEXUAL HARASSMENT DIFFERENT FROM JOKING AROUND?

"If one guy looks at you but you like him, it's flirting. If he gives you the 'creeps,' it's sexual harassment."—Female recruit[7]

"When humor is meant to be taken seriously, it's no joke. "—Lionel Strachey

THERE ARE TWO BASIC types of sexual harassment: the Quid Pro Quo and the hostile work environment. The Quid Pro Quo form of sexual harassment involves the misuse of power: a superior letting a subordinate know that career advancement is based on sexual favors, and if they are not forthcoming the subordinate will be punished. An example of a hostile work environment is a setting where pornography is easily visible and sexually explicit language and behaviors, such as "grab ass," are common. Women who are offended by these behaviors are usually told they are prudes, or lesbians or lack a sense of humor. Men who find these behaviors inappropriate in the work place are accused of not being "real men" or of being homosexuals.

When Captain Claudia Kennedy entered military intelligence school, her male instructor included in each classroom presentation several slides of naked women and cartoons of women having sex with barnyard animals. When Kennedy complained to the instructor, he ignored her. When she complained to the instructor's commander, "He smiled condescendingly. 'Captain, you just don't have a sense of humor.'"[8] Despite her alleged lack of humor, Captain Kennedy went on to become three-star General Kennedy, the Deputy Chief of Staff for Army Intelligence. In the General's assessment, "The goal of sexual harassment is power, control, and dominance, not affection and desire."[9]

Frank G. Williams provided additional evidence that sexual harassment is not merely joking around, but actually a form of punishment, when he wrote in *Navy Times*, "So the U.S. Navy is having a problem with sexual harassment. Well, what does anyone expect? When women go where they do not belong, sexual harassment is the logical result."[10]

Some veterans bemoan the good old days when people could take a joke and things weren't taken so seriously. A Women's Army Corps veteran wrote in a posting, "Old vs. New Morality and Sexual Harassment":

Could it have been that some of us simply overlooked some of the "attentions" or "harrassments" [sic] during our tours of duty in WWII? We certainly didn't come to the service filled with TV presentations of ugliness and mental abuse between the sexes, so we lacked the expectation that we would be mistreated. In the absence of an out and out physical attack, I don't believe I would have recognized "harrassment" [sic] if it were present. In retrospect, if viewed by today's standards, I probably experienced plenty of it.[11]

She implies that contemporary personnel are hypervigilant for harassment because of "TV presentations of ugliness and mental abuse between the sexes." But then she goes on to acknowledge that, short of a "physical attack," she wouldn't have recognized harassment when it occurred. This illustrates that if one does not have a term for a concept it is difficult to recognize when it occurs and then communicate it to others. Before the widespread use of the term "harassment," the euphemism "attention" was used.

TAILHOOK: CONDUCT UNBECOMING AN OFFICER AND A GENTLEMAN[12]

THE EVENTS THAT TOOK place in the 1970s to the 1990s, at the Navy and Marine pilots convention known as Tailhook, are among the most public examples of sexual abuse in a military setting. The convention, named after the device that assists airplanes landing on short runways, began in 1956 as a low-key affair but became progressively more rowdy with each passing year. In 1962, the town of San Diego got sick of the antics and banned the event, so it was moved to Las Vegas, where breaking a waitress's leg while attempting to toss her into a swimming pool and dropping a piano from the fifteenth story of a hotel were accepted as good-natured fun. Another custom that became a routine part of the convention was "ball walking," which involved letting one's scrotum hang out of one's pants while strolling around the convention site. By 1985 the practice of ball walking had become such a popular practice that T-shirts which read, "HANG 'EM IF YOU GOT 'EM" were sold on site. When word of this behavior became public, it was justified as a military "custom."[13] In the civilian world a man walking around a hotel with genitals exposed is a criminal act known as exhibitionism.

Senior officers were aware of what took place at Tailhook because they themselves were in attendance and responsible for some of the stranger acts. Vice Admiral Jack Ready was happy to demonstrate his ability to drink a beer while standing on his head. Admiral Bear Taylor showed up to the convention dressed as a Civil War general, complete with a horse, which he rode *into* the hotel. John Francis Lehman Jr., no less than Secretary of the Navy, liked to have a naked stripper dance over him as he lay on the floor, while other attendees cheered him on. With role models such as these, attendees began to think they were entitled to do whatever they wanted, and the citizens of America ought to fund it as well. The aviators who were not within driving distance were flown there on military transports, or flew "their" F-14s or A-6s to the event. The military's estimate of the cost of fuel, maintenance, and wear and tear on planes of this type is $3,000 per hour.[14] Some pilots flew government planes all the way from the East Coast to the convention. In addition to flying the taxpayers' planes to the event, many of the officers were also drawing a per diem, so that U.S. taxpayers not only funded their partying but also paid the officers while they partied.[15]

Even commanders who did not personally attend the convention knew what took place, because military newspapers published yearly summaries of the events. In 1990 a base newspaper reported that none of the officers who had attended "were convicted of any crimes, felonies, that is." The article went on to describe the convention as "characterized by celebration, joviality, and debauchery." In one suite alone, fifteen cases of liquor, forty kegs of beer, and 450 gallons of margaritas containing 315 liters of tequila were consumed.

Most Americans had never head of the Tailhook Association until 1991, when Las Vegas did not live up to its motto, "What happens in Vegas, stays in Vegas." The incidents that took place at Tailhook that year were no different than those of others years, except that they became public knowledge.

As in previous years, the third floor hallway was the site of "the Gauntlet," where male officers lined both sides of the hall waiting for a woman to approach, then two male officers would get behind her to prevent her from escaping once the men began grabbing her breasts and crotch and attempting to remove her clothing. Hotel security had learned from past experience to protect their female security personnel by keeping them off the notorious third floor. Other women were not so fortunate. By the time this convention was over, at least eighty-three women had been sexually assaulted. Many of the women made it clear they did not welcome such treatment by screaming, kicking, and punching. Since some of the officers had their penises exposed, the women thought they were about to be gang raped. The female victims included civilians, Naval and Air Force officers, government officials, spouses of military personnel, and a teenage girl who was provided with enough liquor that she passed out. She was stripped naked, lifted into the air, and passed down the line from officer to officer to be fondled before being left on the floor in a semiconscious state. Seven men were also sexually assaulted.

After it was all over, the President of the Tailhook Association, Captain Rick Ludwig, sent a letter to the members noting the convention was "the most successful" and senior leadership had been "thoroughly impressed and immensely enjoyed their time." He did mention "five separate reports of young ladies, several of whom had nothing to do with Tailhook," had been "verbally abused, had drinks thrown on them, were physically abused, and were sexually molested." When word of this letter became public, Naval official Lawrence Garrett, stated, "No man who holds a commission in this Navy will ever subject a woman to the kind of abuse in evidence at Tailhook '91 with impunity." Sean O'Keefe, another Naval official, held a press conference and announced, "Sex harassment will not be tolerated, and those who don't get the message will be driven from our ranks." President George H. Bush invited Lieutenant Paula Coughlin, one of the women assaulted, to dinner in the White House and assured her that justice would be done. A task force was formed to investigate the matter and met twenty-one times over a five-month period.

Over one million dollars was spent to question more than 1,500 officers of the 5,000 who had attended the convention. However, the Secretary of the Navy, Lawrence Garrett, Vice Admiral Richard Dunleavy, the Chief of Naval Aviation, and the seventy-one admirals who attended the convention were not interviewed. The Inspector General, George Davis, attempted to interview these high-ranking personnel but was told by higher-ups that such questioning would not be useful to the investigation. A several-hundred-page report was released indicating was there enough evidence to file charges under the Uniform

Code of Military Justice for crimes that included conduct unbecoming an officer, indecent exposure, indecent assaults, making false statements to investigators (lying), and obstruction of justice. Naval Judge Captain William Vest Jr. noted that Admiral Frank Delso had lied under oath and manipulated the investigations so as to "shield his own personal involvement in Tailhook '91."[16] The Admiral's punishment was to retire two months earlier than he had planned. Despite having enough evidence to charge over 300 officers with crimes, only seventy were recommended for disciplinary action. All but one were junior officers. No high-ranking personnel were held accountable. Higher-ups insisted that, even though Captain Rick Ludwig, the President of the Tailhook Association, who had written the letter after the convention, was not the senior officer in attendance, he ought to be held accountable for any misbehavior that took place. He was so distressed by the way his comrades ostracized him that he ended up in a psychiatric hospital.

After two years, the Navy and the Department of Defense had completed a total of seven investigations that cost U.S. taxpayers three million dollars. The Marines who had been charged with crimes were cleared or given nonjudicial punishments. Of the 120 Naval personnel charged, 50 percent of the cases were thrown out for lack of evidence, and most of the rest resulted in a letter of caution and forfeiture of pay. Despite the lack of any meaningful action taken, Admiral Frank Kelso went to far as to claim, "Something like Tailhook is not going to happen again. Tailhook also brought to light the fact that we had an institutional problem in how we treated women." [17] He spoke in the past tense, as if change had taken place. He was being far too optimistic. Institutional change had not taken place, and sexual abuse would continue in the Navy and the rest of the armed forces.

"Information from a variety of sources indicates that sexual harassment continues to be a serious organizational problem for the U.S. Navy."—Sexual Harassment in the Active-Duty Navy[18]

IS SEXUAL HARASSMENT STILL A PROBLEM IN THE U.S. MILITARY?

NOT EVERYONE BELIEVES sexual harassment is a serious problem in the military. Marie DeYoung wrote of Sergeant Major Brenda Hoster, who had accused a male sergeant of kissing her against her will and soliciting sex.

> [She] has become the poster girl for all of the women in the Army who
> have hidden their own professional incompetence behind bizarre alle-
> gations of sexual misconduct or sexual harassment. These women have
> done nothing to further the cause of equality or to secure the place of
> women in combat, unless we are willing to agree that women can defeat
> the enemy soldier, who would foolishly touch them inappropriately in
> battle, with million-dollar lawsuits.[19]

Sexual harassment is not a new problem in the military. It has existed as long as there has been a military. A survey of female nurses in Vietnam found that more than 50 percent had been sexually harassed, which included unwanted sexual remarks, touches, and receiving requests for sex.[20]

The military has repeatedly surveyed personnel about sexual harass-ment, and the results have consistently been disheartening: "Inappropri-ate behaviors are commonplace throughout the Army. In many cases, however, soldiers subjected to such behaviors do not equate them with sexual harassment. Further, soldiers seem to accept such behaviors as a normal part of Army life."[21] In 1977, even though only 14 percent of military personnel who had been harassed reported it to any superior, the reported rate was still higher than in nonmilitary government work-places.[22] By 1988 the rate of reporting had dropped to only 10 percent.[23] A 1995 Pentagon survey revealed that more than half of the 50,000 female military respondents surveyed reported they had been sexually harassed.[24] Twenty-eight years after the first harassment study, more than half of women attending the military academies had been the victims of sexual harassment, including jokes, inappropriate gestures, or promises of better treatment in exchange for sexual favors.[25]

One servicemember went so far as to say there was, "an overall climate in which sexual harassment is the norm rather than the excep-tion."[26] Only 1 percent agreed with the statement, "I don't think any women really experience sexual harassment anymore." When asked if they thought a woman's appearance or adherence to gender-role expectations increased the likelihood she would be sexually harassed, 38 percent of the subjects believed women who were more feminine were more likely to be sexually harassed than women who appeared more masculine, but most (58 percent) thought it didn't matter how a woman looked or how she behaved.

Rates of sexual harassment in the ranks consistently remain well above civilian rates.[27] Surveys by both military and civilian researchers find that 69 percent of military women are sexually harassed, 64 percent of women consider it a problem, and 76 percent believe that military leaders have not done enough to address it.[28]

The military sees sexual harassment primarily as a bureaucratic problem that can be remedied through written policies; if they officially forbid it, then it will cease to exist. Secretary of Defense William J. Perry stated in a news briefing,

> Our policy on sexual harassment is crystal clear. We believe that sexual harassment is wrong, ethically and morally. We believe it is wrong from the point of view of military discipline. And we believe it is wrong from the point of view of maintaining proper respect in the chain of command. And for all of these reasons therefore, we have a zero tolerance for sexual harassment."[29]

In the *Soldiers' Manual of Common Tasks*, Army personnel are informed they "must behave in accordance with the Army's Equal Opportunity (EO) and Sexual Harassment policies, take actions to maintain an environment free from unlawful discrimination and sexual harassment, and report behaviors that violate the EO and Sex Harassment policies." Furthermore these behaviors are expected in "on and off duty settings both in the field and in garrison."[30] Unfortunately, like most human-to-human problems, unless the underlying psychological motivations are addressed, these policies will have little impact.

COMMON TYPES OF SEXUAL HARASSMENT

MANY PEOPLE MISTAKENLY believe that most sexual harassment are merely jokes or comments. But research has found that, of those military personnel who report being subjected to sexual harassment, only a very small percentage reported only being verbally harassed (9 percent females, 3 percent males), 30 percent of females and 17 percent of males reported pressure for sexual acts, sexual assault, or actual rape.[31] The most common form of sexual harassment is accusing a woman of being a lesbian because she is unwilling to have sex with her male comrades. Sidebar 10-2 shows types of harassment reported by service members, a majority of whom experienced two or more forms (88 percent female, 73 percent male). In many cases the mistreatment was not an isolated incident, nor was there only one offender.

Sidebar 10-2

TYPES OF SEXUAL HARASSMENT REPORTED BY MILITARY PERSONNEL[32]

Type of Harassment	Female Victims	Male Victims
Sexual teasing, jokes, remarks, or questions	82 percent	74 percent
Sexually suggestive looks, gestures, or body language	69 percent	58 percent
Touching, leaning over, cornering, pinching, or brushing against of a deliberate sexual nature	60 percent	51 percent
Whistles, calls, hoots, or yells	59 percent	27 percent

AN EXAMPLE OF SEXUAL HARASSMENT

IN CAPTAIN DOROTHY MACKEY'S story (Part II) she briefly described some of the harassment she endured while in the Air Force. What follows are descriptions of the harassment taken from one of the court documents related to her lawsuit.[33] At their first meeting her superior locked the door to his office while she was alone with him. He often "ogled" her, made comments when she wore her skirted uniform, stood very close to her, inquired about her perfume and make-up, engaged in "unwanted touching," and made sexual comments in her presence. She complained that another of her supervisors often stared at her breasts, made comments about her slender waist and her appearance in the skirted uniform. During meetings he leaned back in his chair so that he could see under the table when she wore her skirted uniform. Without permission he massaged her neck touched her ankles and legs, and he placed his hands around her waist "in order to measure it." He invited her to a bar off base late one evening for the stated purpose of working on her 'resume.' She met him at the bar, but when she started to leave he physically prevented her from entering her car. After she resigned, both former supervisors gave unfavorable assessments of her work to prospective employers.[34]

> *"The Panel concludes that the human relations environment of the Army is not conducive to engendering dignity and respect among us. We are firmly convinced that leadership is the fundamental issue. Passive leadership has allowed sexual harassment to persist; active leadership can bring about change to eradicate it."*—The Secretary of the Army's Senior Review Panel Report on Sexual Harassment[35]

WHO HARASSES WHOM?

WHILE THE DEPARTMENT of Defense has found that women are more likely than men to be sexually harassed, and usually by men; when men are sexually harassed it is also usually by other men.[36] Female military personnel are much more likely than male personnel to be sexually harassed by a superior, whereas males are more likely to be sexually harassed by peers.

Some people mistakenly believe the problem of sexual harassment will be eliminated when the ratio of males to females in an organization reaches some critical mass. They believe, since rates of sexual harassment are highest in organizations that are "male dominated," an increase in the number of women will dilute the organizational culture that supports or even encourages sexual harassment. It is not the ratio of men to women that contributes to the prevalence of sexual harassment in the military, but the gender-role expectations. In any unit where men are viewed as superior to women, and femininity is disparaged, the unit culture is "male dominated" regardless of the ratio of men to women.[37] A unit in which females outnumbered males would still be more likely to experience sexual harassment by men if those men were hypermasculine than a unit where there were fewer women than men but those men were not hypermasculine.

Further evidence that the root of harassment is not merely men and women working in the same environment comes from a Department of Defense survey that found civilians hired to work in a military setting engaged in less sexual harassment of coworkers than did active military personnel. In other words, even within a military setting, civilians were less abusive than servicemembers.

The fact that when men are sexually harassed the perpetrator is usually a man makes it easy to conclude that male homosexuals are harassing heterosexual men. However, the vast majority of men committing sexual harassment, even toward other men, are heterosexuals. When it comes to homosexuals and sexual harassment, homosexuals are much more likely to be the target of harassment than to be the perpetrators.[38] Not only are they harassed at higher rates, the intensity and forms of harassment directed at them tend to be more severe.[39]

TYPES OF HARASSERS[*]
Misperceiving Harassers

"*A woman's no is no proof of her objection.*"—Evan Esar[40]

MEN IN THIS CATEGORY are described as being naïve about relationships, so they misread even simple, polite interactions as having sexual content. They have no malicious intent; they merely think that the workplace is an appropriate location for finding sexual partners. They repeatedly ask coworkers for dates or sex, and misinterpret women declining their offers as a message to try harder.

"*You can always tell how much a girl wants you to kiss her by the strenuous objection she sets up.*"—Evan Esar[41]

Exploitive Harassers
These men often engage in harassing behaviors of women or men in

---

[*] All these types are based on research that focused on men as harassers. This is not to say that women do not engage in harassing behavior, merely that I am not aware of research on women who engage in harassment.

order to bolster their hypermasculine standing in the eyes of onlookers who also endorse this type of masculinity.[42] They believe male-female relationships are adversarial, see having power over a woman as erotic, and the more power one has over a woman the more attractive she becomes. These men are willing to use power and authority for obtaining sex. They are not only at risk for engaging in sexual harassment but for sexual assault as well. They have "pro-rape attitudes which allow them to use violence (without guilt) for obtaining sex. They believe that, "women accept and even enjoy male domination, even when it means physical coercion," that "women who dress in sexy clothes are asking to be raped," and "most women would enjoy being raped."[43]

Misogynistic Harassers

This type can be summarized as men "who dislike or despise women," and are "not so much expressing a desire to have sex with someone in the workplace but…expressing hostile or negative feelings" toward members of that sex.[44] One of the major reasons they want to include pornography in the workplace is the very fact that it bothers most women. These men engage in disrespectful sexual language about females and their abilities in the presence of women, with the intent of offending them. The purpose of the hostile work environment is to punish and drive away women who are "invading" a place that "rightfully" belongs only to men. Misogynistic harassers have been compared to racists; just as Jim Crow laws and violence toward African Americans was designed to keep them "in their place," sexual harassment is the "technology of sexism." [45]

THE NEGATIVE EFFECTS OF SEXUAL HARASSMENT

"The cost of sexual harassment is high, in reduced mission effectiveness, in the suffering of victims, and in wasted resources."—Dick Cheney, Office of the Secretary of Defense[46]

Sexual harassment in the military may be more disturbing than in the civilian workplace, since many service members live on military property and therefore their harassers, particularly if they are high-ranking, have access to them and their "home," so there is no safe place.

Research on female military personnel found that only one percent of women thought they benefited professionally from sexual attention.[47] Of those who claimed to have experienced sexual harassment, 58 percent noted it had led to emotional distress, including loss of self-esteem, a lowered opinion of men, and damage to their emotional and physical health. Diminished quality and quantity of work, poor attitude, and a decrease in attendance were reported by 43 percent.[48] Eight percent stated the effects were so great as to damage their relationships with their spouses and other family members. A majority indicated it created a less favorable attitude toward their comrades and toward the military as an organization. Department of Defense research found that for both females and males, sexual harassment results in negative effects to psychological well-being, physical health, job performance, and job satisfaction.[49] Nineteen percent of women and 8 percent of men who resisted sexual harassment reported it led to work assignments or conditions worsening, inaccurate job performance reports, or denial of promotions.[50]

The first two columns of Sidebar 10-1 show the negative effects on the individual being harassed, while the third column indicates the price the military pays for the existence of harassment.

Research has found that leaders who tolerate sexual harassment within their units are creating an environment in which sexual assault is more likely to take place. A Veterans Affairs report stated, "Officer leadership played an important role in the military environment and safety of women." The study found that officers who permitted sexual harassment saw four times the level of rapes in their units.[51]

Sidebar 10-1
NEGATIVE EFFECTS OF SEXUAL ABUSE[52]

Psychological	Physiological	Work Related
Fear and anxiety	Sleep disturbances	Impaired concentration
Depression	Nausea	Increased absenteeism
Confusion	Dizziness	Decreased confidence in coworkers
Sense of helplessness	Headaches	Decreased work satisfaction

Psychological	Physiological	Work Related
Sense of powerlessness	Fatigue	Negative feeling about work
Anger and bitterness	Ulcers	Decreased commitment to organization
Decreased life satisfaction	Tremors	Increased job turnover
Stress	Weight loss	
Social withdrawal	Increased reactivity	
Loneliness	Dental problems e.g. tooth grinding	
Irritability		
Self-blame	Increased frequency of Respiratory infections	
Increased suspiciousness	Increased frequency of Urinary tract infections	
Emotional numbing	Disruptions in relationships	
Decreased sex drive	Difficulty functioning sexually	
Disturbances in body Image	Overeating or undereating	
Uncontrolled crying	Increased use of tobacco, alcohol and other drugs	
Recurrent nightmares		

A SIMPLE STANDARD

"Better lose a jest than a friend."—Thomas Fuller[53]

THERE ARE THOSE WHO complain they are afraid to use humor or be playful, that all the fun has been taken out of life in an attempt to be "politically correct." They fear that the most innocent joke will be taken wrong and they will be wrongly accused of sexual harassment. "How is anyone to know what's all right to do?" they wonder. One standard that could be employed is, prior to saying or doing something, ask oneself, would I do this if one of my family or someone whom I want to respect me were present? Would I want someone else to do to someone I love what I am considering doing? If the answer is no, then in all likelihood the behavior is inappropriate.

11

SEXUAL ASSAULT WITHIN THE RANKS

"The truth is rarely pure and never simple."—Oscar Wilde

REASONS WHY UNDERSTANDING SEXUAL ASSAULT IS DIFFICULT
Lack of Definition

UNTIL RECENTLY IT WAS IMPOSSIBLE to determine how often sexual assault occurred between comrades, because the military did not collect information on the topic. For the first twenty years that women attended the Air Force Academy, no data on sexual assaults were collected.[1] Of course it was unfeasible to attempt to collect data when the military had no accepted definition of sexual assault. In 2004 the Pentagon put Brigadier General K. C. McClain in charge of the newly created Joint Task Force for Sexual Assault Prevention and Response. She sought to develop a military-wide definition of sexual assault, one that would be clear, in plain English, and apply to current military law.[2] But as of January 2005, the Department of Defense still did not have "a clear Department-wide definition of sexual assault for training and educational purposes," which contributed to "confusion and uncertainty about what actions constitute" sexual harassment, sexual assault, and other sex-related offenses.[3, 4]

The Belief That Most Claims of Sexual Assault Are False

There are those who believe claims of sexual assault in the military are greatly exaggerated. A male Army criminal investigator wrote:

Here is a very typical scenario, and if you called the Special Agent in Charge of most any Army post's CID office, you could confirm what I am writing. Young female soldier, 18-20 years old, becomes friendly with an equally young male soldier. Their friendliness is considerably enhanced by their good friend, Al K. Hall (say it fast). They wind up in his barracks room or other private place. Neither are [sic] in full possession of their faculties. They have sexual relations. Later—in many cases, weeks later—the female soldier accuses the male soldier of rape. There is absolutely no physical evidence of any kind. The male soldier claims the sex was totally consensual. They both admit they were drunk. There are no witnesses. A female CID agent told me that this scenario was so commonplace at her post that she and her office categorized them as "Fort Bliss rapes" to distinguish them from the real kind. In my tenure in command I had at least 80 young women claim they had been raped. All but three were false, the claims used being used as an excuse for not obeying some other instruction or in some cases as retribution against the man for some offense she took for some other reason.[5]

Army Captain Marie deYoung believes women use the "abuse excuse" to avoid taking responsibility for their own behavior.[6] In her view, "[M]any women tender false allegations of rape or sexual harassment to deflect attention from their own misconduct, or to obtain postcoital birth control."[7] She also maintains, "False allegations are a symptom of women's emotional problems that are exacerbated by ill-suited military occupations."[8]

According to the Federal Bureau of Investigation, only 8 percent of civilian rape allegations as false.[9] Not only do women rarely make false reports of sexual assault, but even women who have experienced an act that fits the legal definition of sexual assault do not perceive what happened as rape. Women who experienced less severe physical injuries or had been using alcohol prior to the event were not likely to depict what happened as rape. Not perceiving the experience as rape did not spare them from having psychological consequences; those who thought of their experiences as something other than rape, and women who perceived themselves as having been raped, had similar psychological reactions, and both groups scored worse on psychological measures than did women who had not been sexually assaulted.[10]

Women who experience "date rape" are much more likely to think of what happened as something other than sexual assault than are women who were attacked by a stranger. In cases of date rape, at first everything appeared to be going fine—the man was respectful and appeared interested in the woman as a person. Since she has not yet perceived any threat to herself, she believed she was safe and willingly agreed to take part in acts, such as accepting a ride, that will later be seen by her and others as evidence that she was "asking for it" or "wanted it."[11]

It Is Underreported

"This is the most underreported crime in our society."—Pentagon spokesman Roger Kaplan describing a 2006 report that sexual assault in the military was up 40 percent.[12]

For a variety of reasons, sexual assault in both civilian and military settings is a vastly underreported crime. The National Crime Victimization Surveys indicated that only one in three sexual assaults against persons twelve or older are reported to law enforcement.[13] A three-year study of over 4,000 women found that only 16 percent of those raped reported the crime to authorities.[14] The figures on sexual assault represent the number reported, not the actual number that occur. According to Dr. Susan Gluck Mezey, sexual assault is "one of the nation's most underreported crimes," and the actual number of assaults is two to three times greater than the number *reported.*[15] In a 1990 Navy study, only one out of ten females who said they had been sexually assaulted reported it to the police or Master at Arms.[16] In 1994, the Department of Veterans Affairs determined only 31 percent of rapes were reported to military officials.[17] More recently, the Miles Foundation, a nongovernment group that assists military personnel who have been abused, found that, of the American service members who had been sexually assaulted by comrades while in Iraq, Kuwait, Afghanistan, and Bahrain, only 20 percent had reported the crime to military officials. Instead, service members turned to a civilian organization for assistance, because they feared they would be mistreated by the military if they reported the events.[18]

Incarcerated rapists report they never expected to end up in prison for their crime, because they counted on victims not contacting police, or not getting convicted even if charged with sexual assault. In the words of the interviewers, "These men perceived rape as a rewarding low-risk act."[19] In civilian courts, only 2 percent of those charged with sexual assault are convicted and imprisoned, and those on average serve only half of their original sentence.[20] In a military setting, when sexual assault takes place in a combat zone, the victim and witnesses can be eliminated simply by killing them. In 2006 an American soldier admitted that he and four comrades raped a fifteen-year-old Iraqi girl, killed her, and murdered three of her family who witnessed them entering their home.[21]

Reasons Not to Report

Victims do not report sexual assault to the authorities because they fear that it will lead to further sexual victimization by the offender; other forms of retribution by the offender or the offender's friends; prosecution of the offender, who is a family member, friend, or coworker; not being believed; being traumatized by the criminal justice system process; and shame if friends, family members, or the media learn of the assault. There is more shame associated with being a victim of a sex crime than other types of crimes. Persons whose cars are stolen are not usually told, "Well, that's what you get for having a nice car," or, "Maybe you were drunk and gave him the car but later changed your mind and then pretended it was stolen." However, victims of sex crimes commonly are told, overtly or covertly, they are lying, wanted what happened, or are responsible for what happened. Women who report being sexually assaulted are still viewed as damaged goods if they are believed, or as sluts if they are not believed. Men who report being sexually assaulted are thought not to be real men, since they did not successfully fight off the attackers, or thought to be homosexuals who wanted what happened.

Military personnel face all the same obstacles to reporting as civilians, but also have additional factors that make reporting even more precarious. They must report to their employer, an assault that likely took place on military property, was perpetrated by one or more service members, perhaps even a superior—and risk being accused of fraternizing or engaging in homosexual behavior, being prosecuted, and discharged. According to Colonel Janis Karpinski, the military doesn't make it easy to report a sex crime. The Army provided personnel stationed in the

Middle East with a toll-free telephone number to report sexual assaults, but few personnel had access to a telephone. In addition, those who were able to make a call could not actually speak with a person, because even after a six-month period during which more than eighty-three incidents of sexual assault in Iraq and Kuwait were reported the twenty-four-hour rape hotline was still answered by a machine that told callers to leave a message.[22] Several times in June of 2006 I went to the official Marines website to see how easy it would be for a victim of sexual abuse to make a report. Every time I attempted access to the section "Sexual Assault Prevention and Response Office" the only response was "Error 500–Unknown host."

It Wasn't Really Rape Because…

In sexual assault cases that come to court martial, the defense attorney will often argue that the events were consensual sex and not an assault. This defense is particularly effective if the alleged victim asked the assailant to use a condom to protect against sexually transmitted disease or pregnancy. Some assailants (10 to 20 percent) wear a condom without being asked, to avoid leaving behind DNA evidence.[23]

One might think that, if a victim of sexual abuse knows the identity of the person who committed the act, the victim would be more able and willing to report the crime. However, the opposite is true, because most people conceptualize rape as an act that takes place between strangers. When asked, 27 percent of female college students disclosed they had been "forced to have sexual intercourse in a dating situation," but when asked if they had "ever been raped," only 3 percent responded yes. When male college students were asked if they had ever "victimized women while on a date," 15 percent admitted they had. But when asked if they had ever "raped a woman," less than 1 percent of them acknowledged they had.[24] Many people assume sexual abuse perpetrated by someone known to the victim is less traumatic than sexual abuse at the hands of a stranger. Yet research on victims of both crimes finds that the resulting psychological problems are very similar.[25] In fact, in some cases those who have been sexually abused by an acquaintance have more severe reactions than for those abused by a stranger.[26]

Males As Victims

> *"Everyone is happy when Johnny comes marching home again, but Johnny may bring home some horrible secrets that have nothing to do with his combat experience."*—Editorial, *Florida Today*[27]

> *"In some respects the situation facing male rape victims today is not so different from that which faced female victims about two centuries ago."*—Susan Estrich[28]

Solzman's writing on rape as a weapon of war refers to sexual assault as a "gender-specific war crime," and in *War's Dirty Secret* the sexual assault of women during war is described as "the best-kept secret." Both authors completely overlooked the fact that males are also victims of sexual assault.[29] In 1949, the Fourth Geneva Convention provided the first explicit international prohibition of sexual assault. Although it states that all civilians ought to be protected against violence, it only mentions children and women when addressing sexual assault in articles 27 and 77:

> Article 27: "Parties to a conflict must respect children, provide them with any care or aid they require, and protect them from any form of indecent assault."[30]
>
> Article 77: "Female civilians in an occupied territory, internees, and refugees must be protected against any attack on their honor, including rape, enforced prostitution, or any form of indecent assault."[31]

In 2004, reporters from the *Denver Post* interviewed sixty service members who had been sexually abused while on active duty. Not one of those interviewed was a man.[32] Michael Scarce in *Male On Male Rape: The Hidden Toll of Stigma and Shame*, explained why so many have failed to notice male victims.

> The intense shame and stigma attached to adult male rape arguably exceeds that of the rape of women, which has, only within the last twenty years, become a widely acknowledged and public issue. . . . We can easily believe that a child might not be able to defend himself against an adult, but the sexual violation of a man may come as something of a shock, for

men have traditionally been expected to defend their own boundaries and limits while maintaining control, especially sexual control, of their own bodies. When this does not occur, when other men rape men, society tends to silence and erase them rather than acknowledge the vulnerability of masculinity and manhood.[33]

The military has been no better than civilian organizations at realizing the extent of sexual victimization of males. Under the *Uniform Military Code of Justice*, rape is defined as "[A]n act of sexual intercourse with a female not his wife, by force and without consent." Carnal knowledge is "an act of sexual intercourse with a female not his wife who has not attained the age of sixteen years." Notice that nowhere in either definition is it possible for a male to be the victim of rape. The sexual assault of males was not defined in American military law until 1992.[34]

Another example of the military not conceptualizing men as possible victims of sexual assault is the content of the POW survival training that pilots receive. When women pilots entered this program they were given additional training that was not offered to male personnel: Female pilots were briefed on ways to cope with rape and other forms of sexual abuse. The instructors seemed oblivious to the fact that males can also be sexually tortured.[35]

Conditions are no better in the twenty-first century. In 2003, Lieutenant General John R. Dallager, the Superintendent of the Air Force Academy, noted that a survey of the Air Force Academy cadets showed that "While a large majority, 80 percent, of the Wing has faith in our [sexual assault prevention] programs, 29 percent of the second-class women cadets and 59 percent of the first-class women cadets did not." Apparently it didn't occur to him to mention what male cadets thought of how the Academy would respond if they were to report being sexually victimized.

When newspaper reporter Alan Snel was doing research for a story on sexual abuse of males in the military, he formally requested information from the military bases in Florida, including Eglin and Patrick Air Force Bases, and the Navy base in Jacksonville. He was told that in the past twenty years not a single case of sexual assault involving a male victim had ever been reported.[36] The key word is "reported." A Pentagon study found that 9 percent of the reported victims of sexual assault in the armed forces in 2002 and 2003 were men, and fellow servicemen had assaulted them.[37] Charles S. Abell, the Principal Deputy Under Secretary of Defense for Personnel and Readiness, acknowledged that the figures only represented the reported assaults, not the number that occurred: "We recognize that sexual assaults are seriously underreported, and we have no reason to doubt that it is even more so in the case of male victims."[38]

One reason servicemen hesitate to report sexual assault is the fear of being labeled a homosexual and facing dishonorable discharge from the military. Since sodomy is a military crime, some men who were sexually assaulted do not report the assault for fear that military authorities might decide what took place was not an assault but a consensual act, and file a charge of sodomy. Those males whose penis became erect during the assault are particularly at risk for being told they enjoyed the experience and thus have no right to claim it was assault. Sex researchers Drs. William Masters and Virginia Johnson noted years ago that involuntary penile erections occur for many reasons other than sexual excitement, including the muscle stress that occurs during unwanted anal penetration during an assault. [39]

According to Dr. Nicholas Groth, an expert on sexual offenders, some assailants want to get their victim to ejaculate because, for the rapist, it symbolizes their complete sexual control over their victim's body and can be offered as evidence that the victim enjoyed the act, making a charge of sexual assault inappropriate.[40] Since ejaculation is not always within conscious control, but rather can be an involuntary physiological reaction, rapists are able to succeed at getting their male victims to ejaculate. Bewildered by his physiological response during the sexual assault, the victim is afraid to report the event for fear his response will be used against him.

Sexual desire is virtually never identified as a reason to engage in sexual assault.[41] The vast majority of assailants have access to willing female sexual partners. Furthermore, in the majority of male-to-male sexual assaults, the assailant does not ejaculate.[42] Nearly every study done on men who sexually assault men finds that the motivation was some combination of anger, desire to experience power over another person, and a wish to degrade and humiliate someone. One method of terrorizing the victim is to tell him that he has been infected with the virus that causes AIDS. In a survey of males who had been sexually assaulted, 65 percent reported their assailant(s) had claimed to purposely infect them with HIV.[43]

In a study of male military personnel who had been sexually assaulted, 85 percent of them reported there were multiple assailants involved in the assault.[44] Gang rapes tend to last longer and involve more physical trauma than lone-assailant assault and explain why male victims of sexual assault often score higher on measures of trauma than do women. Half of the servicemen who were sexually assaulted by comrades were so distressed by the experience they sought discharge from the military.[45]

REPORTS OF SEXUAL ASSAULT IN THE U.S. MILITARY

"Sexual assault will not be tolerated in the Department of Defense."—Defense Secretary Donald H. Rumsfeld[46]

"Sexual trauma is a serious problem for women and men serving in current deployments."—Dr. Matthew J. Friedman on U.S. troops in Afghanistan and Iraq[47]

It would be comforting to believe that sexual abuse is something that only took place in the distant past but is not a part of the contemporary military. However, this is not the case. Sexual abuse continues to take place in all branches of the military—during peacetime and wartime, on foreign soil and within our borders. The risk of being sexually abused by a service member begins even before enlistment. In the Army alone, which accounts for nearly half of the military, 722 recruiters have been charged with sexually abusing enlistees since 1996. In 2005, fifty-three Army recruiters were disciplined for sexual misconduct with potential enlistees. Nor is the Army the only branch to have a problem with recruiters. In 2005, at least twelve Air Force, eighteen Navy, and eighteen Marine recruiters were disciplined for sexual misconduct with young people who were considering enlisting. This means, across all branches, that one in two hundred recruiters have been found guilty of sexual misconduct with potential enlistees. How many more have never been reported? Most of the reported victims were females ages sixteen to eighteen, who were raped in various settings, including in U.S. government offices and military vehicles. When asked to comment on the results of the investigation, Defense Department spokesperson Lieutenant Colonel Ellen Krenke explained that, although the military spends over $1.5 billion a year on recruiting efforts, the Pentagon does not track sexual misconduct among recruiters.

It was not until the 1990s that the issue of sexual assault in the American military got any significant attention when, during Congressional hearings, witnesses estimated that American servicemen had sexually assaulted approximately 200,000 women.[48] In 1993 the Veterans Administration began developing sexual trauma counseling programs, due to the large numbers of female veterans seeking help related to their experiences of sexual abuse while in the military.[49] After the 1997 sex scandal at the Aberdeen Proving Ground, the Army set up a hotline to take reports of sexual misconduct. Over 5,000 women called, leading to 325 investigations of sexual misconduct at installations around the world.[50] In 1999, the Veterans Administration conducted an extensive survey of treatment records at 1,300 VA facilities from the previous sixty years. By 2002, 1.67 million files had been examined and 22,500 male victims of sexual trauma had been identified. This means at least one in 100 servicemen experienced sexual trauma at the hands of peers or superiors. The number of victims is very likely higher, but nearly 24,000 men refused to answer if they had ever been sexually abused. Furthermore, up to 24.5 million veterans have never used the VA medical system, so their experiences could not be included in the reported numbers.[51]

From 1999 to 2002, the number of attempted sexual assaults reported to the Army Criminal Investigative Division increased by 19 percent, and the number of reported completed rapes increased by 25 percent.[52] This increase was not due to an increase in the number of Army personnel on active duty, because the number of personnel, including reservists, during this period rose by less than 6 percent.[53] In 2003, 27 percent of female veterans surveyed indicated they had been raped or experienced an attempted rape during their military service.[54] A 2004 Defense Department investigation found one-fifth of the women at the Air Force Academy reported experiencing an attempted sexual assault.[55] In 2004, more than 50 prcent of the rapes reported to military officials involved an alleged assault by at least one member of the American military against another service person.[56] A 2005 Defense Department survey of women currently attending America's military academies found that one in seven female cadets had been sexually assaulted since becoming a cadet or midshipman, but very few lodged complaints.[57] In the first year of the war in Iraq, there were 112 reports of sexual assaults by U.S. armed forces in Iraq and Afghanistan; by 2006 the number had grown to over 500, and almost all involved American servicewomen being attacked by U.S. servicemen.[58]

SEXUAL ASSAULT AND OTHER VIOLENT CRIMES

One might speculate that the rates of sexual abuse and other crimes would be lower for military personnel when compared to civilians because military life is highly structured, personnel are under greater surveillance than most citizens, freedom of movement is reduced (particularly for those living on base), the opportunities to use drugs (other than alcohol) are reduced, there are few convicted felons, and the value the military places on discipline and honorable behavior is high.[*] Given all these factors, it makes sense the rates of nonsexual violent crimes for service members are substantially lower than the rates for civilians. At the end of World War II, the rate of reported military rapes was 366 percent higher than that of the reported civilian rape. During this same time period the rate for murder was nearly the same as the civilian rates and aggravated assault was 27 percent lower than that of civilian assault.[59]

By the 1990s, 4 percent of the women who responded to a survey from the Department of Defense reported they had been sexually assaulted while in the military.[60] However, other research found rates between 23 percent and 31 percent—more than seven times higher than the military's figures and three times that found in civilian settings (7 percent).[61] The Department of Veteran Affairs found that from 1994 to 2004, 21 percent of servicewomen had been raped and 30 percent had experienced attempted rape. During this same period the civilian figures for these crimes were 18 perent.[62] In the U.S. military prisons, one

---

[*] In the 1990s nearly half of the recruits enlisting in the Marine Corps did so under a waiver for illegal drug use and other crimes, or for medical or psychological problems (Ricks, 1997).

out of three military men are there for having committed sexual assault. Conviction for sexual assault is the most common reason veterans are incarcerated in civilian prisons. Veterans are incarcerated for the crime of sexual assault at twice the rate of civilians.[63] In combat theaters the rate of sexual assault perpetrated by military personnel increases to the point where it exceeds the civilian level, even though other violent crimes do not.[64] In 1991 in the Persian Gulf theater the rate of sexual assault by military personnel was ten times the rate in the civilian world.[65]

12

THE IMPACT OF SEXUAL ABUSE

DOES SEXUAL ABUSE IMPACT MILITARY PERSONNEL DIFFERENTLY THAN CIVILIANS?

THE SURGEON GENERAL observed: "Women in the military are not necessarily representative of the 'average' American woman. A military career is still not considered a traditional path for women, and women who choose a military career may have a different 'willingness to take risk' than women in the general population. They may not react like the 'average' woman in the civilian setting."[1] This sounds as if he is indicating that servicewomen are less negatively impacted by sexual assault than civilians. However, he was addressing female prisoners of war coping with sexual abuse perpetrated by the enemy, not by comrades. Female veterans deployed overseas in the first Gulf War reported high levels of sexual abuse from their male comrades: 66 percent experienced verbal harassment, 33 percent endured physical forms of harassment, and 23 percent were sexually assaulted. This abuse increased the likelihood of developing Post Traumatic Stress Disorder more than did combat experience, and the more sexual abuse suffered the more likely the victims were to develop PTSD.[2]

ARE THE EFFECTS OF SEXUAL HARASSMENT & SEXUAL ASSAULT SIMILAR?

RESEARCHERS HAVE COMPARED the reactions of women sexually harassed with those who were sexually assaulted and found both differences and similarities. Women who had been sexually harassed during military service had "a heightened feeling of betrayal and disillusionment" that continued long after they were discharged. Women who had been sexually assaulted while in the military tended to have higher levels of guilt and shame about their experience than did the women who had been harassed. Both groups of women believed that other people viewed them as "unchaste" or "bad" women.[3]

THE IMPACT OF SEXUAL ABUSE

"Sexual rape, exploitation, and humiliation are common forms of torture because they so quickly accomplish torture's goal—to destroy the victims' sense of self, to leave them broken, battered, and ashamed."—D. A. Johnson[4]

THE PERSONAL STORIES in Part II portray how the lives of victims of sexual abuse and their families are profoundly damaged. Bruises, lacerations, and other wounds heal at the same rate whether they are the result of an automobile accident or a sexual assault. But sexual abuse is not something that randomly occurs; it is something that is intentionally done to a person, and the resulting psychological wounds heal very slowly, if they heal at all. Time alone does not heal such wounds; sexual assault survivors still had more psychological symptoms fourteen years after the attacks than similar persons who had never been sexually assaulted, and sexually assaulted men reported more psychological and physical problems than did sexually assaulted women.[5,6] The higher level of problems may be due to the fact that when men are sexually assaulted the assailant(s) are much more likely to use a weapon in the attack, so in addition to the trauma of the sexual assault, there is the fear of being killed.[7]

Even after surviving the original attack, death can still result. When adult females who had survived rape or attempted rape were compared with those who had never been victimized, thoughts of suicide were two to six times more common for victims as were suicide attempts (rape 44 percent, attempted rape 29.5 percent).[8]

The war in the Middle East brought a new way that sexual assault, or the fear of it, could lead to death. American Colonel Janis Karpinski claimed that several American servicewomen in Iraq died of dehydration because they were afraid they would be sexually assaulted by American servicemen if they went to the women's latrine after dark. Women were vulnerable because the latrine for female soldiers at Camp Victory was far from their barracks and had no lights near it. Karpinski alleged that a physician reported, in a briefing for the Coalition's Joint Task Force, that because women were afraid to go out after dark they were not drinking liquids after midday, and in un-air-conditioned quarters in 120 degree heat some had died in their sleep from dehydration.[9]

"What does it say about us as a people, as a nation, as the foremost military in the world when our women soldiers sometimes have more to fear from their fellow soldiers than from the enemy?"—Senator Susan Collins, Armed Services Committee[10]

The Initial Reaction Stage

The impact of sexual assault varies over time, and not every person will react the same way. But there is a common pattern.

Immediately following the assault, victims are primarily focused on the physical aspects of the assault: the pain caused by wounds inflicted during the attack and exposure to sexually transmitted diseases.[11] But soon their focus changes. Army Ranger Lieutenant Colonel Grossman observed, "In rape the psychological harm usually far exceeds the physical injury. The trauma of rape, like that of combat, involves minimal fear of death or injury; far more damaging is the impotence, shock, and horror in being so hated and despised as to be debased and abused by a fellow human being."[12] Men in particular are not prepared to conceive of themselves as victims of sexual abuse, wondering, "How could this happen to me? I'm a trained fighter!"

Fear persists: "What if they come find me again? Will they kill me to shut me up?" Being sexually assaulted is not something most people expect to experience, so once it occurs there is an intense sense of vulnerability. The victim begins to ruminate, "It could happen again. I couldn't stop this attack. I won't be able to stop the next one. If I can be raped by members of my own unit, there is no safe place." In Gregory's story (Part II), long after the assault he continued to be fearful and kept a bayonet in his bed in case he was attacked again.

Guilt causes victims to replay the events and second-guess their actions: "Did I do something to invite this? Was it because I had been drinking? I shouldn't have accepted the offer of a ride back to the base. I should have fought back harder." Whereas the focus of guilt is on what the victim did or didn't do, shame focuses on the victim's self-image: "I'm disgusting"; "I'm nothing but a worthless slut"; "I'm not a real man if I let this happen to me." Some victims use the word "humiliation" rather than shame to describe what they are experiencing. After being assaulted Gregory wrote *Despised:*

Weird

Perverted

Sick

Words that describe me...

This was not who I was supposed to be

Not how I was raised

I am not a man

I am something else

Something to be despised[13]

Both male and female victims express a desire for retribution. This is particularly difficult on the victim when the perpetrator is a comrade, or worse, a superior. When the ability to engage in revenge is thwarted by circumstance, it often leads to misdirected anger. The victim's anger can be directed outward at family members who had nothing to do with the assault but are a safe target, or inward at oneself. A sign of misdirected anger is the woman who is angry toward all men because she was raped, or the man who hates homosexuals because he believes the man who sexually assaulted him must be a homosexual.

The Reorganization Stage

Even without treatment most victims move into the reorganization stage between four months and one year after the abuse. Or course, if the abuse is ongoing, then the progression from the initial stage is disrupted. In the reorganization stage the victim is less focused on the possibility of another attack from the original perpetrator, but tends to have a more generalized anxiety of being attacked by "someone," so the victim is constantly searching for signs of danger. Those victims who continue to suffer from flashbacks become hypervigilant for cues in their surroundings that might trigger them and try to restrict the places they will go. Unlike a civilian, who may be able to completely avoid the perpetrator and the place where the assault took place, a service member may be obliged to interact with the perpetrator or return to the site of the assault.

Hypervigilance takes a toll on the body, not just the mind. The National Vietnam Veterans Readjustment Survey found that veterans with Post-Traumatic Stress Disorder reported more chronic physical health problems than other veterans, including sustained muscle tension, rapid heartbeat, and other symptoms related to always being on high alert.[14] When compared to women without PTSD, those with PTSD reported more physical health problems, including obesity, smoking, irritable bowel syndrome, fibromyalgia, chronic pelvic pain, polycystic ovary disease, asthma, cervical cancer, and stroke. They also reported higher levels of psychiatric problems and substance abuse.[15] It is common for victims to attempt to medicate their anxiety, depression, and emotional pain with alcohol. The Department of Veterans Affairs reported 23 percent of women seeking treatment for depression and alcohol abuse had been sexually assaulted while on active duty.[16]

One of the most devastating effects of sexual abuse is the sense of loss suffered by the victim. Three common losses are one's image of the military as a place of honor and comradeship; one's self-image as an invincible warrior; and belief in a just, loving God.

Post-Traumatic Stress Disorder

Post-Traumatic Stress Disorder first gained widespread attention when it appeared in the *Diagnostic and Statistical Manual of Mental Disorders* published by the American Psychiatric Association in 1980. Originally this diagnosis was only used when the traumatic event was combat. Of course, the symptoms now called PTSD existed prior to 1980, but different terms were used. During and after the American Civil War it was called "soldier's heart."[17] In World War I it was known as "shell shock." During World War II these same symptoms were called "war neurosis" or "combat fatigue."[18]

In the post–Vietnam years, as more civilian clinicians became familiar with the symptoms of PTSD they began to realize that some sexual assault survivors were experiencing PTSD. Sixty-three percent of female veterans being treated for PTSD at a VA clinic reported physical sexual harassment during military service, and 43 percent reported rape or attempted rape. Most had served in either the Vietnam or first Gulf War, and 12 percent had directly been exposed to enemy fire. This research found sexual harassment and rape are more likely to cause PTSD than other stresses linked to military service—even combat—and that the combination of sexual abuse and combat created the highest risk of developing PTSD. [19] In 2005 researchers examined the health records of more than 30,000 1991 Gulf War veterans and identified over 1,300 who came home with PTSD. The two most common experiences that triggered the PTSD for both women and men were "high combat exposure and sexual harassment/assault."[20]

Similarities Between Combat Trauma and Sexual Trauma

Research on the impact of combat can inform us about the effects of sexual abuse. During the early years of the Korean War the rate of psychiatric casualties was nearly seven times higher than the average rate during World War II. In later years, when the lines stabilized so that the threat of being attacked by the enemy from the rear was reduced, the rate of psychiatric casualties in Korea went down to a level lower than that of World War II. Lieutenant Colonel Grossman explained, "The *potential* of close-up, inescapable, *inter*personal hatred and aggression is more effective and has greater impact on the morale of the soldier than the *presence* of inescapable, *im*personal death and destruction.[21] This is an important finding, because sexual assault, particularly when committed by one's comrades, is a "close-up, inescapable, interpersonal" act of hatred and aggression that is quite likely to produce psychological casualties.

Some of the symptoms of PTSD are more difficult for military personnel to deal with than they are for civilians. Civilians who are sexually abused at their place of residence or employment can move or resign, but military personnel do not have this level of freedom.

Many survivors of sexual assault have a sense of a foreshortened future—an expectation that he or she will not have a normal life span and therefore will not live long enough to enjoy the things most people desire such as a career. This makes it difficult to take the necessary steps to be successful in the military and is viewed by others as mere laziness.

Some survivors of sexual abuse have difficulty falling or staying asleep, so they use alcohol and other drugs, such as sleep aids, which can lead to drug abuse and dependency. If illegal drugs are being used, particularly on base, these persons risk destroying their military careers and they risk imprisonment.

In civilian life, outbursts of anger at a superior can get one fired, but in a military setting such an action can lead to a charge of insubordination and serious consequences.

Many occupational specialties in the military, even in peacetime, involve dangerous situations. The military utilizes large equipment that can easily cause dismemberment and death. Personnel must be alert and able to concentrate in order to remain safe and also not to endanger their comrades. The symptoms of PTSD make it difficult for an individual to function in a demanding environment such as the military.

THE IMPACT OF SEXUAL ABUSE ON THE VICTIM'S FAMILY

The Real Me: *Those who love me/Know my secrets/Not sure/I can live with that*—Gregory Helle, U.S. Army, SP5[22]

SEXUAL ABUSE ALWAYS creates more than one victim. The loved ones of the victim are themselves victimized. They too have a sense of vulnerability, fear, and anger. In Part II, Annie describes how her life was negatively impacted when her husband was sexually assaulted: "There are times when I get my feelings hurt because I need some sign of emotion or attention from my husband and I don't get it. He is so traumatized by what happened to him that he has a hard time relating to others.... Not only is my husband being cheated out of a normal life but also I feel like I'm being cheated out of the love and tenderness I should be getting from my husband. I'm angry with the men who did this to him and got away with it. Not only does he have to suffer because of what happened to him, but I do too."

Just as there are patterns to the ways sexual abuse victims react, so too there are common responses shown by family members.[23] When family members first learn of sexual abuse, they may not understand the events as abuse. Particularly if the perpetrator is someone known to the victim, such as a superior, and family members don't understand the misuse of power and authority, they may think the victim was nothing more than a willing participant. A sexual abuse survivor may not report the abuse for fear a spouse will find out what happened and blame the survivor for a betrayal of the marriage vows.

Even when the family does not blame the victim, there is still much to be distressed over. Many people view the military with great respect, even love. To learn that someone in a cherished organization abused one's loved one can cast a shadow over key events in the past, present, and future. The treasured memory of one's child successfully completing boot camp is now tainted because the officer who made such a stirring speech at the event is now remembered only as the perpetrator of sexual abuse.

Not only can learning of sexual abuse change the image of a single individual, the anger and hurt can infect one's view of the entire military as a trusted organization. This response is particularly common in situations in which the military's response to the disclosure of the abuse appears to be more of an effort to sweep the problem under the rug, or protect the perpetrator at the expense of the victim. Family members wonder, where else might trust be misplaced? This leads to second-guessing oneself, authority figures, and other institutions. Family members may become hypervigilant for the "hidden" meanings in events, looking for signs that abuse is taking place.

FACTORS THAT AFFECT THE IMPACT OF SEXUAL ABUSE

"RANK HAS ITS PRIVILAGES": THE BELIEF THAT THE SYSTEM IS CORRUPT

UNFORTUNATELY, IT ONLY TAKES a few high-profile cases of sexual abuse to negatively affect the reputation of the military, and in the previous two decades many have become public. Among the cases of abuse that became widely known are:

- Eight male instructors being disciplined at Lackland Air Force base for sexually abusing female recruits.[1]
- Five high-ranking officers making headlines for inappropriate conduct with women. One, while an aide at the White House, made improper comments about his female staff's bodies. Two were charged with adultery, and one of them was accused of stalking a subordinate who wanted to end their affair. The most embarrassing case involved the highest-ranking naval officer to face court martial since World War II. He was accused of sexually harassing female subordinates while in charge of the office for the prevention of sexual harassment in the Navy.*
- Staff Sergeant Delmar Simpson was found guilty of eighteen out of nineteen counts of rape in a military trial. His victims were six women trainees at the Army's Aberdeen Proving Ground. Simpson was only the first of twelve Aberdeen drill instructors to face court martial for sexual misconduct.[2]

---

* This case appeared to be an incidence of revenge on the part of a number of high-ranking officials who wished to punish the defendant for his enthusiastic performance of his job. Although he was later acquitted the damage to the reputation of the Navy remained.

- Senior enlisted soldier (Army) Gene C. McKinney was court martialed on nineteen criminal charges, most related to sexual misconduct. He as found guilty of one count of obstructing justice, reprimanded, and reduced in grade to master sergeant before retirement.[3]

- More than 100 officers sexually harassed and assaulted dozens of women and men at the 1991 Tailhook Convention.[4] One of the members of the Naval Investigative Service (responsible for investigating the scandal) was removed from the case after he addressed one of the victims as "Sweet Cakes" and sexually propositioned her.[5]

- Specialist Lorenzo M. Tarrence was convicted of rape and sentenced to ninety days in jail. The same year, another soldier as given twice that sentence for committing adultery with a willing partner.[6]

- Four-star general Kevin Byrnes was dismissed as the head of the Army Training and Doctrine Command because he violated a direct order from the Army Chief of Staff, General Peter Schoomaker, by continuing to have an adulterous relationship.[7]

- Brigadier General Larry G. Smith was nominated to be the Deputy Inspector General of the Army, which investigates sexual harassment by senior officers. Three-star general Claudia Kennedy, the Deputy Chief of Staff for Army Intelligence, accused him of engaging in the sexual abuse. When the Inspector General substantiated her claim, General Smith was officially reprimanded and retired immediately.[8]

- Cadet Beth Davis resigned from the Air Force Academy, claiming she was punished for reporting being raped by a fellow cadet. She received a demerit for having sex in a dorm, but her alleged attacker was not prosecuted.[9]

- Air Force General Counsel Mary L. Walker released a report that found "no systemic acceptance of sexual assault at the Academy" nor "institutional avoidance of responsibility." However, the Department of Defense found that, even though leaders had known about "serious sexual misconduct problems" at the Academy for at least ten years, they failed to conduct proper investigations or make long-range plans to deal with sexual abuse, despite having received warnings from their own Office of Special Investigations, the Air Force Surgeon General, and the Armed Services Committee of the U.S. Senate. The authors concluded "a chasm of leadership...helped create an environment in which sexual assault became a part of life at the Academy."[10]

- The Panel to Review Sexual Misconduct Allegations at the U.S. Air Force Academy was formed and included Anita K. Blair, founder of the Independent Women's Forum, which opposes the admittance of women to the Virginia Military Institute, and Amy McCarthy, who publicly stated that abuse allegations from female cadets were suspect because some engaged in "high-risk behaviors."[11]

- Major General Thomas Ficus, the Air Force's top lawyer, was investigated for alleged "inappropriate conduct" with a member of his staff.[12]

- Air Force Brigadier General Richard S. Hassan, the former director of the Air Force Senior Leader Management Office, who oversaw the career development of senior service leaders, was demoted to colonel because he sexually harassed female subordinates, engaged in unprofessional relationships, and created a hostile work environment by making sexual advances toward women in his office, suggesting they wear more revealing clothing, and sending sexually explicit e-mail and graphic photographs via his government computer.[13]

These events can be understood two ways: either the military takes sexual abuse seriously and prosecutes offenders, even officers, or the military is filled with sexual predators, of whom only a few are ever confronted with their deeds and fewer still are punished. The latter is the conclusion of many sexual abuse victims. In the Army, only 12 percent of those who had been sexually harassed used the formal complaint system, because they believed the reporting system was merely in place "to protect the chain of command as opposed to assisting soldiers":[14]

In effect, the system stigmatizes an individual for reporting. Frequently, complainants find that their working conditions worsen once a complaint is surfaced. Soldiers who complain are often ostracized by other soldiers in their unit and/or by their chain of command, or find themselves being transferred to another unit. In effect, victims are re-victimized by the system. The individual soldier, as a result, often chooses to simply put up with the harassment.[15]

NOT HOLDING OFFENDERS ACCOUNTABLE

THE MILITARY HAS ALSO been reluctant to bring charges against those accused of sex crimes. Imagine the cries of outrage if the ship of a foreign nation docked at an American port spilling forth drunken sailors who began harassing and raping American citizens. No such outcry was heard in 1992 when the U.S. Navy ship *Duncan* docked in the American port of Sitka, Alaska. While the ship was in harbor there were so many reports of drunken sailors sexually harassing women, having sex with underage girls, and committing sexual assault, that civilian authorities held an emergency meeting to make the town off-limits to all sailors. For nearly four years the Navy refused to take action on the reported crimes. Finally, in 1996, a civilian grand jury indicted a sailor and an officer for the sexual assault of a fourteen-year-old girl.[16]

At Annapolis, a review of the midshipmen accused of sexual assault from 1998 to 2006 found that only two were convicted, and in one of these cases the conviction was in a civilian court.[17] In the civilian criminal justice system, four out of five of those arrested for sexual assault are prosecuted. But in the military, from 1994 through 2004, twice as many personnel accused of sex crimes were given administrative punishment instead of being court-martialed. This means 5,000 accused sex offenders were never tried. When the military uses administrative punishment instead of court martial, the offender does not face prison time or dishonorable discharge but is merely given a reprimand, ordered to counseling, reduced in rank, or fined.[18] Even repeat offenders were allowed to resign, with only administrative reprimands that allowed them to return to the civilian world with no criminal record.[19]

In military trials where the most serious charge for which the defendant was convicted was rape, the median sentence for Marines was thirteen years, while in the Navy it was just five years. Sometimes the punishment is measured in mere months. Kori Hansler, a 19-year-old sailor, was attacked, beaten, raped, sodomized, infected with venereal disease, impregnated, and eventually gave birth to the child. Her assailants—two shipmates—were court martialed and found guilty of conspiracy to commit an indecent act, indecent acts, and sodomy. Donnel D. Taylor was given a bad-conduct discharge and sentenced to nine *months* confinement with time off for time served during the trial. His accomplice, Damanys Degrant, recieved a bad-conduct discharge and six months of confinement with time off for time served.[20]

CONTEXT MATTERS

SEXUAL ABUSE DOESN'T occur in a vacuum; it is takes place in the context of a culture. Dr. Paul Farmer, in *Pathologies of Power*, explained, "Human rights violations are not accidents; they are not random in distribution or effect. Rights violations are, rather, symptoms of deeper pathologies of power and are linked intimately to the social conditions that so often determine who will suffer abuse and who will be shielded from harm."

When Army and the Air Force academies began admitting female cadets, there were protests, harassment, predictions of failure for the women, and damage to the standards of the institutions Neither the civilian press nor the naysayers at the academies gave any attention to the fact that, years before, the U.S. Merchant Marines and the U.S. Coast Guard had admitted women, had classes that contained 30 percent female cadets, and did so with relatively little fuss.[21] Unlike at West Point, these female cadets did not have to endure their male comrades ejaculating into the women's dresser drawers when they were out of their rooms or sabers covered with ketchup driven into their mattresses.[22]

SECONDARY VICTIMIZATION: WHERE IS THE JUSTICE?

"[T]he far-reaching role of commanding officers in the court-martialing process remains the greatest barrier to operating a fair system of criminal justice."—The Cox Commission, 2001[23]

" 'Military justice' is often an oxymoron."—Dr. Donna Dean, Navy veteran and rape survivor[24]

LIEUTENANT COLONEL DAVE GROSSMAN summarized the research findings on trauma: "In study after study two factors show up again and again as critical to the magnitude of the post-traumatic response. First and most obvious is the intensity of the initial trauma. The second and less obvious but absolutely vital factor is the nature of the social support structure available to the traumatized individual."[25] In far too many cases, instead of justice, victims experience a second "assault" in the form of betrayal by comrades and superiors. Not bringing charges against offenders, allowing them to resign or retire rather than face court martial, and imposing light punishment or none all contribute to secondary victimization. The victim gets the message that the reputation of the offender and the military as a whole is more important than the physical and emotional suffering of the victim.

When Lieutenant Paula Coughlin resigned from the Navy, she did so not because she had been sexually abused during the 1991 Tailhook Convention, but because of the way she had been treated by her comrades for disclosing the abuse. She mistakenly believed her superiors would take appropriate action. But investigating was half-hearted, and she was ostracized, maligned, and ridiculed by her comrades. It was this treatment that led her to end her promising career. In her resignation letter she wrote, "I feel continued service would be detrimental to my physical, mental, and emotional health. The physical attack on me by naval aviators at the 1991 Tailhook convention, and the covert and overt attacks on me that followed have stripped me of my ability to serve."[26]

An Army veteran wrote of her experience of secondary victimization after she was attacked by two comrades, who had placed duct tape on her mouth to muffle her screams as they assaulted her. After repeatedly raping and sodomizing her they removed the tape and orally assaulted her. When they finally left her alone, she was bruised on her breasts, legs, and neck from being tied down, choked, and bitten. She dressed and found the officer of the day and the noncommissioned officer of the day, to report what she had suffered. They laughed at her, telling her she should be grateful for a hot night of sex with two guys at once. They told her she wasn't really hurt and should just go take a nap. As they left her, they informed her she ought to "expect more of the same since she was a lady-in-the-military" and had therefore "signed on for a tour of duty to satisfy the men of the Army."[27]

The Department of Defense publication *Policy on Prevention and Response to Sexual Assault* summarized the situation: "Our studies and consultations showed that we need to: improve victim protection, treat victims with dignity and respect, and offer victims the medical treatment, care and counseling they deserve."[28] In 1997, a report by the National Summit on Women Veterans Issues urged the Department of Defense to create treatment programs for sexual assault, and a violence response process outside the normal chain of command, because the usual chain of command was not effective. The report also recommended the Veterans Administration permit initial medical treatment, counseling, and referrals regardless of eligibility determinations, because the cumbersome process of application and evaluation interfered with victims getting timely treatment for the effects of the sexual abuse they had experienced while serving in the military.[29] In 2004, an Army task force found that allegations of sexual assault in the U.S. Army had climbed steadily over the preceding five years, that there were weak prevention efforts, slow investigations, inadequate field reporting, and poor managerial oversight.[30] That same year the Defense Department acknowledged that victims inadequately supported legally and psychologically, and that the victims' comrades and superiors routinely hampered investigations into the crimes.[31] It appears that far too many in the military have greater devotion to image maintenance under the guise of "Duty, Honor, Country" than they do to "Life, Liberty and Justice for all."[32]

THE AIR FORCE ACADEMY: "A CULTURE OF RAPE"

IN 2003, THE MEDIA was abuzz with the stories of 142 former and current cadets who alleged they had been sexually assaulted and that the leadership was minimizing the assaults and covering up the factors at the school that contributed to the abuse. These events provide an excellent example of secondary victimization.

When the scandal became public the superintendent of the academy, Lieutenant General John R. Dallager, issued a statement.

I want to assure you that the issue of sexual assault has my personal attention and the highest interest of the Air Force leadership. Above all, you
should know that, throughout the Air Force at large and at the Academy,
there is zero tolerance for sexual assault, and any and all perpetrators will
be brought to justice and disciplined appropriately."[33]

Despite these reassurances, there were zero convictions.[34] No wonder
29 percent of the female cadets in the second class and 59 percent of
women in the first class did not have faith in the sexual abuse reduction
program at the Academy.[35]

What led U.S. Congresswoman Diana DeGette to describe the academy
as a "culture of rape?"[36] Perhaps it was the Defense Department Inspector
General's report that 80 percent of all sexual assaults went unreported at
the academy, yet it still had a higher rate of reported sexual assault than
civilian colleges (more than 7 percent vs. less than 2 percent).[37]

Perhaps it was this kind of even. When the class of 1979, the final
all-male class at the school, returned to campus for a reunion, academy
teachers and officers (up to the rank of colonel) wore baseball caps bearing LCWB ("Last Class With Balls" or "Last Class Without Bitches").[38]
LCWB lit up the scoreboard for all 54,000 spectators to see, and LCWB
appeared in huge letters on the hillside overlooking the campus.[39] Just a
playful joke? If LCWN stood for "Last Class Without Niggers," would
it be perceived as a harmless prank?

The Air Force general counsel stated there was "no systematic acceptance of sexual assault at the Academy [or] institutional avoidance of
responsibility."[40] However, Inspector General Joseph E. Schmitz came to
a much different conclusion: "We conclude that the overall root cause
of the sexual assault problems at the Air Force Academy was the failure
of successive chains of command over the past 10 years to acknowledge
the severity of the problem,"[41] which "helped create an environment in
which sexual assault became a part of life at the Academy."[42] As a result
of this report, the acting superintendent, General Weida, was removed.

The Price of Admission?
At the academy's website, under the words "Mission and Values," it reads:

"The universal guiding principle for all cadets, officers, and NCOs will be honor, integrity, and mutual respect that is Academy tradition. . . . The climate we strive to achieve at the Air Force Academy is one which takes appropriate action to deter, stop, or report the criminal actions of a few that sully the reputation of themselves, their fellow cadets, and the United States Air Force."[43]

Inspiring words indeed. How well has the academy lived up to these ideals? Ask Cadet Fullilove, who seemed like an ideal officer candidate, whose application showed excellent grades in high school and included letters of recommendation from the vice president and president of the U.S. The commander of in-patient and emergency services at the academy hospital was Colonel Shafer, the proud parent of Cadet Fullilove. The cadet could do 100 one-arm push-ups. The otherwise outstanding application had but one flaw: Fullilove was a woman. She herself did not consider her sex a flaw, nor did her mother, Colonel Shafer, a twenty-year Air Force veteran. But in 1999 their opinion of women was in the minority at the academy. Upon entering the academy, she was told by some female graduates, "If you get raped, don't tell anyone, because they'll [the administration] find a way to get you kicked out." Current female cadets told her, "Expect getting raped, and if it doesn't happen to you, you're one of the rare ones," and, "If you want a chance to stay here, if you want to graduate, you don't tell. You just deal with it."[44]

After only six months, Sharon Fullilove had left the academy because a fellow cadet she knew and trusted raped her. She resigned from the academy but reported the crime. Investigators accused her of making it up and informed her mother that they considered the whole thing a lie. Even after she had reported the rape, the academy's hotline for reporting sexual abuse was still being answered by none other than the man she accused of raping her.[45]

I GET BY WITH A LITTLE HELP FROM MY FRIENDS

WOMEN VETERANS WHO had been harassed or assaulted and returned to a supportive community had much lower rates of Post-Traumatic Stress Disorder than those who encountered hostility and isolation.[46] Units with high cohesion and high regard for their leaders have fewer psychological and physical problems that do units with low cohesion and low regard for the leaders, even when units include persons with extensive trauma histories.[47] In one study nearly all of the service members had experienced at least one traumatic event (92 percent males and 91 percent females). Half of the women and 6 percent of the men had been sexually assaulted. Over a third of the women had been raped more than once. Although most of these traumatic events had occurred prior to enlistment, the level of unit cohesion had significant impact on the mental and physical health of personnel. It is clear that the proper military experience can be helpful in reducing the negative impact of trauma on personnel. It is also clear that the wrong military environment has the opposite effect.

FALSE BELIEFS THAT CONTRIBUTE TO SECONDARY VICTIMIZATION

SOME OF THE MOST COMMON and destructive myths concerning sexual assault are:

- Some women have fantasies of being raped, therefore all women really want to be raped;[48]
- Women mean "yes" even when they are saying "no";
- Women who have already had sexual experience are not psychologically harmed as much by being sexually assaulted are as virgins;
- Only persons who ask for it get raped. Those who are sexually assaulted bring it on themselves because of their dress, attitude, or other behaviors;
- Being sexually assaulted by an acquaintance is less disturbing than being raped by a stranger;
- Any person who really wanted to, particularly someone with military training, could resist a rapist, even one with a weapon;
- If a man gets an erection or ejaculates during a so-called rape, then it means he liked it therefore he wasn't rape, and he must be gay;
- Homosexual men are not harmed by being sexually assaulted because they must have already experienced anal penetration;[49]
- Females who were sexually active prior to the alleged sexual assault have less moral integrity, therefore their testimony is sus-

pect. However, evidence of male heterosexual promiscuity is not an indication of poor morality, therefore it should not affect the believability of his testimony; [50]

- A victim of interracial rape is more responsible for being raped than a victim who is raped by an offender of the same race;[51]
- African-American women are more responsible for being raped, and experience fewer traumas as a result of being attacked, than Caucasian victims, because they are more promiscuous than Caucasian women.[52]

14

THE OFFENDER MENTALITY

"Many ill-adjusted, antisocial young men ended up in our ranks."—Brigadier General Bernard Trainer[1]

WHEN THE MILITARY first began to address the use of illegal drugs within the ranks, it became clear that commanders' stereotypes of drug abusers interfered with accurate identification of drug abusers. This was not something found in only a few naïve commanders, it was a military-wide stereotype that drug users could easily be identified because they would be obviously incapacitated. When functioning personnel tested positive for illegal drugs, commanders refused to believe the test results.[2] A similar problem exists in addressing sexual abuse: Military leaders' stereotypes of what a sexual abuser is make it difficult for them to believe their personnel are capable of sexual abuse and make it impossible for them to identify their own behavior as abusive. How could a colonel who, during a public ceremony, pinned first-lieutenant bars on the collar of a female soldier and then kissed her on the mouth, respond appropriately when one of his officers was accused of engaging in sexual harassment?[3]

Most people believe that those who sexually abuse are unlike anyone they know. It is common when someone has been accused of sexually abusing an adult for coworkers to exclaim, "He couldn't have done that! I've known him for years. He's not the type." Similarly, much of the general public believes that anyone who would sexually abuse a child is a monster and easily identified. Therefore, when a prominent member of the community is accused, they react with disbelief. They assume anyone who would abuse children would be incapable of holding a position of high status in society. In fact, many persons in high-status roles have been found guilty of sexually abusing children; there is even a book written on the topic, *The Socially Skilled Child Molester*.[4]

"The accused's general good military character is a pertinent character trait if there is any nexus, however strained or slight, between the circumstances surrounding the crime and the military. The defense, in most cases, and certainly in every 'military' offense prosecution, will probably consider offering a 'good soldier defense' by presenting evidence of the accused's good military character."—156th Officer Basic Course[5]

According to the Association for the Treatment of Sexual Abusers, "Sexual perpetrators represent an extremely diverse group of offenders in educational, income, and racial background, as well as personality and coping skills."[6] Those who exclaim, "You'd have to be crazy to rape somebody," might be surprised that only 5 percent of rapists were psychotic at the time of the offense.[7]

Although sexual assault has serious negative effects on the victim, the offender suffers few, if any, unpleasant effects.[8] Some men convicted of sexual assault were afraid of being caught or felt sorry for themselves, but only 8 percent felt guilty, and just two out of 114 expressed any concern for their victims. The rest stated they felt good, relieved, or it improved their self-image.[9] Since they do not experience guilt as a result of their actions, they are not internally motivated to change their antisocial behaviors. It is only when they are held accountable by others that there is any hope for behavior change.

AN ACT OF HOSTILITY

"Virtually every study indicates that men rape men out of anger or an attempt to overpower, humiliate, and degrade their victims rather than out of lust, passion, or sexual desire."—Michael Scarce[10]

SEXUAL ASSAULT IS NOT due to a lack access to willing sexual partners. Some offenders prefer assaulting a stranger rather than having sex with a willing partner: "With rape, I felt totally in charge. I'm bashful, timid. When a woman wanted to give me normal sex, I was intimidated. In the rapes, I was totally in control, she totally submissive." [11]

If the primary goal was merely sexual contact, then the level of violence seen in many assaults would be unnecessary. Victims are beaten, humiliated, degraded, and threatened, even after they cease to resist. Following the sexual portion of the assault, assailants still continue to beat and threaten victims. Assaults often include acts that are not normally a part of voluntary sexual encounters, such as being urinated on and having dangerous objects thrust into the vagina or rectum. [12]

JUSTIFYING SEXUAL ABUSE

OFFENDERS OFFER SEVERAL justifications for their actions.[*] Many of them claim that the mere fact of being men grants them the privilege to punish women who "misbehave."

Intoxication

The rate of intoxicated offenders is lower in military cases than in civilian cases (52 percent vs. 61 percent). [13] In both settings the more intoxicated the victim the more likely the assault will lead to penetration and physical injury. [14]

Burglaries and car thieves who are intoxicated at the time of their offenses are still held accountable for their actions. Nor is it a legitimate defense to claim, because the victim was intoxicated at the time of the theft, that the criminal should not be held accountable. However, in sexual assault cases both these claims are made.

Uncontrollable Sexual Desire: "I Couldn't Help Myself"

"The sex drive demands an outlet, especially with the young men. It cannot be stopped."—Ken Good, anthropologist[15]

Dr. Good's claim that men have a virtually uncontrollable sexual desire that must be satisfied regardless of the consequences is one of the most pervasive myths regarding sexual assault. When members of the military

---

[*] My nomination for most interesting justification for sexual assault goes to the Hindu priest who when charged with raping and impregnating a woman who came to him for spiritual counseling, claimed the alleged victim had been his wife in a past life and God had brought them back together again so the act should not be considered rape (Bishop, 2005).

make such a claim it is an interesting justification, because military men tend to pride themselves on being disciplined, to the point of being able to control their natural urge to flee when faced with enemy fire. Yet they will claim they were overcome by lust and couldn't stop themselves. Further evidence against the "once it got started I couldn't stop" justification for sexual assault is that it is typically not a spontaneous act: 71 percent of sexual assaults are planned in advance.[16] In other words, sexual assault is usually not done, "in the heat of passion," but in a cold, calculated manner.

Blame the Victim

Supposedly, "nice girls" don't get raped, so it follows that the woman "wanted it" or "was asking for it," and is unworthy of respect or sympathy despite the physical injuries that often accompany assaults. Indications of "asking for it" include hitchhiking and walking alone at night.

Seductress / "Cock Tease"

This rationalization insists that some women get sick satisfaction out of "leading men on" by dressing or acting provocatively and then "rejecting them." One rapist described his experience: A "lot of times a woman knows that she's looking really good and she'll use that and flaunt it, and it makes me feel like she's laughing at me and I feel *degraded*."[17]

Another form is the woman who is 'too aloof," meaning that she doesn't respond to sexual overtures, thereby indicating she "thinks she is better than everyone else," should be punished. A rapist explained his actions: "If a woman doesn't want to give it [sex], the man should take it. Women have no right to say no. Women are made to have sex. It's all they are good for."[18]

Rough Sex

The assailant describes the encounter not as an assault but rather as a mutually desired sexual act: "She likes it rough," or "I was only pretending to rape her, we were just acting out a fantasy." In some cases the assailant may grudgingly acknowledge that "things got a little extreme," but he continues to insist that the events were essentially consensual. When victims of sexual assault stop resisting or comply with the demands of the attacker(s), this is viewed as an indication that the victim has relaxed and is now enjoying what is taking place. Even men who use a weapon against their victim make this claim.[19]

Revenge

These assaults are among the most brutal, with high levels of violence, serious injuries, and even death. A woman is raped to punish her partner for something the partner has done to hurt or humiliate the assailant. The assailant views the sexual assault on "another man's woman" as a way to enhance his own masculinity and reduce that of the other man.[20] The women is being treated as a form of property to be damaged, as a way of harming the "owner."

In other cases the victim is a scapegoat for all members of a group (women, homosexuals, an ethnic group).[21] Sexually assaulting one servicewoman is viewed as message to all women thatt they are not welcome, or had better "keep in their place."[22]

Sometimes the victim is a stand-in for a specific woman, whom the assailant wishes to harm but is somehow unavailable (e.g., an ex-wife, mother). Men speak of assaulting their victim as a way to "get even" with a particular woman who has hurt them in some way.[23] That 43 percent of the men stated they preferred a victim who was "significantly older" than they suggests the revenge is directed at their mother or other maternal figure."[24]

Gang Rape, or "Gang Bang"

Common reasons given for engaging in gang rape are to alleviate boredom, increase male camaraderie, and because it is "fun." These same reasons are given by men for verbally harassing women who walk by them on public streets, suggesting that sexual assault is on a continuum with behaviors that have similar psychological underpinnings.[25]

Homosexual Panic

When a male is sexually assaulted by another man, responsibility for the assault is denied because the victim was "acting like a faggot," meaning style of clothing, body build, or being in the wrong place at the wrong time. If the victim was perceived to have sexually approached the assailant, then this is offered as further evidence that the victim deserved to be attacked. Furthermore, the thinking goes, since the victim was a homosexual and therefore must like anal sex, anally raping him should not be considered a serious crime.

SEX OFFENDING IS CHRONIC BEHAVIOR

IT WOULD BE COMFORTING to believe that those who sexually abuse others are somehow caught up in a situation not of their doing—just victim of circumstance, and after the abuse has occurred, they will come to their senses and never engage in abuse again. However, sexual abuse is not an impulsive act but involves long-range planning. Follow-up studies have found that sexual offenders are at high risk for reoffending, with 45 percent of untreated sexual offenders reoffending.[26] Although these rates are considerably lower than rates for other types of violent crimes, sexual offense recidivism rates are vastly underreported. When official records are compared to "unofficial" sources of data, the number of sex offenses revealed was nearly two-and-a-half times higher than the number in official reports.[27] When placed on polygraphs ("lie detectors"), convicted sex offenders with one or two known victims were found to actually have an average of 100 victims and 300 offenses.[28] Another polygraph study found offenders had been committing sex crimes for an average of sixteen years before getting caught.[29] One third of the military Catholic chaplains accused of sexual abuse had already been accused of sexual misconduct before enlisting. Church and court records showed that Catholic officials knew about the misdeeds of some of these men, but did not inform the military before they were commissioned as chaplains.

The number of offenders who victimize both children and adults is extremely high. Although only 6 percent of incarcerated sex offenders admitted to having both child and adult victims, polygraphs indicated 71 percent had abused both children and adults.[30] Therefore the strategy of reassigning known sex offenders to a setting where they won't have easy access to their known type of victim will not prevent further victimization because many offenders target whomever is available. But superiors who do not understand the psychology of offending, or who just want the problem to disappear, merely elicit a promise that "nothing like this will ever happen again" and transfer the offender to another unit or base.

Or worse, the victims will be transferred, giving them the message that what happened was their fault.

The Offender Response

When confronted with overwhelming evidence of their crimes, sex offenders tend to react in a predictable manner. They may concede that they are guilty of minor wrong doing, but they will continue to insist that, because they are otherwise nice, decent men, they were not really being abusive.[31] They will act remorseful but are actually filled with resentment and self-pity, because they see themselves as the real victims in the situation.[32] In other words, they are not upset by what they did, but only that they are being held accountable for their actions.

Below is a progression of responses to an accusation of sexual abuse commonly seen in a military setting. Although not all offenders offer up every one of these defenses, anyone who has reason to interact with those accused of sexual crimes ought to be familiar with this pattern:

- The alleged event(s) never took place. The accuser is lying.
- I wasn't involved. This is a case of mistaken identity.
- I couldn't have done it because of my record, reputation, rank, status, character, etc. I am above reproach. Just ask my character witnesses, and those who spontaneously rush to defend me and attack my accuser.
- The accuser asked for it, wanted it, deserved it. The accuser is nothing more than a willing participant who later changed her/his mind, or a slut or a faggot. Compare my rank, status, reputation, record, and character to my accuser's and you will see mine is more impressive and therefore more believable.
- The alleged events didn't cause harm. The events were just a normal part of human interaction but were misinterpreted by the accuser (who is too sensitive) or were merely a joke (but the accuser has no sense of humor).
- The accuser shouldn't have been offended or frightened. The accuser is different from the rest of us. The accuser is overreacting and being unreasonable. If something as benign as these events is enough to bother the accuser, how can she or he deal with

the enemy? The accuser is too sensitive, can't take a joke, doesn't understand military tradition, is unfit for military service. The real problem is the accuser, not the accused.

- I didn't intend to offend, frighten, or cause harm. I am different from others and therefore I should be treated better.

- I should not be held accountable for my actions because of all the good I've done, my rank, my status, my position, my reputation, imminence of promotion, transfer, or retirement, or the damage it would do to the image of our branch or the military as a whole.

- These events took place a long time ago when norms and standards were different. I've since learned my lesson. It will never happen again therefore, I should not be held accountable.

- The real victim here is our way of life, our traditions, our cohesion, our combat readiness, the image of our branch and the military as a whole. There is a bigger issue at stake here. If I am held accountable for my actions, a much greater harm will be committed.

- I should not face further punishment. I have suffered enough due to the strain of defending myself, facing public humiliation, and the damage to my reputation. I just want to put this all behind me. I just want to get on with my life, my career, and our vital mission.

WHO ARE THE PERPETRATORS OF SEXUAL ABUSE IN THE MILITARY?

PERPETRATORS COME FROM all ethnic groups and religions, and have positions of the highest rank down to those with little status.

Clergy

As difficult as it is for any victim of sexual abuse to stand up to a perpetrator, it is even more difficult when the offender is a respected, powerful member of a hierarchical organization. The situation is further complicated if the perpetrator is clergy. Unfortunately, having religious responsibilities is no guarantee of moral behavior; the reported misconduct rate for military chaplains is higher than for other officers. The majority of chaplains charged with crimes, found guilty, and punished had committed sexual crimes, including molesting the children of military personnel and the harassment or assault of adult personnel. A Navy report found that in a period of only five years nineteen chaplains from twelve denominations had been punished for sexual misconduct.[33] However, although some chaplains were charged, convicted, and sent to prison for sexual crimes, many more avoided prosecution by simply agreeing to quit the military rather than face court martial.[34]

A Few Bad Apples: "They Aren't Like Us"

"If only it were all so simple! If only there were evil people somewhere insidiously committing evil deeds, and it were necessary only to separate them from the rest of us and destroy them. But the line dividing good and evil cuts through the heart of every human being."—Aleksander Solzhenitsyn, *The Gulag Archipelago*

"We have met the enemy and he is us."—*Pogo*[35]

Many people would like to believe that those who commit sexual crimes are evil, mentally ill, or somehow different than the rest of us. One of the most cited research projects related to the ability of normal people to mistreat other people is the Stanford prison simulation in which male Stanford University students were randomly assigned the role of guard or prisoner.[36] The guards were given uniforms, clubs, and whistles and instructed to enforce certain rules in a simulated prison in which fellow students, in the role of prisoners, were locked in barren cells, wearing cheap rubber sandals and shapeless smocks that exposed their bare legs.

It took little more than a day before some of the guards began to actively degrade the prisoners, developing humiliating routines for the prisoners for no apparent reason other than that they had the power to do so. Not all of the guards became abusive, but those who did not merely stood by and did not intervene. In response to the guards' abuse, those in the role of prisoner broke down, became apathetic, or rebelled. The conditions deteriorated so rapidly that the study that had been planned to run for fourteen days was terminated early.

At the end of only six days we had to close down our mock prison because what we saw was frightening. . . . There were dramatic changes in virtually every aspect of their behavior, thinking, and feeling. In less than a week, the experience of imprisonment undid (temporarily) a lifetime of learning; human values were suspended, self-concepts were challenged, and the ugliest, most base, pathological side of human nature surfaced."[37]

What is the lesson of this research? That prison, even a mock one, is a bad place? No, the real lesson of this research is that when average people are placed in a position of authority without adequate training, without a functioning chain of command, and without accountability, what is created are "atrocity conditions."[38] This is what happened in the basement of Stanford University, what happened in Iraq at Abu Ghraib Prison thirty years later, and what will occur again anytime that anyone anywhere is put in these conditions. The lesson is simply that conditions are more likely to change people than people are to change conditions. If we want to reduce abuses of power, we must modify the conditions that contribute to these acts. In order to do this, first we must develop some humility:

> [Y]ou're not different, anything any human being has ever done cannot be alien to you, you can't divorce it! We must break through this 'we-they' idea that our dispositional orientation promotes and understand that the situational forces operating on a person at any given moment could be so powerful as to override everything prior—values, history, biology, family, [and] church.[39]

WHERE IS THE HONOR? — "THE TRUTH? YOU CAN'T HANDLE THE TRUTH!"

"From the halls of Montezuma, to the shores of Tripoli, we fight our country's battles in the air, on land, and sea. First to fight for right and freedom, and to keep our honor clean; We are proud to claim the title of United States Marines."—The Marines' Hymn

IN THE CHAPTER on military culture, honor was listed as a motivation to be a part of the military. But those with an offender mentality twist this concept and use it as justification for engaging in abuse. Honor is the theme of the film *A Few Good Men*.[40] The plot of the film revolves around a "code red," an unofficially encouraged form of punishment where low-ranking personnel beat a "foul-up," or "fuck-fuck," to motivate the failing Marine to "get with the program," and to discourage other Marines from poor performance. In the film two Marines, PFC Dawny and Corporal Dawson, submit a comrade, Willie, to a code red that results in his death and they are facing court martial. One of the defendant's lawyers, Lieutenant Kaffee (played by Tom Cruise), thinks they are innocent because they were following an order, even though it was an illegal one. A second member of the defense team, Sam Wineberg (played by Kevin Pollak), has no sympathy for the accused: "I believe every word of their story—and I think they ought to go to jail for the rest of their lives! They beat up on a weakling! They tortured and tormented a weaker kid! They didn't like him, so they killed him, and why? 'Cause he couldn't run very fast!" He sees no honor in the strong preying on the weak. The third member of the team, Lieutenant Commander Galawa (played by Demi Moore), admires the accused, "Because they stand on the wall, and they say, 'Nothing's going to hurt you tonight, not on my watch.'" She sees honor in the strong protecting the weak.

At the conclusion of the trial the base commander, Colonel Jessup (played by Jack Nicholson) who ordered the code red, is arrested, the two defendants are acquitted of murder but convicted of conduct unbecoming a Marine and dishonorably discharged. PFC Dawny, the younger of the two Marines, protests, "I don't understand. Colonel Jessup said he ordered the code red. What did we do wrong? We did nothing wrong!" But then the other defendant, Corporal Dawson, responds, "Yeah, we did. We were supposed to fight for people who couldn't fight for themselves. We were supposed to fight for Willie." The moral of the film is clear: the measure of one's honor is not how much power one possesses, but how that power is used. There is no honor is using one's power to humiliate those who have less power.

A person with an offender mentality is basically a bully. One can learn how to bully by direct experience or by watching one parent bully the other, or an adult bully a child. From these experiences an outlook on life is developed: "There are two kinds of people in the world, those who abuse and those who get abused, and I'm going to be the one dishing it out, not the one taking it." Whether we refer to these people as bullies, offenders, or perpetrators, their behavior ought not to be ignored. We ought to confront their actions, regardless of their claims of immunity because of tradition or rank and efforts to blame their victims. Even as we confront their actions, we ought to ensure we do not shame and bully them in an attempt to correct their behavior. They have to be told by word and deed that their actions are unacceptable. They have to be provided with alternative behaviors and shown the benefits of the new style of behavior. In other words, make it easier to change than to remain the same. Those unwilling or unable to meet these standards ought to be discharged.

> *"The measure of a man is not his strength; it is the depth of his nobility. The measure of any person is how he or she treats those who are less gifted, less intelligent, and less able."*—Frank Peretti[41]

15

THE IMPACT OF SEXUAL ABUSE ON
THE MILITARY AS A WHOLE

"Meanwhile, sexual harassment complaints, rape complaints, and domestic-violence complaints appear to have blindsided a complacent military. Here again, the military functions about twenty years behind the rest of the country—only now facing issues that rocked the rest of America in the 80s and 90s."—Karen Houppert, *Home Fires Burning*[1]

MOST PEOPLE ACCEPT that sexual abuse harms those individuals who are the target of it. However, many people, including those in the military, do not fully appreciate how the wide spread existence, and tolerance, of sexual abuse within the ranks causes grave damage to the military as a whole. Let us now examine the impact of sexual abuse on the mission of the military.

Enlistment

An organization that enjoys a good reputation will more easily attract new recruits. One important source of new recruits is current personnel. A high percentage of recruits come from military families. Veterans, both male and female, who experience sexual abuse while enlisted are less likely to encourage their offspring to join the military.

Retention

The best way to keep the ranks full is to retain those personnel who are already trained. Sexual abuse leads to personnel leaving the military. Half of the men who were sexually assaulted while in the military desired a discharge.[2] In 2006 the media began to report on servicewomen who had been sexually assaulted by comrades while in Iraq going AWOL and facing court martial rather than face further assaults.

The military not only loses trained personnel who are victims of sexual abuse, but also those personnel who perpetrate sexual abuse are lost. The U.S. Navy has not lost an admiral in combat since 1944, but in an eighteen-month period five members of the top brass were lost due to sex scandals.[3]

Communication

War requires effective and efficient communication or troops die. A unit that has a culture of misogyny and sexual harassment creates two sub-cultures. Where there is one culture for men and one culture for women increases the likelihood miscommunication will take place. That undermines the unit's ability to function as a team and decreases its efficiency and effectiveness.

Readiness

One of the main concerns of military planners, and rightly so, is mission readiness. Anything that is perceived to threaten readiness gets their attention. Sexual abuse in the ranks negatively affected readiness. This not merely my opinion, it is also the conclusion of a Senior Review Panel of the Army. "The Army is an institution grounded in seven core values: honor, integrity, selfless service, courage, loyalty, duty, and respect. When respect for the individual soldier is not maintained, the Army's human relations environment suffers. Combat readiness is directly correlated with a unit's human relations environment...."[4] Sexual abuse violates all seven of these values. The Walter Reed Army Institute of Research studied thirty-four Army companies and found that those units that had high levels of sexual harassment also had lower levels of combat readiness[5]

Morale

"**morale**—the level of psychological and emotional functioning of an individual or group with respect to sense of purpose, confidence, loyalty and ability to accomplish tasks."[6]

Mission readiness is greatly affected by morale. History teaches that a fighting unit with high morale can triumph over a superior force that is handicapped by poor morale. Military psychologists indicate there are several components to morale: individual morale, team spirit, and identification with the immediate commander, with the entire unit, and with the military as a whole.[7] The existence of sexual abuse in the ranks negatively affects all these types of morale. According to research, of the components of morale the most significant one is identification with the immediate commander.[8] Therefore, if the immediate commander is ignoring the existence of sexual abuse, or worse yet, the perpetrator of it, the effect on the morale of the unit can be devastating. When female enlisted personnel and officers who were voluntarily leaving the Navy were asked the most important influence in determining to leave the unit, morale was the most common reason given.

"Any relationship that harms [a] unit's morale, discipline, or efficiency requires action."—Air Force Regulation 36-2909[9]

Discipline

Morale affects discipline. Military planners have long known an undisciplined unit is ineffective and endangers the mission. Combat journalist Christ Hedges observed, "Organized killing is done best by a disciplined, professional army."[10, 11] Captain Danny Kaplan stressed the importance of discipline when he wrote, "The combat role requires a special *style* for applying violence: high discipline, rigidly specified moves, and coordinated behavior."[12] Outbursts of aggression between comrades are not conducive to this necessary level of organization. Misogyny and homophobia contribute to poor discipline and outburst of violence between comrades.

Command Authority

In order for there to be discipline, command authority must first exist. This is the bedrock of military culture. When military leaders ignore, or worse, take part in, sexual abuse it dilutes their authority. Three-Star General Claudia Kennedy, the Deputy Chief of Staff for Army Intelligence, noted this when she wrote, "One's authority is undermined by lack of adherence to institutional values." [13] A commander cannot preach about the importance of military values, then behave in a manner that violates them, and expect to maintain authority. The Walter Reed Army Institute of Research found that those units that had high levels of sexual harassment also had poor relationships between subordinates and superiors. [14]

Respect

A potent way to obtain and maintain command authority is for a leader to behave in a manner that produce respect from subordinates. When cadets first enter West Point they are issued *Reef Points*, a book of maxims they are expected to memorize. One of these quotes is "Qualifications of the Naval Officer" by John Paul Jones:

> It is by no means enough that an officer of the Navy should be a capable mariner. He must be that, of course, but also a great deal more. He should be as well a gentleman of liberal education, refined manners, punctilious courtesy, and the nicest sense of personal humor.
>
> He should be the soul of tact, patience, justice, firmness and charity. No meritorious act of a subordinate should escape his attention or be left to pass without its reward, even if the reward is only a word of approval. Conversely, he should not be blind to a single fault in any subordinate, though at the same time, he should be quick and unfailing to distinguish error from malice, thoughtlessness from in competency, and well meant shortcoming from heedless or stupid blunder.
>
> In one word, every commander should keep constantly before him the great truth, that to be well obeyed, he must be perfectly esteemed.

Contemporary military thinkers continue to emphasis the importance of respect. In its report on sexual harassment the Secretary of the Army's Senior Review Panel stressed the value of respect between members of the military, "Respect encompasses more than the traditional military courtesies that leaders and soldiers observe in deference to rank and position. It is a deep and abiding sense of the human worth of our comrades in arms. In peace, it brings us together as a team and, in war, it holds us together against our enemies." [15]

When asked what makes a man follow a leader into combat Colonel Gerald W. Medsger made it clear he believed respect between comrades was vital to the military:"He doesn't follow you because of the goddamn flag, or motherhood, or God and religion. That son-of-a-bitch follows you because you are the man there that he deeply respects, a man there that is a leader of that damn group and you care for him, and he deeply senses and feels that you care for him."[16] The Colonel is pointing out that for respect to be most effective, it has to exist not just from subordinate to leader, but also from the leader to those of lower rank. Too many so-called leaders are much more concerned about being respected than they are about offering respect to others. In his book on reverence Paul Woodruff wrote on the importance of leadership and respect. He did not focus on the significance of the troops' respect for the leader, but on the leader's respect for the troops. He wrote, "Your respect, if you are a leader, helps your followers feel that they belong in the group and are part of what the group is doing. Your contempt makes them feel left out, overlooked, irrelevant."[17]

One of the most common of the many ceremonies performed in the military is the salute; when a lower ranking individual formally gestures to a person holding higher rank by raising the right hand to the forehead or by presenting arms. Sometimes this is an act empty of any respect. It is done because military law requires it, and to neglect to do it invites punishment. In these cases the junior salutes the rank, but not the officer. Now visualize the same physical moments only this time the salute is given, not only out of obligation, but also as a true sign of respect, even reverence, not merely for the symbol of rank, but for the individual person holding that title. And then the officer returns the salute with an equivalent level of respect. Imagine the awesome power of such a relationship. Such power is not possible when senior personnel use their rank to harass or abuse those under them or ignore when others engage in mistreatment. Only by being just and righteous will officers earn sincere respect. Only then will they be great leaders. Research has found that to be truly effective soldiers must be bonded, not only to one another, but also to their direct commander. Discredited leaders are much less likely to get compliance in combat than are respected leaders.[18] Effective military leaders through history have known that respect is a vital command value. A review panel noted this very thing in a report to the Secretary of the Army.

> What impacts soldiers impacts combat effectiveness. One such factor is the human relations environment in which our soldiers live and work. The Army subscribes to a human relations environment based on dignity and respect. Respect is a bedrock value of both the Army and the Nation. Inherent in American society since the framing of the Declaration of Independence and the United States Constitution, the importance of treating soldiers with dignity and respect is reflected in early military doctrine, regulations, and codes of conduct as a basic tenet of leadership. In 1789, Frederick von Steuben wrote in the *Regulations for the Order and Discipline of the Troops of the United States* that a leader's first priority should be "treating [soldiers] with every possible kindness and humanity, inquiring into their complaints, and when well founded, seeing them redressed."[19]

What was true for General George Washington and the other commanders of the Continental Army during the American Revolution is still true today. Troops who are treated with respect by their commanders, regardless of their rank, will more likely respect that leader, and therefore be more motivated to successfully execute their mission no matter how difficult. A leader cannot expect to be respected if he or she is overlooking sexual abuse within the ranks, since that shows a lack of respect for the troops.

Trust

Respect breeds trust. As with respect, trust goes both ways along the chain of command. An effective unit is one in which the troops trust their commander to do what is right, to take care of them by behaving responsibly and honorably, and the leader trusts the troop to give their best effort toward successfully completing the mission regardless of the challenges involved. A review panel reporting to the Secretary of the Army described the importance of trust within a fighting unit.

> When their leaders and their peers treat soldiers with respect and dignity,

a strong bond develops between them. This bond is founded on mutual trust and serves to cement unit cohesion and to build esprit-de-corps. When this commitment to treating one another with dignity and respect falters, we risk destroying that which we must hold most precious—the indomitable, warfighting spirit of our soldiers.[20]

Simply put, to be effective and efficient military personnel must be able to trust their comrades and their superiors. Trust cannot exist in a unit in which there is sexual abuse.

Loyalty

Respect and trust lead to loyalty. Loyalty is a powerful dynamic. Synonyms for *loyalty* include dependability, steadfastness, allegiance, devotion, faithfulness, and fidelity. A loyal unit is a powerful unit. General Konitzer described the importance of loyalty, "Why is someone willing to risk his life for god and country? Ten percent of the willingness to put your life on the line might be attributed to motivation and another 10 percent to loyalty to the Army as an organization; the remaining 80 percent comes from the willingness of soldiers to risk their lives for each other."[21] A fighting unit that has loyalty to a cause is gong to be much more motivated and effective than a unit consisting of mercenaries whose only loyalty is to themselves and a paycheck. Loyalty cannot be demanded; it must be earned, earned through showing respect and behaving in a trustworthy manner. There is no other way to obtain it.

The power of loyalty is illustrated in the story of the military commander who comes to the gates of a great walled city demanding to speak to the person in charge of the defenders. When the head of the defenders appears on the parapet the enemy commander insists that the city surrender immediately. The defender roars with laughter, exclaiming, "You have only a few hundred warriors while we have high strong walls, thousands of well-armed troops. How can you ever hope to defeat us?" The enemy commander turns to the two warriors next to him and says, "Kill yourselves." Without a moment's hesitation the two men draw their swords and thrust them into their own hearts, killing themselves instantly. After the bodies of his men hit the ground the commander announces, "Yes, I have only a few hundred soldiers, but they are all that loyal to me." At that point the head of defenses sighs and orders his men to open the city gates and begin the process of surrender.

Reputation

Units that have a reputation for quality have high status and attract the best and the brightest personnel. The Marine Corps had a recruiting campaign with the slogan "*Maybe* you can be one of us." They were counting on their reputation for excellence to attract highly qualified personnel to fill the ranks. But when military personnel sexually abuse comrades their crimes damage the hard-earned reputation of the military. Senator Susan Collins expressed this very concern at a meeting of the Armed Services Committee, "What does it say about us as a people, as a nation, as the foremost military in the world when our women soldiers sometimes have more to fear from their fellow soldiers than from the enemy?"[22]

When American personnel are overseas and sexually harass and assault civilians they create a dishonorable reputation for the military, one that damages the image of every member of the organization. A good reputation is a valuable thing, something hard to obtain, and all too easily destroyed. The reputation of the military affects not only the military, but also the country as a whole. When American troops are overseas they are, in the eyes of the citizens of the country in which they are stationed, America. How they behave, or misbehave, determines how the rest of the world will view America. When asked about an embarrassing scandal Marine Commander Krulak answered, "What kills the Marine Corps is Marines who do not act like Marines–Marines who lie, cheat, and steal, who rape little girls on Okinawa. That's what kills the Marine Corps."[23]

Unfortunately, it appears that Marines and Navy sailors have gotten the message that it is more acceptable to engage in sex crimes overseas than it is on American soil. From 1998 to 1995 more Marines and Navy sailors were tried for rapes, child molestations, and other sexual crimes at bases in Japan than at any other U.S. military site in the world. Computer records of Navy and Marine Corps cases showed bases in Japan, which had a total of 41,008 personnel, held 169 court martials for sexual assaults. That is 66 percent more cases than the second-worst location, San Diego, which had more than twice the number of personnel (93,792) but 102 rape cases. [24]

16

THE TIMES, THEY ARE A-CHANGIN'

[The military] is actually one of the most effective organizations in our government; responsive, changing, and highly accountable."—Lieutenant General Claudia Kennedy[1]

"To change anything in the Navy is like punching a feather bed. You punch it with your right, and you punch it with your left until you are finally exhausted, and then you find the damn bed just as it was before you started punching."
—President Franklin D. Roosevelt[2]

CAN THE MILITARY CHANGE?

CAN THE MILITARY CHANGE? Of course. It has and it will continue to change. There was a draft, now there is an all-voluntary military. There were racially segregated units, now there are none. For years it was considered appropriate, good-natured entertainment for white servicemen to darken their faces with ash or grease, pretend to be black men, and perform "minstrel shows." Now that a significant percentage of military personnel are African American, this practice has ceased.

In 1976, when seventeen-year-old Sharon Hanley arrived at the Naval Academy, an upperclassman informed her, "I don't like women at my school, and so I'm going to be on your butt every waking minute. If my plan works you're going to be long gone by the time I graduate." Despite this "welcome," she graduated, and on the thirtieth anniversary of the first class to include women she proudly watched her twin children, a daughter and son, enroll in the academy.[3] By 2006, more than 2,700 women had graduated from the Naval Academy. The women who came the first year were only 6 percent of the class; the percentage in 2006 was nearly 23 percent.[4]

HOW DOES THE MILITARY CHANGE?

ASK THE QUESTION, "How does the military change?" and the only accurate answer has always been, "Reluctantly and slowly." When semi-automatic weapons first became available, some military leaders showed little interest in these new weapons because they thought they would only lead to infantryman wasting ammunition by not properly aiming. Now, rapid-fire rifles are the norm. In World War I, even after the machine gun was invented, military leaders continued to order massive charges against enemy positions, which, armed with this fearsome new weapon, slaughtered men by the hundreds. It was only after literally thousands of men bravely but uselessly died that such foolhardy tactics were abandoned.

When Senator John McCain entered the Naval Academy as part of the class of 1958, he and his fellow cadets were required to take an "outdated" and "stupefyingly dull" course on ship boilers, even though the Navy was already in the nuclear age.[5]

In 1982, the Department of Defense officially terminated the use of the word "dependent" and replaced it with "family member." This change was made because many of the women married to servicemen held jobs, so they were not solely dependent on the military for their income. More women were enlisting, and their husbands also held outside employment. Despite the official change in the lexicon fifteen years earlier, the 1997 *Handbook for Military Families* still used the term "dependent," even though in its introduction the authors themselves state, "The word 'dependent' is no longer officially acceptable in everyday military speech."[6]

In the early 1990s, with the introduction of the "Don't Ask, Don't Tell" policy, the secretary of defense ordered the removal from enlistment forms of the question "Are you a homosexual or bisexual?" Despite this unequivocal directive, it took three years to be implemented by most branches of the military.[7] The Air Force seems to be the branch of the military that has the most difficulty changing. Five years after the directive to eliminate the sexual orientation question, Air Force recruiters were stilling using enlistment forms that contained the prohibited question.[8]

In 2003, more than a quarter of a century after the first female cadets were admitted, a survey of male Air Force cadets found 22 percent of them still did not believe women should be permitted to enroll at the academy.[9]

"In a large organization, one whose roots are deep in the substance of the nation, change is necessarily slow—almost glacial."—Lieutenant General Victor H. Krulak, on change in the military[10]

WHEN DOES THE MILITARY CHANGE?

WHEN DOES THE MILITARY change? Simply put, when change is in its best interest. Prior to World War II, African-American men were relegated to support positions within the military, since they were viewed as unfit for combat. However, when the military became desperate for fighters, African Americans were sent into combat and proved themselves to be effective warriors. When military leaders cannot get enough of their preferred personnel they will set aside, at least temporarily, their stereotypes and biases in order to complete the mission. During World War I, the Red Cross proposed accepting female African Americans into nursing positions, but the surgeon general vetoed the plan. However, when a massive epidemic led to a nursing shortage, the Army Nurse Corps finally accepted black nurses. At first they were only permitted to treat black servicemen, but when the need for nursing staff became great enough toward the end of the war, they were allowed to treat whites as well. Once the war was over, no more black nurses were accepted into the nursing ranks.[11] The problem with the military is not that it won't change, but that it won't stay changed.*

During the Vietnam War, 35 percent of Army troops used heroin, and 20 percent were addicted. By 1971, the number of troops hospitalized for drug-related problems was four times that of those hospitalized for

---

* This is one case in which the military eventually stayed changed; by 1982 the head of the U.S. Army Nurses Corps was Hazel Johnson, a woman of African-American decent (Enole, 1983).

combat injuries.[12] In the 1980s, 47 percent of Navy personnel were smoking marijuana and 11 percent were regularly snorting cocaine.[13] Illegal drug use had been grounds for discharge, but the number of personnel using these substances was so massive that an amnesty program was offered to those who agreed to treatment.[14]

More recently the Army has eased its restrictions on the types of tattoos recruits allowed. Prior to 2006 soldiers were not permitted to have tattoos on their hands or the back of the neck. But with 30 percent of Americans between the ages of twenty-five and thirty-four having tattoos, the ban on these tattoos was making recruitment more difficult. Military sociologist David Segal explained the change in policy: "If norms change, the military has to adapt to the change or get left behind."[15] Now all personnel are allowed to have tattoos on their necks as long as they aren't visible in dress uniforms, and female personnel are permitted to have permanent make-up on their eyelids and eyebrows.

CONSTANT CHANGE IS HERE TO STAY

NOW THAT THE MILITARY has become successful at recruiting females, some of the aspects of military culture have become obsolete, and a majority of the *men* enlisting are interested in change. As early as 1997, 61 percent of male recruits preferred training in units with both males and females.[16] There has been a dramatic increase in the number of dual-career military families. Servicemen married to servicewomen are less tolerant of the military mistreating women.

Like it or not, the military is going to change so that it can attract enough personnel, or the draft will have to be reinstated. The military is going to have to attract new recruits because, according to an article in *Stars and Stripes,* morale in the ranks has been low and is going down. More than half of deployed soldiers reported they wouldn't be reenlisting.[17]

SIMILARITIES BETWEEN MILITARY CULTURE AND THE ADDICTIVE MENTALITY

WRITING ABOUT THE MILITARY culture has reminded me of treating drug addicts; both groups engage in euphoric recall, denial, minimization, rationalization, justification. Drug addicts and organizations change only when the consequences of not changing become greater than the pay-offs for staying the same.

SIMILARITIES IN THE THINKING OF DRUG ADDICTS AND MILITARY LEADERSHIP

Euphoric Recall

- *Drug Addicts:* I miss the old days when getting high didn't cause me any problems, and was fun.
- *Military Leadership:* I miss the good old days when men were men. There were no faggots before the military got feminized.

Denial

- *Drug Addicts:* Problem? I don't have a drug problem!
- *Military Leadership:* Problem? We don't have a problem with sexual abuse!

Minimization

- *Drug Addicts:* It's not that bad. It used to be worse. I don't need any help, particularly from a psychologist.
- *Military Leadership:* It's not that bad. It used to be worse. I don't need any help, particularly from civilians.

Rationalization

- *Drug Addicts:* I have to get high. If you've never done drugs, you just can't understand.
- *Military Leadership:* It has always been this way, and it must stay this way. If you have never been in the military, you can't understand.

Justification

- *Drug Addicts:* Sure, I said I wanted to get sober, but that was when I was facing jail time. But now that I'm off probation, why shouldn't I get high?
- *Military Leadership:* Certainly, we reluctantly accepted the services of blacks, women, and homosexuals, but that was during a national emergency. You can't expect us to continue with that practice now that the crisis is over.

AN EXAMPLE OF THE MILITARY SUCCESSFULLY CHANGING: THE INTEGRATION OF AFRICAN AMERICANS

IN MOST PEOPLE'S MINDS, the racial integration of the American armed forces first occurred during the Korean War on orders from President Truman.* They would be surprised to learn that the first American army, the Continental Army, that fought the British in the American Revolution, was racially integrated.† At the outbreak of war Washington thought he would have no trouble filling the ranks with willing, fit white men. He ordered that "neither Negroes, boys unable to bear arms, nor old men unfit to endure the fatigues of the campaign, are to be enlisted."[18] However, within a few months, General Washington, like many leaders to follow, would have to decide between his biases and victory on the battlefield. When it became all too apparent that he could not enlist adequate numbers of white men, he decided to accept the services of black men as soldiers. He wrote the Continental Congress to inform them that he had begun to accept "free negroes" [sic] as paid soldiers, but added he realized this was a departure of the vote of the war council that had directed him when enlisting soldiers to "reject all slaves & by a great Majority [sic] to reject Negroes altogether," and ended, "[I]f disapproved of by Congress, I will put a stop to it."[19] Congress wisely allowed him to continue enlisting black men, thereby obtaining enough troops to defeat the British. However, once the war was won, it was decided that blacks and whites serving together was bad for morale, and the practice was ended for decades.

> "I told him [Lt. Colonel Campbell C. Johnson] 'Eleanor [Roosevelt] says we gotta take in Negroes, and we are just scared to death, we've never had any in [the Marine Corps], we don't know how to handle them, we are afraid of them.'"
> —General Ray A. Robinson [20]

All branches of the military had high-ranking personnel who resisted racial segregation, even after President Harry S. Truman signed Executive Order 9981, which read:

---

* I focus on the integration of African-American troops into the U.S. military because there was never an organized outcry at the idea of including Americans of Asian decent or other racial groups like there was when it was suggested that blacks and whites serve in the same units.

† The famous painting of General George Washington crossing the Delaware River with his troops portrays a black soldier to the left of Washington.

Whereas it is essential that there be maintained in the armed services of the United States the highest standards of democracy, with equality of treatment and opportunity for all those who serve in our country's defense:

Now, therefore, by virtue of the authority vested in me as President of the United States, and as Commander in Chief of the armed services, it is hereby ordered as follows:

1. It is hereby declared to be the policy of the President that there shall be equality of treatment and opportunity for all persons in the armed services without regard to race, color, religion or national origin.* This policy shall be put into effect as rapidly as possible, having due regard to the time required to effectuate any necessary changes without impairing efficiency or morale.†

Two years after the order, the Army had opened a mere seven more military occupations to Negroes.[21] Morris J. MacGregor Jr., of the historical division of the Joint Chiefs of Staff, described the resistance to complying with integration.

Resisting the pressure for change was a solid block of officials in the services which held out for the retention of traditional policies of racial exclusion or segregation. Professed loyalty to military tradition was all too often a cloak for prejudice, and prejudice, of course, was prevalent in all the services just as it was in American society. At the same time traditionalism simply reflected the natural inclination of any large, inbred bureaucracy to preserve the privileges and order of any earlier time. Basically, the military traditionalists—that is, most senior officials and commanders of the armed forces and their allies in Congress—took the position that black servicemen were difficult to train and undependable in battle.[22]

White military leaders claimed Negro troops would degrade mission effectiveness because blacks were difficult to train (stupid), could not be kept from falling asleep (lazy), could not be trusted to remain at their positions (irresponsible), and were fearful at night (cowards). [23]

---

* Equality based on sex was not mentioned.
† Most historians agree that "as rapidly as possible" turned out to require the formation of another committee and over twenty years of effort.

For years white military leaders attempted to control the influence of African Americans through three methods. First, the standards for enlistment for blacks were set higher than the standards for whites. Secondly, quotas that limited the number of blacks who would be permitted to enlist, regardless of their qualifications or the need for personnel, were imposed. The Marine quota was one black for every thirty whites accepted.[24] Even following the attack on Pearl Harbor, medical examiners were told to disqualify "colored applicants" during their enlistment physicals.[25] Major General Thomas Holcomb publicly declared that Negroes did not have the "right to enlist in the Marines" and "If it were a question of having a Marine Corps of 5,000 whites or 250,000 Negroes, I would rather have the whites."[26]

Restricting the roles blacks could fulfill controlled those blacks who managed to enlist. Policies forbid them from obtaining flight training, serving on combat ships, or being honor guards at military funerals. They were not allowed into positions of authority where they might come in contact with white civilians, since whites would object to being subject to orders from blacks. The Navy even went so far as to form the Stewards' Branch, whose all-black members served white officers as butlers and drivers. Even when the Navy had over 7,500 unfilled openings for stewards, no whites were assigned these duties.[27] There would not be a white steward until 1953.

Black soldiers were not part of the occupational forces in Germany after World War II, because American officials did not want to offend German citizens who viewed nonwhites as inferior.

Another reason for restricting where African Americans could serve was the fear that they would be better treated by the citizens of the host country than they were by their fellow Americans, which would make them less subservient when they returned to the States. Furthermore, there was the risk that they would be sexual with white women. When asked for guidance on how to respond to African-American military personnel who were seeking permission to wed white women, European Theater Chaplain L. C. Tiernan announced, "The permission to marry in such a case would be to create a state of concubinage* which

---

* "concubine n. a woman who lives with a man and has a sexual relationship with him but is not married to him." Encarta World English Dictionary, 1999.

is definitely bad for social conditions and does reflect discredit on the service."[28] These interracial marriages would not be seen as legitimate by many state governments when the soldier returned home with his new bride. Alvin M. Owsley, commander of the American Legion, wrote to General Dwight D. Eisenhower to complain that if these men dared to return to America, they "very likely are on their way to be hanged or to be burned alive at public lynchings by the white men of the South."[29]

As late as the 1960s, national cemeteries were segregated by race. When the National Association for the Advancement of Colored People (NAACP) complained that the practice of segregated military cemeteries was "un-American and un-democratic," the quartermaster general explained that to open all sections of the national cemeteries to the dead of all races would "constitute a breach of faith with the next of kin of those now interred."[30]

Historically, military commanders had directed military personnel to comply with local standards such as using the "whites only" or "colored only" drinking fountains. In 1956, the Secretary of the Air Force, Harold E. Talbott, informed military commanders they were to promote good relations with local authorities by "requiring" servicemen to conform with local law and custom, "regardless of their own convictions or personal beliefs."[31] A black Air Force pilot stationed at Craig Air Force Base who refused to comply with Alabama State law by moving to the rear of the bus and was discharged from the service.[32]

In 1962, President John F. Kennedy announced the creation of the President's Committee on Equality of Opportunity in the Armed Forces. It went further than had President Truman's Committee in that it recommended that military base commanders stop complying with the racist traditions of the local communities near the bases.

Fortunately, not everyone resisted the racial integration of the military. Major General Laurence S. Kuter boldly informed his subordinates, "Judgment, leadership, and ingenuity are demanded. Commanders who cannot cope with the integration of Negroes into formerly white units or activities will have no place in the Air Force structure."[33] In 1963, the office of the Secretary of Defense, on the fifteenth anniversary of Truman's executive order, sent out a directive that read in part: "Every military commander has the responsibility to oppose discriminatory practices affecting his men and their dependents and to foster equal opportunity for them, not only in areas under his immediate control, but also in nearby communities where they may live or gather in off-duty hours."[34]

As this brief history illustrates, a major lesson that can be learned from the process of racial integration is that change takes time.

> *"The armed forces of the United States cannot now reverse the process that has made blacks full partners in the racially integrated military establishment. Nor is there any incentive to do so. Racial integration, considered a dangerous social experiment as recently as the 1940's, has worked, improving the morale and efficiency of all the services."*—Bernard C. Nalty[35]

Comparing the Racial Integration of the Military and the Acceptance of Women and Homosexuals Serving

J. H. Anderson protested: "Advocates of putting women in combat and maintaining gender-integrated boot camp often cite the racial integration of the armed forces as precedent. This approach is fundamentally flawed. Restrictions preventing women from serving in infantry, armor, and artillery units in no way are comparable to odious discrimination, based on race. Despite the fact that skin color, unlike gender, has no bearing on a unit's military potential, proponents of gender-integrated basic training and women in combat have appropriated civil rights terminology, to mute concerns over their potential costs to military cohesion and readiness."[36]

A similar argument was made by General Colin L. Powell, Chairman of the Joint Chiefs of Staff: "I can assure you I need no reminders concerning the history, African Americans in the defense of their Nation and the tribulations they faced. I am a part of that history. Skin color is a benign, nonbehavioral characteristic. Sexual orientation is perhaps the most profound of human behavioral characteristics. Comparison of the two is a convenient but invalid argument."[37] General Powell dismissed the comparison between race and sexual orientation, just as Mr. Anderson discounted the comparison of race and sex. But no racist would agree that race is a benign characteristic. Try telling a member of the Ku Klux Klan that race is a neutral characteristic. To a racist, race is *the* defining characteristic of a person. Similarly, to someone who is sexist, sex is the defining characteristic of a person.

The arguments used to discriminate against African Americans are strikingly similar, if not identical, to the arguments currently used to discriminate against women and homosexuals. When African Americans sought to join the armed forces during World Wars I and II, military leadership limited the number of black men who could enlist and restricted their roles to stewards, drivers, and laborers. When women made efforts to join the military, the leadership ensured that female personnel would not exceed 2 percent of the ranks. Women's roles were restricted to nursing and secretarial work. The ban on women serving in combat roles has caused bitterness in female personnel, who have objected to not being allowed to fully serve, while simultaneously causing male personnel to resent women getting stateside or rear echelon posting that did not take them away from family for long periods of time or place them in hardship situations. The identical dynamic was identified in 1944 by James Forrestal, then Secretary of the Navy: "The Negroes resent the fact that they are not assigned to general service billets, and white personnel resent the fact that Negroes have been given less hazardous assignments ashore."[38]

Female personnel have been discriminated against when they engaged in behaviors that are not stereotypically feminine, such as being too assertive. In 1945 Lieutenant Colonel Marcus H. Ray complained that white officers, particularly those from the South, promoted Negro enlisted men who conformed to racist stereotypes, but those who exhibited attributes normally associated with leadership potential, such as self-reliance and self-respect, were viewed as uppity and punished.[39]

In the recent past women were prevented from being in positions of authority in the military, particularly those where they would out-rank male personnel. Into the 1960s women in the Army were not allowed to command men or rise higher than the rank of colonel.[40] From 1922 to 1932 blacks were excluded from the Navy by a clause in enlistment regulations; Naval leaders claimed integration was impractical, since blacks would be "unable to maintain discipline among white subordinates with the result that teamwork, harmony, and ship's efficiency" would suffer.[41]

Initially, when it was proposed that female personnel be admitted to West Point, a "separate but equal" proposal was presented as an alternative to full integration.[42] This was also the tactic racial segregationists used to keep African Americans from fully being a part of American society.

Until recently, women have been banned from getting training in many military occupations because they would not be allowed to put these types of training into practice since they were forbidden from serving in combat zones. In the past the Navy insisted that blacks could not be allowed to obtain certain training because the Navy's "training and distribution system demanded that a man in any particular rating be available for any duty required of that rating in any ship or activity in the Navy."[43]

A nearly identical pattern of objection to accepting the existence of homosexual personnel has existed in military thinking. Military leaders claim that known homosexuals will damage morale, be rejected by their comrades, and be ineffective leaders. Major Randel Webb, USMC warned, "The services have adopted policies opposing homosexuals primarily because they are a threat to good order and discipline. . . . Homosexuals would be harassed, and discriminated against. . . . [There would be] morale and retention problems that would be caused by people who leave in disgust, and reduced effectiveness of homosexual officers and NCOs handling contemptuous subordinates. . . ."[44] Identical claims were made concerning interactions between blacks and whites. When whites balked at having to work alongside blacks they were reminded by higher-ups that "our prejudices must be subordinated to our traditional unfailing obedience to orders"[45] The Bureau of Naval Personnel assigned white officers from the South to command black sailors because of their "understanding" of how to interact with "Negro sailors." There was even an official pamphlet released by the Bureau of Naval Personnel titled *Guide to the Command of Negro Personnel*.[46]

Opponents of women and homosexuals in the military have insisted that in order for the military to function it must have cohesion. Certainly being able to function as a unit is essential to military success. However, military research has shown that effective cohesion is not necessarily the result of every member of the group being the same. The office of the Secretary of Defense and the National Defense Research Institute

identified two important forms of cohesion: social cohesion, or camaraderie, which occurs when members of a group are buddies and enjoy
spending time together; and task cohesion that occurs when members
of a unit are committed to a common goal. Ideally, a unit would have
both types of cohesion, but task cohesion is a better predictor of success
than social cohesion.[47]

It is clear the military has made progress in overcoming racial stereotypes and discrimination. Both the military and America as a society are
the better for it. African-Americans males have proven themselves and
been accepted into the military, and eventually so too will women and
homosexuals. Many other countries have already stopped discriminating against female and homosexual military personnel. In almost all
cases policy changes have come about due to pressure from outside the
military establishment. This pressure has come primarily from grass-roots
organizations of family members, supportive political representatives, and
discharged service personnel. In all cases these changes have met with
resistance from within the military and conservative civilian groups.[48]
Despite this resistance, no country that has eliminated their ban on
openly homosexual personnel serving has reversed this decision, nor
have any of their armed forces collapsed.

It appears that the military is one of the last bastion of homophobia
in America. In 1995 only 4 percent of Fortune 500 companies provided
domestic partner benefits for gay couples. Only ten years later, 43 percent of
these companies provided such benefits. Of the top fifty companies, all but
one provide nondiscrimination protections for their gay employees.[49]

In 2002, when reporters were doing a story on whether baseball was
"ready for gay players," they asked Yankees pitcher Mike Mussina if he
would accept a gay teammate. He responded, "I'm going to make the
assumption that I already have."[50]

Many colleges and universities offer courses on homosexuality.
DePaul University, a Catholic school, offers so many courses on the
topic that students can minor in "Lesbian, Gay, Bisexual, Transgendered,
and Queer Studies."[51]

More and more religious organizations are accepting homosexuals as
full members. Go to Texas, not exactly a hotbed of liberal thinking, and
you'll find the Dallas Cathedral of Hope, one of the largest religious struc-

tures in the country, with close to 4,000 predominantly gay congregants. One of the largest organizations for gays in the country is the Metropolitan Community Church, with over 40,000 active members. Nearly every faith now has an explicitly gay organization associated with it, such as Dignity for gay Catholics and Bet Mishpachah for gay Jews. In many mainstream Protestant churches, and among Reform Jews, such groups don't exist because the integration of gay believers is now commonplace. In the words of Andrew Sullivan, "These groups bring gays together in a context where sexuality is less a feature of identity than faith, where the interaction of bodies is less central than the community of souls."[52]

SIMILAR OBJECTIONS TO HOMOSEXUALS AND AFRICAN AMERICANS SERVING IN THE MILITARY

African Americans

- Their inclusion will lead to violence.
- Their inclusion is a social experiment.
- Their inclusion is being imposed on an unwilling military by civilians.
- They are naturally inferior.
- Their inclusion will damage the morale of Caucasians. Caucasians should not be forced to share quarters with racial inferiors.
- They will disrupt the effectiveness of the military because whites will refuse to take orders from "coons."

Homosexuals

- Their inclusion will lead to violence.
- Their inclusion is a social experiment.
- Their inclusion is being imposed on an unwilling military by civilians.
- They are unnatural.
- Their inclusion will damage the morale of heterosexuals.
- Heterosexuals should not be forced to share quarters with homosexuals.
- They will disrupt the effectiveness of the military because real men will refuse to take orders from "fags."

WHO'S IN CHARGE HERE?

MUCH OF THE TIME the military changes only when required to do so by the civilian government, and even then reluctantly, even defiantly. When writing about the reluctance of the military to take direction from the government, Alfred McCoy quipped, "We should not ask why the military 'rebels against its civilian masters, but why it ever obeys them.' The answer to this latter question is obvious: the military obeys only when it wants to."[53] But let all of us, military and civilian, always keep in mind that since the founding of America the military has always been subject to the civilian government, not the other way around. Secretary of the Army Togo West reminded all concerned, "The fact is that the United States Army does not belong to me or to the Secretary of Defense. As proud as we are of them, it does not belong to our soldiers or our NCOs or our officers. It belongs to the American people. And as such, it should espouse the values of the people to whom it belongs."[54]

POP QUIZ

Identify That Dangerous Group

Does the quotation refer to African Americans, women, or homosexuals?

1. "One of the surest ways to break down the morale of the Army and to destroy its efficiency is to integrate [them]."[55]

2. "The lifeblood of a soldier is masculinity, bravery, and gallantry. The battlefield soldier is inspired to risk all by fighting with comrades whose attributes conform to his view of manhood.... And it is inarguable that the majority of a fighting force would be psychologically and emotionally deflated by the close presence of [them]."[56]

3. "The big problems arise after work or training hours, in living quarters and social events."[57]

4. "The stability of the Army came first; changes would have to be made slowly, without risking the menace of disruption. An attempt to mix [them] in the Army seemed to most officers a dangerous move bordering on irresponsibility."[58]

5. "Maybe you could find one [of them] in 10,000 who could lead in combat, but [that person] would be a freak, and the Military Academy is not being run for freaks."[59]

6. "Allowing them in would destroy the Marine Corps, something no enemy has been able to do in over two hundred years."[60]

7. "Many inside the military think their institution has suffered too many hits in recent years. The institution already faces fundamental changes and cut backs and more change now will be hard to accept."[61]

8. Their attempt to join the Corps is merely an effort "to break into a club that doesn't want them." Their admission to the Corps would be "absolutely tragic." Rather than trying to be Marines they should "satisfy their aspirations" by serving in the Army.[62]

9. "I would never openly harass [them,] but I hope they understand they are not welcome here."[63]

10. I would be unwilling to serve in the military "with a _____ by my side. Rather I should die a thousand times, and see Old Glory trampled in the dirt never to rise again, than to see this beloved land of ours become degraded by _____."[64]

11. "In these times of major crises throughout the world it is a mistake to try to provide social reforms for the armed services. . . . The result may be to injure them at a time when the world looks to us for strength and courage."[65]

12. Allowing them in "will increase the rate of crime committed by service [members], including rape and sodomy."[66] "To change would destroy morale, and impair preparations for national defense."[67]

13. "The incidence of syphilis, gonorrhea, chancre, and all other venereal diseases is appallingly higher among [them]."[68]

14. "To survive in a killing field, a warrior has to believe he's invincible, that he's wearing golden armor; that he can buck 1,000-to-1 odds and live. To think that way, he has to be macho. Fairly or unfairly, [they] threaten that macho. When it goes, the warrior starts thinking, 'maybe I won't make it.' And from that moment, the unit goes to hell."[69]

15. "In an infantry battalion is the very last place they would be put. There is no branch of the service that requires more character and a higher degree of morale than the infantry."[70]

16. "The close and intimate conditions of life aboard ships, the necessity for the highest possible degree of unity and esprit-de-corps;

the requirement of morale—all these demand that nothing be done which may adversely affect the situation."[71]

17. "[T]he service's enormous size and power should not be used for social experiment, especially during a war."[72]

18. "Morale in the armed forces is a fragile asset. It can be instantly destroyed even by those acting with the best of intentions. History has proven that the degradation of morale quickly leads to the erosion of discipline, diminished performance, poor retention, readiness reduction and recruiting difficulties."[73]

19. "The minute [they] are introduced into general service...the high type of man that we have been getting for the last twenty years will go elsewhere...."[74]

20. "How many men would choose, of their own accord, that their closest associates in sleeping quarters, at mess, and in a gun crew should be ____? How many would accept such conditions, if required to do so, without resentment and just as a matter of course?"[75]

21. "I submit, Mr. President, that if there is any one fundamental and sacred right inherent in every individual in a free state it is the right of choosing the type of people with whom we will associate in our daily lives."[76]

22. "[They] are here at West Point, and they are here to stay. Anyone who cannot support that institutional goal can see me, and I will make arrangements for him to leave."[77]

23. "I found out a lot of them were a lot more cowardly than I expected. I found out some of them were more animalistic than any people I knew. I found out that they really didn't have their shit together."[78]

24. "Civil society protects individual rights, but the military, which protects civil society, must be governed by different rules."[79]

Bonus Question

"It would be ruinous to the morals and disciple of the Corps."[80]

What is "it"?

WHAT THE MILITARY CAN DO TO REDUCE SEXUAL ABUSE AND SECONDARY VICTIMIZATION

IMPROVE ACCOUNTABILITY

UNLIKE CIVILIAN LAW ENFORCEMENT agencies, the Pentagon historically did not keep comprehensive statistics on sexual assaults. In 1988, Congress ordered the military to create a database of all criminal incidents, including sexual assault. Eight years later the Pentagon had failed to develop a database but made a commitment to do so. In 2003 the Pentagon said it was still working on the project. This failure to collect the most basic of data indicates the military is not interested in taking meaningful action on the problem, Furthermore, how can the military determine if its efforts to reduce sexual abuse are effective if it doesn't even have baseline figures?[1]

> *"All organizations depend on the existence of shared meaning and interpretations of reality, which facilitate coordinated action."*—Warren Bennis and Burt Nanus[2]

If the military sincerely wants to reduce sexual abuse in the military, it will need to reduce the two major underlying causes: misogyny and homophobia. During the civil rights movement of the 1960s, Professor Oscar Handlin distinguished between the concepts of desegregation and integration.[3] He viewed desegregation as the removal of legal barriers to equal treatment. Jim Crow laws were widespread in America after

World War II, which made it illegal for Americans of different racial groups to use the same public facilities—drinking fountains, toilets, and swimming pools.

Desegregation can be accomplished by merely signing a bill into law; one day it is illegal for African Americans to ride at the front of the bus, and the next day it is legal.

Integration is much more difficult because it requires that the group formerly discriminated against be provided with equal opportunity in terms of training, rank, promotion, and all other forms of treatment. In others words, they are not merely tolerated, they are actually accepted.

> **integration**—"1. The process of opening a group, community, place, or organization to all, regardless of race, ethnicity, religion, gender, or social class; 2. becoming an accepted member of a group or community; 3. a combination of parts or objects that work together well."[4]

Segregation is obvious, but lack of integration is subtler. The uniforms and equipment issued servicewomen reduce their full functioning. It took until 2004 after much complaining from servicewomen, for the Navy to make skirts optional for female personnel. Up until then, the dress-blue skirt had a narrow cut and no kick pleat, making it nearly impossible to run in it.[5] What motivated Navy leaders to place the gender-role tradition of females in skirts over the safety and effectiveness of personnel? Anyone who looks at most military clothing for males can readily see that function is valued over fashion. Yet military leaders have not seen fit to provide servicewomen with clothing designed to make functioning in the field easier and more comfortable. Currently, military clothing requires women to pull down their lower clothing to squat to urinate. Civilian clothing designers such as Workables for Women already manufacture and sell to civilians heavy-duty clothing with full-length front zippers or wrap-around openings that permit urination without disrobing. But the military has not made use of such practical designs. Even simpler solutions exist but are not utilized. Retail sporting goods stores carry products such as the Freshette™ that permit women to urinate while standing.[6] Some Army exchanges carry these products for sale for female personnel to purchase at their own expense, but what prevents the military from making these devices standard issue to all female personnel?

The 80/20 Principle

The 80/20 principle proposes that for most any condition approximately 20 percent of the people are responsible for 80 percent of its occurrences. Twenty percent of drivers cause 80 percent of traffic accidents, and 20 percent of criminals are responsible for 80 percent of the crimes committed. Likewise, when it comes to positive outcomes, 20 percent of the workers do 80 percent of the work.[7]

To better understand how this concept applies to the military, let's examine another uniformed hierarchical organization licensed to use deadly force—the Los Angeles Police Department. Between 1986 and 1990, 1,800 officers were accused of excessive use of force or other improper tactics. This was approximately 20 percent of the total police force. Of those who were accused of abuse, most (1,400) had only one or two allegations made against them in that four-year period. However, there were 183 officers that had four or five charges, forty-four who had six or seven charges, sixteen who had eight or more charges, and one had sixteen accusations. One officer had thirteen allegations of excessive force made against him, twenty-five documented accounts of inappropriate use of force, including a shooting. Another officer was found to have on his record nineteen nonviolence complains, six excessive use of force allegations, ten police-witnessed inappropriate use of force reports, and three shootings. Still another officer's file contained thirty-five officer-witnessed reports of inappropriate use of force, including striking an arrestee on the back of the neck with the butt of a shotgun "for no apparent reason while arrestee was kneeling and handcuffed," and beating a thirteen-year-old handcuffed arrestee, throwing him from a chair, and kicking him in the back and side of the head.[8] These officers were permitted by their peers and superiors to continue to remain on the force despite their inappropriate behavior being witnessed and documented. The L.A.P.D. did not need new policies; the rules already existed, were clear and known. What was needed was compliance to the guidelines already in place. What the citizens of L.A. needed to protect them from bad cops were good cops doing their job and holding their fellow officers accountable.

The military can learn a valuable lesson from the mistakes of the L.A.P.D. If the leadership wants to reduce sexual abuse within the ranks it could do two things. One, identify the 20 percent of those who commit 80 percent of the sexual abuse and give special attention to modifying their behavior, or failing that, discharging them. Two, identify the 20 percent of the personnel who have the greatest impact on the other 80 percent of their comrades and utilize their ability to change military culture to make it one in which sexual abuse is viewed as antithetical to the values of a free democracy that has been defended by noble men and women who fought and died to protect it.

Policy Versus Attitude

A report issued in 2005 by the Defense Task Force on Sexual Harassment and Violence at the Military Service Academies made forty-four recommendations to reduce sexual abuse, including changing the culture of the military academies by increasing the percentage of female cadets and midshipmen; making women more visible as leaders at the academies by increasing the number of female officers and noncommissioned officers in key posts; and emphasizing the value of women in the military. As an example of not valuing the contributions of women, they noted the course on military history at West Point did not once mention the existence of the Women's Army Corps. The report mentioned that although the military academies provide incoming students with sexual harassment and abuse prevention programs, they are poorly designed, offered at inconvenient times, and usually taught by student instructors, which indicate to new students that the administration views this course as mandated but unimportant.[9]

Whenever policy conflicts with attitude, the victor will be attitude. The culture of any organization is more dependent on the attitudes and behaviors of its members, particularly its leaders, than on written policies. In their best selling book *In Search of Excellence: Lessons from America's Best Run Companies*, authors Thomas Peters and Robert Waterman Jr. insisted the most effective way for managers to motivate their employees to behave in a specific manner was for the managers to behave in that manner. In 1987 the Secretary of the Navy instructed the Commandant of the Marines to convene a task force on how servicewomen were treated.

The task force reported that sexism pervaded the Corps; the policies that were already in place were satisfactory, but the problems were a result of the "attitude of the Corps towards women" and recommended corrective action from the command level on down. Following release of the report in testimony before Congress, Lieutenant General John I. Hudson stated, "Our policies are sound, but our actions in carrying them out were in some instances impeded by attitudes." He suggested that the "Commandant stress the significance and importance of a positive attitude towards women."[10] The Commandant, General Alfred M. Gray Jr., immediately threw his support behind the task force's recommendations that sexism and harassment would not be tolerated and that women would not be excluded from field assignments. In his words, "Women in the Corps are Marines and will be treated as such—with decency, dignity, and respect." However, after issuing these supportive words, he rejected his senior officers' requests to allow female Marines to serve as embassy guard units or as pilots, or to obtain offensive combat training, because it was "not in keeping with the role of women in the Marine Corps' conduct in war."[11] In other words, women could learn to defend themselves with arms (defense combat training), but not obtain training in attacking the enemy. Conditions haven't changed much since the 1980s; as the 2005 Task Force on Sexual Harassment and Violence at the Military Service Academies report showed, little meaningful change had occurred in the attitude of the military toward women.

UTILIZE THE POWER OF CONTENT

IN 1964, AN INFAMOUS CRIME took place in New York City. Kitty Genovese was chased and stabbed by an assailant. There were three attacks over the course of thirty minutes that were witnessed by thirty-eight people from the safety of their windows. None of them telephoned the police or sought to intervene in any way. The apathy shown by Kitty Genovese's neighbors to her deadly plight was seen by many as merely another indication of the emotionally cold, dehumanizing effects of living in a big city. A New Yorker provided this explanation: "It is almost a matter of psychological survival, if one is surrounded and pressed by millions of people, to prevent them from constantly impinging on you, and the only way to do this is to ignore them as often as possible. Indifference to one's neighbor and his troubles is a conditioned reflex in life in New York as it is in other big cities."[12] Many people accepted this explanation of the events. However, two New Yorkers, who also happened to be social psychologists, were convinced there might be more to what happened (or, more accurately, didn't happen). They conducted a series of staged "emergencies" to see if anyone would come to the aid of the person in need. They had a student alone in a room pretend to have an epileptic seizure. In 85 percent of the cases in which there was only one person nearby that person rushed to offer assistance upon overhearing the seizure. However, when there were four persons overhearing the seizure, aid was offered only 31 percent of the time. They found 75 percent of those who witnessed smoke seeping out from under a door would report it to authorities, but only if they were the only person witnessing it. If there were others present, only 38 percent would make a report.[13] Drs. Latane and Darley concluded that when people witness a potential problem and are in a group they believe their responsibility for taking appropriate action is diffused, and the more people present, the more each individual believes his or her own responsibility is reduced. Each person assumes either someone else has already taken the necessary action or an actual problem must not exist because otherwise someone would have taken action by now. In other words, to return to the murder of Genovese, "[T]he lesson is not that no one called despite the fact that thirty-eight people heard her scream; it is that no one called *because* thirty-eight people heard her scream. Ironically, had she been attacked on a lonely street with just one witness, she might have lived."[14] In summary, people are sensitive to the context of an event, so much so that it will drastically affect what they will do or not do, even when it is a matter of life and death. Military personnel are affected by the power of context at least as much as civilians.

Military leaders, like most people, make the mistake psychologists call the fundamental attribution error (FAE).[15] The FAE is the tendency to interpret other people's behavior based on an overestimation of their fundamental character, while simultaneously underestimating the impact of the context in which the behavior takes place. In other words, "What did you expect? That's the kind of person he is," rather than, "What did you expect, given the situation he was in at the time."

A classic example of this dynamic is the study that became known at the Stanford prison experiment because it was conducted at Stanford University, mentioned earlier but so important that it bears repeating.[16] The researchers constructed a mock prison with three six-by-nine-foot cells with steel-barred doors, and a closet made into a solitary confinement cell. The volunteer subjects were given a battery of psychological tests and those who appeared the healthiest were chosen to participate. Half of the subjects were randomly picked to be guards, given uniforms and dark glasses, and told their role was to keep order in the prison. The other half of the subjects were designated prisoners. Actual officers from the local police department went to these subjects' homes, "arrested" them, and transported them, handcuffed in marked police cars, to the station house where they were photographed and finger printed. Then they were taken, blindfolded, to the "prison" where they were told to strip, given a prison uniform with a number on it, and told that number would serve as their only form of identification for the remainder of their incarceration. Then the researchers stepped back to see what would happen. They were conducting the experiment to see if prisons are ghastly places because they are filled with people whose fundamental characters are rotten, or whether something about the prison environment, the context, turns even decent people nasty.

The subjects were free to do as they pleased. They were under no obligation to do anything at all. Both the guards and the prisoners could have just put in their time sitting around, leaving each other alone. But that is not what happened. The first night, even though the prisoners had done nothing wrong, the guards awoke them at two in the morning and made them perform arbitrary tasks, such as push-ups. The next morning the prisoners rebelled. They tore off their identification numbers and attempted to barricade themselves in their cells. The guards responded by spraying the group with a fire extinguisher, stripping them of their prison garb, leaving them naked, and throwing the perceived leader of the rebellion into solitary confinement. When addressing the prisoners, the guards got right in their faces and screamed at them. Their explanation for these actions was, "It was part of the whole atmosphere of terror."[17] The longer the experiment continued the more abusively the guards behaved. One guard later noted, "I think I was positively creative in terms of my mental cruelty."[18] The guards ordered the prisoners to say to one another "I love you," and march up and down the hall in handcuffs with paper bags over their heads. After only thirty-six hours, one of the prisoners became hysterical and was released. Soon another four were released because of "extreme emotional depression, crying, rage, and acute anxiety." One of the prisoners summarized his experience: "I realize now that no matter how together I thought I was inside my head, my prisoner behavior was often less under my control than I realized."[19] Although the experiment was scheduled to run for two weeks, it was called off after only six days. One of the experimenters noted of both the guards and prisoners, "What we were unprepared for was the intensity of the change and the speed at which it happened."[20] Even the psychologists fell victim to the fundamental attribution error, assuming that the fundamental character of normal, mentally healthy persons would be more powerful than the context in which they found themselves, and were shocked to find that situational dynamics overwhelmed an individual's character in an amazingly short time. This experiment helps explain how basically decent people, given the right context, can be swept up and engage in behavior they normally would not think of doing, such as sexual harassment and even assault. It helps explain the maltreatment of female cadets at the Air Force Academy and the abuse of prisoners at Abu Ghraib.

REDUCE THE STIGMA OF PSYCHOLOGICAL SERVICES

AS HAS BEEN PREVIOUSLY STATED, the military is a society unto itself. Military bases have all of the services that are available in even a small town: financial planners, medical, dental, and psychological treatments are all provided. However, the hypermasculine, gung ho, "Army of one" mentality so common to military personnel makes it less likely personnel will make use of psychological services. According to service personnel, the number one barrier to obtaining psychological services is fear of disapproval by superiors. They fear it will be seen as a sign of weakness, lack of moral character, or moral shortcoming, and prevent career advancement. Those returning from combat in Afghanistan and Iraq, who reported suffering symptoms of Post-Traumatic Stress Disorder reported they would not be seeking psychological services for fear of how it would impair their ability to advance in the military.[21] In 2003, four soldiers returned home from Afghanistan and murdered their wives. None of them had previously sought marriage counseling or other psychological services because they thought to do so would be a sign of weakness and damage their careers.[22]

The military's research shows that utilization of psychological services has a significant, positive impact upon mission readiness and effectiveness. In 1999, the Navy began the Psychologists at Sea program that placed a Navy psychologist on board each of the twelve aircraft carrier battle groups, as well as with expeditionary strike groups. Since the placement of psychologists there has been an 87 percent reduction in the rate of medical evacuations, and the number of administrative separations for reasons of mental health have dropped by over 90 percent during deployments.[23]

PROVIDE SUFFICIENT TREATMENT FOR VICTIMS

RESEARCHERS HAVE FOUND that despite having medical personnel and facilities on base, it is common for military personnel who are victims of sexual abuse not to receive even basic medical examinations for exposure to sexually transmitted diseases or be given pregnancy tests.[24] In 1992, the first inpatient treatment program for women veterans with Post-Traumatic Stress Disorder as the result of combat was opened. It was not until a year later that the program began to also treat women who had been sexually assaulted. Unfortunately there were no arrangements for transportation of the women to the treatment center. The women were expected to arrange and pay to get to the site in California. In 2004, Brigadier General K. C. McClain of the Air Force Education and Training Command looked at sexual assault programs at thirteen installations and found that there was no centralized approach to responding to sexual abuse: "[P]eople were reinventing the wheel . . . the individual commands were left to themselves to come up with policy."[25] For many victims of sexual abuse this lack of policy indicates that the leadership is not concerned about the issue of sexual abuse. Therefore, it is not uncommon for military personnel to seek treatment from civilian treatment providers.* Research by the PTSD International Alliance examined

---

* For descriptions of negative experiences see the personal stories in Part II of Annie, Dorothy, Gloria, Gregory, and Raymond. Paula describes helpful treatment from the VA.

utilization of Veteran Administration hospitals by veterans.[26] They found that 85 percent of the veterans utilized VA facilities for general health care. Nearly 21 percent of them found the care to be "excellent," and 45 percent described the medical care as "good." The remainder reported the care as "fair" (21 percent) or "poor" (13 percent). Although the majority of veterans found the general health services acceptable, when it came to those suffering from Post-Traumatic Stress Disorder (PTSD) the rate of satisfaction was greatly reduced. Most (62.5 percent) of these veterans had sought treatment for their disorder at a VA facility, but only 18 percent believed the treatment for PTSD was effective. The majority (82 percent) of those who had obtained treatment from the VA described the care as inadequate. The most common reasons cited for their dissatisfaction were a lack of knowledge of PTSD on the part of treatment providers and difficulty getting appointments in a timely fashion. Even more disturbing is the fact that 22 percent of those with PTSD stated the VA refused to provide treatment because there was no recorded combat incident (25 percent) or seeking treatment could end the service member's career (2 percent). I wonder how many the cases of PTSD that have no recorded combat incident were the result of sexual abuse.

It would seem reasonable to expect that an organization whose function is the treatment of military personnel would have great expertise when it comes to the treatment of combat trauma, but based on the experiences of these veterans this does not appear to be the case. If the VA staff have not been trained to adequately treat combat trauma, how effective are they at treating the effects of sexual abuse?

CHANGE OUTDATED LAWS

IN 2001, A CIVILIAN PANEL of military law experts called for changes in the statute to reflect the unique impact military rank can have on rape cases. What might seem to be consensual sex between a male officer and female subordinate could be a crime if the superior inappropriately wielded his power to punish the victim. To date, no action on the proposal has been taken.[27]

In 1992, Congress passed the Women's Veterans Health Program Act, which mandated that the Veterans Administration address the needs of female veterans who had been sexually abused but only those who sought assistance within two years of being discharged were eligible for treatment. Unfortunately, those whose symptoms did not develop immediately (delayed onset PTSD), those who did not realize their PTSD symptoms were the result of sexual abuse, and those who were too afraid to seek help within two years, were no longer eligible for treatment.[28]

LEARN FROM PREVIOUS SUCCESSES

WERE THE MILITARY to view sexual abuse as serious a threat to mission readiness as it does drug use, it could likely bring about a similar dramatic decrease in the occurrence of sexual abuse. The military's efforts to control recreational drug use (other than alcohol) have been largely effective. Research indicates that prior to enlistment new recruits use drugs at the same rate as other American high school seniors, but when faced with the policy of zero tolerance, combined with education and monitoring, the rate of drug use drops to 3 percent of active duty personnel.[29]

PROVIDE SUFFICIENT TRAINING

A 2005 DEPARTMENT OF DEFENSE report on the military academics found the course on sexual abuse was too limited and poorly integrated, not graded, and was not conducted during regular class times, indicating to the students that it was not important. Furthermore, issues of sexual abuse were not covered in courses on military leadership and ethics.[30] One measure of the importance of an issue is the amount of training an organization is willing to provide on that topic to its personnel. According to the military's studies, training on sexual abuse is inadequate: "Throughout the Army, soldiers who have been victims of inappropriate sexual behavior have reported incidents to professionals and leaders. These same professionals and leaders have not received sufficient training in working with victims and are left to rely on rudimentary perceptions of how victims want to be treated. As a result, victims are reluctant to report inappropriate behaviors for fear of being re-victimized by the very system that was put in place to deal with their complaints. This reluctance contributes to soldiers' lack of trust and confidence in the chain of command and in Army leaders in general."[31] For years in order to determine if a woman who alleged to have been sexually abused should be believed, the Air Force used a checklist developed by Charles

McDowell, a civilian with no specific training in sexual assault, who routinely told the military investigators he was training that "50 percent to 60 percent of rape claims are false."[32] He made this claim despite decades of psychological and criminal justice literature that consistently place the rate of false claims in the single digits.

ELIMINATE STRUCTURAL CONFLICTS OF INTEREST

OUTSIDE THE MILITARY, independent prosecutors determine whether a suspect will stand trial for rape. In the armed forces, commanders make those decisions by weighing evidence involving personnel under their supervision. According to Lynn Hecht Schafran, a former member of a Pentagon advisory group on women's issues, the commanding officer's role in criminal cases discourages victims from filing complaints and blocks valid charges from being prosecuted.[33]

In the 1980s there was a significant change in the way the Air Force responded to suspected substance abuse: Referrals for assessment and treatment became mandatory. Previously, referral for such services was at the discretion of the individual's commander. The discretionary policy had created an interesting pattern.

> Discretionary referral had the potential to set the "bar" quite high to determine how bad is bad enough. Referrals tended to be delayed in identification of substance abuse problems. Individuals in their first term of enlistment (generally the first four years of active duty) and, interestingly enough, individuals nearing retirement were the primary referral groups. Referring those nearing retirement appeared to reflect the extent the individual's alcohol use disorder was known by the commander but had not been addressed earlier. Referrals of mid-career individuals were rare.[34]

This discrepancy was due largely to the importance placed on an individual's military record remaining clean. If someone wishing to make a career of the military were to be referred for assessment, it could easily damage the chances for promotion. Therefore, commanders were overlooking indications of problems until an individual's problem became so severe that it was nearly impossible to ignore. Although some commanders feared this change in policy reduced their authority, it actually came to be seen as a benefit to them, since they were not in a position where they had to pre-diagnose a problem for which they were not trained but could rely on properly trained staff to determine the appropriate course of action.

STOP BLAMING THE VICTIMS

CONSISTENTLY RESEARCH HAS FOUND that military personnel do not report sexual abuse because they fear they will only receive more mistreatment: "Unfortunately, in some instances, soldiers who reported sexually inappropriate behavior to their chain of command or other agencies have been mistreated. Most prominently, such mistreatment included insensitive questioning of the soldier victim, together with the implication that, somehow, the victim, not the perpetrator, created the problem."[35]

Not only are individual victims blamed for the abuse they suffer, but entire groups of people are accused of being the root of problem: "What do you expect when women are permitted to be where they don't belong and aren't welcome?" Or "That's what happens when gays are allowed in the military."

Unfortunately, all too often comrades treat the alleged perpetrator of sexual abuse with respect while the alleged victim is treated with disrespect and isolated. Superiors sometimes reassign the victim in order to "get rid of the problem," while the perpetrator's routine remains undisturbed.

Gwen Dreyer's father and grandfather had graduated from Annapolis, and she had wanted to attend the academy since she was fourteen years old. When she enrolled, she knew many of her male classmates had a misogynistic attitude, even though women had been attending the school for fourteen years. She tolerated them watching pornographic movies in their rooms, exposing their penises to her, and telling her she was "fucking ugly." One night she awoke to find two comrades standing over her. They dragged her from her bed into the men's lavatory, handcuffed her to a urinal, pulled out their penises and threatened to urinate on her. A number of other men watched the events and took no action. One man got a camera so he could photograph what was taking place. When Dreyer complained about the event, her superior showed her the photographs taken during the assault and insisted they showed she was not upset by what was happening. Dreyer was accused of staging a phony assault, as a ploy on her part to leave the academy because she had allegedly been pressured by her father to enroll in the school against her will.[36]

STOP PROTECTING OFFENDERS WITH INTRAMILITARY IMMUNITY: MODIFY THE FERES DOCTRINE

CIVILIANS WHO EXPERIENCE sexual harassment in their workplace can, under Title VII, sue their employer. Civilians who work for the military, when sexually harassed on the job, can sue their employer. Kelly Theriot was a civilian attorney working at the Madigan Army Medical Center. She accused a colonel of sexual harassment, and the Army settled her claim for $500,000.* Had she been a military lawyer working at the same site, with the same responsibilities and the same supervisor, she would have been unable to hold her employer responsible since service members who are sexually harassed by other service members, peers or superiors, cannot sue for damages because of the 1950 Feres Doctrine.[37]

To further illustrate the point, let us examine two nearly identical cases. The first case involves Captain Tammy S. Blakey, a pilot for Continental Airlines who complained that flight crews routinely left pornographic materials in the cockpit, and glued pornographic photos on the bottom of cockpit drawers, in-flight manuals, and other places within the aircraft. Captain Blakey sued Continental Airlines for not taking action and was awarded $350,000 for lost wages and $500,000 for emotional distress. Had she been a military pilot she could not have brought suit when her complaints were ignored.

The second case involves First Lieutenant Julie Clemm, who was assigned to the 90th Fighter Squadron deployed to patrol the no-fly zone over Bosnia. She complained to the Air Force inspector general that pornographic movies were shown on base, an inflated female sex doll was displayed at the Squadron Thanksgiving party, and pornography was posted in public areas of the base and in aircraft. Her complaints were ignored, and she was unable to take civil action because of the

---

* The offender has since been promoted to general.

Feres Doctrine.

Dorothy Mackey's story in Part II also illustrates this strange state of affairs. She alleged that her superiors had sexually abused her, and filed suit when the military did not take sufficient action.[38] In civilian settings, when licensed mental health professionals obtain malpractice insurance, the policy will provide payments for professional mistakes, but will not cover criminal acts such as sexual abuse of patients. But the servicemen Mackey accused of sexually abusing her were given free legal representation by the Department of Justice. These attorneys successfully argued that the alleged offenders were acting within the scope of their employment as government employees and therefore could not be sued. The federal court ruled that even though some of the acts had taken place off government property and after normal working hours the offenders was still within the scope of their employment. The defense attorneys convinced the court to substitute the United States of America as the defendant, replacing the alleged offenders. In other words, the victim was now suing the United States government rather than two individuals. The court then concluded that since the American government was now the defendant, there was no grounds for a suit because under the Feres Doctrine, "the Government is not liable under the Federal Tort Claims Act for injuries to servicemen where the injuries arise out of or are in the course of activity incident to service."[39] The intended goal of the Feres Doctrine was to prevent officers from being sued for the outcome of orders given in the usual and customary course of running a military organization. But the court determined that even when a superior officer is using his position of authority to sexually abuse a subordinate the victim cannot take legal action. The court determined that "Mackey's allegations go directly to the 'management' of the military; they call into question basic choices about the discipline, supervision, and control of a serviceman and are therefore allegations, about which we are prohibited from inquiring." A supervisor sexually abusing someone of lower rank is very different from an officer ordering a subordinate into harm's way in the course of a military action. The first is an illegitimate use of power and therefore ought to be punishable, while the second is a necessary function of military leaders and ought to be protected.

At the end of the twentieth century, when the criminal justice system was unable or unwilling to hold responsible the adults who were sexually abusing children, the civil courts brought the issue to national attention. Only when victims began to prevail in civil suits and obtain awards did organizations, most notably the Catholic Church, begin to take notice and begin meaningful action. The inability of service members to bring suit against those who engage in sexual abuse allows the military to be among the last institutions that systematically protect sexual perpetrators.

DO MORE TO LIVE UP TO THE MILITARY'S STATED VALUES

"All Marines in every instance are expected to employ and live by the principles of responsibility. It means being personally responsible and accountable for one's actions, particularly in relation with other Marines. . . . It means an uncompromising tenacity in guarding the mores and reputation of the world's finest military organization. It means unerring application of the highest standards of personal conduct on the battlefield, in garrison, and on liberty. It means doing nothing to tarnish that proud heritage."—Colonel Humberto "Rod" Rodriguez of the Recruit Training Regiment, to Marines who have just completed basic training.[40]

"The fact is, core values for military leaders and their civilian commander-in-chief remain in effect no matter where they are or what they are doing twenty-four hours a day. When observed by anyone, they must reflect the institution's core values of respect for decency, human dignity, morality, and doing what is right, in or out of uniform, on or off duty."—Admiral Bud Edney, Naval Academy Chair of Leadership[41]

THROUGHOUT THE ENTIRE existence of the American military, leaders of all ranks have stressed to those under their command the importance of having high standards such as the ones mentioned above. These are magnificent ideals, and if they were practiced by all there would be no need for this book.

18

FINAL THOUGHTS

AT LEAST TWO THINGS ought to be clear: Sexual abuse is far too common in the armed forces of America; and the effectiveness and efficiency of the military are gravely compromised by the existence of abuse within the ranks. A significant number of veterans returning from recent wars are experiencing serious mental disorders as a direct result of their experiences in the military. Over 15 percent of veterans retuning from the 1991 Gulf War developed Post Traumatic Stress Disorder.[1] Figures are even higher for veterans returning from Afghanistan and Iraq: 17 percent of them have Post-Traumatic Stress Disorder, Major Depressive Disorder, or Generalized Anxiety Disorder.[2] How many of the symptoms these women and men are experiencing are the result of combat, and how many are suffering from the effects of sexual abuse from their comrades?

Reducing sexual abuse within the ranks is in the best interest of the military. Making the military a safer environment makes it more attractive to potential recruits, and attraction is more cost effective than promotion. Reduction of sexual abuse adds to retention of personnel. In the high-tech military, the cost of training personnel is staggering. It is costly to have to constantly replace and train replacements for personnel who prematurely end their military careers due to sexual abuse. The existence of fewer victims mean fewer financial and emotional costs related to criminal investigations, trials, punishments, and disability claims due to sexual abuse.

Bill Carr, the Deputy Under Secretary for Military Personnel Policy, observed, "It's called the 'voluntary' military, but it's really a 'recruited' military. Walk-ins are only about five percent of our needs. We have to go out and find the other ninety-five percent."[3] With an all-volunteer military, no branch can treat personnel with disdain and hope to survive.

In addition to impacting the lives of American military personnel, reducing sexual abuse within the ranks would improve our image on the world stage. America is very likely to continue to be involved in peacekeeping throughout the foreseeable future. If the U.S. military can't protect its own personnel from one another, how can it be trusted to treat the citizens of other countries with decency?

The military will eventually have to change its stubborn habit of ignoring and covering-up sexual abuse in its ranks. It will do so only when its leaders realize that a culture of misogyny and homophobia is obsolete, not merely because it is morally wrong, but because it negatively affects the ability of the military to fulfill its mission successfully. The sooner they learn this lesson, the closer they will be to creating a more effective and efficient military.

I will let Dr. Donna Dean, a Navy veteran suffering from PTSD as the result of sexual harassment and assault, have the last word. When she and others first publicly disclosed how their comrades had abused them, they were discounted and accused of being nothing more than whining bellyachers. One enraged comrade spitefully exclaimed, "Remember, you all volunteered! None of you were drafted!" To which Dr. Dean retorted, "None of us had volunteered for rape, violence, and dehumanization."[4]

PART II
PERSONAL STORIES

PART II

PERSONAL STORIES

WHAT FOLLOWS ARE GRAPHIC stories of sexual abuse by those who experienced it. Those readers who are survivors of abuse ought to approach these stories with caution, since they are likely to trigger painful memories and emotions. I have included these stories to put a human face on the material covered in Part I. It is all too easy to distance oneself from the impact of sexual abuse by focusing on the facts and figures, and thus lose sight of the terrible toll that sexual abuse takes on people. I also want people who have been sexually abused (and those who have a loved one who has suffered such abuse) to see that they are not alone. Others have walked this difficult road before them, and readers may gain strength and hope through reading the stories of those who came before them.

Some readers will find these stories hard to believe. Others will know their truth all too well. Personally, I wish these stories were not true. However, I have spent too many years listening to clients tell me similar stories to have any doubt that these veterans are writing about actual events. Furthermore, in some cases the veterans sent documentation to support the stories, fearing that otherwise I wouldn't believe them.

I salute the brave women and men whose stories you are about to read.

"An event has happened upon which it is difficult to speak, and impossible to remain silent." —Forgiveness Memorial, Duluth, Minnesota

I came home
No scars on my body
Nothing to show
The wounds inside.
—Gregory Helle, U.S. Army, SP5[1]

Survivor Psalm[2]

I have been victimized.
I was in a fight that was
not a fair fight.
I did not ask for the fight.
I lost.
There is no shame in losing
such fights.
I have reached the stage of
survivor and am no longer a
slave of victim status.
I look back with sadness
rather than hate.
I look forward with hope
rather than despair.
I may never forget, but I need
not constantly remember.
I was a victim.
I am a survivor.
—*Frank Ochberg*

Annie D.

THE WIFE OF A SURVIVOR*

MY NAME IS ANNIE. I'm married to a survivor. Why do I call my husband a survivor? There are a lot of reasons—the biggest one, which has made his life a living hell, was being gang-raped twice during a six-month period during his second hitch in the Army.

This is my second marriage and my husband's fifth. He self-medicated with alcohol a lot during his pervious marriages, so that he wouldn't have to think about what happened to him. He's not drinking anymore. He is trying to work on his problems instead of trying to drown them.

Can you imagine what it's like to want to hold on to, and love, your husband, but you know you can't? I try not to let it bother me too much, but it does. He gets so distant sometimes. He spends a lot of time on the computer by himself. He says it helps take his mind off stuff. But a lot of it is spent looking at porn sites of people doing things he can't do anymore.† That hurts me because sometimes I feel like he would rather be on the computer than be with me. We don't go out much unless we

---

* Annie is the wife of Raymond, whose story begins on page 313. Her name was changed at her request.
† Some survivors of abuse become sexually compulsive or retreat into a world of fantasy, to distract themselves from painful emotions and memories.

have to. He doesn't like crowds and he feels safer at home. I miss going out. I was very active with outside activities before we got married.*

My husband suffers from nightmares, anger, guilt, shame, and other demons that cause him to hurt mentally and emotionally every day. There are times when I get my feelings hurt because I need some sign of emotion or attention from my husband and I don't get it. He is so traumatized by what happened to him that he has a hard time relating to others.

When we first met I thought I had found the man of my dreams. He was so loving, caring, and gentle. Little did I know what horrors hid behind that mask. Finally he let me read the papers on male rape that his counselor had given him. As I read the papers, he stood by the front door waiting for me to throw him out. He had come to think of himself as a throw-away, disposable person. He felt like someone to put out on the curb with the rest of the trash. I guess that's what had happened to him before, not because the others knew what the real problem was, but because they saw what was the result of that problem. I hugged him and told him that it was not his fault. I also told him that we had a problem and I would see that he got the help he needed. He didn't know what to think. It took some time before he could really trust me, but that trust has been building the longer we are together.

I went to work to get him an appointment at our local VA hospital. The result being that they moved him around from one person to another. They had no qualified sexual abuse counselor on staff so they overlooked the cause of his problems and focused only on his alcohol problem, even when he was no longer drinking. Instead of helping, they only made matters worse. He was getting more and more frustrated because they didn't understand why something that happened so long ago was still bothering him. Us.

Finally I suggested we go to someone outside the VA for help. We didn't know how we were going to pay for the treatment, but I knew we had to try. I finally got him in with an experienced sexual abuse counselor. My husband started his long journey to getting the help he needed. Dragging up all those memories was having a terrible affect on

---

* Annie, like many partners of abuse survivors, reduced her own social interactions out of loyalty to her spouse.

him, but he knew it had to be done in order to get better. There were times when I wondered if he would ever get better and if I had made a mistake by marrying him. But I reminded myself how much I loved him and how much he needed my help, my love, and my support.

We finally did get the VA to agree to pay for his outside counselor, only after throwing a lot of fits at the VA and threats to put a piece in the local paper about how they mistreated the veterans. I also got our U.S. Congressman involved with our problems at the VA Now he sees a very caring, qualified counselor at the local VET Center. He feels comfortable with this counselor and feels like he may finally get the help he needs.

I get so angry with the VA because they won't validate what happened to him. We have filed with the VA for disability from Post-Traumatic Stress Disorder; which he suffers very badly, but they turned him down. "Things like that don't happen in the military," they claim! They just treated him like he was making the whole thing up because he never told anyone at the time and he has waited all these years to file a claim.[*] They don't understand what it is like for a man to go through that—and they don't care.

Not only is my husband being cheated out of a normal life, but also I feel like I'm being cheated out of the love and tenderness I should be getting from my husband. I'm angry with the men who did this to him and got away with it. I'm angry with the VA for treating him like a liar who isn't entitled to any benefits for the mental and emotional damage the assaults caused on him. For his second period of service he got a less-than-honorable discharge, and they refuse to change it now, even after we sent them the reason why his behavior changed.[*] They say it has been too long ago. They just don't want to admit that this sort of thing does go on in the military.

I told one of his therapists that for all intents and purposes, it seems like I am living with a walking dead man. I hated to say that, but sometimes that it what it seems like to me. I believe that something vital died within him when those men attacked him. And to go through it twice within a six-month period was enough to cause you to completely shut down mentally and emotionally.

---

[*] It is common that victims of sexual assault, particularly males, do not disclose the experience at the time of the event. Many wait years before telling anyone or take the secret to their grave.

[†] One of the consequences of a less-than-honorable discharge, besides the insult to the veteran, is that his or her reputation is tarnished. Therefore he or she is viewed as a less-than credible witness if a hearing or other legal processing is held.

It's hard to see him get so depressed and know that all I can do is be here for him and support him. I would love to see him happy, enjoy life and love, and be free of the nightmares, the terror, the hopelessness, and the shame he lives with every day. It's hard seeing the pain my husband lives with. His manhood—in his mind—was violently taken from him. He feels like less of a man and no matter how hard I try to convince him otherwise, he still feels the same.

He feels especially bad because he has finally come to the place where he wants to have an intimate relationship with me, but he can't. Those demons won't release his mind, and being intimate brings back flashbacks of the assaults. That is hard on me, too, because I love my husband very much. But I know that I can't force the issue because that would only make him feel worse. Not only does he have to suffer because of what happened to him but I do too.

It's hard to love someone who feels like they are worthless and filled with so much pain and anger. But I refuse to give up on him or on us. I live with the hope that some day his therapy will help him see that what happened to him was not his fault and he has a right to live a happy life.

For others who are married to someone who has gone through this hell, I have some advice:

- Love him and don't stop—he can't help being the way he is.
- Understand that it was NOT his fault.
- Be understanding and don't demand what he can't give.
- Be very supportive—this is very important to his healing.
- Take an active part in his healing process—it concerns both of you.
- If he is self medicating—there is a reason; try to get him some help.

In closing, just let me say that it is horrible that these brave men who went into the military to fight for our freedom had their whole world ruined by some selfish man or men who chose to destroy the self-respect, the pride, and the manhood of these wonderful men. The VA needs to be more concerned and willing to help these men instead of treating them as less than human and placing the blame on them. They need to put themselves in these men's place, and realize the devastation that these men have to live with daily.

This is an Open Letter to the Veterans Administration and the Military Review Board

How dare you dismiss not only my husband but also the untold numbers of other past and present military personnel who have suffered sexual abuse while doing their duty serving their country! Because they never told anyone or did tell but somehow the reports "got lost somewhere" does NOT mean it didn't happen! How many of you would go around telling people how you were violated, mentally and emotionally broken either by a person or persons known or unknown to you? Is that something you would write home about? I think not! I think you would do what a lot of these survivors have done, do whatever you could to block out the memory of what happened.

When they do decide to come forward to the VA for the disability they deserve, what happens? They are treated like liars, drunks, and are labeled unfit for benefits. They drag out the whole process to discourage you; put roadblocks at every turn to keep you from getting what you rightly deserve.

You are supposed to be there to help our veterans, NOT deprive them of what's owed them for the horrors they suffered. These veterans have had their whole lives ruined because of what happened to them while they were serving and protecting their country. They were there when their country called for their help. But when they ask for what's due them for having their lives destroyed their country turns its back on them and a blind eye to military sexual abuse. You repay them by closing down the only successful program for treating males who were sexually abused while in the military. The real reason this was closed was because too much about sexual abuse in the military was coming to the public forefront. And the VA didn't like that. You turn them down for disability benefits for their PTSD caused by the abuse, "that doesn't happen in the military" you say. You treat them like they are less than human. I believe the military term is expendable. For my husband and all the others, "THANKS FOR NOTHING!"

Annie
The wife of a survivor.

Dean

ALTHOUGH IT IS EXTREMELY difficult to actually write down this memory, I need to do this for myself and other male victims of sexual assault in the military. I learned during my therapy there were military veterans who were raped as far back as World War II, Korean War, Vietnam, and even the Persian Gulf War. As difficult as it is to write down this memory, I do it as therapy for my own state of mind. The subject, male rape or sexual assault, is a rarely mentioned subject in our society even today, although many boys have come forward about sexual abuse in the church, and female victims from the Air Force Academy have spoken out.

Most men would be wise to never confess being raped. From an early age we have been programmed or brainwashed to be tough, macho, especially in the military environment. Is male rape worse for a male victim? Personally, I believe so. After being raped by more than just one attacker, I had many problems, not just mentally but also physically. I often questioned my sexual identity. Was I attracted to other males?

* Name changed at his request.

The military environment develops the conditions for male sexual assaults, for such sexual behaviors to occur. Mostly young males join, enlist, usually soon after high school. The living conditions in the barracks consist of extremely close confines with other males, deprived of any female company for extended times. The barracks are filled with half-naked men flexing their muscles and showing off. They have private conversations about personal issues. These conditions all throughout military service form a special trust and bond between men unlike any institution in the world. The comradeship can never be broken.

The Assault

As long as I live, I will never forget what happened. It was the most traumatic, terrifying, degrading, humiliating experience ever. Yes, this does happen to men, but hardly ever gets reported.

That night I went to the base movie theater with my buddy. We had been through boot camp and infantry training together. After the movie we were walking back toward the barracks when a military police vehicle approached us with three military police inside. They stopped us and asked where we were going. From the beginning I had a real bad feeling inside my head. They asked to see our ID cards. We were wearing only our PT clothes (sweats), so we had no pockets and had left our IDs in the barracks. One of the MPs was real big; he grabbed me and put handcuffs on my buddy and me. They put us in the back of the van. I remember it had no windows. I thought, "Something is not right with this picture."

They drove us to a remote area and took us into a small building. The interior had a few chairs and a few bunk beds. My buddy and I were then handcuffed to a bench. They started harassing my buddy about his haircut. One of the Marines got a clipper and shaved our heads. The MPs started laughing at us. I initially thought, "Okay, it's over. They were doing some stupid Marine stuff, and they will let us go."

Then they started to pull down our sweatpants and underwear. When my friend tried to resist, the three Marines jumped on him and cut off his T-shirt with a knife. They took off their cammies (uniforms). They started masturbating. They sat on my buddy, holding him down. One went to the latrine and got some liquid soap. He used it to stick his fingers in my buddy's butt. I could not believe this was actually happening. They forced him to perform oral sex on them. I was forced to watch him being sexually assaulted by three guys, all at the same time.* He was raped in an animalistic, savage assault. So much built up anger and aggression. My buddy yelled and screamed. It was frightening and absolutely terrifying to witness. It was frustrating to be physically restrained and unable to stop it.

Then the lights were turned off. Two Marines came over to me. I was still handcuffed to the bench. One of them removed his belt and wrapped it around my neck. I thought he was going to kill me.† He pulled out his penis and forced me to perform oral sex on him. He cut off my shirt with the knife. It was dark and I was facing the wall, so I couldn't see, but I could hear my buddy being raped and his terrible screams.

The other Marine came over and grabbed my testicles real hard. I was in so much pain. He had one hand on my balls to control me as he entered me. As I felt his penis penetrate me I started to scream and yell. I almost passed out from the pain. He took his time fucking me real hard. It hurt so bad. I started to cry. I wanted to escape this torture. I wanted to kill them.

I remember looking over my shoulder at the moment of his ejaculation. My rapist appeared almost in a frenzy, almost as if he thought I was enjoying being raped. I'm certain this is a fantasy of all rapists.

They took turns fucking me for a long time. The real big guy seemed to fuck me the hardest, almost as a punishment. I was relieved when the last of his seed spurted into my butt, because now it would be over, but now a part of his manhood would be in me forever. They ejaculated on me and rubbed their semen all over my body. The smell of body odor and semen in that room I will never forget.

The most humiliating and degrading act was when they performed oral sex on me. Two of them were holding me down. I was trying hard not to ejaculate.‡ I hated everything that was done to me.

I heard my buddy whimpering like an injured animal. They told him to shut up or they were going to fuck him again. When I saw my buddy covered with semen and bite marks all over his young body, I was in shock.

---

* According to the American Psychiatric Association, Post-Traumatic Stress Disorder can develop from witnessing another person being abused.

† For some survivors of sexual assault the most traumatic aspect of the experience is facing death. For others the most damaging aspect of the assault is the helplessness or humiliation.

‡ Survivors will sometimes view the fact of erection or ejaculation as an indication of compliance or even willingness, and in some case perpetrators have used this argument in their defense, claiming the physical contact was not an assault but a mutually consensual sexual act.

Two of the Marines took us into a shower and raped us again. They told us if we ever told anyone they would come find us and kill us in the middle of the night. After having been repeatedly attacked and brutally raped, I had no doubt in my mind that they were capable of killing us.

When we were let go, my buddy and I made a pact never to tell anyone about this incident. When we got back to the barracks, I saw my body in the mirror. It was covered with bruises and hickeys. Did I deserve to be raped in such a brutal and aggressive manner? Why do males do these things? I used to think it just happened in prisons or juvenile detention centers, or boys being molested by priests. I remember thinking, "God, how did this happen? How could I have been so naïve? I let several guys fuck me." I tried to rationalize it; we were restrained, handcuffed, physically overpowered. I didn't talk to anybody about what happened. Instead I worked out several times a week. I became bigger and real muscular.

Very soon after we were raped my buddy attempted suicide. The damage that has been done to me was not just physical but mental as well. The idea of being dominated goes against my whole image of a masculine male. I was beyond disgraced. How could this have happened? It was a real-life, true nightmare. I was not a small guy. I was in good physical shape. Why were we selected? What about my future? How could I ever reveal such a shameful act? I even questioned my own sexual identity. I never really questioned it until I was raped. Then I began to remember, when I was in high school, there was one guy who used to grab my crotch. He would slap my butt. He made comments about how I had "a nice body," stuff like that.

I have since learned some things about my aggressors. Two of them were cousins who were encouraged to join the Marine Corps directly out of a juvenile detention facility. I learned that their own sexual history included having been raped several times starting at age fifteen.* I received many letters from one of my rapists from Fort Leavenworth Kansas Federal Prison. He told me he "deserved to get fucked again." What a sad situation.

The only reason my particular case was ever revealed was because the same Marines raped a sailor. His uncle was a U.S. Congressman. At

---

* Although most sexual abuse survivors do not go on to inflict pain on others, some survivors go on to perpetrate. They develop a repetition compulsion in which they are driven to repeat what was done to them in the past, only in the present they are the ones dominating not the ones being dominated.

first the Marine Corps attempted to call what was done to us "a hazing incident."* I was never offered any type of counseling.

I have had many problems: drug use, alcohol abuse, and issues with my sexual identity. I still have nightmares. I will never ever again look at the military as I did when I first enlisted as an innocent young man. Sexual assault happens in the military. It is the untold dirty little secret the military does not want to mention to the general public.

I regret not having gone to counseling soon after I was raped. It took me almost seven years to get counseling. I hope anyone else who has been sexually abused seeks help. I am grateful that I have a good therapist who believes in me. She told me I am not alone, that there are many other military veterans who have been sexually assaulted who never told a soul. Recently my buddy who was assaulted with me went to the Veterans Administration to seek counseling. I pray it helps him. I hope others may somehow find the strength and courage to come forward to tell someone what happened to them. It was extremely difficult to come forward to tell anyone this story, but I'm sure I'm not alone.

---

* This is too often the response of the military and other organizations to a disclosure of sexual abuse. When faced with overwhelming evidence and pressure from a member of Congress, the Marine Corps will grudgingly acknowledge that something took place, but seeks to minimize the event by describing it as a hazing, not an assault.

The Reverend Dorothy Mackey

SEXUALLY HARASSED BY HER SUPERIORS AND SEXUALLY ASSAULTED BY COMRADES

MORE THAN NINETEEN YEARS after the start of these events, how do I summarize them? It is hard to know where to begin; it is so difficult, anguishing and incomprehensible, being raped and abused while in the service of my nation by members of my own military.

While I still support the men and women of the military who went in with all the right intentions and have maintained their personal honor and integrity, I cannot sanction or condone their exploitation by rogue members of our military and government leadership.

My story began as a contracted ROTC student in college. During my entrance exam in 1983, at the recruiting exam center, an Army 0-6 Colonel sexually abused me during my ob-gyn exam. Simply put, his exam of me was vicious, angry, and hurtful.* It clearly was outside his oath as a doctor to "First, do no harm." This was my introduction into the military and in hindsight, was a dubious warning. In my head and body I felt violated, but at the time no one spoke publicly about doctors abusing patients. I didn't know what to do, so I just buried the memory and focused on my desire to succeed professionally based solely on my skills, talent, and willingness to work hard. I graduated from college and

---

* The abuse in this case was not what the physician did, but how he did it.

was commissioned a Second Lieutenant. I was told by my instructor as I graduated from administrators school that I was an "exceptional leader and would go far."

The next nine years I would continue both my official, and unofficial, Air Force training. As it turned out, there were several sets of rules I needed to learn:

- The official rules written down as regulations are for show to the public.
- The official rules that stated any breach of them would be swiftly and harshly dealt with. These were the ones used to scare people into keeping quiet.
- The unofficial rules override all the official rules. These included the rules that allowed a person to get away with anything, if that individual knew the right people or had the right background. If you were an Air Force academy graduate, combat or test pilot, you could get away with doing things against official policy—even criminal acts.

My first assignment was to an Air Force base on which the wing commander was being forced to retire because he had turned a group of female enlisted women on the base into his personal prostitution ring. Despite this, he went out with all his benefits and a parade! In protest of his criminal conduct I refused to march in the parade.

This was only the beginning of my realization that the treatment of military personnel by military personnel is often abusive and unnecessarily demeaning. In the next four years I would learn more of the subtle, and not so subtle, unwritten military rules that took precedence over the military rules I had agreed to follow when I enlisted.

Each combat fighter squadron had caustic, disrespectful songs that the new combat crews were required to learn. One song's lyrics included, "sucking and biting your mother's tits, ra ra fuck." On more than one occasion drunken fighter pilots would sing these lewd songs at base functions without regard to the presence of guests. There was also destruction of government property (in the tens of thousands of dollars), use of prostitutes by troops, and violations of all kinds of official rules and morals. It appeared that the entire senior leadership, as high as a wing commander, ignored and even condoned many of these behaviors.

As a female officer and commander, there was a great deal of pressure to be exceptional. It is often said in the military that we military women have to work ten times harder than our male counterparts, and we still do not get recognized for our achievements. Despite this, I was selected into a leadership position and transferred into a command position with enlisted members. But during my introduction to my new boss I was informed that I had three strikes against me—I was "petite, blond and a woman."

It was during this assignment that I was sexually abused two more times. The first time was by another military doctor during a mandatory ob-gyn appointment. After my experience with the previous military physician, I hated ob-gyn appointments. I was very nervous about going to the appointment, and would sweat profusely, but I was required to go. This doctor was one I had been to before and he had shown no unusual behavior in the past. In fact, he would explain to me what he would do prior in the next step of the exam, what type of pressure I would feel, which made me feel safer. However, during this exam, without preparation or warning, he thrust his finger in my anus. I felt stunned and wanted to kick him in the face, but once again I was vulnerable with my feet in stirrups. I numbed out and had the overwhelming sense there was nobody I could safely tell who would believe me. It was not long after this second experience with a physician that a woman in my squadron came to me and told me of her sexual abuse by a military doctor during an ob-gyn that was excessively rough and caused bruising. She had never before told anyone about her experience.

My next assailant was a first sergeant who had been a trusted colleague with over twenty-six years of military service. Our mutual supervisor thought this sergeant walked on water. I knew and worked with this man for two years before he assaulted me. He had even helped to train me. One of the strongest components of the military training is, "You can trust all of the men and women around you," but it is also this training that sets up victims of military crimes to keep quiet.

On a picnic with squadron members, someone pulled out a bottle of tequila. One of my personal rules was to never drink in front of my people. I was a lightweight when it came to alcohol and I very well knew my limit. I decided to have a couple of shots, but I was still well within my allotted amount.*

The squadron began a game of volleyball, and I joined in knowing I would sweat out the alcohol. The First Sergeant stood on the sidelines, cheering on the team. As my team rotated positions I recall asking for a drink of water. The First Sergeant handed me his drink. He assured me there was no alcohol. I took a large drink, only to taste the very strong alcohol going down my throat. I told him very sternly, "No alcohol, water only." As I continued to play, he approached me again, apologized for his behavior, and handed me a glass, assuring me it contained no alcohol. However, after taking a large drink, I once again tasted alcohol. Soon I was unable to focus or walk.† I felt very sick. The First Sergeant led me into a nearby building and then to the men's latrine, where I violently threw up for over an hour while he stood in the doorway and laughed. I was afraid as I threw up that I was going to pass out and drown in the toilet. I was so sick it was like I had been poisoned.

When I finally stopped vomiting the First Sergeant took me to his room and placed me on his bed, where I passed out. I recall waking up to at least four senior NCOs playing cards on the floor of the room; they laughed at me, as I passed out again.

The next time I awoke, the First Sergeant was on top of me, his hand in my pants, his finger penetrating me, his tongue in my ear. I recalled saying, "No," only to pass out again. I have no idea how I got out of that room, let alone got back to my quarters, but I did.

In my role as a commander I reported to the base prosecutor incidences of sexual abuse of children and military women by U.S. military men that came to may attention. Not only did the prosecutor refuse to investigate these crimes, but also the entire chain of command refused to take action. Since I had already seen repeated indifference to abuse and other crimes, even by senior leadership, I did not tell anyone about what was done to me. There was no truly safe person, or place, to make a report.

In my last year of service I worked directly for a full colonel and a lieutenant colonel. These two officers were the military's complaint

---

* The fact that Dorothy is seen voluntarily consuming alcohol could easily be used to claim that the sexual contact which later takes place between her and the sergeant was not rape but merely consensual sex between equals.

† All of this was witnessed by the other members of the squadron, so if charges had been filed against the sergeant, he could have called them as witnesses to testify that Dorothy was so intoxicated she could barely function.

system known as the Inspector General. The colonel was also the "Zero Tolerance" officer.* Despite their roles, I saw how they buried evidence of military personnel physically and sexually abusing children and spouses. These officers took personal pleasure in groping and grabbing me. Every day they sexually touched me between six and twenty times. Furthermore they threatened my career and to imprison me in a military psychiatric ward. I tried to overcome their continuous abuses by working harder, accomplishing more, and being nominated for awards and honors. The torment, humiliation, and the sexual, physical, mental, emotional, and psychological abuse they perpetrated on me were as devastating as all of my earlier abuses and rape. I resigned from the military because I feared these men would rape me or worse. On my last day in service, the colonel laughed at me and said, "I knew my touching bothered you."

In the years that followed my resignation from the military, I sought legal assistance from the Justice Department to prosecute my last two assailants, but they refused to help me. I also sought emotional help for the trauma of the abuse. I initially sought help from my local Veterans Administration, only to be run through a gauntlet of abuse there. My abuse there included: interviews with a series of four doctors who did not know anything about rape; a psychiatrist who refused to document in my record the abuses disclosed because he claimed if he did so I would never get a job; a female ob-gyn who, in the middle of an exam, left the room with the door open as civilians were passing by; and a VA worker who screamed, "I don't care if you were raped in the military, I won't help you get your disability." Regional VA headquarters also exacerbated my trauma by their continual loss of documents when I was filing my disability claim, forcing me to reexperience the trauma by having to rewrite descriptions of what happened.† I described my years of flashbacks concerning the attacks by my last two bosses and my days of emotional despondency, but I was repeatedly refused any disability payment. I was offered various types of medications, most of which I turned down with the exception of antidepressants.‡

---

* The fact that these two men were in positions of authority related to preventing and investigating sexual abuse is ironic but not unheard of. This makes their victims' claims of sexual abuse seem unbelievable. The perpetrator will appear above reproach because of his position.

† On numerous occasions I have heard of veterans making disability claims related to sexual abuse being told their records had been lost or portions of their files had gone missing.

‡ There are three main reasons for medication being the primary, if not only, treatment offered by the Veterans Administration and other military settings. First, in order to treat the effects of abuse, the abuse would have to be acknowledged and that is potentially unpopular, if not dangerous. Secondly, these settings tend to overwhelmingly use a medical model to explain human problems; therefore, a medical solution such as medication is viewed as the logical treatment option. Finally, most treatment providers know little or nothing about how to treat trauma-related problems.

Eventually I was provided with a female nurse for a therapist, but she had no training related to sexual abuse and trauma.[*] Furthermore, I was told by two women vets, who had also been sexually abused while in the military, that this nurse yelled at them for having any connection to me because I was speaking out publicly about sexual abuse in the military.[†]

After I had twice placed a gun to my head, I knew I needed competent help, so I located a civilian inpatient treatment center that truly saved my life.[‡] I found an attorney who filed a civil suit against my last two assailants. To my amazement, the Justice Department, with my tax dollars, provided free legal aid to my abusers. In court, the Justice Department argued that my case should not be allowed to come to trial because it would breech our national security policy and "disrupt good order, morale, and discipline of the military." Twice I witnessed my case rise to the Supreme Court, once against my assailants, once against the U.S. and its policies that allow for immunity for those who committed these crimes. Twice I witnessed my nation's highest court let criminals go free and sanction abuse by the military by claiming protection of our national security policy. I recall my devastation when the Supreme Court gave them immunity. It was clear to me that everything I had believed in—everything I was taught about this nation—was a lie. What I wasn't prepared for was the emotions that came up from yet another revictimization and betrayal. It was like a bomb going off in my soul.

I made a commitment to myself, and God, to do something about the abuse. I decided to speak up until I was heard. In March 1997, on the lawn of the U.S. Congress with several U.S. Congresswomen present, the formation of STAAAMP, Inc. (Survivors Take Action Against Abuse by Military Personnel), was announced. It was an amazing day, as one after another, military women and men spoke honestly about rape and other sexual abuse. This was not to be the end of my story, but the beginning, with each day, a new beginning.

---

[*] Unfortunately, despite the prevalence of sexual abuse in both the civilian world and in military settings, most mental health treatment providers, even those with graduate degrees, have little or no training in the assessment and treatment of trauma.

[†] Those who have a vested interest in covering-up the existence and extent of sexual abuse in the military often seek to socially isolate and label those who speak out as troublemakers or disloyal to the service.

[‡] Unfortunately, the first time many victims of sexual abuse finally come to the attention of mental-health-treatment providers is when they are suicidal or incapacitated by depression or anxiety. The most unfortunate aspect of all this is that they are likely to be treated only for the symptoms that are the result of their experiences of abuse. The cause of their suffering the abuse is going undetected and untreated.

Gloria J. Williams

SEXUALLY ASSAULTED BY A
CIVILIAN WHILE ENLISTED

I WAS NINETEEN when I joined the U.S. Army. Being African American
and young, I wanted to better my life and thought the military was the
way for me. Initially I got off to a rough start after basic training. I was
going to school as an administration specialist and I felt my "superiors"
were being abusive. So I went AWOL. I was given an Article 15, then
transferred. I started school again, this time as a financial specialist.

One day, I left the post, which was an "open-post," with a civilian
I had met a few weeks prior. I had been drinking at the time, but was
not drunk. He drove to a secluded place and tried to have sex with me.
I fought with him until he put a knife to my throat. I knew without a
doubt that I was going to die that night. My whole life flashed before
me as he raped me. He proceeded to take me back to the base. No
words were exchanged as he dropped me off, as if this was routine for
him—obviously, he had raped more than once. I later learned he had a
prior record of rape at gunpoint. The night they arrested him, he was
back on the base and had another young servicewoman in his car.

I went to my room and cried, a feeling of death inside me. I had more
to drink; then I called the police, who came and took me to the military
hospital. I told them exactly what happened, and identified the rapist.

The civilian police became involved because he was not in the military. Once I told them I had been drinking that night, they suddenly

shifted the way they had been treating me. Now it was as if I "deserved it." Although they never came out and said it, they implied it.

Eventually I was given an honorable discharge, but was told it was because I was "unable to adjust to military life." I was also told the rape was a result of "my own willful misconduct due to alcohol abuse."[*]

When I sought help at the local Veterans Administration I was treated as if I were a leper. I never heard from the VA after undergoing a psychiatric examination. I got absolutely no useful assistance from the VA. Matter of fact, I felt like I was raped all over again.

For two years, in order to cope with what had happened, I drank and drank. I tried working many jobs, but walked off many of them. I could not maintain a relationship with a man, nor did I want to. My weight went up and then down. I isolated myself from my family.

I blamed myself for the rape, but I always fantasized about killing the person who raped me. I carried this vision for many years, along with guilt, shame, anxiety, and depression. Nightmares and fear of being raped again were constant, as deep rage permeated my spirit. I tried to ignore my feelings, but they would come up and scare the hell out of me; the pain of it was raw, raw, raw. My rage verbally exploded on my daughter and on bystanders.

I entered a substance abuse treatment program, began attending Alcoholics Anonymous meetings, and stopped drinking. Had I not gotten sober I believe my life would have been worse, which is exactly what the military wanted. They wanted me to drink/drug myself to death so they wouldn't have to deal with me. One less black woman veteran to deal with.

My biological family never knew about the rape until last year. I finally shared it with my sisters and mom. My mom does not understand; due to her religious upbringing she always takes the side of the "man."

In 1998, I had a nervous breakdown, unable to cope anymore, unable to work anymore, and unable to fight the demons.[†] I called the VA hospital and told them what happen to me in 1981. They told me to reopen my claim and seek help in the PTSD clinic. I didn't know about PTSD; I just thought something was wrong with me.

---

[*] This is referred to as secondary victimization, and for some victims it is the aspect of the abuse they find most disturbing.

[†] "Nervous breakdown" often is a term used by nonpsychological personnel to describe the effects of being overwhelmed by PTSD.

I told the staff I never heard back from the VA in 1984 after the exam, and hadn't returned because I felt like I was the criminal and I could not go through that kind of treatment anymore.

Being that I was young, black, and female, I had many barriers stacked against me, but I not only had documentation of the rape in my file but also had my own copy of it. At first I was granted 50 percent disability, but I appealed and was granted 70 percent. I appealed again and was eventually granted 100 percent disability due to PTSD.

My life changed on November 11, 1981, when I was raped with a knife to my throat and lived to talk about it. My "journey" was forever altered, and the military has never taken any responsibility for the altering. Now it is years later, but the "assault" continues. The denial, the cover-ups, the racism, the sexism, the literal hatred of women, all continue.

Gregory A. Helle, U.S. Army, SP5

SEXUALLY ASSAULTED BY A COMRADE IN A COMBAT ZONE

THIS IS MY LIFE, a portrayal of the personal hell caused by sexual assault and trauma. But there is more to my story and it all combines to make me who I am today.

As a high school senior in 1968, news of the Vietnam War was a daily event. In small town Iowa, service to your county was very important. Even before graduation, I had enlisted in the Army and had volunteered for duty in Vietnam. I was a naïve eighteen-year-old boy straight off the farm. John Wayne molded my understanding of war. I thought I was invincible. My terror began immediately upon landing, as the airport was being mortared while we taxied up the runway. We watched the explosions praying that one would not hit us. As we rushed off the plane, running by the metal caskets on the runway, we knew this was real, not some distant war on TV.

It became even more real when one night on guard duty, I was in the unlucky position to spot a gook working his way through the wire. I watched him for what seemed like hours, hoping he would go away. He didn't, so I emptied my clip into him. I watched as my bullets blew him apart. When we picked up his mangled body in the morning, I discovered that he could not have been more than eighteen, probably much younger. I knew that I was the one who took his life. I had done the unthinkable. I had broken a sacred commandment.

When not on duty I would be drinking with my buddies. I did not want to feel motions or what I have seen and what I have done. I used alcohol and drugs to numb myself. One June night in 1969, I had been out drinking with my buds. I don't remember if it was in an EM (Enlisted Man's) club or just behind a bunker. Wherever it was, I went to my bunk intoxicated. I know that this was in my bunk in Long Bien. My room was on the second floor, southwest corner. The "room" was open, with only a four-foot wall around it. There were two bunks in the room. I am not sure if I had a roommate at the time.

Sometime during the night I was awakened. I remember wondering what was happening and soon realized that my boxers were being pulled off. I had no clue what was happening. Then I remember my legs being forced apart. I remember trying to turn over but being forced back down, and the pain of him forcing himself into me. It seemed like he pounded me forever.

The next thing I remember it was morning. I was naked. My attacker was a fellow soldier and was bunked across the hall from me. Now I hated him and wanted to kill him.

Throughout the first day I was bleeding anally and having pain with bowel movements, but I wanted his fluids out of me. I felt so ashamed. I felt afraid. I was so confused. I had no clue why any man would want to fuck anyone in the ass, male or female. Sex was normal. This was not.

Reporting what had happened did not enter my mind, because I was not totally sure what had happened to me. I was confused. I was drunk, unable to stop it, and I had just lain there and taken it. I was to blame for letting this happen to me. I felt a weakness had caused this, and being weak was not an option. I could not face my buds if they were to find out.

He was Hispanic, and the Hispanic soldiers stuck close together. We all knew about eliminating bad officers; "friendly fire" was not always friendly. I knew an "accident" could happen to me at any time. My world totally changed forever. I had already learned not to trust any Vietnamese man, woman, or child because they might be Viet Cong. Now I could not even trust my fellow soldiers. I feared my own comrades more than I feared the enemy. I did not know who would hurt me. I was always in the rear on patrols; I did not want a loaded gun behind me. I was totally alone. I kept a knife strapped to my bunk at all times. It was not going to happen again.

This has not changed over the years. I still have a knife close to my bed because nowhere is safe.

When I left home for 'Nam, my dream was to become a minister. I wrote a letter to my wife in early July telling her that I had decided not to go into the ministry. I was filled with too much shame, too many fears, and had broken too many commandments. I cursed God for putting me here. I had killed, which plagued me daily. I was also afraid I was homosexual, which would be totally unforgivable by my God. My faith was not shaken—it was shattered.

The war continued. I could have left after a year, but I extended twice. I did not want to come home alive. The fear of what I had seen and the shame of what I had done and what was done to me were overwhelming.

When I got home, I was so angry my brothers were afraid of me, and there were the nightmares of all the things that happened. I did not tell anyone in my family anything about 'Nam. What had happened to me was a secret I was going to take to the grave with me.

I coped by throwing myself into my work. I received my four-year degree in three years. I received my CPA (Certified Public Accountant) designation and strove for jobs that required long hours. Even though I was technically capable, I found myself getting fired or suddenly "laid off." I distrusted my superiors. I had a hair-trigger temper. I was not a team player; I needed to be in control, I would not play the game. I knew I had a temper but thought I was just a bastard.

I lived mostly in my own head, not letting anyone get close enough to really know me, even my wife. My mood would swing wildly on a moment's notice, which kept people at a distance. I avoided all Vietnam veterans. I wanted nothing to do with a vet. My wife took the brunt of my attempts to prove that I was a man—a *heterosexual* man. I was very sexually demanding. The rape always haunted me, and always will. I cannot to this day define what a man is, but I have always been sure that I fell short of what a man should be.

In 1986, I was at a Boy Scout camp with my troop. As we were lined up for the morning flag ceremony, an adult Scout shot a toy cannon. I found myself face down in the mud. I tried to laugh it off, saying I had just slipped. I couldn't tell anyone I was reliving the events of the war all over again.

I first heard about Post-Traumatic Stress Disorder (PTSD) when I went to see a psychologist. I saw him a few times and he prescribed some medications. I started to feel better, so I stopped seeing him and I stopped taking the medications. I was a man; I did not need these things. I could handle this by myself.

But I was still afraid of everything and everybody. Suicidal thoughts ran through my mind. In May 1969, I decided to attend a presentation at the local vet center where the symptoms of PTSD were described, and I realized they were describing me.

At the vet center I met Jerry, the man who saved my life. He seemed to understand me and what was going on with me. I described my combat traumas. I had not told the psychologist at EAP about my rape, I was afraid of this memory. For some reason I felt I had to tell Jerry. I think I was afraid it would come out accidentally, but I insisted that it was not a problem for me and I did not want to talk about it anymore.

I got back on medication and started seeing Jerry every other week. I was given the label PTSD and could not find a way to run from it. The pain, panic, and isolation I felt were very real and very disabling. I wanted to run, but had nowhere to go. I panicked often, unable to control the rush of emotions. My nightmares scared my wife. I began to drink very heavily. I told them some of the combat stuff, but kept my biggest secret close to my heart. I hoped that I could just get treatment for the combat trauma and never have to talk about the rape. That was a secret that was for me alone.

In November 1999, I attended a ceremony at the Iowa Vietnam Wall. This turned out to be more than I could handle. I returned home, loaded my rifle, drank a lot of beer, and was ready to run away from my problems forever. I did not want to die; I just could not handle the pain anymore. I remember what it looked like when a man is shot in the head and I could not do this to my wife in our home, so instead of pulling the trigger I called Jerry and asked him to get me into the best treatment he knew in the VA system.

In January 2000 I entered the treatment program at the National Center for PTSD in Menlo Park, CA. I believed I was not as sick as the other vets there. I was wrong. Everyone was expected to pick three traumas to discuss in group therapy. I chose mine, and the rape was not one of them. I was terrified that my fellow veterans would reject me, since being raped was not combat trauma, it was a weakness. It was very difficult to tell my stories but I made it through it. When we were leaving, the psychologist grabbed me by the arm, looked me in the eye, and said, "There is something else you need to talk about, isn't there?" He had listened to me in other groups and somehow put the pieces together. This scared the hell out of me. How could someone know my deepest secret? I had no intention of bringing it out. I was scared, scared of being less than a man. The next day I agreed to tell the others about my rape. I was so scared that my peers would reject me. This was still a man's place, and this made me less of a man. Instead of rejection I was accepted, even though I had failed to stop the rape.

When I entered treatment I thought I would be there for six weeks, but it lasted three months. I had faced my monsters and I had survived. I promised them in California that I would tell my wife about the rape when I got home. After many months I found the courage. She said, "I knew there was more to that story." For years I had told her a story about a man who tried to touch me but that I knocked him through a wall.

I began attending a local group for men with sexual trauma. Although trauma was very different from the rest, it was good to be in a group. One night it was especially tough, and I left the meeting very upset. My roommate when I was in the California program and I had become very good friends. We had been talking regularly since I left California, supporting each other. I was upset, and he was my buddy, so I called him and I told him for the first time about the rape. About a week later I received a letter from him. In that letter he basically said not to call him, write him, or come out and see him. The rejection was total and complete. In 'Nam, when you made a mistake, someone died. I felt I had made a huge mistake and I had lost another buddy. Although he was not dead, I had killed a friendship. I was devastated.

Jerry got me into a mental hospital. My panic attacks were coming more often and were more serious. I was never sure what would bring back a rush memories and emotions. Sometimes it was the heat, an overgrown area, sounds and smells, and sometimes I just had no clue. I would either bang my head against a wall or cut on myself with a hunting knife. I think the physical pain brought me a step closer to reality and away from all the emotional pain.

Then I was arrested for the first time in my life for trying to hire a prostitute. It devastated me to be handcuffed and locked up for such a stupid act, especially since my police officer daughter saw me at the station. My wife bailed me out and never said much. That was the night I told my daughter about the rape. She was concerned about that but also really angry for what I had done to her mother. Telling my son later that week was even harder. How could my male child accept me as his father after he knew what I had done? His response was, "That makes a lot of things make more sense."

I was making plans to disappear to Arkansas and live alone in the hills. I wanted to be totally alone. I wanted to desert my family. I wanted to run away from me. Jerry found a program for sexual abuse at the VA hospital in Bay Pines, Florida, but had to fight a lot of red tape because the VA did not want to help me. They wanted absolute proof that I had experienced something in a war zone that could have caused PTSD. I did not blame my government for how my life has been diminished because of the war; I just wanted them to believe me and offer me the help that I so desperately needed.

In August 2001, I went to Florida. I was a dead man walking, my options were running out. I would not survive. There I met Roger. The first time we met, without even needing to interview me, he told me all about myself. He knew that I feared people, how I would isolate and act out in destructive ways. He knew me. I did not want anybody to know me that well. Hell, *I* didn't know me that well. He told me I was not crazy, I was not mentally ill; I was normally reacting to an abnormal event. His compassion, along with his professionalism, gave me some hope.

In the program I met other men who were not afraid to admit to their rapes, men who served in the Marines, Air Force, Navy, Army, and Coast Guard. It had happened to all of them. And it screwed up their lives like it had mine. I was not the only one that experienced rape in the military. I started to feel that I was not alone.

There was also a women's program there. There was one young lady named Linda who I got talking with, and I knew from the grapevine that she was in the women's sexual trauma program. For some reason, I trusted her. I told her why I was there—hell, she already knew. We would spend hours discussing what had happened to us and how it was fucking up our lives. It was amazing how similar we were. It was fantastic to be able to discuss rape openly with both men and women.

I will never be that eighteen-year-old boy that went to Vietnam. But I am coping. I know that I will be on medications the rest of my life. I know I will need counseling. I still have trouble over the summer because of all the anniversaries of my traumas, and the heat of the summer does not help. The treatment people tell me this is as good as it gets.

The man who raped me took so much from me. It is difficult to express the hell I have lived for over thirty years or the hell that continues to torture me day after day. I will never be free of his control over me. I will never be free. I dream about grabbing my rapist by the hair, slitting his throat, and looking in his eyes why he slowly dies. I want him to know who took his life, since he took mine. I know that the teachings of Jesus tell me to forgive this man. But so far I cannot. I do not hate the Vietnamese, but I do hate him. The lifetime effect of his act is worse than death. I would want him to know the hell I have lived and continue to live.

I still struggle with my spirituality. I am trying to attend church, but crowds often panic me. A few months ago I finally took communion. I know in my mind that my God forgives me, but I cannot forgive myself. I cannot forgive the things I did. I cannot forgive myself for letting the rape happen. I struggle. My pastor understands and is patient with me.

I must also continue my fight with the VA system. They do not want to really help veterans. They do not want to admit that anything bad happens to men at war (or even at peace). They look at veterans as a drain on their budget, not as the public they are to serve. I will continue to fight for the help I need. However, I am also seeing a psychologist outside the VA, since it is so hard to get appointments within the system. This is a real shame for our country.

Despite all this, I am so much better now thanks to Roger and his program. I am a much better husband and dad now. I needed to write my book and this story with my real name. It happened, and I cannot be ashamed and carry the guilt of that act anymore. I am a real man. I want the readers of my story to know this is a real story. I know there are many brothers out there who experience what I did and have not sought help. I also know that this is still happening. I want to encourage all my brothers to seek help. The shame of telling your story is less than the pain you carry. The burden can be lightened. The past cannot be changed, but the future can be improved. There is hope for a more normal life. Those who love us will accept us. Those who are opposed are probably hiding their own demons. There is hope.

VIOLATED[4]

What gives a man
The right to violate
Another man
So shamefully
To take something away
That cannot be replaced
To destroy a man's future
To take away his manhood
The act seems so small
So insignificant
But the burden it has brought
Is more than I can bear
Anger
Rage
Frustration
All part of what I feel
Suicidal
Over what I lost
Pain always there
I don't know how to put this in the past
Where it belongs
How to stuff it back
Deep
Forever

Jon

ABUSE OF POWER AND AUTHORITY

I ENLISTED IN THE United States Marine Corps when I turned eighteen years old. During high school I was active in sports, the R.O.T.C. [Reserve Officer Training Corps], the football team, and the wrestling team. Both of my foster parents were in the U.S. Navy. I decided to join the Corps because of their dedication and sharp uniforms, and to stay physically fit.

I thought being a U.S. Marine would be a good place to get a start, but while I was on my first deployment, my girlfriend got pregnant from having sex with two other Marines. I got into a lot of trouble when I learned about this; I went AWOL for sixty days.

Finally I turned myself in to authorities at a Navy base. I was taken to the brig by the MPs. They ordered me to go into the head and shave my face. Then they ordered me to go report to the Navy Corpsman for a physical exam. The corpsman told me to take a seat in a barber's chair. Two Marines handcuffed me to the chair. The corpsman shaved my head. Then they uncuffed me and told me I would have to give a urine sample to test for drugs. While still cuffed I was escorted into a room with a small toilet and shower. Suddenly I was pushed to the floor. They tore off all my civilian clothes. I was scared shitless. They ordered me to piss in a bottle. One guy held the bottle for me while my hands were cuffed behind my back. They were laughing and told me "to get used to not being in control." The Marine guard standing behind me took a flex cuff* and placed it around my testicles. A belt was put around my waist. They told me, "not to try anything stupid." My hands were attached to the restraint belt in front of me. I remember them asking me if I had "ever been fucked before." They stuffed toilet paper in my mouth. When I felt a hard penis against my butt I realized they weren't just playing around. I started to cry. Someone stuck a finger up my butt and used liquid soap to lubricate my ass. When the first penis went in my butt I was trying to scream because it hurt so bad. After he was done, two other guards raped me. I was forced to perform oral sex on them too. When one of them forced his penis down my throat, I vomited. He ejaculated down my throat. I hated it.

Then they took me to a metal bench and told me to lie on my back. They ejaculated on my face and chest. One of them grabbed my testicles so hard I almost passed out from the pain. Then he placed an electric stun gun on my testicles and told me that if I ever told anyone, they were going to kill me. They told me I belonged to them from now on. I was terrified because there was no doubt in my mind they would get me again.

Then I was taken back to the corpsman's office. They were all grinning with sick, sadistic looks. The corpsman was aware of what they just had done to me. He had on rubber gloves and told me to bend over. He shoved a tube up my ass and gave me an enema.† He told me to "get used to the brig." I was ordered to get up on the exam table and forced to give him oral sex. I was crying again. He was smiling and holding onto my ears while he moved his penis in my mouth.

After that I was assaulted many other times, sometimes even by other prisoners. I was raped in the shower many times. Sometimes, when a new prisoner arrived, the guards would take me to "the rape room." They would force me to perform oral sex on the new detainees. They took photos of me engaged in sexual acts.‡

---

* Plastic wire tie.
† This was likely done to eliminate any DNA evidence left behind from the anal assaults.
‡ Photographs and video tapes are useful in at least three ways: first, as aids for masturbation for the assailants at a later date; second, as proof that the assault took place which can be shown to others who value domination; and finally, for use in black-mailing or ensuring the silence of the victim.

When I was close to being released from the brig, a real big Marine took me in a government vehicle on "a trash pickup." Instead, I was taken to a house on base. When I asked what was going on he told me to "shut up." He took me into the house where three Marines were real high on some drug. They told me they had also taken Viagra. A guy with a video camera came in, and they told me to take off my cammies. Then they were all over me like animals. I was raped for many hours by at least five Marines. They would spread their semen on my chest and stomach. They called me female names when they were on top of me. When they finished using my body, one guy pissed on my face. They were real sick. I hated those bastards.

The entire thing was videotaped. I hated the whole scene, but I had learned from the previous rapes not to cry. I just let them fuck me because I am certain if I had put up any resistance they would have killed me.

A few days later a Navy chaplain finally came to visit me. After seven months of being raped I didn't bother to tell him what had happened to me in this hell on earth. Until very recently I never ever told a soul what my fellow Marines did to me.

After being released I have had many mental problems, especially about my own sexual identity, sexual orientation, and masculinity. When I got back in the barracks I began to have sex with other Marines. Since I had turned twenty-one years old I could buy alcohol and I would give it new, younger recruits. Once they were intoxicated, I would pull down their shorts and perform oral sex on them. I was a male slut.

Recently, I read an article in the local paper about an ex-Marine accused of sexually assaulting two active Marines. He got them intoxicated and sodomized them. He was one of the brig guards who had sexually assaulted me. They were real young Marines, just like I was when I got raped in the brig. Their rapist was caught because one of the Marines told another Marine another military guy fucked him off base. The civilian authorities obtained a search warrant and found many photos and videos of Marines being assaulted, including myself. When he goes to trial I must somehow get the strength and courage to testify again him and the other guards for what they did.

I'm starting to get my act together. I'm going back to school and I'm still on active reserve. I will never recover completely from what has been done to me physically and mentally. I encourage other military veterans to seek mental help and go forward with their lives. I am still proud to be a Marine.*

---

* Despite his painful experiences at the hands of other Marines, he remains loyal to the Corps. In my experience, this is not unusual. Loyalty to the military is strong and survives even through repeated abuse and neglect.

Lynda K. Arneson Dokken

USMC DISABLED VETERAN, SERVICE-CONNECTED FOR PTSD SEXUALLY HARASSED AND ASSAULTED

I WAS IN JUNIOR HIGH SCHOOL when John F. Kennedy was president. I took to heart his speech about doing something for your country. When the military recruiters came in my school during my senior year, I knew I want to join the service. At that time women had to be over twenty-one to join without a parent's permission; be high school graduates; and have higher test scores then men. Since I was under the age limit, I got my mother to sign the necessary papers. After high school graduation I was sworn into the Marine Corps.

I found boot camp to be fairly easy since I was physically fit. I was able to handle the mind games since my childhood had been tough. Once I completed boot camp I applied to secretarial school. Even though I had secretarial training in high school I was not accepted into the military's training program. I was told I was not "attractive" enough. Instead they sent me to supply-clerk school.

I was really excited about supply school. The first few weeks were great. My classmates and I went to classes but also had time to do fun things. But then things changed. One of my friends was a young

Puerto Rican woman. She was dating a black man. Both of them received notes from the local Ku Klux Klan threatening their lives if they ever went out together again. Our class instructors, supervisors, and officers told us if they ever caught us going out with a black man, they would take a knife and cut an "N" into our faces and do other horrible things to us.*

I was terrified to even look at any men for fear they would target me. I spent nights fearing the next day and not knowing if someone would take what I was doing in the wrong way. These men made it very clear to me that if I had sex with a black man, whether it was consensual or rape, not only would I be marked by a scar where everyone could see it, but also white men would never have anything to do with me again. I believed them. I came from a tiny town and had never experienced such racial hatred. With all the fear I was experiencing, my grades at the school dropped dramatically. I graduated, but at the bottom of my class. I was so relieved when I got through school and was sent to a series of bases, one after the other.

The men I worked around would ask me out, and if I refused, they would tell me I was "one of those kind of women," meaning gay. They had a running bet as to who could get me into bed. They would daily harass me with catcalls, vulgar statements, etc.

One day after I had been serving about a year, I went into the NCO club. A group of four males asked me to join them. I told them politely that I was there to meet a friend (which was true). One of the men stood up and grabbed me by my wrist and would not let go. When I again refused, the men made threats about what they would do to me when they found me alone. They told me in detail that they would assault me, rape me, and that as a result I would never want to have sex with another man. I was terrified and kept trying to get away, but I was held there by the strong grip on my wrist. Finally someone came into the room, and the man let go of me. I fled to the women's barracks and hid there for the rest of the weekend.

I was unable to tell anyone about what happened because I was afraid I would be blamed for what happened. The only time I left the barracks

---

* "N" for "nigger lover."

in the next two weeks was to go to work and the chow hall. I kept looking all around me.

Finally, after several weeks, I did venture out to see my friend. While I was visiting her I noticed it was getting dark, so I left her and hurried back to the barracks. I took a shortcut thinking I would get back to the barracks a lot sooner. Suddenly, I heard footsteps behind me. With intense fear I started walking faster. The faster I walked the faster came the footsteps behind me. I started to run. Just as I turned my head to see who it was, they grabbed me by the shoulder and shoved me into a recessed doorway. To this day, I have almost total amnesia about how many [attackers] there were. The only thing I can remember is that there was at least one man with a knife and that I was raped.

I don't know how I got back to the barracks, nor do I know if my clothes were dirty or torn. But I do know that those men had found me. I did not report the assault because I had seen what had happened to another woman who had reported an attack. The authorities repeatedly accused her of bringing it on herself.* I could not go through that.

I have checked my military file for any clues about the event. I never had a sick call in the first seven months I was in the service. But after the assault I had twenty-two sick calls in only five months. I gained over twenty pounds. I stopped taking showers. It got to the point where I was supervised for several weeks to insure that I was bathing. This was terribly humiliating for me because I had always been good about personal hygiene in the past. I stayed in the barracks except when I had to go out. I went out only in groups and only with women, even to the chow hall.

I caught mononucleosis and was put on light duty. They assigned me to the commissary filling orders. The male sergeant that I worked for started coming on to me the day I arrived. He told me if I would have sex with him, he would give me good marks on my evaluation that would help me get promoted.† I told him I didn't want to be involved with him because he was married. But despite my refusals, he would call me into his office, back me up against the wall, stand inches from my face, and go into long detailed descriptions of what he wanted me to do sexually to him. I can remember the smell of his body to this day.

---

* Authorities who do not want to acknowledge the prevalence of sexual assault sometimes use this rationale to explain away cases that are brought to their attention. This "blame the victim" strategy is effective.

† The *Quid Pro Quo* type of sexual harassment.

The sergeant finally reported to the major of the women's platoon that I was not obeying orders. She called me in, and I told her what was going on. She just laughed and told me not to worry about it. She directed me to my direct supervisor, a female staff sergeant. When I told her what was going on at the commissary, she told me if I would have sex with her, then she would take care of my problem with the male Sergeant. She tried to get me to touch her sexually right then and there. After refusing her offer I decided I was not safe in the military and wanted out. I was getting so desperate that I even made several suicide attempts. I found a man who had just gotten back from Vietnam who would marry and impregnate me so I could get discharged from the Marines.

My life has been chaotic since then. I had two children by the man I married. He was an angry man. He used to put guns to my head and threaten me with a knife. He would say, "I'll kill you if you even look at another man." After over six years of this, he volunteered to go back to Vietnam and I was able to get away from him. But I was so physically ill I couldn't take care of my two children. My kidney was four times its normal size due to an assault I experienced from my husband. My in-laws agreed to take care of my children, but only if I gave up my parental rights. I was so ill that I thought I might die, so I signed over custody of my six- and seven-year-old children to them, and they took them to the other side of the continent.

I somehow managed to go back to school. I graduated with a university degree at age forty. I got a job working in a corrections office. I was successful at this job for over seven years, but then one day I was pinned behind my desk by a correctional client who physically resembled one of the attackers who raped me. He laughed at me when I was afraid and began shaking like a leaf.

That night I started imaging myself cutting my face and scarring it with a big "N" where everyone would see it.

I was able to make it through the rest of the week, but I had these terrible feelings and felt totally apart from my body. A few days later I started cutting into my arm with a razor, looking for veins so I would bleed a lot. A couple of days later it was getting worse, so I called my estranged husband, who took me to hospital. I spent the next week in a psychiatric hospital. After I was discharged, I started cutting again, so I ended up back in the same hospital. They sent me to the VA psychiatric ward. My husband couldn't deal with my destructive behavior and divorced me.

Over the next three years, I was hospitalized numerous times. I bled myself so much that I had to have blood transfusions several times. Once I nearly died from the loss of blood.

I had never harmed myself until my first breakdown. I was forty-seven then. The head psychiatrist at the VA continuously asked me why I had not started cutting myself earlier in life. He thought my only problem was being a Borderline Personality Disorder. Two of the women psychiatrists thought my cutting was related to my trauma and gave me the diagnosis Post-Traumatic Stress Disorder.

I cannot tell you how humiliating it was for me to be treated the way I was at the VA hospital. Once, a physician began sewing up my wound where I had cut myself before the anesthesia had taken effect. As he pushed the needle into my skin he kept asking me, "Can you feel this?" When I told him it hurt he replied, "Maybe now you will find something better to do." When I got an infection in the places I had cut, a different VA physician examined me. He tore out the stitches while telling me, "Maybe now you will not cut again."

Another time, I was told to take off all my clothes and sit in a seclusion room. I was not given a robe or gown to wear. I sat there sobbing, trying to cover my body with my hands because I knew the camera in this room was connected to the monitor at the front desk, and I knew from experience that both staff and patients could easily see the monitor.

I finally decided I was never going to get better living in an area that had so many triggers, so I decided to move. I had heard there was a good VA hospital where I could get treated with respect and dignity, so I moved close to it.

For a long time the sun did not shine at all for me. Still, now, I have times when my life is filled with the shadows of yesterday. Many times I have begged God to take me. But each morning I would wake up praying to make it through the day. I have lived alone the past eighteen months, and I still fear making new friends or going new places. Despite all this, my life is getting better.

How can I explain to anyone, be they counselors, doctors, or others, that I never cut to get attention? I learned to hate the attention I got when I had to go to Urgent Care or get bandages changed. How degrading it was to be treated as less than human and shamed before the entire world.

Not everyone who cuts is Borderline. Not everyone who cuts is seeking attention. Not everyone who cuts is stupid and has nothing better to do in life. Sometimes, even we do not understand why it started or why we keep doing it. It is two years since I have cut or injured myself. I cannot tell you why I stopped anymore than why I started in the first place.

Please don't judge us with narrow attitudes. We are human. We hurt. We cry. We have suffered in life. We need more understanding, more empathy, and more help to get past the self-destructive stages, past the nightmares and daymares that plague us, and past the fear that makes us dread tomorrow. We need someone to believe in us and give us a name beyond mental illness, be it Borderline Personality Disorder or PTSD.

I want others to know that there is hope beyond the horizon, even for those who are self-destructive. We have the right to have a better life and to love ourselves enough not to try to destroy ourselves. We don't have to go through life playing the victim and should strive for being true survivors. It is important for us to learn to believe in ourselves and know we can make our own road to the future—to learn even when it is cloudy the sun is shining somewhere.

We cannot weigh our hurt against someone else's. While I worked for the veteran's employment office, I was told by my male superior I would not make a good veteran representative because I had never been to war. I responded, "Oh, I have been to war, just not the same war you went through."

Emancipation[5]

With my head thrown back,
I stood facing life,
With stubborn, blazing eyes.
"I will make it,"
I cried out in passion.
I will step beyond,
Any limitations
And break free,

From yesterday's chains,
Go beyond
Today's vague promises;
And march towards,
Tomorrow's future;
Until I am,
The vision I seek.

Paula C.

LONG-TERM SEXUAL ABUSE BY A SUPERIOR

I JOINED THE NAVY at age twenty-one. After boot camp and "A" school, I went to my first duty station. Then my life went downhill. I don't remember dates or the sequence of the timeline, as my memory has been affected, but many details are still crystal clear.[*] My problems started when the new second in command transferred into our unit. The senior chief seemed harmless at first; he was much older than me and I knew nothing of his reputation. I was young and trusting, passive, and had been taught to respect authority and obey orders. At a unit party, I had too much to drink to drive home, and he offered to make sure I got home all right. I was flattered by his concern. Once he got me into my apartment, he changed. I remember feeling uncomfortable and intimidated by him. By the time I realized what he was after, he had gotten me onto my bed. I was in no condition to give consent or to say no, and since he was in the direct chain of command and of superior rank, I was afraid of the repercussions if I fought back.[†] I thought once he got what he wanted, this would be the end of it. I was wrong.

---

[*] Memory is one area where the legal system and the mental health system come in conflict. Courts are very interested in facts such as dates and times in order to determine whether to press charges and to assign guilt. Mental health systems are more interested in the effect of an experience. Disturbance of memory, particularly for details, is a hallmark of trauma. When those who have been assaulted testify, inability to recall dates or other details can be interpreted as a sign of dishonesty rather than an effect of trauma.

[†] In civilian life, the man could easily claim the sex was consensual, even though she was intoxicated. In the military, even if Paula had given consent, it would be fraternization, which is forbidden regardless of marital status or supervisory linkage.

The situation got worse. I was too embarrassed and ashamed to let anyone know what he had done to me. I just wanted to forget the whole thing, but he now had me under his control.

As I came to know him better, I learned he was generally mean, nasty, verbally abusive, and frequently hung-over. He hated women and felt they had no place in the Navy, saying, "Women are good for only one thing and that is to be flat on their backs." He used intimidation and threats to ensure my silence and to continue using me as he pleased. He threatened to ruin my career and make my life hell if I told anyone anything, saying things like, "It's my word against yours; no one is going to take the word of an E-4 over the word of an E-8."* By now I was terrified of him and felt totally helpless.

The sexual abuse escalated over the months. I remember fragments of numerous occasions. He would come find me, drag me to his office, lock the door, and pull me down to perform oral sex on him.

Hoping to avoid him, I stopped going out and stayed in my apartment, but he would show up there, usually drunk. If I didn't hurry up and open the door, he threatened to break the window to let himself in. He was always verbally abusive, sadistic, and into rough sex. I hated every minute of it and would just lie there until he was done with me. One time, he got ticked off that I wasn't being an enthusiastic participant. When he got off of me, he said, "You sure are a lousy fuck."

Another time, he told me we were going out and to wear a dress. He took me to an adult theater. We sat in the back and watched a porno movie while he had his hand up under my dress and had me fondle his penis. Afterward, he drove me home and there he raped me yet again.

I was scared to death of becoming pregnant. Since Navy Medical would not consider me for sterilization, I felt I had to take matters into my own hands. In May 1979, I went to an abortion clinic where they performed a tubal ligation. I even had to ask the senior chief for the seventy-two-hour liberty to schedule the surgery. I had the procedure on a Friday and had to report to work on Monday morning. I was in a lot of pain, with a two-inch incision in my abdomen, and could not do anything at all. Yet, he would not excuse me to recuperate, and I was left with a really bad scar.

* Forms of rank, with E-8 being superior.

The trauma was taking its toll on me. I became withdrawn and depressed. I was drinking frequently and heavily. I even carried a flask in my Navy-issue purse so I could have a couple shots in the morning, just to get through the day. I took care not to run into the senior chief and if I had to report to him, I made sure I was not alone and stood near the door so it could stay open. I felt very alone and afraid all the time. I wondered if my peers noticed my behavior and if anyone suspected what was going on, but I was too afraid of his revenge to confide in anyone.

I considered going up the chain of command for help, but that was impossible in this case. I could not trust our commanding officer either, since he had a reputation for cheating on his wife. He went along on one of our road trips to observe our unit. That night, after everyone had retired to their motel rooms, he came and knocked on my door. I knew it was him and did not open the door. With everything I had been going through, I had learned to be a lot less trusting. I asked him what he wanted, and he invited me to his room for a drink. I made up an excuse and turned down his proposition. I was convinced that the senior chief had bragged to him about what an easy target I was.

I felt completely trapped, and felt like my life was spiraling downward. I didn't know how much more I could take or what to do about it. The chief finally pushed me beyond my limit when he came up with the sick idea of pimping me out to other chiefs. He was going to set it up for me to have sex with them and even collect money from them. That was the last straw. I had to draw the line and summoned up the courage to refuse his demands. At this point I just didn't care what happened to me anymore. Even if he hurt me or dragged my reputation through the mud, I had had enough torment. I guess he realized I meant it, because after that, the harassment let up. I still had to be very careful to avoid him and I lived in constant fear. He still would instill terror in me with a certain look or whispered comment.

In 1980, a new E-4 transferred into our unit. His apartment was two buildings from mine, and we started carpooling to work. We hung out together and became friends. When our relationship developed into a long-term commitment, I felt it was important to be honest and have no secrets, so I told him about my sterilization and the abuse I suffered from the senior chief. I then learned that he had his own reasons for hating the man from past experiences. He cornered the senior chief in his office one day and warned him that if he ever came near me again, he would kill him. We all had to attend the senior chief's retirement ceremony, and I fantasized about spitting in his face and telling everyone what a perverted, dirty old man he was. We never spoke of him again, and I completely blocked out that terrible year and tried to move on with my life. I married my knight in shining armor in December 1980.

In 1983, we transferred to NETC, Newport (Rhode Island). We weathered some difficult times, but he was always there for me, protecting me from the stresses of Navy life. Before leaving Newport in 1987, I had made it to petty officer first class, but was also battling weight problems and high blood pressure. We were moved back to Memphis, TN.

Being back at the old Memphis building started triggering long-buried memories. I felt nervous and often had this vague feeling of impending doom. In addition to being assigned to numerous regular duties, I was also assigned the duty of supply petty officer, a difficult, time-consuming job with awesome financial responsibility. My supply office was the same room that, eight years ago, was senior chief's office. I had a lot of trouble concentrating and I couldn't get the hang of the supply accounts. My anxiety became overwhelming. I started having nightmares and not sleeping. I became exhausted and was having crying spells, anxiety attacks, and flashbacks almost every day. I got so depressed, I thought I was having a nervous breakdown, so I finally went to sick call to the psych deptartment. My symptoms were chalked up to job stress and I went to the master chief and told him I could not handle the supply job; it was too overwhelming for me. The fact that he was very disappointed in me made me feel worse. I continued to have a low threshold for any type of stress or confrontation, which would set off a panic attack, causing all the horrible memories to come flooding back. This was to be my last tour of duty. My weight was out of control, my nerves were shot, and I knew I would not pass the next reenlistment physical. I had always planned to serve a full twenty years, but it was not to be. I left the Navy in February 1990.

These traumatic experiences have had a profound effect on my life and continue to do so. The drinking problem, which I have since overcome, was a direct result of the repeated abuse. I have been dealing with fear and anxiety for years, never connecting why I would fall apart so easily. I have trouble with sleeping, waking up numerous times each night, often from disturbing nightmares and drenched in sweat, so I am always fatigued. The smallest thing startles me when I'm not expecting it, and I have an obsessive, compulsive behavior about checking the locks at home. I check the doors anywhere from twenty to fifty times a day even though I know they are locked. I have two dogs and security alarms on both my home and vehicle, which gives me some peace of mind. I have agoraphobia, in that I feel safest when at home. I never go out alone after dark and at times can barely force myself to leave the house. I'm always afraid of what's going to happen to me next out there that will set off a panic attack. I have trouble focusing on tasks at hand and have noticed my memory getting worse and worse. I am obsessed with stories of women in peril, especially rape or abuse. I have to know how others dealt with it and survived and could I have done something differently.

My sexual desire is nonexistent, much to the chagrin of my patient and understanding husband. I have no self-esteem and I use being overweight as a way to protect myself, by not being desirable to men. Different reminders set off flashbacks. I remember the Tailhook scandal in the news, and having intense feelings of bitterness and repressed anger. Any kind of stress is a trigger. It starts out where I feel nervous, frustrated, or overwhelmed by some type of conflict or confrontation. Once it escalates to a panic attack, I am unable to control it. My throat constricts, I have trouble breathing, my heart pounds, and my mind floods with every bad thing that ever happened to me. At best, I am reduced to tears; at worst, I become hysterical. Afterward I am completely drained and unable to function for the rest of the day.

It took many years before I could talk about the trauma. I finally reported it to the VA, even though I still have a fear that that man is out there somewhere and will hunt me down because I told. I wish I knew if he was still alive, because if he isn't, my mind could be put at ease, and I wouldn't be so scared anymore. The stress finally took a physical toll on me: in April 1997, I ended up in the emergency room twice with a peptic ulcer. I was quite ill for two months. I realized then that I had to get help and called the VA who put me touch with the mental health department. Meds have helped and therapy has helped me to understand myself better and why I feel the way I do.

I have heard lots of horror stories about dealing with the VA. I belong to a women vets support group on the Internet, which I have found to be very rewarding and enlightening. It's nice to have others with similar experiences and understanding to relate to. I feel lucky that I have always been treated with respect by the staff at the Oakland Park Outpatient Clinic and at the hospital in Miami. The psychiatrists and social workers that I have been assigned to were especially helpful and instrumental in my attaining a positive outcome of my claim, and I was referred to a really good veterans service officer, who took care of filing all the paperwork and documentation. Everyone along the way was always encouraging and said I "had a great case. . . . It was just a matter of time." Of course the most frustrating part was the waiting; the process dragged on for so long, since the system is woefully backlogged. Getting timely appointments is also a challenge as they are always understaffed and overworked. The system is not perfect, but I have never been treated badly. Plus, I wish I had not waited so many years to come forward and finally report it. I could have received compensation and treatment so much sooner. It was just so hard to finally take that first step. The strongest feelings I had when I won my claims were relief and validation. I felt like the truth was out and acknowledged by the government, and that the compensation they awarded was to try to make it up to me for the psychiatric injuries I suffered while serving my country. It gave me a sense of closure, and I could finally begin healing.

Until recently, I was able to hold down a part-time job in the same company with my husband. I was able to get by at work because he was my boss and still my protector. I dreaded every time the phone rang, fearful that I would have to deal with an irate customer or get yelled at.

In 2000, a volatile situation occurred at work and sent me into a total relapse. My PTSD symptoms rebounded worse than ever. I woke up every single morning with my stomach in knots. I was agitated and angry and would have flashbacks and panic attacks as I tried to get ready for work. The closer it got to time to leave the house, the worse I felt. I had to take a tranquilizer just to force myself to drive the forty-five minutes to the office. This would happen only during the work week, but not on the weekends,. I finally realized what I had to do to get relief: get back into therapy and quit my job, as stress is my primary trigger. I left my job for health reasons and have stayed at home ever since. I feel less nervous and fearful, and since then I have had very few major panic attacks. However, I am still always fatigued and have a difficult time functioning during the day, as I am still having nightmares or disturbed sleep every night. My problems with memory and concentration keep me from going back out in the working world; there are too many mean people out there and I can't handle being around them.

Since there is no cure for PTSD, I have learned to cope with it by avoiding any stress that triggers the flashbacks, panic attacks, etc. For now I am concentrating on feeling safe and I am using this time to continue therapy and to feel better. I have gotten to the point where I am putting myself first.

The trauma I experienced was not a single event; it was repeated and ongoing for the better part of a year. It wasn't just the rapes and abuse done to me physically; it was also the brainwashing by the chief. A couple of years ago, my husband heard from a Navy buddy that senior chief K. was dead. I sure wish I could confirm that as fact, as it would give me peace of mind to know he is not still out there somewhere. Thank you for letting me tell my story.

Rachel Johnson[*]

SEXUALLY ABUSED AS A CHILD BY HER STEPFATHER; SEXUALLY ABUSED BY A SERIES OF MILITARY SUPERIORS

THERE IN THE SMALL, cramped apartment I shared with my family I sat hunched over, frozen across the kitchen table from my stepfather. My eyes fixed firmly on a neatly framed photo hanging alone on the wall. It was 1977, and I was on the threshold of puberty. Our eyes never met, but I was acutely aware of his long, labored breaths, each executed with more effort than the last. I watched helplessly as the man my mother married (over my objections) just one year before moved his hands between his legs, caressing his crotch repeatedly.

I remember him walking toward me, three months later, each step more ominous than the last. He was moving toward me with his genitals exposed in one hand, gripping a fist full of dollars in the other. He called out to me, "Do you need any money?" I looked past him, down the hall, hoping against hope that someone would awaken to disrupt this dreadful scene, see what I saw, perhaps feel what I felt—total repulsion and horror. But it was not to be. I hurried out the door moments later, passively declining the offer of money.[†]

---

[*] Name changed at her request.
[†] It is common for victims of childhood sexual abuse to go on as adults to experience sexual harassment and other forms of sexual abuse.

Later that afternoon, I reached out from a pay phone to my mother's sister. I relayed my experiences and disclosed overwhelming fears of returning home. Would he touch me next time, attack me, threaten me? I feared the worst was yet to come.

That evening I arrived home and sensed immediately that all was not well with my mother. There was a look of disdain on her face as she looked at me and in a very somber voice said, "He's getting out of here, but I know you did something to entice him." The words cut me like a knife.

I recall being in my early twenties, a proud member of the communications aquadron of the U.S. Air Force, stationed at my first duty assignment. I enjoyed my assigned duties as a ground radio operator and worked diligently to perform at full capacity from the outset of my tour. I felt a sense of cohesion with my fellow service members. One day, during my participation in a squadron picnic, the unit's noncommissioned officer in charge, Sergeant Briggs, stood behind me as I was conversing with other service members. Suddenly, he blurted out to me, "Nice ass!" I turned to face him, and he covered his mouth in a gesture of embarrassment. Many of the enlisted members (mostly male) were seated and a few of them laughed openly. Sergeant Briggs never apologized. I was confused about what action I should take and worried that if I openly expressed disagreement, it might somehow be used against me.

I felt humiliated and hurt, but to a great extent, responsible for what happened. I spent the remainder of my year-long tour avoiding interaction with both peers and superiors. I never resolved such feelings during my tour. At the end of my tour, I felt as though I left the base behind, but not my feelings associated with my experience there.

It was during my second tour of duty at another base that I accepted a car ride on base to my residence off-base from the squadron's first sergeant, Staton. He approached me as I was standing in front of a base facility waiting for my boyfriend to pick me up. He smiled, inquired as to my status, and offered to take me home in his vehicle. I accepted. When we arrived, I don't recall the circumstances that led to his being inside my apartment, but I recall him walking toward me and then leaning against me, then starting to undo my clothes. I repeatedly asked him to stop, but he ignored me. I remember being near the kitchen when he maneuvered me to the floor, proceeded to undo my pants, and enter me. I remember saying, "No" and thinking, "This is not happening." All at once it was over, and he was gone. I do not have any memories of what took place afterward except that he never acknowledged the incident and I felt that if I did, my Air Force career would somehow be jeopardized. When I told my boyfriend that Sergeant Staton had given me a ride home that day, he was angry with me, so I did not disclose the incident to him because I was afraid and ashamed of how he would view me. I also feared that he might report the incident, which in turn might jeopardize my Air Force career.

On another occasion, I was required to participate in a base-wide exercise involving full chemical warfare gear. I remember being heavily laden with a web belt, canteen, hand-held radio, camouflage uniform and helmet. When the exercise was complete, an Air Force enlisted male offered me a ride home. I don't recall the circumstances regarding his entering my home, but I recall that, once inside, he grabbed me from behind, turned me around, and pushed me to the floor. I had all my exercise gear on and so did he. I felt as if I was in a fog as I protested his actions and pleaded with him to stop. He ignored me and kept repeating in a calm, low voice, "It's going to be all right." He positioned himself over me, had me pinned down and with one hand proceeded to unzip his pants, then mine, and entered me. When he was finished, he left me on the floor and walked out of the door. I do not recall ever seeing him on base ever again. However, by coincidence, during my last tour of duty I traveled to another base in close proximity where I noticed this same individual walking nearby. Our eyes met. He greeted me, and the conversation was brief and strained for me. At no point did he ever acknowledge what he had done to me. I walked away from him and never saw him again.

On still another occasion, I was the passenger in the vehicle of a high-ranking enlisted male. I do not recall the circumstances that led to my being in his vehicle, but I do recall him stopping his vehicle in an isolated area, reaching over to me in the passenger seat, grabbing the back of my neck while unzipping his pants, and forcing my head down between his legs. I told him to stop and, as I looked up at him, I remember him smiling down at me and ignoring me. He kept my face positioned down in his crotch area and, with his private parts exposed, forced me to perform oral sex. I do not remember his name, nor how the situation ended. I only remember feeling ashamed and feeling as if what happened was my fault alone.

Today, over fifteen years after these deplorable experiences, I frequently find myself emotionally gripped by lingering, conflicting feelings of sadness, anger, guilt, and confusion. Sadness and anger because I have been victimized. Guilt and confusion because of my role in the situation. Could I have done something differently to influence the outcomes?

All too often, I am transformed into an unidentified being, full of explosive, uncontained rage. In the aftermath, I am emotionally spent, psychologically imprisoned behind stone-cold, impenetrable walls. At times, I long to escape a world immersed in painful truths too difficult to bear. But I have found that the sun does indeed rise. I am able to catch glimpses of it from time to time.

Raymond D.[*]

ABUSED AS A CHILD AND TWICE
GANG-RAPED AS AN ADULT

RAY'S STORY APPEARS in a format that is different from the previous stories. He found it too emotionally painful to write his story in narrative form. Therefore I sent him some questions for him to respond to. Once he had responded to these, we talked by telephone.

WHAT HAPPENED?

In 1975 I was brutally gang-r——-ed.

This is the way Raymond wrote his description. He was so ashamed of what happened, he couldn't bring himself to write out the word rape. Raymond's assaults took place during his second enlistment period. He had been honorably discharged and returned to civilian life. Then he later reenlisted. The first assault took place while Raymond was posted in a remote area. Several men jumped him from behind. He decided not to fight back because he felt "a cold object" on his neck that he believed was the barrel of a weapon. Fellow soldiers then sexually assaulted him.

---

* Name changed at his request. Raymond is the husband of Annie, whose story appears earlier in this book.

The second assault took place two years later. He left an on-base club and was sexually assaulted by four soldiers, one of whom he recognized from the first attack.

WHO DID IT?

The perpetrators were other [American] soldiers.

WHAT WERE THE FIRST EFFECTS?

Having already suffered years of childhood abuse,s being brutally gang-r——-ed only added to my anger and hatred. Once again people had caused me to feel more hurt and pain. People enjoyed abusing me. My abuse gave them a deep feeling of pleasure in their lives. As a result of this attack and the effects it caused, I ended up going AWOL. My only thoughts were getting away from anything and everyone.

DID YOU TELL ANYONE?

No, I did not tell anyone about my attacks. Keep in mind it was during the 1970s and the fact that I was in the military, reporting it would have caused me even more harm.

Following the assault, Raymond returned to his assigned barracks. After several days, he left the post without authorization. He was gone for five days, during which he consumed alcohol "the whole time."

When I did finally return from being AWOL, I again suffered at the hands of people; I faced court martial and was sent to a retraining brigade, a part of the military prison system. While being punished for going AWOL, I was again gang-r——-ed. I had not yet sorted through the first attack and then it happened a second time.

The second assault took place when he left an on-base club and was sexually assaulted by four soldiers, one of whom he recognized from the first attack.

I told no one of this second attack. Who was there to tell? After being gang-r——-ed twice in a six-month period, I went off the deep end and no longer cared. People and their years of different abuses had finally accomplished what they had hoped

for, the total destruction of a human life. They had succeeded in their goal. They
had succeeded 100 percent.

Following the second assault, Ray went AWOL for forty-five days.
When he returned, he met with the company commander, but was
too ashamed to tell him about the assault. He did hint at the personal
nature of his motivation by saying, "Due to the nature of my reason, I
can't discuss it with you." Raymond's sergeant spoke on his behalf at the
court-martial proceedings, saying Raymond had been "an exemplary
soldier and something terrible must have happened to cause him to violate military law." Raymond was discharged with Bad Conduct status.

DID YOU SEEK HELP FROM THE VETERANS ADMINISTRATION?

I turned to the VA system for help. But I ended up regretting seeking their help.
"Stupid" me had forgotten doing so meant being around people again. Why would
I want that? People had already done so much for me in my life! The people in the
VA system who tried to help were few and far between, almost nonexistent.

WHAT WERE THE LONG-TERM EFFECTS?

As a direct result of all the abuses I suffered, so much was stolen from me: I never
had a childhood; I went through broken marriages and families and years of alcohol
abuse to block out all the "fine and wonderful" moments of my life. I have learned
a valuable lesson in life: trust only yourself and never the enemy. That's exactly
what I saw and believe the military and society is to me—the enemy. Their only
purpose was to bring about my total destruction. Then and only then would they
feel happy and content in a job well done. Now can you understand my feelings
toward society as a whole? Probably not! But then, if you can't, it won't surprise
me. Very few understand. I've never had friends in life. I have no desire to be part
of society. After all, have I not already had enough of society? Of course I have!

I've learned so much from my abuses. Things like hate, anger, resentment, and
isolation. Even the "wonderful and warm" feeling that abandonment leaves. Wow!
Am I blessed in life? Through my many years of abuse I have been given such
"precious gifts" from society. I would love to tell society how much I appreciate
each and every one of them. But for some unknown reason, I just can't seem to
find the appropriate words. At times I feel like saying "Thank you" to them. But
then I remember they deserve better than that. Sure they do.

ABOUT THE CONTRIBUTORS

Gregory A. Helle is the author of *A Walk in Hell: The Other Side of War.* He served in Vietnam as a U.S. Army, SP5.

Reverend Dorothy H. Mackey is the executive director and cofounder of Survivors Take Action Against Abuse by Military Personnel, Inc. (STAAAMP), which was founded in 1997. Rev. Mackey graduated from the Air Force Institute of Technology with advanced studies in Acquisition Management/Contract Negotiations. She has a master's degree in public administration, graduating Summa Cum Laude from Troy State University, and a bachelor's of science in criminal justice/political science from the University of Akron. While in ROTC she entered the U.S. Air Force as a Second Lieutenant and served from 1983 through 1992, rising to the rank of Captain and Commander. Her military and civilian awards and recognitions include *Who's Who of Women Executives*, nomination as

Federal Women's Supervisor of the Year, the U.S. Air Force Commendation Medal, and the U.S. Air Force Achievement Medal. Her work in the field of abuse within the military has led the print and broadcast media to seek her out on numerous occasions. She has spoken to audiences throughout the world, including the East Asian Pacific Women's Summit on U.S. Military Abuses, the Women's Feminist Majority Conference on U.S. Military Abuses, the Peace Conference concerning East Asian Abuses by U.S. Military members.

END NOTES

CHAPTER ONE

1. Woods & Mahoney, 1994, p. 16.
2. Speech, Marines Not Taught to Hate, given to the Committee on Armed Services, January 1962.
3. Janda, 2002, p. xi.
4. Braudy, 2003, p. xix.
5. Kennedy, 2001, p. 12.
6. Jeffers & Levitan, 1971, p. 186.
7. Gerzon, 1982, p. 28.
8. Motten, 2003.
9. Hightower, 2005.
10. Woulfe, 1998.
11. Ricks, 1997.
12. Da Cruz, 1987, p. 23.
13. Woulfe, 1998.
14. *Star Tribune*, 11/13/05, p. AA7.
15. Powell, 2000, p. 70.
16. Ricks, 1997, p. 20.
17. Zeeland, 1996, p. 158.
18. Hedges, 2002, p. 3.
19. Kennedy, 2001, p. xix.
20. Wood & Mahoney, 1994, p. 161.
21. Zeeland, 1996, p. 48.
22. Manchester, 1983, p. 391.
23. Wood & Mahoney, 1994, p. 16.
24. Da Cruz, 1987, p. 38.
25. Dubbert, 1979, p. 76; 192.
26. Gerzon, 1982, p. 93.
27. Miedzian, 1991, p. 22.
28. Lawlisee, 1988, p. 86.
29. Calendo, 1982, p. 64.

CHAPTER TWO

1. Cox, 1999, p. 168.
2. Benedict, 1959, p. 12.
3. Ricks, 1997, p. 65.
4. Shalit, 1988, p. 317.
5. Ibid.
6. Ibid.
7. Ricks, 1997, p. 78.
8. Dyer, 1985, p. 115–116.
9. Anderson, 1997.
10. Da Cruz, 1987.
11. Shay, 1994, p. 151.
12. Burke, 1996, p. 214.
13. Da Cruz, 1987, p. 79.
14. Ricks, 1997, p. 86.
15. Da Cruz, 1987, p. 41.
16. Powell, 2000.
17. Janda, 2002, pp. 88; 92.
18. Naval Terminology, Jargon and Slang

http://www.hazegray.org/fag/slang

19. G.I.jargon.com.

20. Ibid.

21. Da Cruz, 1987, p. 59.

22. Ricks, 1997, p. 150.

23. Pers. comm.

24. Zeeland, 1996, p. 28.

25. Huxley, 1939.

26. Grossman, 1995.

27. Sheldrake, 2003, pp. 140-141.

28. "Bob MacGowan" is a fictitious name used to protect his identity. CNN Presents: *Fit To Kill*, October 26, 2003.

29. Francke, 1997.

30. Hersh, 1970, p. 185.

31. Brownmiller, 1975.

32. *War As I Knew It*, p. 23.

33. Copelon, 1994, p. 213.

34. Hersh, 1970.

35. Brownmiller, 1975, p. 53.

36. Nanking International Relief Committee, 1938.

37. Chang, 1997.

38. *Horror in the East*, The History Channel, March 8, 2005.

39. Shanor & Hogue, 1996, 197.

40. Da Cruz, 1987, 14.

41. Da Cruz, 1987.

42. Ricks, 1997, p. 71.

43. Grossman, 1995, p. 143.

44. Terry, 1985.

45. *http://abcnews.go.com/sections/GMA/World/Iraq_Abuse_Davis_040514-1.html*

46. Archard, 1998.

47. Ibid., p. 51.

48. Rhem, 2001.

49. MacKinnon, 1982.

50. Pateman, 1988; 1989.

51. Archard, 1998, p. 36.

52. Dyer, 1985, p. 147.

53. Nelson, 1983, p. 142.

54. Saar & Novak, 2005, p. 108.

55. Dyer, 1985, p. 152.

56. LeShan, 2002.

57. Joint Doctrine Division, J-7, Joint Staff.

58. Vistica, 1995.

59. Zeeland, 1996, p. 163.

60. Orloff v. Willoughby, 345 U.S. 83, 94 (1953).

61. Vistica, 1995, p. 417.

62. *Final report of the Independent Panel to Review DoD Detention Operations* August 2004, p. 18.

63. Investigation of Abu Ghraib Prison and 205th Military Intelligence Brigade.

64. Wood & Mahoney, 1994, p. 9.

65. Burke, 2004.

66. Anderson, 1997.

67. Clark Hine, 1989.

68. Wood & Mahoney, 1994.

69. Ricks, 1997.

70. Toner, 2006.

71. O'Hare & O'Donohue, 1998, based on Finkelhor, 1984.

72. Pryor, 1995.

73. Ibid.

CHAPTER THREE

1. Gutek, 1985; Gruber, 1997.

2. Zeeland, 1996, p. 33.

3. Kennedy, 2001.

4. Kahn, 1984, p. 238.

5. Military Resource Center, 1995.

6. Resolution 3, June 9-11, 1998, Salt Lake City, UT.

7. Katzenstein, 1998, p. 50.

8. Dean, 1997; 1999. The military-pornography alliance.

9. Johnson, 2004, p. AA6.; Badger, 2004.

10. Maloney, 1947, pp. 26-27.

11. Gerzon, 1982, p. 31.

12. Kaplan, 2003, p. 203.

13. Dinter, 1985.
14. Showalter, 1987.
15. Herman, 1992, p. 54.
16. Wood & Mahoney, 1994.
17. Burke, 1996.
18. Dingfelder, 2005, p. 10.
19. Hatheway, 2001.
20. Matthews, 1996.
21. Archard, 1998.
22. Powell, 2000, p. 145.
23. Goddard, 2004.
24. Kaplan, 2003.
25. Kimmel & Messner, 1995, xiii.
26. McBride, 1995, pp. 43-44.
27. *http://www.geocities.com*
28. Grossman, 1995, pp. 307-308.
29. Burke, 2004, pp. xi-xii.
30. Francke, 1997, p. 95.
31. Shilts, 1993, p. 133.
32. Powell, 2000, p. 142.
33. Schmitt, 2005.
34. Levy, 1989.
35. Capt. Ted Triebel, U. S. Navy, interviewed by Morris, 2000.
36. Morris, 1982, pp. 202-203. She became aware of these facts because she was special consultant to the Secretary of the Army.
37. Ibid.
38. Ibid.
39. Truman, Tokar & Fischer, 1996, p. 559.
40. Malamuth & Sockloskie, Koss & Tanaka, 1991; Mosher & Anderson, 1986; Quackenbush, 1989; Riedel, 1993; Tieger, 1981.
41. Sanday, 1981, p. 25.
42. Costin, 1985; Fischer, 1986; Hudson & Ricketts, 1988; Malamuth & Sockloskie, Koss & Tanaka, 1991; Mosher & Anderson, 1986; Quackenbush, 1989; Riedel, 1993; Sanday, 1981; Stark, 1991; Thompson, Grisanti, Pleck, 1985; Tieger, 1981.
43. Opotow, 2005, p. 127.
44. Francke, 1997, p. 260.
45. Testimony before the House Armed Services Committee, February 1984.
46. Holm, 1992, p. 381-382.
47. Fussell, 1989, p. 130.

CHAPTER FOUR

1. Barkalow, & Raab, 1990, p. 31.
2. Nuwer, 1990.
3. MacArthur, 1964, p. 25.
4. Finkel, 2004.
5. Nuwer, 2004.
6. Zeeland, 1996, p. 95.
7. Burke, 2004.
8. Zeeland, 1996.
9. Zeeland, 1996.
10. Lenny, 1949, p. 136.
11. Knudson, 1981.
12. Knudson, 1981.
13. Knudson, 1981.
14. Janda, 2002, p. 99.
15. Webb, 1979, p. 148.
16. Coulthard-Clark, 1984, p. 125.
17. McCain, 1999, pp. 120-121.
18. Knudson, 1981.
19. Barkalow & Raab, 1990, p. 36.
20. Reber, 1985, p. 657.
21. Nuwer, 2004, p. 143.
22. *Bugle Notes*, p. 39.
23. Statement by General Paul Kern, Commanding General, United States Army Materiel Command Before the Armed Services Committee, United States Senate on the Investigation Of the 205th Military Intellence Bridgade At Abu Ghraib Prison, Iraq, Second Session, 108th Congress, September 9th, 2004, p. 8.
24. Hersh, 2004, p. 22.
25. Kern, 2004, p. 7.
26. Ayala, 2004.

27. *AR 15-6 Investigation of Abu Ghraib Prison and 205th Military Intelligence Brigade*, p. 10.

28. Witt, 2004.

29. Black, 2004, p. A-20.

30. *AR 15-6 investigation of MG Fay*, paragraph 11, p. 45.

31. Embser-Herbert, 2004.

32. Jones, 2005, p. 11.

33. Saar & Novak, 2005.

34. Protocol I, Art. 75, http://www.globalissuesgroup.com/geneva/protocol2.html#4.

35. *Geneva Convention, Relative to the Treatment of Prisoners of War*. Office of the United Nations High Commissioner for Human Rights, Geneva, Switzerland, p. 6

36. The Lieber Code of 1863, Correspondence, Orders, Reports, and Returns of the Union Authorities from January 1 to December 31, 1863, #7 O.R., Series III, Volume III.

37. Burke, 2004.

38. Zagorin, 2005.

39. Woodruff, 2001, p. 179.

CHAPTER FIVE

1. Moon, 1997.

2. Ibid.

3. Ibid.

4. Matsui, 1984,

5. Lehr, 1993, p. 89.

6. Enloe, 1996, p. 15.

7. Moon, 1997.

8. Butler, 2000.

9. Powell, 2000, p. 130.

10. Costello, 1985.

11. USFK Civil Affairs Conference, March 2, 1973, and USFK Civil Affairs Conference, September 28, 1973, cited in Moon, 1997,

12. Vistica, 1995.

13. Powell, 2000.

14. Winick & Kinsie, 1971; Loory, 1973.

15. Vistica, 1995.

16. Brandt, 1985.

17. *Pacific Stars and Stripes*, July 3, 1977.

18. Army Regulation #600-240; Air Force Regulation # 211-18.

19. Moon, 1997, p. 118.

20. Vistica, 1995, p. 193.

21. Humphrey, et al., 1970.

22. Moon, 1997, p. 23.

23. Zuger, 1998.

24. *Population Representation in the Military Services*, Chapter 2, http://www.dod.mil/prhome/poprep2002/chapter2/c2_education.htm.

25. Army Office of the Deputy Chief of Staff for Personnel, Human Relations Directorate, Department of Defense, Anti-Child Prostitute Briefing, January 22, 1998.

26. Fred Pang, Assistant Secretary of Defense, U.S. Department of Defense, Washington, D.C., Memorandum for Assistant Secretary of the Navy (Manpower and Reserve Affairs), Assistant Secretary of the Air Force (Manpower, Reserve Affairs, Installations, and Environment), Subject: Anti-Child Prostitution Effort, 30 July 1996.

27. Enloe, 1989.

28. Seifert, 1994, p. 64.

29. de Schmidt, 1991, p. 110.

CHAPTER SIX

1. Enloe, 1983.
2. Campbell, Garza, et al., 2003.
3. Lloyd, 2002.
4. Freudenheim, 1988.
5. Reiss & Ross, 1993.
6. July 26-29, 2002, *http://hometown.aol.com/milesfdn/myhomepage/index.html*
7. Fisher et al., 2005.
8. McFarlane et al., 2005.
9. Dingfelder, 2006.
10. Enloe, 2000, p. 189.
11. Meyer, 2003.
12. Untitled typescript at Clark University, Worcester, MA. Quoted in Enloe, 2000, p. 168.
13. Ibid., 1983.
14. Hosek, et al, 2002.
15. U.S. Army Community and Family Support Center, 2001.
16. Weinstein & Merderer,
17. The Court's *McCarty* decision of 1980 was met by the legislative branch in 1982 with the passage of the Uniformed Services Former Spouses' Protection Act that returned to the state courts the question of how military benefits would be treated in cases of divorce.
18. Lehr, 1993, italics added.
19. Laurier, 2004.
20. Houppert, 2005.
21. Ember & Ember, 1997.
22. Hicks Stiehm, 1999, p. 285.
23. Kim, et al., 1976.
24. Enloe, 1983, p. 87.
25. Jenkins, 1999.
26. GAO, 1979.
27. U.S. Department of Defense Task Force on Domestic Violence, 2003.
28. Department of the Army, 2004.
29. Laurier, 2004.
30. Ring, 2005.
31. Maguen, Suvak, & Litz, 2006.

CHAPTER SEVEN

1. Van Creveld, 1994, p. 88.
2. Williams, 2005.
3. Casey, 2006, Elliot, 2006.
4. D'Amico, 1998, p. 119.
5. Depaux, 1998.
6. Reeves, 1996.
7. Barkalow, & Raab, 1990, p. 23.
8. Ambrose, 1997.
9. Walters, 2005.
10. Murphy, 1978, p. 75.
11. Burke, 2004.
12. Secretary of the Army, 1997, p. 62.
13. Kennedy, 2001, p. 274.
14. Pfluke, 1999.
15. Peach, 1996.
16. Noakes, 1998.
17. Holm, 1992.
18. Francke, 1997; Manning, 1999; Spears, 1998.
19. Francke, 1997.
20. Janofsky & Schemo, 2003.
21. deYoung, 1999, p. xii.
22. William, & Khouzam Skelton, 1995.
23. Kang & Hyams, 2005, p. 1289.
24. U.S. Senate, 1991, p. 895.
25. Dyer, 1985, p. 130.
26. Griesse & Stiters, 1982.
27. Haskell, 2001.
28. Peach, 1996, p. 161.
29. Mitchell, 1998, p. 56.
30. Mitchell, 1998, page 160.
31. Leonard, 1994, p. 16.
32. Treadwell, 1953.
33. Hertbert, 1988.
34. Barkalow, & Raab, 1990.
35. Solaro, 1999.
36. Pennington, 1997.
37. Rupp, 1978, p. 98.

38. Da Cruz, 1987.
39. Campbell & D'Amico, 1999.
40. *Rolling Stone,* January 26, 1995.
41. Center For Military Readiness, *http://www.cmrlink.org/WomenInCombat.*
42. Heimark, 1997, p. 5.
43. Baxandall, Gordon, & Reverby, 1976, pp.75-76.
44. Zeeland, 1996, p. 164.
45. Powell, 2000.
46. March 27 *National Review.*
47. Cook, 2003.
48. Cornum, 1996, p. 12.
49. *The Times,*1996.
50. *The Independent,* 1996.
51. Wright, 1982, p. 74.
52. Treadwell, 1954, p. 25.
53. Price, 1991.
54. Holm, 1992.
55. Herbert, 1988.
56. Campbell, 1990.
57. Resolution 3, June 9-11, Salt Lake City, UT.
58. Janda, 2002, p. 101.
59. Embser-Herbert, 2004.
60. Nabors, 1982, p. 60.
61. D'Amico, 1998.
62. Dunbar, 1992.
63. Alvarez, 2006; Casey, 2006.
64. Grant DePaw, 1981.
65. Hicks Stiehm, 1999, p. 279.
66. Dunbar, 1992, p. 2.
67. Goldstein, 2001.
68. Woulfe, 1998.
69. Kennedy, 2001.
70. Francke, 1997.
71. Bird, 1989.
72. Peach, 1996.
73. Hanley Disher, 1998.
74. Cornum, 1996.
75. Francke, 1997.
76. Holm, 1992, p. 433.
77. Mitchell, 1998.
78. Pers. comm. with St. Paul, Minnesota, recruitment office.
79. Holm, 1992.
80. Ibid.
81. Mitchell, 1998.
82. Peach, 1997.
83. Dean, 1997.
84. Bingham, 2003.
85. Air Force Flight Rules Driving Women Out of the Service, *San Francisco Chronicle*, March 28, 1989.
86. Bradley, *A General's Life.*
87. Mitchell, 1998. p. 5.
88. Leonard, 1994, p. 16.
89. Campbell, 1990.
90. Goldstein, 2001, p. 314.
91. Van Devanter, 1983, p. 32.
92. St. George, 2006, p. 8A.
93. Francke, 1997, p. 161.
94. Dean, 1997, p. 45.
95. Williams, 2005, p. 13.
96. Williams, 2005.
97. Herbert, 1998, p. 55.
98. Shilts, 1993, p. 596.
99. Herbert, 1988, p. 26.
100. Barrett, et al.; Herbert, 1998.
101. Dunivin, 1988.
102. Herbert, 1998, p. 75.
103. Kennedy, 2001, p. 32.
104. Herbert, 1998, p. 106.
105. Herbert, 1998.
106. Frankel, 2004.
107. Based on Herbert, 1998.
108. Anderson, 1997.
109. Jeffers & Levitan, 1971, p. 206.
110. Woulfe, 1998.
111. Da Cruz, 1987.
112. Woulfe, 1998, p. 130.
113. Fleming, 1994, p. 11.
114. Sledge, 1980.
115. Jeffers & Levitan, 1971, pp. 38-39.
116. Quoted in Rick's 1997, p. 90.
117. Jeffers & Levitan, 1971, p.xiv.
118. Jeffers & Levitan, 1971.

119. Ibid.
120. Ibid.
121. Woulfe, 1998.
122. Ricks, 1997, p. 48.
123. Secretary of the Army, 1997, p. 40.
124. Hull, Scott, & Smith, 1982.
125. Wood & Mahoney, 1994.
126. Hicks Stiehm, 1999.
127. United States Military Academy, November 17, 1975, p. 17.
128. Burke, 2004, p. x.
129. Wood & Mahoney, 1994.
130. Holm, 1992.
131. Gaskin & Hawlins, 2003.
132. Hicks Stiehm, 1988.

133. Peach, 1996, p. 166.
134. 1992, pp. 47–48.
135. Harrell & Miller, 1997, p. 101.
136. Pinch, 1982.
137. Rovella, 1998.
138. Donnelly, 1994, p. 10.
139. Villalon, 2004.
140. Williams, 2005.
141. Johnson, 2006.
142. Johnson, 2006, p. 33.
143. Maccoby, 1998.
144. Mitchell, 1996.
145. Cornum, 1996, p. 20.
146. Clarke, 1981.

CHAPTER EIGHT

1. Nazi Persecution of Homosexuals, 1933–1945, United States Holocaust Memorial Museum, Washington, D.C.
2. A.P.A., 1994, p. 770.
3. Campbell & D'Amico, 1999.
4. Pine, 1994.
5. Lehne, 1989, p. 416.
6. Saghir & Robins, 1973.
7. Lehne, 1978; Sorensen, 1973.
8. Clinton & Gore, 1992.
9. RAND, 1993, p. xvii.
10. Servicemembers Legal Defense Network, *http://www.sldn.org/templates/dont/record.html?section=42&record=749*
11. Enloe, 2000.
12. Felien, 2005.
13. Moradi, 2006.
14. Servicemembers Legal Defense Network, fund raising letter, Fall 2006.
15. Hatheway, 2001.
16. Humphrey, 1990, p. 231.
17. Benecke & Dodge, 1996.
18. Vasile, 2005.
19. Braudy, 2003.
20. Lehring, 2003.
21. Ronner, Amy, 2005. Ronner, A.D. (2005). *Homophobia and The Law.*

Washington, DC: American Psychological Association.
22. Shilts, 1993.
23. Lehring, 2003.
24. Department of Defense, 1982 (written in 1981, went into effect 1982).
25. Garner, 1999.
26. *Robinson v. California* 370 U.S. 660 (1962).
27. Rivera, 1991, p. 85.
28. Richard P. Watson, Lieutenant v. William S. Cohen, Secretary of Defense; John Dalton, Secretary of the Navy; United States of America
29. Ibid.
30. Department of Defense, 1982.
31. Longenecker, 1992, p. 19.
32. Weinberg & Williams, 1974.
33. Walzer, 2000.
34. Kaplan, 2003.
35. Gross, 1990, p. 24.
36. Servicemembers Legal Defense Network Historical Timeline of "*Don't Ask, Don't Tell, Don't Pursue, Don't Harass,*" www.sldn.org.
37. Humphrey, 1990, p. 265.
38. Belkin, 2004, p. 3.

39. Belkin, & Evans, 2000.
40. Zeeland, 1996, p. 161.
41. Zeeland, 1993, p. 15, Italics in the original.
42. Williams, 2005, p. 22.
43. *CSSMM*, Vol. 4 (1), Fall, 2002.
44. Ari Bianco, 1996, p. 50.
45. Associated Press, July 9, 1993.
46. Ibid.
47. Nation Public Radio, 1997, quoted in de Young, 1999, p. 39.
48. United States v. Marcey at 141.
49. Brown, 1993.
50. Servicemembers Legal Defense Network Historical Timeline of "*Don't Ask, Don't Tell, Don't Pursue, Don't Harass,*" www.sldn.org.
51. Crittenden, 1957.
52. RAND, 1993; McDaniel, 1989, p. iii.
53. Ari Bianco, 1996, p. 52.
54. Hackworth, 1992, p. 27.
55. Belkin, 2004, p. 3.
56. *CSSMM*, Vol. 4 (3), Spring 2003.
57. Orange, 2003.
58. Wood & Mahoney, 1994.
59. Ricks, 1997.
60. Gonsiorek, 1991, pp. 118–119.
61. Rivera, 1991, p. 87; McDaniel, 1989.
62. Baldor, 2006; *www.military.com/news.*
63. Testimony before the Republican Study Committee on Homosexuals in the Armed Forces, December, 1992.
64. Churchill, 1967.
65. Kinsey, Pomeroy, & Martin, 1948.
66. Lehne, 1989, p. 419.
67. Bacevich, 1993, p. 43.
68. *Holy Bible*, 1962, Philadelphia: A.J. Holman Company, p. 112.
69. Goldman v. Weinberger 475 US 503 (1985).
70. *Los Angeles Times*, May 21, 1995.
71. Committee for Public Education and Religious Liberty v. Nyquist.
72. Servicemembers Legal Defense Network Historical Timeline of "*Don't Ask, Don't Tell, Don't Pursue, Don't Harass,*" www.sldn.org.
73. Ibid.
74. Thomas, 2004, p. 2
75. Based on Humphrey, 1990, quotes from p. 40.
76. Moskos, Williams, & Segal, 2000.
77. Kaplan, 2003. Moskos, Williams and Segal, 2000; Dandeker, 2000; Soeters & van der Meulen, 1999.
78. *CSSMM*, vol. 4 (3), Spring 2003.
79. Evans, 2003.
80. Meinhold v. U.S. Department of Defense, 1993.
81. Meinhold, 2001.
82. *CSSMM*, Vol. 4 (2), Winter, 2003.
83. Elliott, 2006.
84. Sheridan Embser-Herbert, 2005.
85. Gross, 1993, p. A5.
86. DePauw, 1988.; Thomas, & Thomas. 1996.
87. Benecke & Dodge, 1996, p. 85.
88. Bawer, 1993.
89. Childress, 1997.
90. Report estimates financial cost of "Don't Ask, Don't Tell," Center for the Study of Sexual Minorities in the Military, vol. 7 (2): 1, Winter 2006.
91. *CSSMM* Releases data on discharged medical specialists. Center for the Study of Sexual Minorities in the Military, vol. 7 (2): 1, Winter 2006.
92. Zeeland, 1996, p. 26.
93. Bicknell, 2000.
94. NBC *Meet the Press* transcript, June 15, 2003.
95. West Pointer Wins First-Ever Military Award for Challenging Gay Ban, August 9, 2006, *www.gaymilitary.ucsb. edu.*
96. Childress, 1997.
97. Andrew Holmes, First Lieutenant, Plaintiff-Appellee, v. California Army

National Guard Defendants-Appellants, And Richard P. Watson, Lieutenant, Plaintiff-Appellant, v. William S. Cohen, Secretary of Defense; John Dalton, Secretary of the Navy; United States of America, Defendants-Appellees.

98. Graves, 1991,

99. Goldwater, 1993, p. A23.

100. Speech, "Marines Not Taught to Hate," given to the Committee on Armed Services, January 1962.

CHAPTER NINE

1. Martin et al. (2000).

2. Hindelang, 1976; King, King, Foy, & Gudanowski, 1996; Kulka, Schlenger, & Fairbanks, 1990; Martin, Rosen, Durand, Stretch, & Knudson, 1998; Sampson, & Lauritsen, 1993 and; Zawitz, Klaus, & Bachman, 1993.

3. Tolson, n.d., p. 8.

4. Finkelhor, Hotaling, Lewis, & Smith, 1990.

5. Maker, et al., 2001.

6. Elliott, Mok, & Briere, 2004.

7. Lalumiere, et al., 2005.

8. Bremner, Southwick, Johnson, Yehuda, & Charney, 1993; Engel, Engel, Campbell, McFall, Russo, & Katon, 1993; Zaidi & Foy, 1994.

9. Shay, 1994.

10. Ricks, 1997, p. 29.

CHAPTER TEN

1. Army Sexual Harassment Incidents at Aberdeen Proving Ground and Sexual Harassment Policies within the Department of Defense, Committee on Armed Services, U.S. Senate, 105th Cong., 1st Session, February 4, 1997, p. 14.

2. Secretary of the Army, 1997. p. 56.

3. Foote & Goodman-Delahunty, 2005.

4. MacKinnon, 1979.

5. Meritor v. Vinson (Meritor Savings Bank, FSB v. Vinson).

6. Oncale v. Sundowner Offshore Services, Inc. See Martin 2000 for a first-person account.

7. Secretary of the Army, 1997, pp. 81-82.

8. Kennedy, 2001, p. 66.

9. Ibid., p. 296.

10. Williams, 1992, p. 22.

11. Briggs, 1997.

12. Vistica, 1995.

13. McMichael, 1997.

14. Vistica, 1995.

15. Ibid.

16. Ibid., p. 379.

17. Ibid., p. 372.

18. Culbertson, Rosenfeld, & Newell, 1993.

19. DeYoung, 1999, p. xi.

20. Jacobs, 1991.

21. Secretary of the Army, 1997, p. 56.

22. Foote & Goodman-Delahunty, 2005.

23. Laurier, 2004.

24. http://www.wsws.org/public_html/prioriss/iwb12-2/army.htm

25. Daniel de Vise "Defense Dept. Surveys Academy Sex Assaults" 3/19/05 http://www.washingtonpost.com/ac2/wp-dyn/A48335-2005Mar18; http://news.yahoo.com/news\?tmpl=story&u=afp/usmilitarywomen.

26. Sheridan Embser-Herbert, 2005, p. 224.

27. Firestone & Harris, 1999; Nelson, 2002; Sheridan Embser-Herbert, 2005.

28. Sheridan Embser-Herbert, 2005.

29. Perry, 1996.

30. www.ArmyStudyGuide.com., 2001.

31. Martindale, 1988.

32. Based on Martindale, 1988.

33. ELECTRONIC CITATION: 1998 FED App. 0284P (6th Cir.) File Name: 98a0284p.06 United States Court of Appeals for the Sixth Circuit Dorothy Mackey, Plaintiff-Appellee, v. David W. Milam, Travis Elmore, and United States of America, Defendants-Appellants. No. 97-3859 Appeal from the United States District Court for the Southern District of Ohio at Dayton. No. 96-00140—Susan J. Dlott, District Judge. Argued: June 11, 1998. Decided and Filed: September 10, 1998.

34. Taken from majority opinion section.

35. Secretary of the Army, 1997.p. 2.

36. Magley, Waldo, Drasgow, and Fitzgerald, 1999.

37. Gruber & Morgan, 2005, p. xii.

38. Magley, et al, 1999; Herek, 1989.

39. Herek, et al., 1997.

40. Esar, 1968, p. 557.

41. Ibid.

42. Stockdale, 1998.

43. Pryor & Stoller, 1994, p. 167.

44. Foote & Goodman-Delahunty, 2005, p. 30; 31-33.

45. Franke, 1997; Foote & Goodman-Delahunty, 2005, p. 44.

46. Cheney, 1991.

47. Martindale, 1988.

48. Pryor, 1995.

49. Magley, Waldo, Drasgow, & Fitzgerald, 1999.

50. Martindale, 1988.

51. Sadler, Booth, Cook, Bradley, & Doebbeling, 2003.

52. Foote & Goodman-Delahunty, 2005, p. 133.

53. Fuller, 1732, p. 915.

CHAPTER ELEVEN

1. Janofsky & Schemo, 2003.

2. White, 2004.

3. Department of Defense, p. 8.

4. Ibid.

5. *http://www.donaldsensing.com/2003_08_01_archive*.

6. DeYoung, 1999, p. 314.

7. Ibid., p. xii.

8. Ibid., p. 237.

9. National Crime Victim's Survey, Bureau of Justice Statistics, 1997; 1999.

10. McMullin & White, 2006.

11. Churchill, 1993.

12. *Newsweek*, March 27, 2006, p. 23.

13. Center for Sex Offender Management (2001). *Recidivism of Sex Offenders*. Office of Justice Programs, U.S. Department of Justice, A Project of the Office of Justice Programs, U.S. Department of Justice, *http://www.csom.org/pubs/recid-sexof.html*.

14. Kilpatrick, Edmunds, & Seymour, 1992.

15. Gluck Mezey, 2003.

16. Navy Women's Study Group, (1991).

17. Department of Veterans Affairs. Undersecretary of Defense for Personnel. Abuse Victims Study, Department of Defense, 1994.

18. Biddle, 2004.

19. Scully and Marolla, 1995, p. 71.

20. Gluck Mezey, 2003.

21. Iraq war vet charged with murder, rape of Iraqis. CNN.com, July 3, 2006.

22. Cohn, 2006.

23. Scarce, 1997.

24. Miller & Marshall, 1987.

25. Koss, Dinero, Seibel, & Cox, 1988.

26. Muehlenhard, & Linton, 1987.

27. Our View, *Florida Today*, uncredited editorial, 1/19/03, 10A.

28. Scarce, 1997, p. vii.

29. Solzman, 2000, p. 87.

30. *http://www.globalissuesgroup.com/geneva/protocol2.html#4.*

31. Ibid.

32. Herdy & Moffeit, 2004.

33. Scarce, 1997, p.9.

34. 10 U.S.C. § 920[1994] amending 10 U.S.C. § 920[1988].

35. Francke, 1997.

36. Snel, 2003.

37. Jacobs, S. (2004).

38. Ibid.

39. Masters & Johnson, 1966.

40. Groth & Birnbaum, 1979.

41. Scarce, 1997.

42. Ibid.

43. Hillman, 1991.

44. Goyer & Eddleman, 1984.

45. Hunter, 1996.

46. Lumpkin, 2004.

47. Friedman, 2005, p. 1287.

48. Laurier, 2004.

49. Wilborn, 1998.

50. MacNeil/Lehrer Productions, 1997.

51. Snel, 2003.

52. Laurier, 2004.

53. Smith, 2004.

54. Laurier, 2004.

55. Ibid.

56. Lumpkin, 2005.

57. Daniel de Vise, Defense Dept. Surveys Academy Sex Assaults, 3/19/05, *http://www.washingtonpost.com/ac2/wp-dyn/A48335-2005Mar18; http://news.yahoo.com/news/usmilitarywomen.*

58. Laurier, 2004; MSNBC, March 9, 2004; St. George, 2006c.

59. Morris, 2000.

60. Bastian, Lancaster, & Reyst, 1996.

61. Hankin, et al. 1999.

62. Laurier, 2004.

63. US Justice Department, Office of Justice Programs, Bureau of Justice Statistics Special Report Veterans in Prison or Jail, January NCJ 178888, Revised 9/29/00 facts cover time period from 1985–1998.

64. Morris, 2000.

65. MSNBC, March 9, 2004.

CHAPTER TWELVE

1. Office of the Surgeon General, 1995, p. 435.

2. Wolfe, et al., 1998.

3. Wilborn, 1998.

4. Johnson, 2004, AA4.

5. Elliott, Mok, Briere, 2004.

6. Briere, 1995,

7. Scarce, 1997.

8. Kilpatrick, et al., 1985.

9. Cohn, 2006.

10. *http://www.msnbc.msn.com/id/4490652.*

11. McMullen, 1990.

12. Grossman, 1995, p. 77.

13. Helle, 2002, p. 141.

14. Litz, Keane, Fisher, Marx, & Monaco, 1992; Wolfe, Schnurr, Brown, & Furey, 1994; Friedman, Schnurr, & McDonagh-Coyle, 1994; Wolfe J., Brown P. J., & Buscela, M. L., 1992.

15. Dobie, et al. 2004.

16. Rhem, 2001.

17. Marmar & Horwitz, 1988.

18. Martin & Campbell, 1999.

19. Wilborn, 1998.

20. Kang, Dalager, et al., 2005.

21. Grossman, 1995, p. 81. Italics in the original.

22. Helle, 2002, p. 126.

23. Anonymous, 2005.

CHAPTER THIRTEEN

1. Gleick, 1996, p. 29.
2. MacNeil/Lehrer Productions, 1997.
3. Kennedy, 2001, p. xvi.
4. Vistica, 1995.
5. *Newsweek,* August 10, 1992, p. 35.
6. Carollo, Nesmith, & Jaspin, 1997.
7. Fired General disobeyed order, *Saint Paul Pioneer Press,* August 13, p. 6.
8. Kennedy, 2001, p. xiii.
9. Sarche, 2004.
10. Gomstyn, 2003.
11. Gomstyn, 2003.
12. *U.S. News & World Report,* 2004.
13. *http://www.washingtonpost.com/wpdyn/content/article/2006/02/08/AR2006020802025.html.*
14. Secretary of the Army, 1997. p. 47.
15. Ibid.
16. Carollo, 1998.
17. Trials Rare After Charges of Sex Assault at Annapolis, *New York Times,* 3/19/06.
18. Herdy & Moffeit, 2004.
19. Laurier, J., 2004.
20. Herdy & Moffeit, 2004.
21. Campbell & D'Amico, 1999.
22. Backalow, 1990.
23. Laurier, J., 2004.
24. Dean, 1997, p. 60.
25. Grossman, 1995, p. 285.

26. Zimmerman, 1995, p. 275.
27. Dean, 1997, pp. 50.
28. P, 7.
29. Wilborn, 1998.
30. Smith, 2004.
31. Laurier, J., 2004.
32. Galloway & Johnson, 19, p. 22.
33. Dallager, 2003.
34. Laurier, 2004.
35. Dallager, 2003.
36. Foster, 2003.
37. Janofsky & Schemo, 2003.
38. Ibid.
39. Ibid.
40. Bingham, 2003, p. 166.
41. Sarche, 2004.
42. Bingham, 2003, p. 194.
43. Agenda for Change-Policy Directives and Initiatives, March 26, 2003, *http://www.usafa.af.mil/agenda.cfm.*
44. Janofsky & Schemo, 2003, p. A17.
45. Ibid.
46. Wilborn, 1998.
47. Martin et al., 2000.
48. Kanin, 1982.
49. Burt, 1991.
50. Archard, 1998.
51. George & Martinez, 2002.
52. Hall, 1998; Willis, 1997.

CHAPTER FOURTEEN

1. Ricks, 1997, p. 22.
2. Newsome, 1999.
3. Barkalow & Raab, 1990, 1990.
4. Van Dam, 2006.
5. Officer Basic Course, p. AA-7
6. Association for the Treatment of Sexual Abusers, 2004.
7. Able, et al., 1980.
8. Smithyman, 1978.
9. Scully and Marolla, 1995, p. 70.
10. Scarce, 1997, pp. 18-19.

11. Scully and Marolla, 1995
12. Jackson, 1995.
13. Testa, Vazile-Tamsen, & Livingston, 2004.
14. Ibid.
15. Good, 1991, p. 115.
16. Amir, 1971.
17. Beneke, 1983, p. 43.
18. Scully & Marolla, 1995, p. 71.
19. Ibid.
20. Griffin, 1971.

21. Scully & Marolla, 1995, p. 63.
22. Weiss & Borges, 1973.
23. Scully & Marolla, 1995.
24. Ibid., p. 72.
25. Benard & Schlaffer, 1984.
26. Association for the Treatment of Sexual Abusers, 2004.
27. Rice & Harris, 1995 a & b; Bynum, Decarter, Matson, & Onley, 2001; Marshall & Barbaree, 1990.
28. Ahlmeyer, Heil, McKee, & English, 2000.
29. Ahlmeyer, English, & Simons, 1999.

30. Ibid.
31. Scully & Marolla, 1984.
32. Carlson, 1990.
33. Kelly, 2002.
34. Ibid.
35. Walt Kelly, *http://www.planetwaves.net/pogo.html*.
36. Zimbardo, 1970, 1971.
37. Ibid., p. 3.
38. White, 2004, p. 13.
39. Bruck, 1976.
40. Sorkin, 1990.
41. Peretti, 2000, p. 155.

CHAPTER FIFTEEN

1. Houppert, 2005, p. 226.
2. Hunter, 1996.
3. Heimark, 1997.
4. Secretary of the Army, 1997, p. 15.
5. Noone, 1999.
6. Shafritz, Todd, & Robertson, 1989.
7. Shalit, 1988; Motowildo & Borman, 1977.
8. Shatan, 1977.
9. U.S. Air Force Regulation 36-2909.
10. Hedges, 2002, p. 9.
11. Herbert, 1998, p. 128.
12. Kaplan, 2003, p. 183.
13. Kennedy, 2001, p. 41.
14. Noone, 1999.

15. *The Secretary of the Army's Senior Review Panel Report On Sexual Harassment,* The Secretary of the Army, 1997, pp. 11-12.
16. Ellis & Moore, 1974, p. 78.
17. Woodruff, 2001, p. 200.
18. Shalit, 1988.
19. *The Secretary of the Army's Senior Review Panel Report On Sexual Harassment,* Secretary of the Army, 1997, p.11.
20. Ibid., pp. 11-12.
21. Burke, 2004, p. 9.
22. MSNBC, March 9, 2004.
23. Ricks, 1997, p. 264.
24. Carollo, & Nesmith, 1995.

CHAPTER SIXTEEN

1. Kennedy, 2001, p. xv.
2. Vistica, 1995, p. 12.
3. St. George, 2006.
4. Ibid.
5. McCain, 1999, p. 119.
6. Drewry Lehr, 1999, p. 120.
7. Servicemembers Legal Defense Network, 1998.
8. Servicemembers Legal Defense Network Historical Timeline of "Don't Ask, Don't Tell, Don't Pursue, Don't Harass," *www.sldn.org*.

9. Sarche, 2004.
10. Woulfe, 1998, p. ix.
11. Lorraine Underwood, "Minority Women and the Military" at the Women's Equality Action League, Washington, DC, June 1979.
12. Maclear, 1981.
13. Vistica, 1995.
14. Garmise, 1991.
15. Hoffman, 2006, p. A8.
16. Harrell & Miller, 1997.
17. Houppert, 2005.

18. Ellis, 2005, p. 99.

19. Ibid.

20. USMC Oral History Interview, General Ray A. Robinson, USMC Ret. 18-19 March, 1968, p. 136, History Division, HQMC.

21. Memo, Truman Library 23 April 1950.

22. MacGregor, 1981, p. 610.

23. Martin, 1951; Ibid.

24. MacGregor, 1981.

25. Memo, Officer in Charge, Eastern Recruiting Division, 16 January, 1942, subject: Colored Applicants for Enlistment in the Marine Corps, WP 11991, MC files.

26. Navy General Board, "Plan for the Expansion of the USMC," 18, April, 1941 (No. 139), Recs of Gen. Bd. OpNavArchives.

27. MacGregor, 1981.

28. Astor, 1998, p. 315.

29. Ibid., p. 316.

30. Memo, GMG for DcofS, 15 April 1947.

31. Secretary of the Air Force 24 May 1956 AF file 202-36, Fair Employment Program.

32. Memo, 3380th Tactical Training Wing, Keesler AFB, July 1953, Subject: Administrative Reprimand.

33. Secretary of the Air Force files, Headquarters Letter #9, 1 May 1949.

34. Department of Defense Directive 5120.36, 26 July 1963.

35. Nalty, 1986, p. 356.

36. Anderson, 1997.

37. Letter to Congresswoman Patricia Schroeder, May 8, 1992.

38. Memorandum from James Forrestal to the president, May 20, 1944, MacGregor, 1981, p. 84.

39. Letter from Ray to Truman Gibson, 14 May 1945, quoted in MacGregor, 1981, p. 133.

40. Kennedy, 2001.

41. MacGregor, 1981, p. 59.

42. Janda, 2002, p. 35.

43. MacGregor, 1981, p.60.

44. Humphrey, 1990, p. 265.

45. Conference with Regard to Negro Personnel, held at Headquarters, Fifth Naval District, 26 October 1943.

46. Naval Personnel, 15092, 12 February 1944.

47. Burke, 1996.

48. D'Amico, 1996.

49. Sullivan, 2005.

50. Lemon, 2002.

51. Soukup, E. (2006). Catholic and Queer. *Newsweek*, 2/27, p. 12.

52. Sullivan, 2005.

53. McCoy, 1995, p. 692.

54. March 21, 1996, quoted in Burke, 2004, p. 143.

55. Hanson W. Balkwin, in the *New York Times*, August 1948, on African Americans. Striking Parallels. *Washington Post*, Nov. 20, 1992, p. 14.

56. Legal scholar Bruce Fein on homosexuals in Shilts, 1993, p. 281.

57. General Omar Bradley on African Americans, Fahy Committee testimony, p. 68.

58. Military historian Morris J. MacGregor Jr. on African Americans, MacGregor, 1981, p.143.

59. General William Westmoreland, speaking of women in *Family Week*, September 25, 1976.

60. Marine Corps Commandant Barrows testifying in 1991 at Congressional hearing on women in combat roles (U.S. Senate, 1991, p. 897).

61. Marcia Stepanek on homosexuals, Stepanek, 1992.

62. Major General Thomas Holcomb, Commandant of the Marine Corps, 1942, on African American men who sought to enlist in the Marines, Enlist-

ment of Men of Colored Race (201), 23 Jan 1942, Hearing before the General Board of the Navy.

63. Male West Point cadet on the admission of women, Francke, 1997, p. 205.

64. U.S. Senator Robert Byrd (D–West Virginia) in a 1945 letter on serving in the military with "race mongrels"(African Americans), Planin, 2005, A4.

65. Congressman Overton Brooks on African Americans, Congressional Record, Appendix, July 27, 1948, p. A4650.

66. Georgia Senator Richard Russell on African Americans, 1948, Ari Bianco, 1996, p. 50.

67. Morris J. MacGregor Jr., Historical Division of the Joint Chiefs of Staff, on African Americans, MacGregor, 1981.

68. Georgia Senator Richard Russell on African Americans, 1948, Ari Bianco, 1996, p. 51. The rate for blacks was 1,186 cases per 1000 men, while the rate for whites was only 139 cases per 1,000 men. *Occupational Monograph of the Eighth Army in Japan*, History Division. Rates for June 1946. By the 1950s the rates had become equivalent.

69. David H. Hackworth on homosexuals. Hackworth, 1992, p. 27.

70. Lt. General Thomas Holcomb, USMC on African Americans, Hearing before the General Board of the Navy, January 23, 1942.

71. Majority report, committee appointed by the Secretary of the Navy, December 24, 1941 on the inte-gration of African Americans.

72. Morris J. MacGregor Jr., Historical Division of the Joint Chiefs of Staff on the integration of African American men, MacGregor, 1981, p. 17.

73. Charles Jackson of the Non Commissioned Officers Association, statement before the Republican Study Committee on Homosexuals in the Armed Forces, December 9, 1992.

74. Capt. F.E.M. Whiting, General Board of the Navy on African Americans, January 23, 1942.

75. Memorandum, Chairman of the General Board of the Navy #420 on African Americans.

76. Senator Russell proposing an amendment to guarentee military personnel would be allowed to choose only with members of their own race, *Congressional Record*, Senate, June 8, 1948, p. 7355–6.

77. General Andrew Goodpaster, superintendent of West Point, on the admission of female cadets in 1976, Backalow, 1990, p. 63.

78. Specialist 5 Harold "Light Bulb" Bryant, Combat Engineer, Vietnam, on white people, Bryant, 1984.

79. Samuel G. Cockerham et al., Presidential Commission on the Assignment of Women in the Armed Forces, November 1992, p. 45.

80. Statement made by the Superintendent of West Point when he learned in 1863 that Congress planned to have a road built to the academy, thereby reducing the isolation of the campus, *Officers & Gentlemen*, p. 34.

CHAPTER SEVENTEEN

1. *http://www.usatoday.com/news/opinion/ editorials/2003-04-16-our-view_x.htm*.
2. "Leading Others, Managing Yourself," Leaders: The Strategies for Taking Charge, 1985.
3. Handlin, 1966.
4. *Encarta World English Dictionary*, 1999.
5. Stoughton, 2004.
6. Dean, 1997.
7. Koch, 1998.
8. Gladwell, 2006, p. 98.
9. , Editorial/Opinion, "Military academies and sex abuse: 15 years of failure." *USA Today*, 8/25/05; "Two Academies Faulted on treatment of women." *New York Times*, 8/26/05.
10. Testimony before the House Armed Services Subcommittee on Personnel and Compensation, February 4, 1988.
11. Moore, 1988, p. 1.
12. Rosenthal, 1964.
13. Darky & Latane, 1968.
14. Gladwell, 2002, p. 28.
15. Nisbett & Ross, 1991.
16. Haney, Banks, & Zimbardo, 1973.
17. CBS *60 Minutes*, The Stanford Prison Experiment, August 30, 1998.
18. Ibid.
19. Ibid.
20. Ibid.
21. Hoge, et al., 2004.
22. Teague, 2003.
23. Sammons, 2005.
24. Lumpkin, 2004
25. White, 2004.
26. Ierace, K. (2005). Letter to Congress. May 8. *www. ptsdpeace.org.*
27. *http://www.usatoday.com/news/opinion/ editorials/2003-04-16-our-view_x.htm*
28. Dean, 1997.
29. Romberg, et al., 1993; Bray, 1996.
30. Walters, 2005.
31. Secretary of the Army, 1997. p. 31.
32. Dean, 1997, p. 59.
33. *http://www.usatoday.com/news/opinion/ editorials/2003-04-16-our-view_x.htm*
34. Newsome, 1999, p. 93.
35. Secretary of the Army, 1997. p. 46.
36. Vistica, 1995.
37. Feres v. United States, 340 U.S. 135 (1950).
38. United States Court of Appeals for the Sixth Circuit, Electronic Citation: 1998 Fed App. 0284p (6th Cir.) File Name: 98a0284p.06, Dorothy Mackey, Plaintiff-Appellee, v. David W. Milam, Travis Elmore, and United States of America, Defendants-Appellants.
39. Feres v. United States, 340 U.S. 135 (1950).
40. Ricks, 1997, p. 216.
41. Edney, 1998.

CHAPTER EIGHTEEN

1. Kang, et al., 2003.
2. Kang & Hyams, 2005.
3. Toobin, 2005, p. 35.
4. Dean, 1999, p. 9.

PART TWO

1 Helle, 2002, p. 37.
2. Copyright Frank Ochberg, MD & Gift From Within. Used with permission.
3. Helle, 2002. Mr. Helle's book is available for purchasing at www.ptsdalliance.biz and all proceeds do go to the PTSD Alliance.
4. *Emancipation*, Copyright 2003, Lynda K. Dokken. Used with permission.

BIBLIOGRAPHY

Able, G., J. Becker, & L. Skinner. 1980. Aggressive Behavior and Sex. *Psychiatric Clinics of North America*, 3: 133–151.

Abrams, A. 1918. Homosexuality: A Military Menace. *Medical review of Reviews*, 24: 528–529.

Ahlmeyer, S., P. Heil, B. McKee, and K. English. 2000. The impact of polygraphy on admissions of victims and offenses in adult sexual offenders. *Sexual Abuse: A Journal of Research and Treatment*, 12 (2), 123–138.

Ahlmeyer, S., K. English & D. Simons. 1999. The impact of polygraphy on admissions of crossover offending behavior in adult sexual offenders. Presentation at the Association for the Treatment of Sexual Abusers, 18th Annual Research and Treatment Conference, Lake Buena Vista, FL.

Alvarez, L. 2006. Jane, We Hardly Knew Ye Died. New York Times, 9/24, pp. 1 & 4.

Ambrose, S.E. 1997. *Citizen Soldiers: The US Army from the Normandy Beaches to the Bulge to the Surrender of Germany June 7, 1944-May 7, 1945*. New York: Simon & Schuster.

American Psychiatric Association. 1994. *Diagnostic and Statistical Manual of Mental Disorders*, 4th ed. Washington, DC.

Amir, M. 1971. *Patterns in Forcible Rape*. Chicago, IL: University of Chicago Press.

Anderson, J. H. 1997. Boot Camp or Summer Camp? Restoring Rigorous Standards to Basic Training. *http://www.heritage.org/Research/PoliticalPhilosophy/BG1147.cfm*.

Anonymous. 2005. Clergy Sexual Abuse-Victim's Spouses are Abused Too. *Tamar Talks*, September, pp. 3 & 4.

Archard, D. 1998. *Sexual Consent*. Boulder, CO: Westview Press.

Ari Bianco, D. 1996. Echoes of Prejudice: The Debate Over Race & Sexuality in the

Armed Forces. In C.A. Rimmerman (ed.) *Gay Rights, Military Wrongs: Political Perspectives on Lesbians and Gays in the Military*. NY: Garland Publishing, pp. 47–70.

ArmyStudyGuide.com. 2001. *Soldiers Manual of Common Tasks*. Skill Level 1 STP 21-1-SMCT, Comply with the Army's Equal Opportunity and Sexual Harassment Policies, 805C-0EO-1391(SL1), http://smct.armystudyguide.com/Skill_Level_1/805C-0EO-1391.htm.

The Association for the Treatment of Sexual Abusers. 2004. Ten Things You Should Know About Sex Offenders and Treatment. *http://www.atsa.com/ppTenThings.html*

Astor, G. 1998. *The Right to Fight: A History of African Americans in the Military*. Novato, CA: Presidio.

Ayala, L. 2004. U.S. forces tortured Iraqis, general says: Army report ties 46 to abuses at Abu Ghraib. MSNBC-TV, August 25.

Bacevich, A.J. 1993. Military culture and effectiveness. *Society*, 31 (1), 43–48.

Badger, T. QA. 2004. Abu Ghraib prisoners recount jailer's abuse. *St. Paul Pioneer Press*, January 12, p. 3A.

Baldor, L.C. 2006. Pentagon Lists Homosexuality As Disorder. June 20, Fox News.

Barkalow, C. & Raab, A.1990. In the Men's House: An Inside Account of Life in the Army. New York: Poseidon.

Bastian, L., A. Lancaster, & H. Reyst . 1996. *The Department of Defense 1995 Sexual Harassment Survey*. Arlington, VA: Defense manpower Data Center.

Bawer, B. 1993. *A Place at the Table: The Gay Individual in American Society*, New York: Poseidon Press.

Baxandall, R., L. Gordon, & S. Reverby. 1976. *America's Working Women: A Documentary History, 1600 to the Present*. New York: Vintage Books.

Belkin, A. 2004. In reply to "Legitimate Debate, or Gay Propaganda?" *Center for the Study of Sexual Minorities in the Military*, Spring, Volume 5 (3): 3–4.

Belkin, A., & L.R., Evans. 2000. *The Effects of Including Gay and Lesbian Soldiers in the British Armed Forces: Appraising the Evidence*. Santa Barbara, CA: The Center for the Study of Sexual Minorities in the Military.

Benard, C. & E., Schlaffer. 1984. The Man On The Street: Why He Harasses. In A. Jaggar & P. Rothenberg (Eds.) *Feminist Frameworks*. New York: McGraw-Hill.

Benecke, M. M., & K. S. Dodge. 1996. Military Women: Casualties of the Armed Forces' War on Lesbians and Gay Men. In C.A. Rimmerman (ed.) *Gay Rights, Military Wrongs: Political Perspectives on Lesbians and Gays in the Military*. New York: Garland Publishing, pp. 71–108.

Benedict, R. 1959. *Patterns of Culture*. Boston: Houghton Mifflin.

Beneke, T. 1983. *Men on Rape*. New York: St. Martin's.

Bicknell, Jr., J. W.2000. "Study of Naval Officers' Attitudes Toward Homosexuals in the Military" (submitted for the degree of Master of Science in Management, Naval Postgraduate School, Monterey, California, March).

Biddle, J. 2004. Military Sex Assault Likened to 'Friendly Fire.' *http://www.reuters.com/newsArticle*.

Bingham, C. 2003. Code of dishonor. *Vanity Fair*, Dec. pp. 164–194.

Bird, J. 1989. Special Report. *Air Force Times*, December 4.

Bishop, J. 2005. Rape rap priest 'told victim she was former-life wife.' January 14. http://iccroydon.icnetwork.co.uk/news/croydon/tm.

Black, E. 2004. Pressure mounts against coercive interrogations. Star Tribune. May 16, A1 & A20.

Brandt, A. M. 1985. *No Magic Bullet: A Social History of Venereal Disease in the United States since 1880*. New York: Oxford University Press.

Braudy, L. 2003. *From Chivalry to Terrorism: War and the Changing Nature of Masculinity*. New York: Alfred A. Knopf.

Bremner, J.D., S. M. Southwick, D. J. Johnson, R. Yehuda, & D. S. Charney. 1993. Childhood physical abuse and combat-related post-traumatic stress disorder in Vietnam veterans. *American Journal of Psychiatry*, 150:235–239.

Briggs, R.V. 1997. Comment: Old vs [sic] New Morality and Sexual Harassment. March 20.

Brownmiller, S. 1975. *Against our will: Men, women, and rape*. New York: Bantam Books.

Bruck, C. 1976. Zimbardo: Solving the maze. *Human Behavior*, April, pp. 25–31.

Bureau of Justice Statistics. 1997. Criminal Victimization in the United States, 1994. Washington, DC: Bureau of Justice Statistics, U.S. Department of Justice.

Bureau of Justice Statistics. March 1985. The Crime of Rape. Washington, DC: Bureau of Justice Statistics, U.S. Department of Justice.

Burke, C. 1996. Pernicious Cohesion. In Judith Hicks Stiehm (Ed.). *It's Our Military, Too! Women and the U.S. Military*, Philadelphia: Temple University Press, 1996. pp. 205–219.

Burke, C. 2004. *Camp All-American, Hanoi Jane, and the High-and-Tight: Gender, Folklore, and Changing Military Culture*. Boston: Beacon Press.

Burt, M. R. 1991. Rape Myths and Acquaintance Rape. In A. Parrot & L. Bechhofer (eds). *Acquaintance Rape: The Hidden Crime*. New York: John Wiley, pp. 26–40.

Bulter, J. S. 2000. Militarized Prostitution: The Untold Story (USA). In Llewellyn Barstow, A. (Ed.) pp. 204–232, *War's Dirty Secret: Rape, Prostitution, and Other Crimes Against Women*. Cleveland, OH: The Pilgrim Press.

Bynum, T. M., Decarter, S., Matson, & C., Onley. 2001. *Recidivism of Sex Offenders. Center for Sex Offender Management*. Office of Justice Programs, U.S. Department of Justice. http://www.csom.org/pubs/recidsexof.html.

Bryant, H. 1984. In W. Terry (Ed.) *Bloods: An Oral History of the Vietnam War by Black Veterans*. New York: Random House. pp. 18-32.

Calendo, J. 1982. Down in Oceanside. *In Touch*, September, p. 64.

Campbell, J. C., M. A. Garza, A. C. Gielen, P. O'Campo, J. Kub, J. Dienemann, A. S. Jones, & E. Jafar. 2003. Intimate Partner Violence and Abuse Among Active Duty Military Women. *Violence Against Women*; Sept., Vol. 9 Issue 9, pp. 1072–1092.

Carlson, S. 1990. The Victim/Perpetrator: Turning Points in Therapy. In M. Hunter (Ed.) *The Sexually Abused Male: Application of Treatment Strategies*. pp. 249–266. New York: Lexington Books.

Carollo, R. 1998. Oklahoma Board May Help Military Doctors Keep Jobs, *Dayton Daily News* (OH) January 24, p. 8A.

Carollo, R., J. Nesmith, & E. Jaspin. 1997. Army Treated Rape As Lesser Crime. *Dayton Daily News*, January 12, p. 1A.

Casey, M. J. 2006. Then and Now, Female Soldiers Just Do Their Jobs. *New York Times*, 11/9, p. A26.

Chang, I. 1997. *The Rape of Nanking: The Forgotten Holocaust of World War II*. New York: Basic.

Cheney, D. 1991. *Department of Defense Strategies to Eradicate Sexual Harassment in the Military and Civilian Environment*, Office of the Secretary of Defense memo.

Childress, K. 1997. Conduct Unbecoming: Third Annual Report on "Don't Ask, Don't Tell, Don't Pursue": Executive Summary Staff Attorney, Washington, DC: Service-members Legal Defense Network.

Churchill, S. D. 1993. The Lived Meaning of Date Rape: Seeing Through the Eyes of the Victim. *Family Violence & Sexual Assault Bulletin*, 9(1): 20–23.

Churchill, W. 1967. *Homosexual Behavior Among Males: A Cross-cultural and Cross-species Investigation*. New York: Hawthorn.

Clark Hine, D. 1981. Mabel Seaton Stater: The Integration of Black Nurses in the Armed Forces, World War II. Presentation at the Berkshire Conference of Women Historians, Vassar College, June.

Clarke, M. 1981. Letter to the editor. *Army Times*, September 21.

Clinton, B. & A. Gore Jr. 1992. *Putting People First: How We Can All Change America*. New York: Times Books.

Cohn, M. 2006. Military Hides Cause of Women Soldiers' Deaths. http://www.truthout. org/docs_2006/013006J.shtml.

Cook, G. 2003. POWs Likely to Endure Sexual Assault. April 6. http://www.womense-news.org/article.cfm/dyn/aid/1281/context/cover/.

Copelon, R. 1994. Resurfacing Gender: Reconceptualizing Crimes Against Women in Time of War. In A. Stiglmayer (Ed.) *Mass Rape*.

Cornum, R. 2000. The Prisoner of War Experience. The Health Care of Women in Military Settings. Operational Obstetrics & Gynecology. http://www.vnh.org/OBGYN/ POW.htm.

———. 1996. Soldiering: The enemy doesn't care if you're female. In Judith Hicks Stiehm (Ed.). *It's Our Military, Too! Women and the U.S. Military*. Philadelphia: Temple University Press, 1996, pp. 3–23.

Costello, J. 1985. *Virtue Under Fire: How World War II Changed Our Social and Sexual Attitudes*. Boston: Little, Brown.

Costin, F. 1985. Beliefs about rape and women's social roles. *Archives of Sexual Behavior*, 14: 319–325.

Coulthard-Clark, C. D. 1984. *Duntroon: The Royal Military College of Australia*. Sydney: Allen & Unwin.

Cox, J. 1999. The Role of Social Work in Policy Practice. In J. G. Daley (Ed.) *Social Work Practice in the Military*. New York: The Haworth Press, pp. 165–176.

Crittenden, S.H. (Chairman) 1957. *Report of the Board Appointed to Prepare and Submit Recommendations to the Secretary of the Navy for the Revision of Policies, Procedures, and Directives Dealing with Homosexuality*. Washington, DC: Government Printing Office.

Culbertson, A. L., P. Rosenfeld & C. E. Newell. 1993. *Sexual Harassment in the Active-Du Navy: Findings from the 1991 Navy-Wide Survey.*

D'Amico, F. 1998. Feminist Perspectives on Women Warriors. In L. A. Lorentzen & J. Turpin (eds.) *The Women & War Reader,* pp. 119–125.

Da Cruz, D. 1987. *Boot: The Inside Story of How a Few Good Men Became Today's Marines.* New York: St. Martin's Press.

Dallager, J. R. 2003. Superintendent addresses issue of sexual assault. http://www.usafa. edu/sexualassault.cfm 3/18/03.

Dalton, J. H. 1997. Holistic Navy Approach to Curbing Sexual Harassment. Defense Issues 12, no. 8: 1–4 '97. Remarks before the Senate Armed Services Committee, February 4.

Dandeker, C. 2000. "New Times for the Military: Some Sociological Remarks on the Changing Role and Structure of the Armed Forces of the Advanced Societies." *British Journal of Sociology* 45 (1994): 637–654.

———. 2000. "The United Kingdom: The Overstretched Military." In *The Postmodern Military,* ed. Charles. C. Moskos, John Allen Williams, and David R. Segal. Oxford: Oxford University Press, 2000, 32–50.

Darley, J., & B. Latane. 1968. Bystander Interventions in Emergencies: Diffusion of Responsibility. *Journal of Personality and Social Psychology,* 8: 377–383.

De Schmidt, A. C. 1991. Voices of Hope and Anger: Women Resisting Militarization. In *The Sun Never Sets: Confronting the Network of Foreign U.S. Military Bases.* Boston, MA: South End Press.

Dean, D., M. 1997. Warriors Without Weapons: The Victimization of Military Women. Pasadena, MD: Minerva Center.

Dean, D. M. 1999. Autobiography: Warriors without weapons. In F. D'Amico & L. Weinstein (Eds.) *Gender Camouflage: Women and the U.S. Military* pp. 90–95, New York: New York University Press.

Department of the Army. 2004. *The Army Family Advocacy Program* (Army regulation 608-18). Headquarters, Washington, DC.

Department of Defense. 2004. *Final report of the Independent Panel to Review DoD Detention Operations.* Washington, DC: Author.

———. 2005. *DoD Policy on Prevention and Response to Sexual Assault.*

DePauw, Linda Grant. 1988. Gender as stigma: Probing some sensitive issues. Minerva, 6(1):29–43.

———. 1998. *Battle Cries and Lullabies: Women in War from Prehistory to the Present.* University of Oklahoma Press.

DeYoung, M. 1999. *This Woman's Army: The Dynamics of Sex and Violence in the Military.* Central Point, Oregon: Hellgate Press.

Dingfelder, S. 2005. Social comparison can highlight similarities as well as differences. *Monitor on Psychology,* June, 36(6): 10.

Dingfelder, S. 2006. Violence in the home takes many forms. *Monitor on Psychology,* Oct., 37(9):18.

Dinter, E. 1985. *Hero or Coward: Pressures Facing the Soldier in Battle.* Totowa, NJ: Frank Cass.

BIBLIOGRAPHY

obie, D. J., D.R. Kivlahan, C. Maynard, K.R. Bush, T.M. Davis, & K.A. Bradley. 2004. Post Traumatic Stress Disorder in Female Veterans: Association With Self-reported Health Problems and Functional Impairment. Archives of Internal Medicine; Vol. 164 (4): 394–400.

Donnelly, E. 1994. Opinion. *San Diego Union-Tribune*, May 29, p. G-1.

Drewry Lehr, D. 1999. Military Wives, In F. D'Amico & L. Weinstein (Eds.) *Gender Camouflage: Women and the U.S. Military* pp. 117-131, New York: New York University Press.

Dubbert, J. L. 1979. *A Man's Place*. Englewood Cliffs, NJ: Prentice-Hall.

Dunbar, Cynthia. 1992. "Toward a Gender-Blind Military," *Harvard International Review*, vol. 15, no. 1, Fall, pp.52–55.

Dunivin, K. O. 1988. There's men, there's women, and there's me: The role and status of military women. *Minerva: Quarterly Report on Women and the Military*. VI (2): 43–68.

Dyer, G. 1985. *War*. New York: Crown Publishing.

Edney, L. 1998. Testimony before the House Judiciary Committee, December 1, 1998.

Elliott, A. 2006. For Recruiter Speaking Arabic, Saying 'Go Army' Is A Hard Job. *New York Times*, Oct. 6, pp. A1 & A10.

Elliott, D. M., D. S. Mok, & J. Briere. 2004. Adult sexual assault: Prevalence, symptomatology, and sex differences in the general population. *Journal of Trauma Stress*, June, 17(3):203–11.

Elliott, S. 2006. Army's New Battle Cry Aims at Potential Recruits. *New York Times*, 11/9, C3.

Ellis, J. J. 2005. Washington takes charge. *Smithsonian*, January, 53(10):92–103.

Ember, M. & C .R. Ember. 1994. Cross-Cultural Studies of War and Peace: Recent Acheivements and Future Possibilities. In Reyna & Downs (eds.), pp. 185–208.

Embser-Herbert, M. S. 2004. When Women Abuse Power, Too. www.washingtonpost.com. May 14.

Engel, C. C., A. L. Engel, S. J. Campbell, M. R. McFall, J. Russo, & W. Katon. 1993. Post Traumatic stress disorder symptoms and precombat sexual and physical abuse in Desert Storm veterans. *Journal of Nervous Mental Disorders*, 181:683-688.

Enloe, C. 1983. *Does Khaki Become You?: The Militarization of Women's Lives*. Boston: South End Press.

———. 1989. Bananas, Beeches and Bases: Making Feminist Sense of International Politics. Berkeley: University of California Press.

———. 1996. Spoils of War. *Ms Magazine*. March/April, p. 15.

———. 2000. *Maneuvers: The International Politics of Militarizing Women's Lives*. Berkeley, CA: University of California Press.

Esar, E. 1968. *20,000 Quips & Quotes*. New York: Barnes & Noble.

Felien, E. 2005. Do you want to get married? *Pulse of the Twin Cities*, 9 (3): 5.

Field, R. L. "The Black Midshipman at the U.S. Naval Academy" *US Naval Proceedings* (April 1973): 28–36.

Finkel, M. A. 2004. Traumatic Injuries Caused by Hazing. In H. Nuwer (Ed.) *The Hazing Reader*. Bloomington: Indiana University Press, pp. 171–183.

Finkelhor, D. 1984. *Child Sexual Abuse: New Theory and Research*. New York: Free Press.

Firestone, J. M. and R. J. Harris. 1999. Changes in patterns of sexual harassment in the U.S. military: A comparison of the 1988 and 1995 DoD surveys. *Armed Forces and Society*, 25(4): 425–445.

———. 1994. Sexual Harassment in the U. S. Military: Individualized and Environmental Contexts. *Armed Forces and Society* 21:25–43 Fall.

Fischer, G. J. 1986. College student attitudes towards forcible date rape: Cognitive predictors. *Archives of Sexual Behavior*, 15: 457–466.

Fisher, W. A., S. S. Singh, P. A. Shuper, M., Carey, F. Otchet, D. Maclean-Brine, D. DalBello, & J. Gunter. 2005. Characteristics of women undergoing repeat induced abortion. CMAJ Mar 1; 172(5):637–641.

Fleming, K. 1994. *Corps in Crisis*. South Carolina Press.

Foote, W. E. & J. Goodman-Delahunty. 2005. *Evaluating Sexual Harassment*. Washington, DC: American Psychological Association.

Foster, D. 2003. A 'culture of rape.' *Rocky Mountain* News, March 15, http://rockymountainnews.com/drmn/state/article/0,1299, DRMN_21_1813924,00.html.

Frank, T. 2004. *American Soldier*. New York: HarperCollins.

Frankel, L. 2004. *Nice Girls Don't Get The Corner Office*.

Freudenheim, M. 1988. Employers act to stop family violence. *New York Times*, August 23, A1 & D5.

Friedman, M. J. 2005. *New England Journal of Medicine*, 352(13): 1287–1290.

Friedman, M. J., P. P. Schnurr, & A. McDonagh-Coyle. 1994. Post-traumatic stress disorder in the military veteran. Psychiatric Clinics of North America. 17:263–277.

Fuller, T. 1732. *Gnomologia: Adages and Proverbs*.

Fussell, P. 1989. *Wartime* Oxford: Oxford University Press.

Galloway, K. B., & B. R. Johnson .19?. *West Point: America's Power Fraternity*.

Garmise, G. 1991. Twenty years ago today: U.S. in a tunnel without end. *The VVA Veteran*, 11:7.

Garner, B. A. (Ed.). 1999. *Black's Law Dictionary, 7th ed.* West Group.

Gaskin, C., & V. Hawkins. 2003. *Samurai: From Roning to Ninjas, The Fiercest Warriors in Japanese History*. New York: Barnes & Noble Books.

General Accounting Office. 1979. *Military Child Advocacy Programs: Victims of Neglect*. Washington, DC: Author.

Geneva Convention Relative to the Protection of Civilian Persons in Time of War, August 12, 1949.

George, W. H., & L. J. Martinez. 2002. Victim blaming in rape: Effects of victim and perpetrator race, type of rape, and participant racism. *Psychology of Women Quarterly*, 26(2): 110–119.

Gerzon, M. 1982. *A Choice of Heroes: The Changing Face of American Manhood*. Boston, MA: Houghton Mifflin.

Gladwell, M. 2002. *The Tipping Point: How Little Things Can Make a Big Difference*. New York: Little, Brown, & Co.

———. 2006. Million-dollar Murray. *The New Yorker*, 2/13, pp. 96–107.

Gleick, E. 1996. "Scandal in the Military," *Time*, November 25, p. 29.

Gluck Mezey, S. 2003. Rape. *World Book* CD edition.

Goddard, J. 2004. A grim virtual reality. *Metro* September 22, p. 15.

Goldstein, J. S. 2001. *War and Gender*. New York: Cambridge University Press.

Goldwater, B. 1993. The Gay Ban: Just Plain Un-American. *Washington Post*, June 10, p. A23.

Gomstyn, A. 2003. Air Force Officials Ignored Warnings About Sexual Assaults at Academy for a Decade, Says Panel Created by Congress. *Chronicle of Higher Education;* Vol. 50 Issue 6, p. A37.

Gonsiorek, J. C. 1991. The Empirical Basis for the Demise of the Illness Model of Homosexuality. In J. C. Gonsiorek & J.D. Weinrich (Eds.) *Homosexuality: Research Implications for Public Policy*. Thousand Oaks, CA: Sage Publications, pp. 115–136.

Goyer, P. F., & H. C. Eddleman. 1984. Same-sex rape of nonincarcerated men. *American Journal of Psychiatry*. 141(4): 576–579.

Grant DePaw, L. 1981. Women in combat: The revolutionary war experience, *Armed Forces and Society*, 2(21): 216.

Graves, A. 1991. Barney Frank Grills Colin Powell on Military Gay Ban. *Philadelphia Gay News*, Feb. 21.

Griffin, S. 1971. Rape: The All-American Crime. *Ramparts*, 10: 26–35.

Grossman, D. 1995. *On Killing: The Psychological Cost of Learning to Kill In War and Society*. Boston, MA: Little, Brown, & Co.

Groth, A. Nicholas, & B. A. Birnbaum. 1979. Men Who Rape: The Psychology of the Offender. New York: Plenum.

Gruber, J. E. 1997. An epidemiology of sexual harassment: Evidence from North America and Europe. In W. O'Donohue (Ed.) *Sexual Harassment: Theory, Research, and Treatment*, pp. 84–98. Needham Heights, MA Allyn & Bacon.

Gruber, J. E. & P. Morgan (Eds.). 2005. *In the Company of Men: Male Dominance & Sexual Harassment*. Boston, MA: Northeastern University Press.

Gutek, B. A. 1985. *Sex and the Workplace:* San Francisco: Jossey-Bass.

Hackworth, D. H. 1992. The Key Issue is Trust: Clinton Should Review the Gay Question. *Newsweek*, November 23, p. 27.

Hall, C. A., 1998. White counselors' attributions and diagnosis as a function of victim race and attribution about rape. *Dissertation Abstracts Internationals*, 58: (08), 748B–749B.

Handlin, O. 1966. The goals of integration. *Daedalus*, 95:270.

Haney, C., C. Banks, & P. K. Zimbardo. 1973. Interpersonal Dynamics in a Simulated Prison. *International Journal of Criminology and Penology*, 1: 73.

Hankin, C. S., K. M. Skinner, L. M. Sullivan, D. R. Millere, S. Frayne, & T. J. Tripp. 1999. Prevalence of depressive and alcohol abuse symptoms among women VA outpatients who report experiencing sexual assault while in the military. *Journal of Traumatic Stress*, 12, 601–612.

Hanley Disher, S. 1998. *First Class: Women Join the Ranks at the Naval Academy*. Annapolis: Naval Institute Press.

Harrell, M. C., & L. L. Miller. 1997. *New Opportunities for Military Women: Effects upon*

Readiness, Cohesion, and Morale. Washington, DC: National Defense Research Institute, Rand Corporation.

Haskell, B. 2001. First Women Graduates from Sniper School. *The Beam,* April 27. *http://dcmilitary.com/airforce/beam/6_17/national_news/6893-I.html.*

Hedges, C. 2002. *War: A Force That Gives Us Meaning.* New York: Public Affairs.

Heimark, K. K. 1997. Sexual Harassment in the United States Navy: A New Pair of Glasses. *Naval Law Review,* 44 (223).

Herbert, M. S. 1998. *Camouflage Isn't Only for Combat: Gender, Sexuality, and Women in the Military.* New York: New York University Press.

Herdy, A., & M. Moffeit. 2004. Betrayal in the Ranks. *The Denver Post,* January 15-25.

Herek, G. M. 1989. Hate crimes against lesbians and gay men: Issues for research and policy. *American Psychologist,* 44: 948–955.

Herek, G. M., J. R. Gillis, J. C. Cogan & K. E. Glunt. 1997. Hate crimes victimization among lesbian, gay, and bisexual adults: Prevalence, psychological correlates, and methodological issues. *Journal of Interpersonal Violence,* 12: 195–215.

Herman, J. 1992. *Trauma and Recovery.* New York: Basic Books.

Hersh, S. M. 1970. *My Lai 4: A Report on the Massacre and Its Aftermath.* New York: Random House.

Hersh, S. M. 2004. *Chain of Command: The Road From 9/11 to Abu Ghraib.* New York: Harper Collins.

Hicks Stiehm, J. 1999. The Civilian Mind. In Judith Hicks Stiehm (Ed.) *It's Our Military, Too! Women and the U.S. Military,* Philadelphia: Temple University Press, 1996, pp. 270–296.

Hightower, J. 2005 An economic draft. *Pulse of the Twin Cities,* 9(22):11.

Hillman, R. 1991. Adult Male Victims of Sexual Assault: An Underdiagnosed Condition. *International Journal of STD and AIDS,* 2: 24.

Hindelang, M. J. 1976. *Criminal Victimization in Eight American Cities: A Descriptive Analysis of Common Theft and Assault.* Cambridge, MA: Ballinger.

Hoffman, L. 2006. Army eases some of its taboos on tattoos. *Star Tribune,* March 26, p. A8.

Hoge, C. W., C. A. Castro, S. C. Messer, D. McGurk, D .I. Cotting, & R. L. Koffman. 2004. Combat duty in Iraq and Afghanistan mental health problems, and barriers to care. *New England Journal of Medicine,* 351, 13–22.

Holm, J. 1992. *Women in the Military: An Unfinished Revolution.* Revised ed. Novato, CA: Presidio Press.

Hosek, J., B. Asch, C. Fair, C. Martin, & M. Mattock. 2002. *Married to the Military: The Employment and Earnings of Military Wives Compared with Those of Civilian Wives.* Santa Monica: Rand Corporation.

Houppert, Karen. 2005. *Home Fires Burning: Married to the Military-for Better or Worse.* New York: Ballantine.

Hudson, W. W. & W. A. Ricketts. 1980. A strategy for the measurement of homophobia. *Journal of Homosexuality,* 5: 357–372.

Hull, G. T., S. P. Bell, & B. Smith (Eds.). 1982. *All the Women Are White, All the Blacks Are Men, But Some of Us Are Brave: Black Women Studies,* Old Westbury, NY: Feminist Press.

Humphrey, M. A. 1990. *My Country, My Right to Serve: Experiences of Gay Men & Women in the Military, World War II to the Present.* New York: HarperCollins.

Humphrey, R. L., T. Parris, & J. Sheperd. 1970. Troop-Community Relations Research in Korea: Educational Materials. Experimental Draft, prepared for the Office of the Chief of Research and Development, Department of the Army, Spring.

Hunter, D. 1996. Sexual abuse of military recruits should not be tolerated. *Knoxville News-Sentinel*, December 3, p. 22.

Huxley, A. 1939. *The Olive Tree.* New York: Harper & Brothers.

Jackson, S. 1995. The Social Context of Rape: Sexual Scripts and Motivation. In P. Searles & R. J. Berger (Eds.) *Rape and Society: Readings on the Problem of Sexual Assault.* Boulder, CO: Westview Press, pp. 16–27.

Jacobs, M. 1991. Stats and more stats. Letter to the editor, *The VVA Veteran*, 11(3): 5.

Janda, L. 2002. *Stronger than Custom: West Point and the Admission of Women.* Westport, CT: Praeger Publishers.

Janofsky, M., & D. J. Schemo. 2003. Ex-cadet: AT academy, most women raped or molested. *Star Tribune*, March 16, p. A17.

Jeffers, P. & D. Levitan. 1971. *See Parris and Die: Brutality in the U.S. Marines.* New York, New York: Hawthorn.

Jenkins, J. L. 1999. History of Air Force Social Work. In J. G. Daley (ed.) *Social Work Practice in the Military.* New York: Haworth Press, pp. 27–48.

Johnson, D. A. 2004. This torture cries out for U.N. investigation. *Star Tribune*, May 9, AA4 & AA6.

Johnson, S. 2006. Tipping Point. *Newsweek*, Aug. 7, pp. 30–25.

Jones, A. R. 2005. *AR 15-6 Investigation of Abu Ghraib Prison and 205th Military Intelligence Brigade .American Journal of Psychiatry*, 152 (1): 16–21.

Kahn, A. 1984. The power war: Male response to power loss under equality. *Psychology of Women Quarterly*, 8(3), 234–247.

Kang, H. K., N. Dalager, C. Mahan, & E. Ishii. 2005. The Role of Sexual Assault on the Risk of PTSD among Gulf War Veterans. *Annals of Epidemiology*; Mar., Vol. 15 Issue 3, pp. 191–195.

Kang, H. K., & K. Hyams 2005. Mental Health Care needs Among Recent War Veterans. *New England Journal of Medicine*, 352(13): 1289.

Kang, H. K., B. H. Natelson, C. M. Mahan, K. Y. Lee, & F. M. Murphy. 2003. Post Traumatic Stress Disorder and Chronic Fatigue Symptom-like Illness Among Gulf War Veterans: A Population-Based Survey of 30,000 Veterans. *American Journal of Epidemiology*, 157: 141–148.

Kaplan, D. 2003. *Brothers and Others in Arms: The Making of Love and War in Israeli Combat Units.* Binghamton, NY: Harrington Park Press.

Katzenstein, M. F. 1998. *Faithful and Fearless: Moving Feminist Protest Inside the Church and Military.* Princeton, NJ: Princeton University Press.

Kelly, M. 2002. Documents detail Navy chaplains, misconduct, including molestations. Associated Press article found @ Navy Chaplain Corps: *http://www.chaplain.navy.mil/*.

Kennedy, C. J. 2001. *Generally Speaking*. New York: Warner Books.

Kern, P. 2004. Statement by General Paul Kern, Commanding General, United States Army Material Command Before the Armed Services Committee United States Senate on the Investigation of the 205th Military Intelligence Brigade at Abu Ghraib Prison, Iraq, Second Session, 108th Congress, September 9.

Kilpatrick, D. G., C. L. Best, L. J. Veronen, A. E. Amick, L. A. Villeponteauz, and G. A. Ruff 1985. Mental health correlates of criminal victimization: A random community survey. *Journal of Consulting and Clinical Psychology*, 53(6), 866–873.

Kilpatrick, D. G., C. N. Edmunds, & A. Seymour. 1992. Rape in America: A report to the nation. Washington, DC: National Center for Victims of Crime and Crime Victims Research and Treatment Center.

Kim, B. C., A. I. Okamura, N. Ozawa, & V. Forrest. 1976. *Women in Shadows: A Handbook for Service Providers Working With Asian Wives of US Military Personnel*. La Jolla, CA: National Committee Concerned with Asian Wives of US Servicemen.

Kimmel, M. S., & M. A. Messner (eds.). 1995. *Men's Lives*, 3rd ed. Boston: Allyn & Bacon.

Kinsey, A. C., W .B. Pomeroy, & C. E. Martin. 1948/1998. *Sexual Behavior in the Human Male*. Philadelphia: W.B. Saunders; Bloomington, IN: Indiana University Press.

Koch, R. 1998. *The 80/20 Priniciple: The Art of Achieving More with Less*. New York: Bantam.

Knudson, Scott. 1981. The Corps is going to Hell: the decline of hazing at the U.S. Military Academy. Honors paper, Macalester College, MN.

Kulka, R. A., W. E. Schlenger, J. A. Fairbanks, R. L. Hough, B. K. Jordan, C. R. Marmar, & D. S. Weiss. 1990. *Taruma and the Vietnam War Generation: Report of Findings from the National Veterans Readjustment Study*. New York: Brunner/Mazel.

Lalumiere, M. L., G. T. Harris, V. L. Qunisey, & M. E. Rice. 2005. *The Causes of Rape: Understanding Individual Differences in Male Propensity for Sexual Aggression*. Washington, DC : American Psychological Association.

Laurier, J. 2004. North America Reports find pervasive and increasing sexual abuse in the US military. http://www.wsws.org/articles/2004/jun2004/military.

Lawliss, C. 1988. *The Marine Book: A Portrait of America's Military Elite*. New York: Thames and Hudson.

Lehne, G. 1978. Gay male fantasies and realities. *Journal of Social Issues*, 34 (3): 28–37.

Lehne, G. K. 1989. Homophobia Among Men: Supporting and Defining the Male Role. In M.S. Kimmel, & M.A. Messner (Eds.) *Men's Lives*. New York: Macmillan Publishing Co. pp. 416–429.

Lehr. D. M. 1993. Madwoman in the Military's Attic: Mental Health and Defense Department Policy in the Lives of U.S. Air Force Wives. Ph.D. dissertation, Union Institute, Cincinnati, OH.

Lehring, G. L. 2003. *Officially Gay: The Political Construction of Sexuality by the U.S. Military*. Philadelphia: Temple University Press.

Lelyveld, J. 2005. Interrogating Ourselves. *The New York Times Magazine*, June 12, pp. 36–43, 60, 66.

Lemon, B. 2002. Not Out at the Plate. *Sports Illustrated*, June 3, p. 18.

Lenny, J. 1949. *Caste System in the American Army: A Study of the Corps of Engineers and Their West Point System*. New York: Greenburg Publishers.

Leonard, E. D. 1994. *Yankee Women: Gender battles in the Civil War*. New York, NY: W.W. Norton.

LeShan, L. 2002. *The Psychology of War: Comprehending Its Mystique and Its Madness*. New York, NY: Helios Press.

Levy, C. J. 1989. ARVN as faggots: Inverted Warfare in Vietnam. In M. S. Kimmel, & M. A. Messner (Eds.). *Men's Lives*. New York: Macmillan Publishing Co., pp. 200–214.

Llewellyn Barstow, A. (Ed.) 2000. *War's Dirty Secret: Rape, Prostitution, and Other Crimes Against Women*. Cleveland, OH: The Pilgrim Press.

Lloyd, D.W. 2002. Opening Remarks. Department of Defense Symposium On Domestic Violence Prevention Research, May 13.

Longenecker, V. S. 1992. Facts of Fear from the foxhole: An individual Study Project. USAWC Military Studies Program Paper, 15 April.

Loory, S. H. 1973. *Defeated: Inside America's Military* Machine. New York: Random House.

Lumpkin, J. J. 2004. Air Force Academy Implicated in Sex Abuse, Associated Press, December 7, http://www.allheadlinenews.com/articles.

———. 2004. Pentagon Probes Sex Assaults Involving Troops in Iraq, Associated Press, Feb. 7.

———. 2005. 1,700 Military-Related Sex Assaults Reported. Associated Press Sat May 7, 6:47 a.m. ET.

MacArthur, D. 1964. *Reminiscences*. New York: McGraw-Hill.

Maccoby, E. E. 1998. *The Two Sexes: Growing Up Apart, Coming Together*. Cambridge, MA: Belknap/Harvard University Press.

MacGregor Jr., Morris J. 1981. *Defense Studies: Integration of the Armed Forces: 1940–1965*. Center of Military History, United States Army, Washington, DC.

MacKinnon, C. 1979. *Sexual Harassment of Working Women: A Case of Sex Discrimination*. New haven, CT: Yale University Press.

MacKinnon, C. 1982. Feminism, Marxism, Method, and the State. Signs, 7:515–554.

Maclear, M. 1981. *The Ten Thousand Day War*. Vietnam: 1945–1975. New York: St. Martin's Press.

MacNeil/Lehrer Productions 1997. *http://www.pbs.org/newshour/bb/military/army/June97/harassment*.

Magley, V. J., C. R. Waldo, F. Drasgow, & L. F. Fitzgerald. 1999. The Impact of Sexual Harassment on Military Personnel: Is It the Same for Men and Women? *Military Psychology*. Volume: 11. Issue: 3. Page 283. www.questia.com.

Maguen, S., M. Suvak, & B.T. Litz 2006. Predictors and Prevalence of Post Traumatic Stress Disorder among Military Veterans. In C. A. Castro, A. B. Adler, & T. W. Britt (Eds.) *Military Life: Operational Stress*. pp.141–170.

Maker, A.H., M. Kemmelmeir, & C. Peterson. 2001. Child sexual abuse, peer sexual abuse, and sexual assault in adulthood: A multi-risk model of revictimization. *Journal of Traumatic Stress*, 14: 351–368.

Maloney, T. J. (Ed.) 1947. *U.S. Camera*, 1947. U.S. Camera Publications, distributed by Duell, Sloan, & Pearce.

Manchester, W. 1983. *Goodbye Darkness: A Memoir of the War*. Boston: Little, Brown, & Co.

Manning, L. 1999. Data from Women's Research and Education Institute, Washington, DC Personnel communication, November 29, with Goldstein, 2001.

Marmar, C. R., & M. J. Horowitz. 1988. Diagnosis and phase-oriented treatment of post-traumatic stress disorder. In J. Wilson, Z., Harel, & B. Kahana. (Eds.) *Human Adaption to Extreme Stress.* pp. 81–103. New York: Plenum Press.

Martin, H. 1951. "How Do Our Negro Troops Measure Up?" *Saturday Evening Post*, June 16.

Martin, J. A., & S. J. Campbell 1999. The Role of the Social Work Officer in Support of Combat and Noncombat Operations. In J. G. Dale (Ed.) *Social Work Practice in the Military*. New York, NY: The Haworth Press pp. 137–164.

Martin, L., L. N. Rosen, D. B. Durand, K. H. Knudson, & R. H. Stretch. 2000. Psychological and Physical Health Effects of Sexual Assaults and Nonsexual Traumas Among Male and Female United States Army Soldiers. *Behavioral Medicine*. Spring.

———. 1998. Prevalence and timing of sexual assaults in a sample of male and female U.S. Army soldiers. *Military Medicine*, 163:213–216.

Martindale, M. 1988. *Sexual Harassment in the Military: 1988*. Department of Defense, Arlington, VA.

Masters, W. H., & V. E. Johnson 1966. *Human Sexual Response*. Boston: Little, Brown & Company.

Matsui, Y. 1984. Why I Oppose Kisaeng Tours. In K. Barry, C. Bunch, & S. Castley (eds.) *International Feminism: Networking Against Female Sexual Slavery*. New York: International Women's Tribune Center.

Matthews, L. 1996. She asks, she tells. *New York Times*, May 16.

McBride, J. 1995. *War, Battering, and Other Sports: The Gulf Between American Men and Women*. Atlantic Highlands, NJ: Humanities Press.

McCain, J. 1999. *Faith of My Fathers*. New York: Random House.

McCoy, A. 1995. "Same Banana: Hazing and Honor at the Philippine Military Academy." *The Journal of Asian Studies*, Aug. 1, v. 54, n.3, p.689–EOA.

McDaniel, M. A. 1989. Preservice Adjustment of Homosexual and Heterosexual Military Accessions: Implications for Security Clearance Suitability. PERS-TR-89-004. Monterey, CA: Defense Personnel Security Research and Education Center/PERSEREC, January.

McFarlane J., A. Malecha, K. Watson, J. Gist, E. Battem, I. Hall, & S. Smith 2005. Intimate partner sexual assault against women: Frequency, health consequences, and treatment outcomes. *Obstet Gynecol.* Jan; 105(1): 99–108.

McMichael, W. H. 1997. *The Mother of All Hooks: The Story of the U.S. Navy's Tailhook Scandal*. New Brunswick, NJ and London: Transaction Publishers.

McMullen, R. J. 1990. *Male Rape: Breaking the Silence on the Last Taboo*. London: GMP Publishers Ltd.

McMullin, D., & J. W. White. 2006. Long-term effects of labeling a rape experience. *Psychology of Women Quarterly*, 30: 96–105.

McNair, L. D., & H .A. Neville. 1996. African American women survivors of sexual assaualt: The interaction of race and class. *Women & therapy*, 19(3/4): 107–118.

Mediawise. 2005. How to beat up a prostitute. *The Onion*, 41 (5), p. 9.

Meyer, C. 2003. Teenage Warriors, http://www.g2mil.com/married_teenage_warriors.

Miedzian, M. 1991. *Boys Will Be Boys: Breaking the Link Between Masculinity and Violence*. New York: Anchor.

Milgram, S. 1965. Some conditions of obedience and disobedience to authority. *Human Relations*, 18, 57–76.

Milgram, S. 1974. *Obedience to Authority*. New York: Harper & Row.

Military Family Resource Center. 1995. Military Family Demographics, Profile of the Military Family. Arlington, VA: Personnel Support, Families and Education Office of Family Policy.

Mitchell, B. 1996. "The Creation of Army Officers and the Gender Lie: Betty Grable or Frankenstein?" In Judith Hicks Stiehm (Ed.) *It's Our Military, Too! Women and the U.S. Military*, Philadelphia: Temple University Press, 1996, pp. 35–59.

Mitchell, B. 1998. *Women in the Military: Flirting with Disaster*. Washington, DC: Regnery Publishing, Inc.

Moon, K. 1997. *Sex Among Allies: Military Prostitution in U.S.-Korean Relations*. New York: Columbia University Press.

Moore, M. 1988. Top Marine Bars Widening Women's Role. *Washington Post*, April, 26, p. 1.

Moradi, B. 2006. Perceived sexual-orientation-based harassment in military and civilian contexts. *Military Psychology*, 18 (1): 39–60.

Morris, M. 1996. By Force of Arms: Rape, War, and Military Culture. *Duke Law Journal*, 45, 651.

Morris, M. 2000. In War and Peace: Rape, War, and Military Culture. In Llewellyn Barstow, A. (Ed.) *War's Dirty Secret: Rape, Prostitution, and Other Crimes Against Women*. Cleveland, OH: The Pilgrim Press, pp. 167–203.

Mosher, D. L. & R. D. Anderson. 1986. Macho personality, sexual aggression, and reactions to guided imagery of realistic rape. *Journal of Consulting and Clinical Psychology*, 59: 77–94.

Moskos, C. C., J. A. Williams, & David R. Segal, D. R. 2000. *The Postmodern Military: Armed Forces after the Cold War*, Oxford: Oxford University Press.

Motten, J. A. 2003. Influences on Navy Retention, Presentation January 17.

MSNBC. 2004. Sexual assaults in the military: Aside from all the dangers of serving overseas, there is also a threat from within. March 9. *http://www.msnbc.msn.com/id/4490652*.

Muehlenhard, C. L., & M. A. Linton, 1987. Date rape and sexual aggression in dating situations: Incidence and risk factors. *Journal of Counseling Psychology*, 34: 186–196.

Murphy, P. M. 1978. What's a Nice Girl Like You Doing in a Place Like This. *Air University Review*, Sept.-Oct., p. 75.

Nabors, R. L. 1982. Women in the Army: Do they Measure Up? *Military Review*, LXII, no. 10, Oct, p. 60.

Nalty, B. C. 1986. *Strength for the Fight: A History of Black Americans in the Military.* New York: The Free Press.

Nanking International Relief Committee. 1938. *War Damage in the Nanking Area.* Shanghai: The Mercury Press.

Navy Women's Study Group. 1991. *An Update Report on the Progress of Women in the Navy.* Washington, DC: Chief of Naval Operations.

Nelson, J. B. 1983. *Between Two Gardens: Relections On Sexuality And Religious Experience.* Cleveland, OH: The Pilgrim Press.

Newsome, R. 199. Military Social Work Practice in Substance Abuse Programs. In J. G. Daley (Ed.) *Social Work Practice in the Military.* New York: The Haworth Press, pp. 91–254.

Nisbett, R. E., & L. Ross, 1991. *The Person and the Situation.* Philadelphia: Temple University Press.

Nuwer, Hank. 1990. Broken Pledges: the deadly rite of hazing. GA: Longstreet Press.

Nuwer, Hank. 1999. *Wrongs of Passage.* Bloomington, IN: Indiana University Press.

Nuwer, H. 2004. Military Hazing. In H. Nuwer (Ed.) *The Hazing Reader.* Bloomington, IN: Indiana University Press, pp. 140–146.

Office of the Surgeon General. 1995. The Prisoner of War. *Textbook of Military Medicine,* United States Army.

O'Hare, E. A., & W. O'Donohue. 1998. Sexual harassment: Identifying risk factors. *Archives of Sexual Behavior,* 27: 561–580.

Opotow, S. 2005. Hate, Conflict, and Moral Exclusion. In R. J. Sternberg (ed.) *The Psychology of Hate.* Washington, DC: American Psychological Association, pp. 121–153.

Orange, C. 2003. The residue of war raises the risk of PTSD, addiction. *Hazelden Voice,* 8 (2), pp. 1 & 4.

Pateman, C. 1988, *The Sexual Contract.* Stanford, CA: Stanford University Press.

Patton, G. S. Jr. 1947. *War As I Knew It.* Boston: Houghton Mifflin.

Peach, L. J. 1996. Gender Ideology in the Ethics of Wopmen in Combat. In Judith Hicks Stiehm (Ed.) *It's Our Military, Too! Women and the U.S. Military,* Philadelphia: Temple University Press, 1996, pp. 156–194.

Pennington, R. 1997. COMMENT: Sex in the military, again.

Peretti, F. 2000. *The wounded spirit.* Nashville, TN: Word Publishing.

Perry, W. J. 1996. Department of Defense News Briefing, November 13. *http://www.defenselink.mil.*

Pfluke, L. A. 1999. Too Bad She's a Girl . . ." In F. D'Amico & L. Weinstein (Eds.) *Gender Camouflage: Women and the U.S. Military.* New York: New York University Press, pp. 80–83.

Pine, A. 1994. ACLU arm slams Navy's policy on gays. *Los Angeles Times,* August 20, p. A28.

Powell, M. R. 2000. *A World of Hurt: Between Innocence and Arrogance in Vietnam.* Cleveland, OH: Greenleaf Enterprises.

The Presidential Commission on the Assignment of Women in the Armed Forces. 1992. *Report to the President, November 15, 1992.* Washington, DC.

Price, J. 1991. NOW Cites Woman POW, *Washington Times*, Feb. 4.

Pryor, J. B. 1995. The phenomenology of sexual harassment: Why does sexual behavior bother people in the workplace? *Consulting Psychology Journal: Practice & Research*, 47(3): 160–168.

Pryor, J. B., & L. M. Stoller, 1994. Sexual cognition processes in men high in the likelihood to sexually harass. *Personality & Social Psychology Bulletin*, 20: 163–169.

Quackenbush, R. L. 1989. A comparison of androgynous, masculine sex typed, and undifferentiated males on dimensions of attitudes towards rape. *Journal of Research in Personality.* 23: 318–342.

Reber, A. S. 1985. *Dictionary of Psychology.* New York: Penguin Books.

Reeves, C. L. 1996. The Military Woman's Vanguard: Nurses. In J. H. Hicks Stiehm (ed.) *It's Our Military Too! Women and the U.S. Military.* Philadelphia: Temple University Press, pp. 73–114.

Reiss, A. J., & J. A. Roth, (Eds.). 1993. *Understanding and Preventing Violence.* Washington, DC: National Academy Press.

Rhem, K. T. 2001. Services Move to Lower Instances of Rape in the Ranks. American Forces Press Service, 6 April.

Ricks, T. E. 1997. *Making the Corps.* New York: Scribner.

Riedel, R. G. 1993. Effects of pretrial publicity on male and female jurors and judges in a mock rape trial. *Psychology Reports*, 73: 819–832.

Rivera, R. R. 1991. Sexual Orientation and the Law. In J. C. Gonsiorek & J. D. Weinrich (Eds.) *Homosexuality: Research Implications for Public Policy.* Thousand Oaks, CA: Sage Publications, pp. 81–100.

Romberg, R. W., S. B. Needleman, M. Porvaznik, M. Past, & W. Beasley. 1993. Effect of pre-enlistment testing on the confirmed drug-positive rate for Navy recruits. *Military Medicine*, 158 (1): 14–19.

Rosen, L. N., L. Martin. 1996a. The measurement of childhood trauma among male and female soldiers in the U.S. Army. *Military Medicine*, 161:342–345.

———. Impact of childhood abuse history on psychological symptoms among male and female soldiers in the U.S. Army. *Child Abuse & Neglect.* 20:1149–1160.

Rovella, D. E. 1997. Inside the ring. *Washington Times,* Oct. 20, A10.

Rupp, L. J. 1978. *Mobilizing Women for War: German and American Propaganda, 1934–1945.* Princeton, NJ: Princeton University Press.

Saar, E., & V. Novak. 2005. *Inside The Wire.* New York: Penguin Books.

Sadler, A. G., B. M. Booth, B. L. Cook, N. Bradley, B. N. Doebbeling. 2003. Factors associated with women's risk of rape in the military environment. *American Journal of Industrial Medicine*, 43(3): 262–273.

Saghir, M., & E. Robins, 1973. *Male and Female Homosexuality: A Comprehensive Investigation.* Baltimore: William & Wilkins.

St. George, D. 2006. Women mark 30 years of gains at Annapolis. *St. Paul Pioneer Press*, July 16, 1A & 8A.

———. 30 Years of growth for academy's women. *Honolulu Advertiser,* July 17, B4.

————. Iraq vet, sex harassment victim . . . deserter? *St. Paul Pioneer Press*, Nov. 20, pp. 1A &10A.

Sammons, M.T. 2005. Psychology in the Public Sector: Addressing the Psychological Effects of Combat in the U.S Navy. *American Psychologist*, Nov. 6 (8): 899–909.

Sampson, R.J., & J. L Lauritsen. 1993.Violent victimization and offending: Individual, situational, and community-level risk factors. In: A. J. Reiss Jr. & J.A. Roth (eds.) *Understanding and Preventing Violence: Social Influences.* Washington, DC: National Academy Press, 31–114.

Sanday, P. 1981.The Socio-cultural Context of Rape: A Cross-cultural Study. *Journal of Social Issues*, 37: 5/27.

Sarche, J. 2004. Pentagon report critical of the role of commanders at the Air Force Academy blasted as inadequate. AP Online. December 8.

Scarce, M. 1997. *Male on Male Rape: The Hidden Toll of Stigma and Shame.* New York: Insight Books.

Schmitt, E. 2005. Army opens inquiry into treatment of dead Taliban. *Star Tribune,* Oct. 20, A17.

Scully, D., & J. Marolla. 1995. "Riding the Bull at Gilley's": Convicted Rapists Describe the Rewards of Rape. In P. Searles & R. J. Berger (Eds.) *Rape and Society: Readings on the Problem of Sexual Assault.* Boulder, CO: Westview Press. pp. 58–73.

Secretary of the Army. 1997. *The Secretary of the Army's Senior Review Panel Report on Sexual Harassment, Volume One.*

Seifert, R. 1994.War and Rape: A Preliminary Analysis. In A. Stiglmayer (ed.) *Mass Rape: The War Against Women in Bosnia-Herzegovina.* Lincoln: University of Nebraska Press, pp. 54–79.

Servicemembers Legal Defense Network. 1998. *Conduct Unbecoming: The Fourth Annual Report on "Don't Ask, Don't Tell, Don't Pursue."* Washington, DC: Servicemembers Legal Defense Network.

Shalit, B. 1988. *The Psychology of Conflict and Combat.* New York: Praeger Publishers.

Shilts, R. 1993. *Conduct Unbecoming: Lesbians & Gays in the U.S. Military Vietnam to the Persian Gulf.* New York: St. Martin's Press.

Shanor, C. C., & L. L. Hogue. 2003. *Military Law.* St. Paul, MN: West Law.

Shatan, C.F. 1977. Bogus Manhood, Bogus Honor: Surrender and Transformation in the United States Marine Corps. *Psychoanalytic Review*, 64: 586–610.

Shay, J. 1994. *Achilles in Vietnam: Combat Trauma and the Undoing of Character.* New York: Scribner.

Sheldrake, R. 2003. *The sense of being stared at.* New York: Crown Publications.

Sheridan Ember-Herbert, M. 2005. A Missing Link: Institutional Homophobia and Sexual Harassment in the U.S. Military. In J. E. Gruber & P. Morgan (Eds.) *In the Company Of Men.* Boston: Northeastern University Press, pp. 215–242.

Shilts, R. 1993. *Conduct Unbecoming.* New York: St. Martin's Press.

Showalter, E. 1987. Rivers and Sassoon: the Inscription of Male Gender Anxieties. In M. R. Higonnet, J. Jenson, S. Michel, & M. Collins Weitz. (eds.) *Behind the Lines: Gender and the Two World Wars.* New Haven, CT: Yale University Press. pp. 61–69.

Sledge, E. 1980. "Peleliu, Neglected battle," *Marine Corps Gazette,* January, Quantico, VA: Marine Corps Association.

Smithyman, S. 1978. *The Undetected Rapist*. Unpublished Ph.D. dissertation, Claremont Graduate School.

Snel, A. 2003. Sex abuse revealed in ranks. *Florida Today*, 1A–6A.

Solaro, E. 1999. Comment: Sexual Violence and the Martial Virtues. August 9.

Sorensen, R. 1973. *Adolescent Sexuality in Contemporary America*. New York: World.

Sorkin, A. 1990. *A Few Good Men*. New York: Samuel French.

Spears, S. 1998. *Call Sign Revlon: The Life and Death of Navy Fighter Pilot Kara Hultgreen*. Annapolis, MD: Naval Institute Press.

Stark, L. P. 1991. Traditional gender role beliefs and individual outcomes: An exploratory analysis, *Sex Roles*, 24: 639–650.

Stepanek, M. 1992. Fear Over Gay Rights Grips Military. *San Francisco Examiner*, Nov. 22.

Stockdale, M. S. 1998. The direct and moderating influence of sexual-harassment pervasiveness, coping strategies, and gender on work-related outcomes. *Psychology of Women Quarterly*, 22: 521–535.

Stoughton, S. 2004. Navy makes skirts optional. *St. Paul Pioneer Press*, October 18, p. 4A.

Sullivan, Andrew. 2005. The End of Gay Culture and the Future of Gay Life. *The New Republic*, November 1, http://www.andrewsullivan.com/main_article.php?artnum=20051101.

Teague, M. 2003. The War Game That Went Too Far. *GQ*, April.

Terry, W. 1985. *Bloods: An Oral History of the Vietnam War*. New York: Presidio.

Testa, M., C. Vazile-Tamsen, & J. A. Livingston. 2004. The Role of Victim and Perpetrator Intoxication on Sexual Assault Outcomes. *Journal of Studies on Alcohol*, May, Vol. 65 Issue 3, pp. 320–329.

Tetreault, M. A. 1988. Gender belief systems and the integration of women in the U.S. military. *Minerva: Quarterly Report on Women in the Military*, 6(1): 44–71.

Thomas, J. 2004. APA task force takes another look at military ad ban. *The National Psychologist*. May/June, p. 2.

Thomas, P. J. & M. D. Thomas. 1996. Integratation of women in the military: Parallels to the progress of homosexuals? In G. Herek, J. Jobe, & R. Carney (Eds.). *Out In Force: Sexual Orrientation and the Military*. Chicago: University of Chicago Press, pp. 65–85.

Thompson, E. H., C. Grisanti, & J.H. Pleck. 1985. Attitudes towards the male role and their correlates. *Sex Roles*, 24: 413–427.

Thompson, Mark. 1994. The Living Room War: As the U.S. Military Shrinks, Family Violence Is on the Rise: Can the Pentagon Do More to Prevent It? *Time*, May 23, p. 48.

Tieger, T. 1981. Self-rated likelihood of raping and the social perception of rape. *Journal of Research in Personality*, 15: 147–158.

Times, The. 1996. Enemies' blunders. September 14, p.12, London.

Tolson, F. Men's *Issues Forum*, 3(2): 8.

Toner, B. 1977. *The Facts of Rape*. London: Arrow Books.

Toner, R. 2006. Who's This 'We,' Non-Soldier Boy? *New York Times*, June 25, p. 3.

Toobin, J. 2005. Sex and the Supremes. *The New Yorker*, August 1, pp. 32–37.

Treadwell, M. E. 1954. *United States Army in World War II, Special Studies: The Women's Army Corps*. Washington, DC: Office of the Chief of Military History, Dept. of the Army.

Truman, Dana, M. Tokar, M. David, & Ann R. Fischer. 1996. Dimensions of masculinity:

Relations to date rape supportive attitudes and sexual aggression in dating situations. *Journal of Counseling & Development*, July/August, 74: 555–562.

United States Military Academy. 1977. *The Fourth Class System.* New York: West Point.

U.S. Army Community and Family Support Center. 2001. "Survey of Army Families IV" Information briefing 12/12/02, slide 22, Q64.

U.S. Department of Defense Task Force on Domestic Violence. 2003. *Defense task force on domestic violence: Third year report 2003.* Washington, DC: U.S. Department of Defense.

U.S. Department of Defense. 1993. *Tailhook '91, Part 2: Events at the 35th Annual Tailhook Symposium.* Washington, DC: U.S. Government Printing Office.

U.S. Department of Justice, Bureau of Justice Statistics. 1992. *Criminal v Victimization In The United States, 1991.* Washington, DC: U.S. Printing Office.

US Justice Department. 2000. *Office of Justice Programs, Bureau of Justice Statistics Special Report Veterans in Prison or Jail,* January NCJ 178888, Revised 9/29/00 facts cover time period from 1985–1998.

United States Merit Systems Protection Board. 1995. Sexual harassment in the federal workplace: Trends, progress, and continuing challenges. Washington, DC: U.S. Government Printing Office.

U.S. News & World Report. 2004. An Affair to Forget? October 11, p. 14.

Van Creveld, M. 1994. Why Men Fight. In L. Freedman (Ed.) *War.* London: Oxford University Press, pp. 88–89.

Van Dam, C. 2006. *The Socially Skilled Child Molester.* New York: The Haworth Press.

Van Devanter, L. 1983. *Home Before Morning,* New York: Beaufort Books.

Vasile, M. A. 2005. The Union Soldier, His Life and Times. *http://www.cwc.lsu.edu/other/other/acw_inf.htm*

Villalon, C. 2004. Cocaine Country. *National Geographic,* Vol 206 (1), July, pp. 34–55.

Vistica, G. L. 1995. *Fall from Glory: The Men Who Sank the U.S. Navy.* New York: Touchstone Books.

Walters, A. K. 2005. Hostile Environment Is Found at Academics. *Chronicle of Higher Education;* Vol. 52 Issue 3, pp. A36–A36.

Walzer, L. 2000. *Between Sodom and Eden: A Gay Journey Through Today's Changing Israel.* New York: Columbia University Press.

Washburn, P. 1993. Women and the Peace Movement. In R. H. Howes & M. R. Stevenson (eds.). *Women and the Use of Military Force.* Boulder, CO: Lynne Rienner, pp. 135–148.

Webb, J. 1979. Women Can't Fight. *Washingtonian.* November, pp. 144–148.

Weinberg, M., & C. Williams. 1974. *Male Homosexuals.* New York: Oxford University Press.

Weiss, K., & S. Borges. 1973. Victimology and Rape: A Case Study of the Legitimate Victim. *Issues in Criminology,* 8: 71–117.

Weinstein, L., & H. Merderer. Blue Navy Blues: Submarine Officers and the Two-person Career, *Wives & Warriors,* pp. 7–16.

White, J. 2004. General Tasked with Combating Sexual Assault, *http://www.washingtonpost.com.*

White, T. W. 2004. Prison abuse in Iraq revives and explains decades-old Stanford study. *The National Psychologist*, July/August, vol. 13(4): 13.

Wilborn, T. 1998. Studies Find Sexual Assault Triggers PTSD. *Disabled American Veteran Magazine*, (5): 41.

William III, P. S., & N. Khouzam Skelton. 1995. Women as Prisoners of War. *Military Medicine*, Vol. 160, No. 11, pp. 558–60.

Williams, F. G. 1992. Sexual harassment: Where does it end? *Navy Times*, July 22, p. 22.

Williams, K. A. 2005. *Love My Rifle More Than You: Young & Female in the U.S. Army*. New York: W. W. Norton.

Williams, R. 2003. Psychiatrist Discusses Abuse, Harassment, Violence Against Military Women. American Forces Press Service, *http://www.defendamerica.mil*.

Willis, G. E. 1997. The Army's Tailhook: Sexual-Assault Case Brings to Mind the Navy's Scandal. *Air Force Times*, 57:17 Mar 10.

Winick, C., & P. M. Kinsie. 1971. *The Lively Commerce*. Chicago: Quadrangle.

Witt, H. 2004. Abu Ghraib guard convicted. *Chicago Tribune*. January 15. p. 1 & 19.

Wolfe, J., P. J. Brown, & M. L. Buscela. 1992. Symptom responses of female Vietnam veterans to Operation Desert Storm. *American Journal of Psychiatry*. 149:676–679.

Wolfe J, P. P. Schnurr, P. J. Brown, & J. Furey. 1994. Post Traumatic stress disorder and war-zone exposure as correlates of perceived health in female Vietnam veterans. *Journal of Consulting Clinical Psychology*. 62:1235–1240.

Wolfe, J., E. J. Sharkansky, J. P. Read, R. Dawson, J. A. Martin, & P. C. Ouimette. 1998. Sexual harassment and assault as predictors of PTSD symptomatology among U.S. female Persian Gulf War personnel. *Journal of Interpersonal Violence*, 13, 40–57.

Wood, D.B., & B. Mahoney. 1994. *A Sense of Values*. Kansas City, MO: Andrews & McMeel.

Woodruff, P. 2001. *Reverence: Renewing a Forgotten Virtue*. New York: Oxford University Press.

Woulfe, J. B. 1998. *Into the Crucible: Making Marines for the 21st Century*. New York: ibooks.

Wright, M. 1982. The Marine Corps Faces the Future. *The New York Times Magazine*, June 20, p. 74.

Zagorin, A. 2005. Another Abu Ghraib? *Time*, Oct. 3, 166 (14):19.

Zagorin, A. & D. Duffy. 2005. Inside the Interrigation of Detainee 063. *Time*, June 20, pp. 26–33.

Zaidi, L. Y., & D. W. Foy. 1994. Childhood abuse experiences and combat-related PTSD. *Journal of Trauma Stress*, 7:33–42.

Zakaria, F. (2005). First Ladies, in The Truest Sense. *Newsweek*, 11/28, p. 39.

Zawitz, M. W., P. A. Klaus, & R. Bachman. 1993. *Highlights from 20 years of surveying crime victims: The National Crime Victimization Survey, 1973–92*. Bureau of Justice Statistics report NCJ-144525. Washington, DC: U.S. Dept of Justice.

Zeeland, S. 1996. *The Masculine Marine: Homoeroticism in the U.S. Marine Corps*. Binghamton, NY: Harrington Park Press.

Zimbardo, P. G. 1970. The human choice: Individuation, reason, and order versus deindividuation, impulse, and chaos. In W.J. Arnold & D. Levine (Eds.) *Nebraska*

Symposium on Motivation, 1969. Lincoln: University of Nebraska Press.

———. 1971. *The psychological power and pathology of imprisonment.* A statement prepared for the U.S. House of Representatives Committee on the Judiciary Subcommittee No. 3: Hearings on Prison Reform, San Francisco, CA, Oct. 25.

Zimmerman, J. 1995. *Tailspin: Women at War in the Wake of Tailhook.* New York: Doubleday.

Zuger, A. 1998. Many Prostitutes Suffer Combat Disorders, Study Finds. *New York Times,* 8/18, C8.